Disenchanted Democracy

Disenchanted Democracy

Chinese Cultural Criticism after 1989

 Ben Xu

ANN ARBOR

THE UNIVERSITY OF MICHIGAN PRESS

Copyright © by the University of Michigan 1999
All rights reserved
Published in the United States of America by
The University of Michigan Press
Manufactured in the United States of America
⊗ Printed on acid-free paper

2002   2001   2000   1999   4   3   2   1

A CIP catalog record for this book is available from the British Library.

Library of Congress Cataloging-in-Publication Data

Xu, Ben, 1950–
    Disenchanted democracy : Chinese criticism after 1989 / Ben Xu.
       p.   cm.
    Includes bibliographical references and index.
    ISBN 0-472-11062-4 (alk. paper)
       1. China—Politics and government—1976–   2. Criticism—Political
aspects—China.   3. Political culture—China.   4.
Intellectuals—China—Political activity.   I. Title.
DS779.26 .X8   1999
320.951—dc21

To my mother and the memory of my father

Preface

My interest in Chinese cultural criticism after 1989 has developed both from my engagement in the ongoing cultural discussion in China since the 1980s and from my continuous concern with the role of intellectuals in Chinese society. Situated on the challenging border between cultural studies and social criticism, my inquiry into cultural criticism focuses on the interaction of ideology, theoretical discourses, and intellectual politics. This enterprise of engagement is not prompted by the certainty of expertise but, rather, accepts the tentativeness and uncertainty inscribed in intellectual action with prudent self-limitation. Given my own participation in the ongoing intellectual debates in China, this book does not pretend to the degree of detachment upheld by some uninvolved observers. Nor does it have as its ideal an exclusive concern of "disinterested" scholarship; it makes no attempt to "objectively" catalogue much that may be admirable in the new trends of the 1990s. Its goal is to present a critical view on the problematic elements of some post-Tiananmen projects while allowing those who approach them differently to develop the resources in ways befitting their own purposes.

I share many of the experiences of other Chinese intellectuals who participated in the cultural discussion of the 1980s, left the country before 1989, and have stayed in the West even though they are still deeply concerned with and write actively about what is happening in China. Like many of them, I must face my own predicament in terms of location, self-positioning, and accountability. I must ask myself, for instance: Why is it the case that one goes elsewhere to theorize about China's problems or writes about them in English? How valid is my criticism of those who remain in China and whose intellectual work is marked by the local site and condition of production and circulation? How are my own specific ambivalences of local and cosmopolitan attachments to be understood? What are the continuing claims of "home," "relevance," or "opposition" on such scholarship? These are questions that concern many Chinese intellectuals working abroad and at home, and they are issues I have been deeply aware of while undertaking this study.

In 1998 my full-length study on post-1989 Chinese cultural issues, *Wenhua piping wang hechu qu? 1989 nian hou de zhongguo wenhua taolun* (Whither cultural criticism? Chinese cultural discussion after 1989), was published in Hong Kong. In that study I focused on five basic aspects of cultural critique: civic consciousness and civil society, socio-political ethics and humanities education, popular culture, political culture, and China's third-world status. The present study differs from that one in perspective and structure. Even writing on what is ostensibly the same subject matter, I find it impossible merely to translate from one language to another because the writing activity that takes place in different language situations is enmeshed in different traditions and locales, not to mention that the works address different audiences. What I can assume as immediately comprehensible or self-explanatory in one language cannot be taken for granted in the other. What is almost common sense in one language may be unspeakable or unsayable in the other. What matters most here is not just a national or vernacular language but, rather, sublanguages with discursive structures, conceptual systems, traditions of argument, and even standards of writing decorum that function as much to communicate concepts and meanings as to constitute issues, raise questions, and mobilize engagement on the part of the intended audience. Writing in two different languages on the same subject matter thus becomes for me an epistemologically and politically enlightening experience. It allows, and often forces, me to clarify my views in a way I would not undertake if I worked in only one language. The writing experience thus becomes not just a bilingual one but also a situated switching between what are almost two modes of knowledge, a process that reinforces differences but also helps to reduce them.

In the process of writing this study in English, I became aware of the constraints, internalized censorship, and taboos that had restricted me when I wrote my book in Chinese, and I began to question whether, in writing about Chinese problems in Chinese for a Chinese audience, one can automatically claim greater authenticity or freedom from ideological contamination. On the other hand, I found the experience of writing that book in Chinese immensely valuable; it quickened my impulse to take more seriously the constraints, taboos, and normality of political correctness associated with writing in English. I can only wonder how the present work might be different if I had not written that earlier book in Chinese.

I am grateful for permission to include in this book the following copyrighted material from my previous publications: "Farewell My Concubine and Its Nativist Critics" (*Quarterly Review of Film and Video* 16, no. 2 [1997]), by Harwood Academic Publishers; "'From Modernity to Chineseness': The Rise of Nativist Theory in China" (*Positions* 6, no. 1 [spring 1998]), by Duke University Press; and "Contesting Memory for Intellectual Self-Positioning: The Nineties' New Cultural Conservatism in China" (*Contemporary Chinese Literature and Culture* 11, no. 1 [spring 1999]), by Ohio State University. I want to thank Monica Clyde, Kirk A. Denton, Edward Friedman, Rosemary Graham, Barry Horwitz, Lydia H. Liu, Norman Springer, Longxi Zhang, and anonymous reviewers for reading parts of an early version of this study and for giving me valuable suggestions. I also owe special thanks to Saint Mary's College of California for generously supporting my work on this book with its Faculty Development Funds.

Contents

Abbreviations   xiii

Introduction   1

Chapter 1   The Crisis of National Identity and the Decline of
Unitary Culture   23

Chapter 2   Retreating from the Public into the Profession   57

Chapter 3   The Postmodern-Postcolonial Stimulus
and the Rise of Chinese Post-ist Theory   88

Chapter 4   The Anxiety of Cross-Cultural Theorizing   129

Chapter 5   Remembering Intellectual Activism in the
Postsocialist-Postcolonial Condition   163

Notes   203

Bibliography   225

Subject Index   251

Name Index   267

Abbreviations

DDZJPL	*Dangdai zuojia pinglun* (Review of contemporary writers)
ESYSJ	*Ershiyi shiji* (Twenty-first century)
GMRB	*Guangming ribao* (Guangming daily)
HZSFXB	*Huazhong shifan daxue xuebao* (Journal of Central China Normal University)
RMRB	*Renmin ribao* (People's daily)
SHWX	*Shanghai wenxue* (Shanghai literature)
WGWXPL	*Waiguo wenxue pinglun* (Foreign literature review)
WLB	*Wenlun bao* (Literary theory news)
WXB	*Wenxue bao* (Literary news)
WXPL	*Wenxue pinglun* (Literary review)
WXZYT	*Wenxue ziyoutan* (Literary free tribune)
WYB	*Wenyi bao* (News of literature and art)
WYLLYJ	*Wenyi lilun yanjiu* (Literary theory research)
WYLYP	*Wenyi lilun yu piping* (Theory and criticism of literature and art)
WYYJ	*Wenyi yanjiu* (Literary and art research)
WYZM	*Wenyi zhengming* (Debates of literature and art)
XHWZ	*Xinhua wenzhai* (Xinhua readers' digest)
ZGWHYJ	*Zhongguo wenhua yanjiu* (Research of Chinese culture)
ZHDSB	*Zhonghua dushu bao* (Chinese reading bulletin)
ZLYGL	*Zhanlue yu guanli* (Strategy and management)

Introduction

Chinese Cultural Discussion after 1989

Beginning in the late 1970s and early 1980s, the post–Cultural Revolution cultural discussion in China has been in search of itself—in search of its pro-enlightenment and pro-democracy premises, its proper procedures, and its distinctive focus of inquiry. Since the crackdown on the pro-democracy movement in 1989 put an end to the liberally oriented "Culture Fever" and imposed more rigid restrictions on the public forum, this search has had all the earmarks of a perplexing journey, immersing many academic intellectuals in a state of confusion and political passivity. Cultural discussion in China has turned away from politically engaged and intellectually oppositional topics: historical and cultural reasons of despotism and tyranny; the urgency of political reform and democracy; the need of social enlightenment and its humanistic values of tolerance, civil liberty, and intellectual freedom; deliberation on the rule of law versus the rule of man; and debate on new authoritarianism versus democracy. Cultural discussion of the 1990s has considerably reshaped its orientation. Most new currents of cultural discussion, by choice or circumstance, have shown either a reconciliation of intellectual inquiry with the prevailing political order or a deliberate avoidance of sensitive sociopolitical issues. In this study I will examine three major trends that indicate such changes: the debate on the humanist spirit (*renwen jingsheng taolun*), the new Chinese national studies (*xin guoxue*), and the postmodern-postcolonial theory, also known as "post-ist studies" (*houxue*).[1]

Cultural discussion in China used to constitute a unique form of cultural criticism or cultural studies, drawing on a tradition of engaged and politically relevant intellectual activism that took shape over the course of China's century-long encounter with the West and its efforts at national reconstruction. The two most exciting and memorable moments of pro-enlightenment and pro-democracy cultural discussion occurred during the New Culture Movement in the beginning decades of this century and the Culture Fever after the Cultural Revolution. These were periods when many Chinese intellectuals faced up to the challenge of cultural reflection and tried to incorporate cultural concerns into their inquiry of the country's social and political modernization. The cultural criticism inscribed in Chinese cultural discussion differs significantly from its Western counterpart, known as "cultural studies," in terms of its historically situated orientations and demands.

After attending a 1995 conference on cultural studies in China, Jonathan Arac was amazed by how the Chinese concept of cultural studies differs from its usage in the West. Arac finds that much of the cultural discussion—in the 1990s, of course—is defined "in relation to the topics of the Postmodern and the Postcolonial, far more than in relation to what most English or American academics would consider 'Cultural Studies'":

> In an intriguing index of comparative international renown, Fredric Jameson and Jean-François Lyotard, as theorists of the postmodern, and Edward Said, as inaugurating postcolonial inquiry, seem far more familiar to [Chinese theorists] than do Raymond Williams or Stuart Hall as fundamental resources for cultural studies. (1997a, 135)

The Chinese cultural discussion is theoretically, sometimes philosophically, oriented, rather than marked by "closely detailed case studies, tending considerably toward the empirical, and discussing cultural productions or activities, not necessarily in print form, that occurred in the present or quite recent past and that were not high on the standard scale of prestige" (136). Western cultural studies have grown out of efforts to comprehend and address the effects of modernity, while Chinese cultural criticism, in contrast, has evolved from the necessity to *accelerate* the process of modernization. Various versions of Western cultural studies, as Lawrence Grossberg, Cary Nelson, and Paula Treichler observe, share the same effort "to understand the processes that have shaped modern and postwar society and culture" (1992, 5). The historical condition, which manifests itself in different Western national contexts and results in distinctive but generically similar cultural-studies traditions, is not the same as the condition in which Chinese cultural criticism finds itself.

With the tremendous changes that have occurred in China since 1989, especially after 1992, a set of new ideas and theoretical orientations has appeared on the Chinese intellectual scene, most of them marked by political evasiveness and disenchantment with democracy. New domestic and international factors have affected much of the intellectual transformation in the 1990s. Domestically, accelerated marketization of Chinese economy and increasing commercialization have brought into the open numerous domestic problems that many people believe may evolve into social chaos and political instability if the country is not brought under the control of a strong authoritarian government. This leads to the popular view that for the sake of stability and economic growth it is worthwhile to sacrifice greater political freedom. After all, the model of Asian modernity—understood as a combination of economic liberalization and political authoritarianism—suits China's own tradition and social conditions better than the Western model, which emphasizes individual rights and political democracy. Internationally, chaos and instability brought about by the dissolution of the Soviet Union and regime changes in Eastern Europe after 1989 present a frightening picture to many Chinese observers. In Eastern Europe and the Soviet Union, when the nature of civil society changed, as when limited reforms in electoral laws allowed for more open debate, the state's authority rapidly cracked. Many Chinese people are afraid that unleashing the public sphere and allowing real debate may lead to a similar collapse in China.

For many Chinese intellectuals these new historical factors are compounded by their particular sense of marginalization and disillusion. Chinese intellectuals in the 1980s played an important role in social enlightenment, not because of a strong institutional base but because of their symbolic role as victims and cultural and moral standard-bearers in an unfree society. Cultural pluralism in the 1990s has undermined this role of the intellectuals. The rise of popular culture and the commercializing and commodifying forces behind it have dramatically marginalized the intellectuals and their elite culture. Being increasingly at the mercy of capital, intellectuals are in the process of changing from the role of critical and oppositional thinkers to that of wage earners and moneymakers. The intellectuals' sense of being marginalized is aggravated by their disillusion with politically engaged, especially pro-democracy, cultural criticism. Since the June 1989 incident, in the view of the public, to talk about enlightenment and democratization has become passé. The assumption is that one cannot still believe in these ideals when they so obviously do not work. On a pragmatic level it clearly means that, whatever it is that Chinese intellectuals do, they are doing it in the context of a discourse that says "democracy does not work or fit in China." And so, in whatever they want to do, they have to take into account the China-West differences in terms of history, cultural tradition, values, and national interests. Anti-Western sentiment developed after Beijing's failure in 1993 to win its bid to host the year 2000 Olympic Games; it has continued to escalate due to the ongoing dispute between China and the United States regarding China's Most Favored Nation (MFN) trading status, China's entry into the World Trade Organization (WTO), and sensitive issues such as human rights, Taiwan, and Tibet. These events have made many Chinese intellectuals who used to be cynical about the government's anti-Western propaganda concur with the official position that there exists a Western conspiracy to contain China. And this has given rise to a commonly held nationalist sentiment among the elite and the general public.

The change in the Chinese intellectual atmosphere in the 1990s often eclipses important questions concerning the relationship between China's formidable post-Tiananmen political-economic reality and its intellectuals' low political morale. How shall cultural critics assess China's political-economic reality, its forced combination of Leninist party-state and economic liberation, its legitimacy, and its rationales? How shall they rethink their own academic and professional endeavor in terms of the aims and obligations of engaged, critical intellectuals under new circumstances? How shall cultural criticism deal with Chinese intellectuals' low political morale regarding democratic changes without ignoring or underestimating the conditions that create it? How can Chinese intellectuals legitimate their social role in the face of the cretinization of the academy? Many Chinese intellectuals have shied away from these questions and ignored the fact that many of their own adjustments have much to do, above all, with the crisis of intellectual activism in the wake of its defeat and demobilization since the Tiananmen period (from June 1989 to early 1992). They often present their own retreat from politically engaged cultural and social critique as a change from frantic radicalism to moderate and realistic thinking, as the maturing of scholarly and professional sense, or as a new wakening from the myth of enlightenment and modernity—in a word, as freely made intellectual choices, rather than twisted options imposed by the undemocratic condition. Because such a self-understanding tends to view forced intellectual adjustments as having been freely arrived at, it downplays the ways in which the repressive political condition curtails intellectual choices in China. As conflict over reality assessment and over the terms of intellectual engagement intensifies and as political challenges emerge within intellectual debate itself, reflection on the current situation and available intellectual options has become one of the focal points of cultural-political debates among Chinese intellectuals.

What Does "Post-1989" Mean in China?

To understand the cultural discussion and its political implications after 1989, one must understand what "after 1989" means. In this book the designation does not only mean a dividing pause in time but also "post-1989," a historical marker of the contemporary state, situation, or condition. History, like perception, suggests a logic in contingency, a reason in unreason; historical forces, like perceptual figures, only come actively into focus through a human endeavor that, by actualizing them, defines them (Merleau-Ponty 1968, 46). Like perception, history can never be construed accurately as a mechanical play of mute factors, whether cultural, economic, or political. History, as surely as perceptual objects, exists only in relation to the individuals that assume it, with a more or less clear consciousness of purpose. History represents a construct of meanings: both history and perception are irreducibly purposeful activities that try to establish a meaningful world.

Post-1989 signifies that 1989 is a year of great importance. This year is important not only for China but also for other areas of the world. It marks the end of the Soviet hegemony in Central and Eastern Europe, from which soon followed the end of the USSR. In the Chinese context 1989 was the year of the Tiananmen incident, which also became a symbol of the brief but darkest period of setback (1989–92) since the post–Cultural Revolution reform. Post-1989 essentially means "post-Tiananmen." For many Chinese the rapid marketization of China's economy, its growing prosperity, and the flourishing of mass culture, explicitly the result of Deng Xiaoping's inspection tour to southern China in early 1992, seem to have heralded the coming of a new era. They are torn between the desire for a better standard of living, ruthless economic competition, the accelerated pace of life, the pressure of commercialization, and conflicts between the old and new, between Chinese and non-Chinese cultures, between new economic reality and old political reflexes. The "being after" embedded in this still emerging new era contains a note of anxiety and unpreparedness, sometimes tinged with regret for the relative simplicity of the old ways or a deep sense of uncertainty.

Many intellectuals are no better prepared than the general public for the arrival of this new era in China. Recovering slowly and gradually from the aftermath and aftershocks of the period following the Tiananmen incident, these intellectuals find themselves stepping into a "post" condition that is not yet recognizable and a "post" mode of history that appears like endless presentness, the seeing through one's own eyes that amounts to ordering time retrospectively. The prefix *post* aligns *post-1989* explicitly or implicitly to different sets of other posts- in various trends of Chinese cultural criticism. Some align this *post* explicitly to the imported *postmodern* and *postcolonial* or to the homebred *post–New Era, post–vernacular Chinese (post-baihua), post-enlightenment,* and so on. Others, shunning or lacking interest in neologism, refer to this *post* implicitly as "post-1980s" or "post–Culture Fever," as in *post-1949, postrevolution,* or *post–Cultural Revolution.*

We can distinguish not only different kinds of conditions that *post-1989* is aligned with but also different referential emphases that the prefix *post* involves. On the one hand, *post* can mark a certain supersession of perception or understanding. When *post-1989* is used as a corollary of *postmodern* and *postcolonial,* these *posts* often refer together to the supersession of outmoded philosophical, aesthetic, and political theories. Postmodernism, for instance, implies going beyond modernist theory as well as a movement beyond a specific point in history, that of modernity. Even when *post* is used as a prefix in *post-1980s* or *post–Culture Fever,* it often implies a sense of supersession. It is not uncommon that Chinese intellectuals in the 1990s use these terms to suggest that their intellectual work is different from and superior to that in the Culture Fever of the 1980s for being more professional or more detached from extra-intellectual interests. On the other hand, *post* can also serve as a signal of periodization, underlining a passage into a new period and a closure of a historical age. In this usage people often resort to alternative terms of periodization, such as *1990s* or *after 1989.*

The year 1989 is not always given significance as a pivotal moment in the use of *posts* that emphasize periodization or supersession. As a matter of fact, much cultural discussion after 1989 opportunistically calls itself "1990s cultural studies," purposefully avoiding association with the politically sensitive year 1989. This erasing of 1989 reminds us of what Ian Gambles calls "forgetting recent history":

> Forgetting recent history is not the same as forgetting the distant past . . . Forgetting [recent history] means distorting the lens through

which we view the present. Consciously or unconsciously, it is an act of denial and repudiation, asserting or imagining that what was, was not, and that what was not, was. It is un-remembering. (1995, 26)

Any witting or unwitting forgetting of 1989 forecloses criticism of the unmitigated violence and repression epitomized by the June 1989 event and the totalitarian power that inflicted them. Counteracting the indifference to 1989, the notion "post-1989" invigorates a narrative in which what happened in June 1989 remains a central point of reference in the march of time from the "pre" to the "post."

Postmodernism in Postsocialist and Posttotalitarian China

In the celebratory and evasive rhetoric of Chinese postmodernism, 1989 is treated as a welcome moment when modernity ends by itself in China, rather than as a traumatic moment when post–Cultural Revolution contestation over the modernity project in China ended in an impasse. In the postmodern rhetoric 1989 is merely an empirical temporal sign that elicits no qualm or pang of conscience; it has little to tell us about the post-Tiananmen reality except that it is a postmodern one. It often oscillates woozily between two different definitions of postmodernism in China. The first definition is a chronological one of periodization. Since the 1980s were the prime time of modernity in China (literary modernism, technological and social modernization, and intellectual enlightenment), and, since the 1990s are felt to be "completely different" from and "after" the 1980s, then they must be the moment of postmodernism (Zhang Yiwu 1997, 247).[2] The second definition is a nonsynchronous and omnipresent one. Postmodernism is a descriptive category of China's mixed temporalities, or hybrid premodern, modern, and postmodern cultures (Wang Ning 1997, 38).[3] While the first definition is obviously mechanical, the second is too trite to count as an insight. The omnipresent postmodernism, with its locus of meaning in global capitalism, is of little value as an argument for the uniqueness of Chinese postmodernism, since it applies to many other third-world societies that exist today (Beverley and Oviedo 1995, 4). If so many third-world societies are characterized by hybridity and nonsynchronicity, then these qualities by themselves cannot serve as a critical standard to distinguish one from another. The cogency of these qualities must be sought somewhere beyond. The

uniqueness and complexity of China's uneven modernity and nonsyn-
chronous development are singularly revealed, among other things, in
China's typical historical events such as the Cultural Revolution and the
Tiananmen incident. At least for this reason, a postmodern survey of
China cannot afford to downplay the "being after" component in rela-
tion to these historical events.

After the Tiananmen incident and from the summer of 1989 to early
1992, China witnessed the return of the ghost of Maoist totalitarianism.
The renewed repression and terror of this dark period resonated with the
deadly echoes of the Tiananmen massacre and cast a long shadow of
political cynicism, apathy, and quietism on China's post-Tiananmen era.
It is not uncommon nowadays, however, for observers of Chinese affairs
to regard the Tiananmen dark period as a short pause that had little
effect on China's irrevocable course of economic reform, social openness,
and cultural pluralism. They tend to believe that, so long as economic
reform continues, the delicate and difficult issue of political democratization, of the reconciliation of economic and political values, can be safely
deferred to a late date. It may be true that commercialism, marketization,
and the rise of a new entrepreneurial class will further reduce the radius
of the Party's power. Yet the problem is that there is no constitutional
guarantee of a political operation that can be counted on to translate liberal economic values into compatible political values and no way of
knowing whether the new autocrats will be, and will thereafter remain,
benevolent and of a character enlightened enough to withstand the corrupting influences of near-absolute power; the possibility exists that the
Maoist ghost will make a new return (Prybyla 1996, 84).[4] From the outset
economic reform was linked to the leadership's determination to safe-
guard and perpetuate the Communist Party's monopoly of political
power. As Deng Xiaoping himself made clear, "Without the economic
results of reform and opening, we [the party] would not have survived
through June 4 [1989]."[5] Although economic liberalization has created
some social and cultural spaces that seem distant from the reach of the
Party's power, it has thus far not affected the Party's absolute value, that
is, its hold on monopolistic power no matter what. The Party's innovated
strategy to implement its unchanged value has produced a mix of systems
that defies formal logic and does not easily fit into existing theoretical
models.

Jean-François Lyotard defines *postmodernism* basically as a not-yet-
recognizable condition after modernism: "The postmodern would be

that which, in the modern, puts forward the unpresentable in presentation itself" (1984, 81). Lyotard suggests that the prefix *post* is a contingent sign, which happens to be attached to modernity in the West but not necessarily so in other contexts. *Post* signals what is not "in principle governed by preestablished rules" or can "be judged according to a determining judgment" or grasped "by applying familiar categories." Entrenched in a not-yet-recognizable condition after the dark period of the Tiananmen incident and facing an uncertain future, China has indeed moved into a post- phase. The questions that remain to be asked are: Is modernity the only historical contingency or social specificity that *post* in China is attached to? If not, what are other elements we must consider in order to have a situated picture of postmodernism in China?

I want to suggest two such elements that should be considered: totalitarianism and socialism. Partly because totalitarianism is a forbidden-zone topic in China and partly because of its Cold War overtones, observers of Chinese affairs in and out of China have avoided using it as a term to describe China's political condition. In contrast to this tendency, I want to stress that China's political system is still undeniably marked by a totalitarian syndrome. In his discussion of the Chinese economic-political system after 1989, Sujian Guo (1995) differentiates between two levels of the totalitarian syndrome. The first is a fundamental level, or dynamic core level, that consists of philosophical absolutism, inevitable goals, official ideology, and the single-party dictatorship. The second is the operative level, or the level of means for taking action. The operative features are changeable, as they have been applied selectively and in varying degrees, but they do not have a decisive effect on the totalitarian regime. The post–Cultural Revolution changes, and for that matter the post-Tiananmen changes in China, take place only on this second level. As is demonstrated by the Party's Four Cardinal Principles—to uphold the socialist road, the dictatorship of the proletariat, the leadership of the Communist Party, and Marxism-Leninism and Mao Zedong thought—the Communist regime is determined to maintain the dynamic core of the totalitarian model, although it has selectively initiated some changes on the operative level. It would be a mistake to interpret changes on the operative level as a transformation of the fundamental components of the totalitarian model. This is not to deny the existence of new official perspectives but rather to contend that the changing official perspectives are important only as post-facto rationalizations or justifications brought on by changing operative necessity.

The other essential element of China's basic condition is socialism. Socialism in China during the Mao regime was composed of three major elements: asceticism, egalitarianism, and statism.[6] They were tied to the Marxist-Maoist orthodoxy of the Communist Party's authoritarian regime. As the market economy is introduced into China's social mechanism, the regime is transforming itself from a coercive to a regulatory body of governance in some economic areas, but in other areas, such as public politics, news media, and civic liberties, the regime remains as coercive as before. The unevenness of change in different areas has much to do with resetting priorities in regard to former Chinese socialist elements. Asceticism and egalitarianism are either completely rejected or severely jeopardized in the post-1989 governmental project; only statism remains as the mainstay of the official ideology. These new developments indicate that China has entered a new phase following its original socialism. We can follow the lead of Paul G. Pickowicz and call this new phase "postsocialist" to underscore the disintegration of socialist legitimacy and credibility in China. *Postsocialism* denotes the massive disillusion of the common people with their actual life condition, the popular perception of the breakdown of the Party's moral authority, and the profound public awareness of the failure of the socialist system and alienation from its alleged moral justification. Moreover, the postsocialist condition is one in which the lack of citizen participation in political affairs and general apathy toward democratic reform form a vicious cycle. This creates a vacuum at the center of political discourse and renders people incapable of envisioning any positive alternative to dysfunctional socialism.

As manifested by the Tiananmen incident, postsocialist ideology in China is congruent and interdependent with the posttotalitarian mode of control and domination. They are interconnected but not identical. Together, however, they indicate a salient quality about the frame of China's present. While the *post* entailed in these terms suggests the death of the socialist vision, it also implies the Party's continuing efforts, in the name of socialism, to ensure monopolistic political power. The concept of a coeval postsocialist and posttotalitarian condition allows us to recognize the Leninist will to power and its largely effective domination and control even in an atmosphere of cynicism and disaffection.

Cultural theories in China after 1989 have by and large been silent on the relationship of cultural criticism to the postsocialist, posttotalitarian condition in which it is entrenched. In this book I want to challenge two kinds of intellectual reaction to China's specific post- condition: one is explicitly or implicitly apologetic, the other meekly evasive. I want to propose an alternative way to respond to and interact with China's status quo, which stresses the importance of democracy in cultural and social thinking. To break the overall patterns of the status quo requires the prior construction of an alternative to it, one that will not automatically develop from its inner logic. New needs and dissenting strata may be spontaneously created by the anomalies of the existing system, but the system has constantly proven itself capable of finding ways partially to satisfy these new needs by absorbing them into its own logic. The logic of the Chinese system now is that democracy must be kept separate from economic modernization and that political modernity (democracy, formal rights, full citizenship, etc.) may actually hinder economic modernization. This is the logic that the pro-democracy cultural critique will challenge. While the 1980s style Culture Fever could, indeed, fade away in the post-Tiananmen era, I believe the disparity between economic and political developments in China presents a new opening for pro-democracy cultural criticism. The democratic message of cultural criticism has the potential to speak to a public that once showed such tremendous support for the pro-democracy movement in 1989. If such a cultural criticism is to be reconstructed, it will be the result of the formulation and consolidation of a different logic, one in which alternatives to existing reality can be advanced.

It is necessary to differentiate between two kinds of unwholesome reaction to the existing order, which combines the Leninist party-state and economic liberalization: one accommodates it; the other does not but is not politically critical of it either. The first kind of reaction defends this combination as inherently valuable and valid, as a worthy model of modernity that must be appreciated on its own terms, such as a "socialist market economy," "socialism of Chinese character," or "China-specific modernity." It assumes, above all, an organic view of society in which the state embodies and is the guardian of the general interests of society, above and against vested interests. Proponents of this parochial model of modernity, though they may differ on various theoretical emphases, argue that "East" (or China) and "West" are two discrete systems of social, political, and economic organization based on enduring cultural traditions and values that transcend social and economic change. In their view, and in an ironic reversal of the Orientalism of nineteenth-century Europe, it is the Chinese, Eastern, or Confucian model that is proving to be superior to Western modernity, which has already entered the impasse of moral and social disintegration. This position informs two major theoretical discourses: neo-authoritarianism and the Chinese post-ist theory. While the former is explicitly concerned with defending Chinese authoritarian rule as culturally and politically legitimate, the latter renders implicit service to it by treating modernity in the Chinese context as nothing but a mystifying notion that is epistemologically false and geopolitically hegemonic. If all the Chinese efforts at political modernization aiming at overcoming despotism, arbitrary authority, social inequality, and servitude are misleading or in vain, if modern values of enlightenment, democracy, and human rights are either deceptive or chimerical, the only thing that really remains, then, is the authoritarian status quo. The only option is to surrender oneself to it.

By contrast, the second kind of reaction to the demoralizing combination of authoritarian control and market economy is less sanguine about its legitimacy and desirability, and, indeed, it is much more sensitive to its many moral problems. Yet many intellectuals who are concerned about China's status quo have good reasons to be fearful about confronting the governmental policy or the state ideology. They seldom fully come to terms with the unfair political-economic system, which is beset with problems of power abuse, monetized graft, corruption, and collusion, or with the single-party rule and its suppression of social and political dissent. Many of them divert their critical energy to two safer channels, discussing the humanist spirit and undertaking Chinese national studies. Advocates of the humanist spirit and practitioners of Chinese national studies describe social problems mostly in moral or professional terms, as the erosion of general moral standards, the disintegration of the intellectual tradition, or the breakdown of professional integrity, values, and norms. Their new strategies of providing indirect criticism and side-of-the-mouth commentary, dressed in the garb of antipolitics, provide a unique model of micropolitics after the death of organic intellectuals.

Of the four theoretical discourses mentioned here, the argument for neo-authoritarianism is the only one that was not newly established in the 1990s. It is not my intention to discuss it in this book, as that has been competently done elsewhere (Sautman 1992; Chen Feng 1997). Suffice it to say that neo-authoritarianism has been related to, but is not identical with, cultural traditionalism in the 1980s and 1990s. Cultural traditionalism can have different political orientations. It can be politically liberal, as in overseas New Confucianism, which seeks points of compatibility between Confucian and liberal values (Tu Weiming 1986, 1992) or stresses the Confucian tradition underlying the work of concerned, engaged, and politically relevant intellectuals (Yu Yingshi 1987, 1993). It can be politically ambiguous, as in mainland Chinese new Confucian studies, which pledge to help promote "socialist spiritual civilization" (Song Zhongfu, Zhao, and Pei 1991).[7] It can also be politically conservative, as in certain "Asian Values" or "Chinese Values" theories that are mobilized by authoritarian regimes as ideological statements of their interests (Ong Jieming et al. 1996). As an apologia of the undemocratic status quo, neo-authoritarianism is more closely related to the third proclivity of cultural traditionalism than the other two, and it has become an active element in the radical/conservative debate of the 1990s.

The other three intellectual trends, the postmodern-postcolonial criticism, the discussion of the humanist spirit, and the new Chinese national studies, have all emerged recently, in the 1990s. Having evolved from, but ignoring, the postsocialist and posttotalitarian condition, these newly formed theoretical orientations have so far eschewed the important problem of democratic construction in China and devoted their energy to some other forms of politics, especially geopolitics, postmodern politics, and academic or professional micropolitics.

On the one hand, postmodern-postcolonial theory attempts to explain away China's problem of democracy with its rhetoric of globalized market and postmodern politics. The framework of globalism has allowed proponents of Chinese post-ist theory to develop a new model of postmodern politics. Yet, as Norbert Lechner notes in his criticism of Latin-American postmodernism, "the risk involved is that postmodern movement of contemporary politics may abandon the notion that society can construct itself in a deliberate manner and that the reduction of politics to a 'political market' may exclude interests and goods that cannot be exchanged in the market," interests and values such as human rights, the sense of belonging together that is rooted in full citizen participation, and the desire for equality, freedom, and justice (qtd. by Brunner 1995, 48).

On the other hand, the humanist spirit discussion and the new Chinese national studies displace China's problems of democracy with pure moral and professional problems. Humanist spiritual and professional inquiries do suggest the existence of some academic areas of micropolitics in which change may finally emanate outward toward the society at large. Yet the monumental problems China faces—endemic corruption, glaring inequalities of wealth, unfair accessibility to social welfare, unequal opportunities for education and employment, suppression of social and political dissent, just to mention a few—require broad-based political solutions. People are asked to be prepared for and to make significant sacrifices (such as massive unemployment) during the transition of the Chinese economic structure and social norms, and to do so there must be some sense of participation from the public and the choice to change.

Pro-Democracy and Postcolonial Criticism in China

To reinvigorate the meek and evasive post-Tiananmen cultural criticism, Chinese intellectuals may find it necessary to rethink and reopen discussion of such traditional categories as "politics," "justice," "private life," "public activity," "citizenship," and "participation." They may also find it too early to give up that part of the enlightenment tradition that seeks to expand the capacity of the people themselves to make decisions that affect the conditions and terms of their lives. I would suggest reasserting in cultural criticism the social vision that favors the democratization of history making and the democratic principle that addresses problems of agency, cultural violence, political repression, and human emancipation. Only then can we hope to fathom how special forms of politics, such as postmodern politics or micropolitics, draw upon some basic ethical-political principles of strength, create out of them new visions of the future, gain from the experiences of their practitioners new critical skills and a broader sense of hope and possibility. While the need for a democratic principle is undeniable, the challenge also must not be underestimated. Here lies the crux of the situation: without the vindication of democratization as a viable oppositional principle, the reconstruction of cultural criticism cannot be completed, but this vindication now seems beyond reach more than ever. While the system of one-party rule will not allow it to happen anytime soon, the newly formed cultural theories cast doubt on its viability and feasibility. In the absence of a democratic principle of social and cultural criticism, there currently appears to be no coherent agenda to which critical intellectuals can turn in order to restructure their stymied cultural criticism.

Besides the unfavorable political condition, cultural criticism engaged with democracy faces another quandary: China's third-world status and the nationalist sentiment regarding its own way of political development. Born of China's encounter with the West and its efforts at national reconstruction, both democracy and nationalism have crossed and recrossed each other at so many vital points that it is essential to describe their intricate interrelations. The relationship of democracy and nationalism in China differs from its counterpart in the West, and, as a component in cultural reflection, it contributes to the uniqueness of the Chinese cultural discussion. As Hans Kohn points out, nationalism, arising in the eighteenth century in Western Europe, emerged simultaneously with democracy and industrialism, "all three closely linked in origin and continuous interaction," marking the advent of modernity (1961, vii). In China the transition from a civilization to a nation, from culturalism to nationalism, cannot be understood outside the context of foreign incursion.

The quest for democracy occurred at best as an afterthought to China's early nationalist effort to emulate the wealth and power of Western countries. In democracy, more than in any other corollary of modernity, Chinese intellectuals feel the pinch of a "time lag" between China and the West.[8] This time lag has consistently marked, or "colonized," China's quest for democracy and its mechanism of enlightenment as mimicry, an effort of emulation with only a secondary status to its "original" Western prototype. The lack of authenticity and genuine agency in that quest has become a stigma that Chinese intellectuals have had to cope with. They have had to share with the intellectuals of many other countries with colonial or quasicolonial experience the sense of the belatedness of their desire to identify with the ideals of progress, democracy, and modernity. To recognize this belatedness as part of China's third-world experience does not necessarily mean holding up Western history as the only model of progress. On the contrary, China can shuttle between different positions to claim a history that faces, but does not reflect, the West.

This seemingly inborn dilemma of democracy in China makes it necessary to conceptualize democracy not as the mere consumption of a Western idea but as a productive process, an endogenous question about good life, good society, and good government as well as about people's power. If we view the inquiry of democracy in China from this perspective, we can shift our critical focus and analytical object from *where* the idea comes from to *how* it is used and under *what* circumstances. We can shift from conceptual content to semiotic activity, from matching the "copy" with the "original," to make sense of the selective process of practice. Such an inquiry about democracy can be conceived in terms of the common structures and interpenetrations of intranational and international forms of coercion, domination, and violence. If so, it will become a meeting place for different forms of anticolonial and antiauthoritarian cultural critiques and between these and other forms of critical activities.

The "postcolonial" thus plays an important role in my interrogation of the post-1989 cultural discussion in China, especially the post-ist cultural theory. Challenging the nativist stance of cultural parochialism and xenophobia, I seek to rehabilitate postcolonial criticism as a form of cultural critique with an ethical-political commitment to human betterment in the third world. Situated in the first- or third-world social context, postcolonial criticism must ground its work in a moral imperative, that is, in opposition to cultural violence exemplified by language, philosophy, science, or ideology that can be used to perpetuate and legitimize tyranny, domination, and injustice. Such criticism must resist both international and intranational forms of cultural violence, what Edwin J. Ruiz (1991) has called the interstructuration of domination.[9] Moreover, in its opposition to all forms of cultural violence, postcolonial criticism must recognize the power of structural determinants in terms of historical-cultural heritage, modes of power, and economic and political institutions. Unlike the more intuitive advocates of third-world cultural revival or revolution, postcolonial cultural critics are more aware of the need for a theory that both recognizes human agency and the need for cultural transformation and, at the same time, accounts for the power of existing material and ideological structures. How to envisage such a theory has become an essential task for Chinese cultural criticism after 1989, and a proper concept of third-world democratization can provide it with a theoretical framework in which the postcolonial can help to advance significantly the dialectic between the third-world consciousness of resistance and structural determinants.

Critics have questioned the applicability of the notion of postcolonialism in China. Rey Chow, for instance, suggests that the two leading themes of "postcolonial politics" do not apply very well to China (1992, 159). The first of these is the Western colonialist "ownership," as well as its political and historical representation, of the third-world geographical space. The second is the third-world cultural and identity distortion authored and authorized by colonialism and Western domination. China—except for marginal areas such as Hong Kong—was never territorially occupied by the European colonial powers. Even when facing foreign incursions, the Chinese retained primary use of their own language, which continued to serve the purposes of writing and historiography and thus of preserving their cultural tradition. From another perspective Arif Dirlik takes postcolonial discourse to task for becoming a "liberating discourse that divorces itself from the material conditions of life [under contemporary] Global Capitalism" (1994b, 99). From Dirlik's Marxist point of view, global capitalism embodies the most essential forms of oppression and inequality faced by people in the third world, and "postcolonialism, in making Eurocentrism into the primary object of criticism, diverts attention from contemporary problems of oppression and inequality to focus on the legacy of the past . . . By denying to capitalism 'foundational' status, the postcolonial argument also suppresses the generation of new forms of power, of oppression and inequality, under contemporary capitalism" (96).

Unlike either Rey Chow or Arif Dirlik, I pursue my inquiry into postcolonial discourse within a framework not of historical colonialism or of globalism but, rather, of democratization. This distinguishes my position in two ways. On the one hand, although I, like Chow, have doubts about the immediate applicability of postcolonial discourse in the Chinese context, I want to stress the pertinence of postcolonial criticism in China as an ethic of opposition against both international and intranational forms of undemocratic politics and relations. On the other hand, although I admire Dirlik's sensitivity to domination and oppression, I tend to see the lack of democracy, rather than global capitalism, as the fundamental source of new forms of domination, oppression, and inequality in China.

Instead of opting for postmodernism, postsocialism, or posttotalitarianism as a self-sufficient framework for understanding and analyzing contemporary China, I would like to propose considering their complementary relations to the notion of the postcolonial. What we probably need is a multidimensional framework, which will help us to apprehend the present historical conjuncture that endows these *post*s with meaningful relations to one another. This is the framework in which we can make sense of the complexity and multiplicity of the *post*s at stake in China today. The post-1989 Chinese condition is too complex, too contradictory, and too dynamic to be isolated and described. The impossibility of using one single descriptive category or framework does not mean, however, that the political, social, and cultural phenomena of the 1990s are beyond understanding. Rather, it means that what is to be understood is precisely how we should stake out different *post*s without pigeonholing them in one single framework or another.

Staking out the *Post*s in Chinese Cultural Criticism

Staking out the *post*s in Chinese cultural criticism after 1989 involves first of all a strong assertion of the priority of democratization. The term *post-1989*, as I stressed before, suggests continuities and discontinuities but emphasizes the new modes and forms of undemocratic practices, not a "beyond." What it particularly watches out for is the suggestion that the quest for democracy and its legitimacy in the 1980s is a matter of the past after 1989. Not all 1980s cultural discussion was politically engaged and critical, but this does not alter the fact that it had a significant body of thought and action that was motivated by democratic inquiry. It is this body of thought and action that must not be lost in the passage from pre- to post-. To say *post* is to say *past;* hence, questions of remembering are inevitably raised when the term *post* is involved. As a signifier of a new historical epoch, *post-1989* should remind us that democracy is as urgently needed today as in the 1980s.

Staking out the *post*s also requires developing a situated interpretation of the ethical-political imperative of postmodern and postcolonial theories. There are two extreme ways to treat these theories: one is to embrace their truth without question, and the other is to reject them as irrelevant to Chinese cultural criticism. The third approach, somewhere between the two, looks for valid intentions behind these theories as critical actions and interprets those intentions for Chinese society. Cultural criticism that inserts itself into the broad postmodern-postcolonial movement seeks to enliven the movement's democratic potential and to work out the implications of this potential for the Chinese social situation. Dick Hebdige's comment regarding his own relationship to postmodernism suggests how a critic can appropriate its democratic potential for a situated interpretation:

> If postmodernism . . . means the opening up to critical discourse of lines of enquiry which were formerly prohibited, of evidence which was previously inadmissible so that new and different questions can be asked and new and other voices can begin asking them; if it means the opening up of institutional and discursive spaces within which more fluid and plural social and sexual identities may

develop; if it means the erosion of triangular formations of power and knowledge with the expert at the apex and the "masses" at the base, if, in a word, it enhances our collective (and democratic) sense of *possibility*, then I for one am a postmodernist. (1988, 226)

In the Chinese context the value of postmodern and other post- theories lies in their role as shifting signifiers that both reflect and contribute to the increasingly complicated and unstable relationship between new theoretical discourses and the dominant official ideology. The important point here is not whether these post- theories should be used or not but how their best insights might be appropriated within a progressive and emancipatory democratic politics.

My own way of engaging with post- theories is to use democratization as a focal point to explore points of connection and contradiction between them and their political implications. I insist that cultural criticism is political in nature. "The political," to borrow a term of Slavoj Žižek,[10] is not limited to one form of cultural discussion or theorizing; all forms of cultural criticism are political, whether or not the participants acknowledge the politics in their work. The political informs their relations to the prevailing conditions, whether favorable or adverse. The political finds its way into the issues and problems that are included or excluded. The political also resides in the discourse of the discussion, in the way intellectuals talk to the common people as equals, talk down to them, or talk only among themselves. The politics of cultural discussion suggests that cultural engagement has political consequences, since the way it is conceptualized and conducted will orient people either to conform and accept their place in the status quo or to think independently and critically, either to submit to or to question the system they live in and the knowledge being offered to them.

A politics of ideas can and must be different from the undemocratic politics of party-state power. Conceived as a strategy of intellectual resistance, a politics of ideas should be informed by the basic values of freedom, equality, and justice. Based on rational argument and on choices freely made on that basis, a politics of ideas opposes the kind of politics that relies on coercive and violent means. To be a critic-intellectual engaged in such politics makes one an ethical thinker, because such politics derives its validity and authority not from its capacity to wield coercive power but from ethical conviction. It argues in the name of the universal good. Unless a politics of ideas is concerned with a human collective large enough for people to feel they belong to it and worthy enough for people to aspire to it by behaving in a certain way, unless a politics of ideas is successful in showing that it is moving people in that direction, and unless it can posit a vindicating telos and present itself as a politics of liberation, it is not likely to possess any persuasive power.

The choice of a politics of ideas over ordinary politics is both a strategic and an ethical choice. It is strategic because it enables those who are marginalized by the current power structure to involve themselves in politics. It is ethical because it is a rejection of party-state power, a rejection based not on the latter's supposed inefficiency or irrationality but on the ethical claim that such power rationalizes domination and repression. A politics of ideas locates itself in a civil society that is neither a monolithic structure nor the site of a life-and-death class struggle. In this public sphere the intellectual's opposition is political in the sense that politics is essentially an "agonal" undertaking, that is, a tension-filled contest revolving around a public relationship steeped in mutual respect, tolerance, and a willingness to let one another "be" (Dallmayr 1984, 9, 116).

With such a view of cultural criticism and politics of ideas I begin, in chapters 1 and 2, to assess the two major humanist-professional approaches after 1989: the humanist spirit debate and new Chinese national studies. I take the view that, despite some humanist-professionalist intellectuals' tendency to divorce themselves from politically sensitive issues, there are some significant—and instructive—moments in which such isolation can be overcome. In my assessment of their political quietism I do not claim that they simply affirm the status quo or that their apathy expresses the intention to delegate social and political responsibility to power holders or to disregard or be resigned to the moral failures of such authorities. Rather, I see in the political withdrawal of humanist-professional intellectuals a feature of political consciousness under undemocratic circumstances. I dispute the effectiveness of such intellectual reactions to adverse conditions, but ineffectiveness in challenging the status quo is not the same as an intended collusion with the dominant official ideology. Although many post-1989 humanist-professional intellectuals have been disoriented by the demise of pro-democracy cultural criticism and unable to maintain their political relevance, they have nevertheless refocused their critical attention and sought new channels for their humanistic ideas and values.

In chapters 3 and 4 I discuss Chinese post-ist theory, another post-Tiananmen trend. Practitioners of Chinese post-ist theory have drawn to a considerable extent upon the perspectives provided by Western post-modern and postcolonial theories and adopted a third-world stance against Western cultural hegemony. They are concerned with the historically new: the rise of mass culture, the rapid maturation of consumer culture and its incorporation with global capitalism, the post–Cold War configuration of cultural conflict, and so on. While sharing their concern with the newly formed experiences and phenomena in the 1990s, I question their way of presenting these experiences and phenomena exclusively in the frame of global capitalism and the China-West dichotomy. Although emphasis on global capitalism allows post-ist theorists to participate in cultural theory at a high level and gives them what appears to be a politically progressive stance, their engagement with issues of national authenticity and global imperialism blinds them to local authoritarianism, which chugs along happily in the absence of any real challengers. The point at issue is not whether we should do post- theories of mass culture, history, national identity, modernity, progress, and so on but whether we can legitimately decontextualize these theories and minimize the postsocialist and posttotalitarian condition of doing these theories in China.

Chinese cultural discussion in the 1990s is characterized not only by new trends in terms of debates and theories but also by certain recollections and reevaluations of the cultural discussion in the 1980s. In chapter 5 I undertake to examine how the contests over memories of the 1980s pro-democracy cultural criticism illustrate the essential role remembering plays in mediating and defining the present intellectual self-positioning, in particular as this contest is manifested in the ongoing debate about cultural radicalism and conservatism. In order for people to control how they define themselves in the present, it is necessary for them to control how they define the past. Memory is a particular relationship to time, and as such it is mediated by the narrative structures through which intellectuals apprehend and render their past experience significant. On the one hand, the existing power relations in a society determine the way memory is controlled and circulated. On the other hand, memory contributes to the perpetuation or challenge of these power relations.

Actively remembering the pro-democracy cultural criticism of the 1980s means looking to the past for the democratic vision and commitment that has been forgotten by the present insipid forms of cultural criticism. It seeks to force revision of existing intellectual ambition by supplying a specially focused perspective about the past. It is not just a carping or biting criticism of the restraining forces outside of the critics themselves. It is a critical mode of thinking that also confronts the amnesia of fatigued intellectuals in flight from their commitment to freedom and resistance. To remember in a critical mode has to do with acknowledging the present conjunction of history, its restraints on alternative possibilities, and its hidden promise of liberation. Critical remembrance of this kind can establish the discursive and ethical referents needed for an ongoing pro-democracy struggle for social change. The subversiveness of such memory is summarized by Sharon Welch in the term *dangerous memory* (1985, 39). Such memory describes a category of remembering that serves both to describe and critique specific histories of oppression "often unaddressed and tacitly tolerated." It is a memory not only of tyranny and injustice but also of freedom and resistance, and, when it has to be forged in the margins of the hegemonic consciousness, it becomes a counter-memory and a form of oppositional criticism.

Chapter 1

The Crisis of National Identity and the Decline of Unitary Culture

Unlike any of the forty years preceding it, 1989 in China will be remembered for the eruption of new democratic enthusiasm and for its suppression by brutal force. The unexpected scope, the unprecedented devastation, and the rapidity with which the pro-democracy movement evolved into a tragic deadlock took the nation by surprise and have precipitated a nationwide crisis, the depth of which it may take many years to fathom. The sudden events of May and June 1989 were fused onto circumstances that had already been agitating the people: corruption and profiteering, bureaucratic inefficiency and unfairness, an unstable and unequal economy, political repression, status hierarchy, and the lack of free speech or of a free press. The cultural discussion of the 1980s raised these issues when it criticized the Cultural Revolution and the pernicious residue of China's tradition of feudalism and despotism.

The crisis of 1989 built gradually since the mid-1980s, when requests for "modernization of the mind," a less openly challenging expression of democratization, were repeatedly made by critical intellectuals and denied by the government. In December 1986 students at the University of Science and Technology in Hefei protested their lack of power to nominate candidates for the People's Congress. This protest heralded student protests on many other campuses, which became a coherent movement across the country. Students called for democracy in their chants during the demonstrations, and their wall posters and placards read, "Down with bureaucratism; return to us democracy" and "Down with autocracy." Some Beijing University posters read, "We want democracy; we want freedom," "We want law; we do not want autocracy," and "Fight for freedom of the press." In other universities the theme was similar: "We will fight for democracy; China should work for the people, not for a small group" (cited in Kwong 1988, 974). Many students participated or were influenced by the then ongoing cultural debates, whose major themes included modernization, humanism, and liberal values of freedom and equality.

In 1988 the appearance of *He shang* (River Elegy), a six-part television series on CCTV and many local television stations, marked a crucial moment in the 1980s cultural discussion when people from all walks of life responded warmly to the questioning of China's feudalist tradition. *He shang* attacked traditional Chinese culture by claiming that some of the country's most revered symbols—the Yellow River, the Great Wall, the dragon, mythic Confucianism—actually represented China's backwardness and passivity, not its greatness. The enormous impact *He shang* had on Chinese audiences nationwide indicated that people's tolerance for the social and political problems associated with the lack of democracy was wearing dangerously thin. The student movement in 1989, which served as the catalyst for Chinese people from all walks of life—including many Communist Party members—was the proverbial straw that broke the back of governmental control.

The Postsocialist Legitimacy Crisis and the Crisis of National Identity

The Tiananmen massacre stunned the country and aggravated the legitimacy crisis in China. What was at stake in the post-1989 legitimacy crisis was not just the political and moral credibility of the government but, more profoundly, how the individual Chinese was henceforth to draw a *worthy* identity from his or her nation. A legitimacy crisis, as Jürgen Habermas says, "is directly an identity crisis" (1975, 46). The question of national identity was vital in the 1980s. When entering the post-Mao period, China suddenly fell from the status of a model of self-reliant socialist development to that of impoverished and underdeveloped power, lagging far behind not only Western countries and Japan but also the small Confucian newly industrialized countries or areas in Asia. This crisis was caused by a sudden reality shock rather than troubled national identification. As a matter of fact, in the late 1970s and early 1980s concern for China's position among the world's nations and the issue of *qiuji* (global membership) had actually become a powerful mobilizing force for national identification. Having overcome this sudden reality shock by a decade of highly successful economic reform, the Communist Party leadership turned violently against some of the sequelae of reform at Tiananmen, plunging the nation into moral chaos and leaving the nation's future course and identity in sinister uncertainty.

National identity, in particular, involves a relationship between the individual and the nation-state. In dynastic China, when neither "nation" nor "state" existed, the relationship was initially conceived of as that of subject and only with the establishment of the republic system as one of citizenship. Yet, whatever the juridical categories used, the state has had to reckon with the existential reality of community, or the society that mediates between the individual and the state. In China this mediating society has been weak, and its function has been served largely by a fused relationship between the state and the people. The state has been a conspicuous piece in the puzzle of how China has responded to the challenge of identity forming: what kind of nation it wants to be has long been the same as what kind of state it wants to be. The frail imperial state structure collapsed in 1911 when the issue of nation was brought to national awareness and the republicans who pushed the Manchu regime aside could not build an effective replacement. Out of the shifting morass of warlordism arose two Leninist state-organizations, the Nationalist Party under Jiang Jieshi and the Communist Party under Mao Zedong. Both were constructed political machines designed to funnel public opinion into a unitary consensus supporting their visions of national identity as well as their policies.

After winning power in 1949, the Communist Party did not sponsor the creation of a new nation-state but became it. The Party's ideology successfully provided resolution to the problem of national identity: China is a Communist country committed to the mission of a better and moral form of society, socialism. The state-people fusion is the condition for the Party to turn its ideology into the basis of national identity. On the people's behalf, and for their own good, the Party monopolizes all political power and exercises total control. Because it serves the people, it does not have to consult them. If the Party's monopoly has prevented the Chinese state from existing as a forum for representing and negotiating competing ideas and interests, that is because the Party represents the unitary will of the People; indeed, the Party is the people. The logic of Party-people or state-people fusion is the parental authority on the part of the party-state and the filial trust on the part of the people, or the nation.

It is not unusual to see the unitary idea of a party-dominated state as typical Leninist social system and to understand the legitimacy involved from this perspective (Manning 1994, 235–36). According to this theory, Leninist systems have been understood as based on a form of legitimacy or social contract that precludes a democratic transformation: "In return for the acceptance of one-Party rule and willingness to close ranks against a variety of internal and external threats, Lenin and his successors promised to prevent foreign military conquest, guarantee economic and social security to the majority, and eliminate starvation and illiteracy" (Kinston-Mann 1988, 10). Although Leninist states actually have also legitimated themselves on charismatic grounds or superpatriotic ones, with the death of the charismatic leader and the decline of immediate hostility, the claim to rule is generally based on socioeconomic performance, or what has been called "social eudaemonic" legitimation (from the Greek word for "happiness"). The mode of legitimation is based on the role of government in providing social and economic benefits for its citizens. For such a system socioeconomic grounds have typically been the single most important basis on which it seeks legitimation (White 1986, 463).

This distinctive legitimation formula and the political-economic tradeoff on which it is based are often described as a "social contract," "social compact," or "social compromise." The regime provides few of the civil liberties that citizens of liberal democracies take for granted: freedom from arbitrary arrest and torture, free speech, an independent press to ferret out corruption, the rule of law and merit criteria for government service, and open, competitive elections to keep power holders accountable. Instead, a Leninist regime promises an ever higher level of socioeconomic welfare, a comprehensive educational and health care system, security of employment and stable prices, modest but steadily rising living standards—all sustained by high and steady rates of economic growth within a framework precluding private ownership or containing market forces. The theory of the Leninist "social contract" believes that it is only when a Party-dominated state becomes unable to deliver the promised benefits that a legitimacy crisis occurs.

The case of China does not fit this theory very comfortably. The famine from 1959 to 1962 as a consequence of the Party's disastrous policy of "Leaping Forward" did not actually ensure a legitimacy crisis in China. Even the catastrophic Cultural Revolution did not cause anything close to the kind of post-1989 legitimacy crisis. We must look for a credible explanation and proper understanding of the post-1989 legitimacy crisis somewhere other than the Leninist "social contract." This legitimacy crisis has its roots in the breakdown of the state-people fusion that used to characterize China's socialist system. The breakdown of the state-people fusion marks the post-1989 legitimacy crisis in China not as a Leninist-socialist crisis but, rather, as a postsocialist crisis.

Here I use the notion "postsocialism" basically as Paul G. Pickowicz uses it, but with some modification to fit it more tightly into my consideration of the post-1989 condition. Before Pickowicz, Arif Dirlik and others have used the notion postsocialism to denote "socialism with Chinese characteristics," a self-styled new theory of socialism claimed by the post-Mao Party elites. Pickowicz uses the concept in a very different way. As he explains:

> [In my use] postsocialism refers neither to the abstract realms of theory and ideology nor to the world of Party elites and official culture. That is, I seek not to evaluate the contemporary Chinese world as it looks from the top down, but to understand the way it looks from the bottom up. My definition of postsocialism deals with the domain of popular perception . . . Those who live in a postsocialist environment are inclined to look upon socialism not as a theory (relatively few people in China know or care much about socialist theory), but as an actual social system that has established a particular economic, political and cultural record over the past fifty years and has affected daily life in various way. (1995, 61)[1]

Used in this sense, postsocialism denotes the massive disillusion of the common people with their actual life condition, the popular perception of the breakdown of the Party's moral authority, and the profound public awareness of the failure of the socialist system and alienation from the false love proclaimed by the parental party-state. The postsocialist condition, as Pickowicz observes, "is not one in which the theory of socialism has been considered and rejected by ordinary people." The postsocialist condition is one in which the lack of citizen participation in the political affairs, apathy toward democratic reform, and mistrust of existing public institutions have obliterated the vision of any alternative to the dysfunctional socialism.

The postsocialist condition does not come about all of a sudden, nor has one single conduct of the Communist Party alienated people of all social classes and given socialism a bad name. It is hard to say exactly when the postsocialist period began. We can certainly find, as Pickowicz does, signs of the disillusion with socialism and the onset of an alienated postsocialist mode of thought and behavior midway through the Cultural Revolution. We have good reason to assume, however, that the scope and intensity of this disillusion and alienation caused by the Cultural Revolution were not as widespread and devastating as Pickowicz believes them to be. The Cultural Revolution did not cause the early popular faith in socialism to vanish, as Pickowicz asserts. The post-Mao Party elites were still able, at least for the first few years after the Cultural Revolution, to blame the failure of Maoist socialism on the Gang of Four. The massive outpouring of genuine hope, political enthusiasm, and social energy immediately after the downfall of the Gang of Four proved that the Party was yet well capable of leading the common people to view the system that had caused their immense suffering as false socialism and to believe that all the previous wrongs could be redressed in the new system of real, humane, and democratic socialism. So far as the popular faith in socialism is concerned, socialism in China did not enter the phase of "post" simultaneously with the advent of the post-Mao age.

Dirlik uses "postsocialism" to name the post-Mao socialism, especially the so-called socialism with Chinese characteristics that has received the status of orthodoxy since it was presented to the Twelfth Congress of the Communist Party of China in 1982 by Deng Xiaoping.[2] The term *postsocialism,* as Dirlik explains, "is intentionally residual, since the historical situation that it is intended to capture conceptually is highly ambiguous in its characteristics" (1989, 364). For Dirlik the ambiguity concerning the Chinese socialism is primarily one of "political metatheory," and the value of postsocialism lies in its challenge to the binary opposition of socialism/capitalism. Although Dirlik's notion of postsocialism is interesting as a socialist theory of postmodern style, it does not explain why socialism was still a popular social vision in China in the years immediately after the Cultural Revolution. In the early years after the Cultural Revolution it was the Party's gesture to reconsider socialism's humanist premises and democratic aspirations, rather than its "articulation of socialism to capitalism," that helped to sustain Chinese people's faith in socialism.[3] It did not take long for the post-Mao Party elites to dash the newly rekindled hope in genuine, humane, and democratic socialism. Their attack on Bai Hua, their repression of the discussion on Marxist humanism, their constraining of intellectual and academic freedom, and their besmirching of demands for democracy as "bourgeois liberalization" and "spiritual pollutions," all in the name of defending socialism in China, contributed to the increasing elusiveness of socialism as a sincere and trustworthy political concept, thereby rendering socialism even more suspect as a mere ideological disguise for totalitarian single-party domination and control.

Dirlik's *postsocialism* is not so much a wrong term as an irrelevant one for understanding the steadily building post-Mao legitimacy crisis that culminated in the May and June events of 1989. And this is why Pickowicz's notion of postsocialism, which emphasizes popular disillusion with socialism rather than the post-Mao definition of socialism by Party elites, is a better description of the situation in China from the late 1980s to the 1990s, although this notion is not very suitable to explain the condition of socialist ideology in the early years after the Cultural Revolution. In Pickowicz's use, as Chris Berry and Mary Ann Farquhar point out, postsocialism marks "the death of socialism and the emergence of something different" (1994, 84). The Tiananmen massacre is certainly the most drastic and decisive event that has forcefully declared the death of socialism in China by destroying once and for all its foundation of state-people fusion. It is this historical event that has rendered significant and crucial the difference between Pickowicz's and Dirlik's concepts of postsocialism. In the present context of my own study, it is a difference not just of theoretical definition but of how relevant the concept of postsocialism is to the purpose of understanding the post-Tiananmen legitimacy crisis.

I use the term *postsocialism* as an integral component of the concept of the post-1989 and the post-Tiananmen age, which is characterized by the posttotalitarian mode of control and domination.[4] While the *post* in *postsocialism* suggests the death of the socialist vision, it also implies the Party's continuing efforts, in the name of socialism, to ensure totalitarian domination and control in ideological and political areas. The concept of postsocialism allows us to recognize such domination and control as effective even in an atmosphere of cynicism and disaffection. Vaclav Havel defines the posttotalitarian regime as one whose voice of power no longer convinces but is still able to enlist the complicity of its subjects in staging the appearance that it does (1986, 45). Fleshing out Havel's insight, Ann Anagnost points out that, in post-1989 China, this complicity is enlisted "by more subtle forms of political terror as well as the redistributive power of the state to imbue the social will with a fetishism of the commodity that is in some respects more total than that of capitalism. If the post-Mao era may be defined as posttotalitarian, the period following June Fourth must count even more so" (1992, 181). Pickowicz emphasizes the tenacity of posttotalitarian control by pointing out, "In postsocialist society, failed institutions remain deeply rooted and continue to have a damaging impact on social, political, economic, and cultural life even though popular alienation is widespread and nonsocialist political forces have emerged" (1994, 83).

The post-1989 legitimacy crisis that does not fit in the model of a crisis of Leninist "social contract" can be understood better in the framework of postsocialism and posttotalitarianism. The breakdown of the foundation of Chinese socialism, the state-people fusion, cuts deeper than any crisis caused by mere material scarcity or lack of economic growth. It affects how the nation looks at itself, for socialist identity has become an integral component of Chinese national self-image since 1949 (Dirlik 1989, 378). Two aspects of this postsocialist legitimacy crisis need to be examined. They are, first, the rift between the state and the nation; and, second, the erosion of national moral vision.

The Rift between the State and the Nation

The first aspect of the post-1989 legitimacy crisis is the deep rift between the state and the nation, which was caused by the evaporation of parental authority on the part of the party-state and the loss of filial trust on the part of the people, or the nation. The parental authority, as Richard Sennett cogently demonstrates in his discussion of political paternalism, is a form of hegemony that is based on "the roles of fathers: protectors, stern judges, the strong" (1980, 54). The roots of practical and symbolic paternalism run deep in Chinese culture and political tradition. Foremost among the pastiche pictures of paternalist authority is the image of a father, a father from a more kindly and stable time, superimposed on the image of a sovereign with heaven's mandate. Paternalism, as Sennett notes, is something more than a passing phase in history: "The fate of this image of authority in the modern world is, in part, ironic. It has passed into the language of revolutionary socialism" (74). The Chinese Communist leaders have long made use of it, and the usage has reached a pinnacle during the Cultural Revolution.[5]

In the post-Mao era, even with the partial de-idolization of Mao, the symbolic basis of the party-state's parental authority remained unchanged. The socialist state run by the Party continued to resort to the concept of a caring parent. The party-state continued to play a parental, protective role to the Chinese people, its government being the people's government, its army being the people's army. Without the use of lethal force by the government against the common people, the parental authority of the party-state would not have collapsed so drastically. The Tiananmen massacre not only breaks the state-people fusion, but, more important, it reveals the nature and hypocrisy of the party-state's parental role. The legitimation of party-state power outside the family appeals to the roles within the family. To the extent this appeal works, those who are subservient are expected to be loyal, appreciative, and passive. The party-state's parental authority holds out a false love to its subjects: "False because the leader cares for these subjects only insofar as it serves his interest" (Sennett 1980, 82). Such authority makes a gift of its obligation and duty to others, and the terms of this gift are wholly in its control.

The logic of state-people fusion underscores the lack of differentiation between state, party-state, nation, and the people. Up until June 4, 1989, no one believed that the people's government would actually order the people's army to open fire on the people. The massacre completely surprised the nation because it was so drastically against what the nation believed itself to be. It shattered the nation's image of its own collective self. After the June 4 event, however, it has become equally difficult for anyone to believe that the state will not do it a second time, a third time, in the future. The creation and continuous strengthening of a special armed force of police (*wujing budui*) after 1989 have deprived people of any possible illusion that the massacre was only a onetime mistake made by some individual incompetent officials, a mistake the Party will not allow again in the future. The sharp contrast between the past of innocent filial trust and the present of alienation and mistrust makes it impossible for many Chinese to identify with the nation-state as they used to. The lethal force the state used against civilians has driven a wedge between the state and the people, destroying the identity linkage between them. By alienating the people, the state has also isolated itself from the nation. As a consequence, national identity in China has become more problematic than ever, for, as Lowell Dittmer and Samuel S. Kim observe, "National identity is the relationship between the state and the nation that obtains when the people of that nation identify with the state" (1991, 13).

The rift between the state and the nation renders questionable the moral content of the national identity as defined by the state. Lowell Dittmer and Samuel S. Kim suggest that a serviceable definition of

national identity requires substantive "content" as well as "boundaries."
In the post-1989 context the content factor is far more significant than the
boundaries factor, since neither China's territorial nor its cultural boundaries were threatened during this time. "National identity," Dittmer and
Kim explain, "should be understood as a predicate nominative rather
than as an abstract noun, as an ongoing process or journey rather than a
fixed set of boundaries, a relationship rather than a free-standing entity
or attribute" (13). To see national identity as a predicate normative and
an ongoing process is to understand it as constitutive and first and foremost axiological and pertaining to value: national identity is not what we
are by nature, by unchangeable determinants, but, rather, what we want
to be because it is good.

China's identity in international society is not a matter of the mixture of primordial qualities but the result of an active and value-oriented
collective choice, which is reflected in the role the country as a whole purposefully takes on. Such a role, as Dittmer and Kim make clear, "is
formed by assimilating the judgments of significant others and then fash-
ioning a specific 'mask' in anticipation of such judgments: an identity is a
repertoire of such roles" (15). National identity partly results from meaningful interaction with its reference group. The reference group contributes to national self-definition by providing it with a certain kind of
international legitimacy. Referring to like-minded significant others
allows a regime to maintain that its domestic social and political order
has international validity. China once sought its significant others in
socialist countries of the Eastern Bloc and then in third-world countries,
though only halfheartedly, because of its dominant Marxist ideology
(Kim 1989, 1990). The Tiananmen massacre and the government's
adamant resistance to international criticism have put China, against the
will of its people, in the company of international outlaws, thus creating
a situation in which many Chinese people are reluctant to respond to
claims for identification by the state with sovereignty over their political
lives, another sign that the post-1989 Chinese state lacks legitimacy.

Besides its international group reference, the notion of national identity can also be understood in philosophical terms as a dynamic one, and
at this point the humanistic definition of "modern identity" made by
Charles Taylor (1985) enters into a necessary relation with the notion of
national identity. To define my national identity is to define what this collective "we" must be in contact with in order to function fully as a particular collective subject and especially to be able to judge, discriminate,

and recognize what really is of worth or importance, both in general and for us as a nation. To say that something is part of our national identity is to say that without it we would be at a loss in making those discriminations that are humanly significant to the nation. Without it we as a collective national subject would lose the sense of what constitutes good, what goal is worth pursuing, what identity fulfillment consists of, and so on. Our national identity helps constitute the horizon within which these discriminations have meaning for the collective human subject.

This horizon is, of course, never fully defined. We find ourselves recurrently engaged in defining and exploring it further. But, given the humanistic values of freedom and equality as the basic elements of modern identity, we have a general sense of where it is to be found. What we call the modern national identity is the modern understanding of what the question of national identity amounts to, where we can look for an answer. Marxist ideology, with its moral premises that, in the final analysis, are not incompatible with the values of freedom and equality, used to provide the moral content necessary for China's national identity as a people's republic of socialism. But the state's use of lethal force against the people has destroyed the state-people fusion, which used to be itself part of the moral content of that Chinese national identity. Having lost much of its credibility, the Marxist-socialist ideology has been replaced to a large extent by the new ideology of nationalism that relies almost completely on primordial determinants such as China's mythical ancestors (Emperors Yan and Huang, in particular), the Chinese language, the indigenous Chinese life, and the essentialized Chinese culture. Such an ideology of nationalism is devoid of modern humanistic principles necessary for constructing a modern collective identity.

The Erosion of the National Moral Vision

The second aspect of the post-1989 legitimacy crisis is the erosion of normative principles in the national moral vision. The normative principles (freedom, equality, human rights, etc.) that help develop and sustain modern national identity and modern individual identity are not of two different kinds. Both modern national identity and modern individual identity are mediated through the common recognition of these normative principles. Such normative principles are particularly important to China as a third-world country because its worthy national identity today is sustained by a world culture that is different from that of the age of feudalism and despotism, a culture that elaborates and maintains a vocabulary of a nation's self-understanding that is also different from that of imperialism and colonialism. This kind of national identity is embedded in an international society (or international relations) in which it has a normative status similar to that of a free human subject in a modern civil society, both predicating self-determination and sovereignty. Contemporary society is now supposed to differ from the one defined by imperialist jungle laws or that defined by unbridled autocracy.[6]

After the success of the Communist Revolution, the national moral vision in China was once based on its socialist ideals of equality and social progress, at least in theory. The post-Tiananmen Chinese regime simply took a great leap backward on the issue of national moral vision. Instead of seeking national identity in a vision of the kind of country China wants to be because it is good, the regime resorts to primordial features of the Chinese in general and the myth of assumed blood ties in particular (the current slogan is "We are all offsprings of Yan and Huang"). The xenophobic nationalist theme of Western intrigue and threat has resurfaced alongside the government's efforts to mobilize public opinion against democratic activists by linking their ideas and actions to foreign sources of inspiration.[7] The mixture of nationalism and ideological orthodoxy explains political and practical conveniences for the central establishment but not any active, future-oriented function of a national moral vision.

The 1989 Tiananmen massacre has drastically deepened and widened the rift between the people and the nation's leadership and indeed the rift within the leadership itself. The common people are unprecedentedly alienated from the leadership and its orthodoxy and are becoming increasingly indifferent to politics and public affairs, to the future of the country, and to what the nation or its culture and tradition may mean to their troubled everyday lives. These troubles indicate something wrong with the tissue of public life: the lack of a sense of belonging together, a sense of sharing something deep that binds them together— meaningful common goals, social vision, national values, and indeed "Chineseness" itself. The identity crisis is a warning sign that the national community itself is facing serious problems regarding how to hold onto its socialist self-image and what kind of community it wants to be because it is good. In that sense the crisis of national identity is also a moral crisis for the whole Chinese society. These crises occur at the time when the consensus-forming mechanism breaks down, when moral skepticism and cynicism spread widely, and when collective goals and visions are unable to form.

It is against this background of the post-1989 legitimacy crisis and the sequential postsocialist national identity crisis that the new trends of cultural discussion after 1989 must be understood. Each of them, however, interprets and understands these crises in its own way. The intellectual trends after 1989 are, of course, not organized or concordant enterprises or movements but, rather, categories of activities, some local, some national, some quite ephemeral, others more permanent. Their adherents are mostly writers, critics, professors, scholars, and university students, on and off university campuses, who are interested in cultural issues and write about them.

New currents of post-1989 cultural discussion are characterized by their divergence about how to account for the lack of collective purpose in the contemporary national life and cultural experience. Writers and critics contributing to the formulation and expression of these new intellectual trends all try to provide their own answers to this question. Different as their apparent answers are, they seem to share a reluctance to tackle the sensitive sociopolitical issues the question itself entails, or, to use an expression common in China, they all "don't want to talk about politics." Ever since the Cultural Revolution, or maybe even earlier, for many Chinese intellectuals the experience of ever-changing political climates and Party policies has given rise to a general suspicion about ideology and politics. The public interest in politics and public affairs was resurrected, albeit cautiously and gradually, in the 1980s, only to sink into an even deeper political apathy after 1989.

General political apathy and withdrawal may be seen in particular as indications of a national identity crisis related to political development. As Lucian Pye points out: "In the process of political development an identity crisis occurs when a community finds that what it had once unquestionably accepted as the physical and psychological definitions of its collective self are no longer acceptable under new historical conditions" (1971, 111). Since the post-1989 official control makes the sociopolitical condition anything but favorable for Chinese intellectuals and other members of the society to redefine who they are in political or politicocultural terms, the crisis of national identity is accelerated and perpetuated. Historically, China has had profound traumatic experiences—for example, the anti-Japanese war, the famine of 1959–62, and even the Cultural Revolution—but such traumatic events did not produce the kind of national identity crisis China has been experiencing after the Tiananmen massacre. The profoundly changed and disoriented state-people and party-people relations have substantially changed the foundation of national identity and made it even more difficult for its political culture form to take shape in China.

Humanist intellectuals, with their concern for the humanistic spirit and its "ultimate concern" (*zhongji guanhuai*), are among those who have reacted most strongly to the current nationwide moral crisis. Yet, instead of recognizing this crisis as reflecting more fundamental crises of national identity and legitimacy, humanist intellectuals see it only as a crisis caused by a free-market economy, mass culture, and decline of public moral standards. They lament it as a "cultural" breakdown, rather than as social disintegration or political alienation. What they tend to ignore is that cultural breakdown ultimately reflects an impasse of values, which can have several aspects. One is the moral decline among both elites and the public. This moral decline is manifested in corruption of Party and government officials, in unrestricted greediness of the professional elites such as actors, artists, writers, teachers, doctors, and in the contagious obsession with moneymaking and philistinism of the public. Another is the breakdown of the minimal normative consensus necessary to bind diverse groups together. While many humanist intellectuals are correct to underline the significance of the cultural crisis and its relation to social malaise, they tend to privilege "culture" over social and political issues as China's most serious problem and deem a unifying culture as the elixir of social reconstruction. Although it may be argued that shared values are the glue of society, defining what those shared cultural values are in China, as anywhere else, is rarely easy, for diverse political, social, professional, and other forces have never stopped struggling to interpret what culture is and to advance competing moral order. Many humanist intellectuals are either unable or unwilling to recognize that it is the erosion of the constitutional fabric and the disintegration of the triad fusion of party-state-people after 1989 that fundamentally underscore the cultural and moral crises that they fear.

To many humanist intellectuals after 1989 the general moral crisis has led toward more specific considerations of three themes: the deterioration of culture and the attempt to overcome this deterioration; the collapse of the traditional polarization of elite and mass cultures and the natural foundation on which a vital cultural tradition has been constructed; and, finally, the quandary of intellectual identity marked by a deep sense of responsibility and noetic legacy but also by the fallen status of academic learning. These three apparently distinct themes turn out to be closely linked, determining the most significant character of discussions of serious/vulgar literatures and intellectuals' moral and ultimate concern, which are also know as the discussion of the humanist spirit in China.

It is not my purpose to provide a complete review of the various elements in the controversy over the humanist spirit. The interested reader can turn to other sources for the purpose.[8] The writings associated with the controversy of the humanist spirit in one way or another are many and diverse, and I can scarcely do them justice here. Important, however, is the recognition that the notion of the humanist spirit includes many issues that should be separated and discussed in different terms. The question is whether the formulation of issues in terms of the humanist spirit has really tackled the problems that have to be faced or whether it has confused the post-1989 social and political situation Chinese intellectuals find themselves in. Perhaps the first task is to unpack the bundle of issues about the loss of unitary culture that results from and perpetuates the decline of the humanist intellectual's authority and about the intellectual's relations to existing institutions and his or her subjectivity as a socially situated agent. I shall stress those issues in which the debates are particularly Chinese—the popularity of so-called hoodlum literature (*pizi wenxue*) exemplified by Wang Shuo's fiction, the threat hoodlum literature and mass culture seem to pose to "serious" writers and their culture, and the humanistic ideal of ultimate concern as a resolution to China's post-1989 social, national, and legitimacy crises defined in purely moralistic terms.

Hoodlum Literature and Serious Literature

Dong Zhilin, in "A Summary of 'the Humanist Spirit' Controversy" (1995), traces the beginning of the controversy to an article published in 1993 by Wang Meng, the famous writer and former minister of cultural affairs, who lost his position because of his sympathetic attitude toward the pro-democracy movement of 1989. In this article "Avoid Nobility" (1993) Wang Meng defends Wang Shuo, a young Beijing writer, against accusations that he is responsible for the spread of hoodlum literature among general Chinese readers and for corrupting them with demoralizing hoodlum values embodied by many of his literary characters, who are seen by many of Wang Shuo's critics as irresponsible, cynical, antisocial, and anti-intellectual. Wang Meng claims that many serious writers hold Wang Shuo and his works in contempt because they have long lived in self-created illusion, seeing themselves as the nation's forerunners, martyrs, teachers, and men of wisdom: "They choose the self-image of all knowing 'elite' and regard themselves as superior to their readers" (1993, 10–11). Therefore, a "vulgar" but immensely popular writer like Wang Shuo becomes all the more valuable as an antidote to the absurd and false heroism and sense of nobility of those self-conceited serious writers. Addressing accusations that Wang Shuo's works are demoralizing and profane, Wang Meng asserts that we should not look for the source of spiritual pollution and corruption in the wrong places; it was not Wang Shuo's works but, rather, endless official political campaigns that have abused and reviled the noble ideals in the Chinese life. "Profanity and abuse," Wang Meng writes, "started from our very life . . . Over and over again our political campaigns have turned all sacred things, from '-ism,' 'loyalty,' 'party membership' to human life, into jokes. Before Wang Shuo plays fool, [those in power] have already fooled everyone of us" (1993, 14).[9] Wang Meng suggests that Wang Shuo should be evaluated and appreciated on Wang Shuo's own terms. If Wang Shuo is not a serious writer, he is at least honest, for Wang Shuo does not write for the wise and the ambitious or for ladies and gentlemen; he writes for the people in the streets. If Wang Shuo's literature has a social function at all, it is probably as an antidote to the hypocritical and selfish serious literature produced in the name of guiding and serving the people (Wang Meng 1994b, 1995).[10] Wang Meng's defense of Wang Shuo was responded to vehemently by many writers and critics, who assaulted Wang Meng for uncritically accepting or even sponsoring the decline of moral and artistic standards of literature and writers in the 1990s and for betraying the tradition of socially responsible intellectuals.

The discussion soon moved from Wang Shuo to more general issues such as the current situation of Chinese literature and what standards critics should use to evaluate it. Most of Wang Meng's opponents hold more or less the same humanist view that literature is fundamentally about people and their ideals and should serve as a humanizing force in society. Literature, as Xie Mian (1995), a Beijing University professor, insists, "should increase and develop man's sensitivity to truth, beauty, and good; it should create a world better than real life." Hong Zicheng (1995), a literary critic, deplores literature's ruined ideals in the 1990s. He recalls the 1980s as a time when the humanist spirit was like a tidal wave that swept China. The tide has receded, and in its wake the shore is littered with all kinds of garbage. "We raise the issue of [a noble] ideal in contemporary literature," Hong writes, "because we are haunted by a painful feeling that, in our 'present' literature, spiritual elements and strength are being sapped. Literature's spiritual independence, writers' commitment to mankind and to society are being ridiculed . . . Human compassion, wisdom, sanity and taste are being derided."[11] Like most humanist intellectuals, Hong is worried about the ongoing and catastrophic effects of these changes on Chinese culture and vows to fight the egregious results of the flight from a literary ideal.

The debate on the humanistic ideal and mission of literature centers on literature's relation to the interest-oriented market mechanism. Critics and writers on both sides of the humanist spirit controversy agree that the market economy is responsible for the fundamental changes in the production and dissemination of literature and in writers' role and status, but they differ sharply about how to estimate the nature of these changes. Many humanist intellectuals are particularly bothered by the corrupting effect a free market has on serious literature and on the self-image and self-expectation of writers. "The crisis of literature is deepening every day," claims Wang Xiaoming (1993, 119), a professor of Eastern China Normal University, "more and more literary periodicals change to commercial direction and new works are deteriorating in quality. The number of appreciative readers is declining and more and more writers and critics are on their way to giving up their profession in order to 'do business.'"[12] Wang Xiaoming's attack on the commercialization of literary production underscores the humanist faith that writers are serious thinkers who should function as stewards of traditional intellectual values. Humanist intellectuals like Wang Xiaoming see market influences as an insidious assault on the mind. They picture themselves as fighters in particular against those who are unwilling to infringe on the market or challenge market values that are now contributing decisively to the erosion of the social fabric. In their view, if writing is the manifestation and purveyor of right reason, of certain norms of decency, of general ethical custom and special intellectual authority, it certainly has to be in the hands of those with whom such a prescription can be trusted.

Opponents to the humanist view, on the other hand, are less sanguine about the noble mission of writing. They are more optimistic about the positive side of a market economy, especially when it is compared with the Soviet-style centralized economy of failed socialism. "It is market," Wang Meng writes, "instead of (centralized) economic planning that shows more respect to man and his active agency," "market is the route to get rid of unnecessary bondage, and that opens more opportunity for education and culture" (1994b, 47).[13] Wang Meng's tactful linking of centralized planned economy with the authoritarian political system drives home the central irony in the humanist critical discourse: humanist intellectuals oppose orthodox Marxism and its centralized political system, but they can think of the market economy only in terms of orthodox Marxism even when orthodox Marxism in China itself seems to have abandoned these terms. Orthodox Marxism used to base its claims of the superiority of the socialist system on its characterization of the capitalist market system as, by its nature, profoundly morally compromised. Market economy, orthodox Marxism has traditionally argued, inevitably inspires a religion of fervent self-interest, a moral climate plagued by deadly avarice, ambition, competitiveness, calculated indifference, and self-interested exploitation of others, all eroding the possibility of civil community.

The debate on culture and its relations to market economy is symbolic of the attempts made by the post-1989 Chinese intellectuals to deal with what they see as the most urgent contemporary problems: the decline of unitary culture and the rise of mass culture, especially in the form of popular literature.[14] For many humanist intellectuals mass culture merits condemnation because it is so integrated with commercial interests. They simply refuse to see mass culture as capable of becoming a unique form of production and circulation of meaning involving the concrete needs and aspirations of the common people. The humanist critique of mass culture usually takes an aesthetic or a moral approach, condemning the shallowness and worthlessness of popular or mass culture and arguing that mass culture is either dictated by a "vulgar taste" in contrast to the "refined taste" of elegant culture or captivated by the consciousness industry, serving to dupe the naive and complacent public.[15] The absolute denial of epistemological, aesthetic, and moral values of mass culture has led many humanist intellectuals to promote serious literature as a sacred culture and as the only possible opposition to the all-devouring consumer culture. Disdain for the vulgar masses and warning against the intrusion of popular culture (*tongsu wenhua*) on the serious culture (*yansu wenhua*) have become the predominant themes of advocacy for the humanist spirit. On the one hand, it takes the vulgar-serious binary to project Wang Shuo as a writer of mass literature even though his works are very popular among the intellectuals as well as common people. On the other hand, it is precisely because Wang Shuo's works do not fit comfortably within the arbitrarily defined category of "vulgar mass literature," that the vulgar-serious and elite-mass binaries and polarizations are subverted and discredited.

In the controversy over the humanist spirit Wang Shuo becomes a symbolic writer, and his fiction also becomes symbolic. Wang Shuo is everything a serious writer is not. He does not have a university degree. He is not a member of the writers' association. And he is not a university employee or an official state writer with a fixed pay. He does not have a place in the established intellectual institution from which one can draw a writer's identity. Wang Shuo and his circle of friends belong to the category labeled by the state as "socially idle people," and his unique symbolic status is largely accountable by his ambivalent identity in the Chinese cultural world. Instead of trying to erase this ambivalence, Wang Shuo seems to enjoy it and deliberately refuses to identify with "writers," who are more likely to be objects of parody and satire for him than of respect and admiration.[16]

Wang Shuo's fiction seems to be everything serious literature is not. His novels and stories are populated by people who, like the writer himself, belong to a nameless sector of the Chinese society. They are simply referred to as *pizi* ("hoodlums" or "hooligans"). The lack of clarity of the meaning of *pizi* in the Chinese language suggests the aberrant character of the person called by this non-name name. It indicates a social subject position whose ambiguity in the institutionalized system of signifiers makes it stand out as sounding and appearing strange. *Pizi* is often rendered as *ruffian or riffraff*, though in contemporary usage it often implies a kind of cleverness and intelligence; in certain contexts *smart-ass* is a suitable rendering. Wang Shuo's fiction seems to bring the obscure *pizi* culture to the foreground all of a sudden. Wang Shuo's stories and films made from them are described as "[literature] written by a *pizi* for *pizi*, *pizi* read them to read about *pizi*; in the end it has given birth to a whole new group of *pizi*."[17] Wang Shuo's fiction contradicts what the serious literature takes for granted. The heroes in his fiction are simply "not part of the intellectual or political elite that people so many of the works of other modern writers. Nor do they belong to the fictionalized peasantry of 'native soil' genre of recent literature and film, nor the angst-ridden urbanities of late Eighties 'new realism literature,' nor are

they the soldiers and workers of the abiding socialist realist literature"
(Barmé 1992, 48).

Wang Shuo and his fiction are unique because they do not fit in the
institutionalized meaning systems that dictate how activities of writing
and reading in China are to be comprehended and evaluated. His work
has a paralyzing effect on critics; according to Wang Ping, it "overturns
the extreme value judgements. Life can no longer be understood in terms
of black and white or good and bad. With Wang Shuo we enter a state of
confusion" (1989, 100). Other unusual Chinese writers and works in the
1990s have captured wide attention, but, however unusual they may be,
they do not subvert and disrupt the existing systems the way Wang Shuo
does. They still work more or less within those systems that allow them
to appear just as unusual. *Feidu* (The Dilapidated Capital City) by Jia
Pingwa is such an example. The book has an unusual intellectual,
Zhuang Zhidie, as its protagonist. Unlike the usual intellectual heroes in
most post–Cultural Revolution literary works, Zhuang Zhidie is not only
morally corrupted, but he also embraces moral corruption as a legitimate
way of life. Yet, unlike the *pizi* characters in Wang Shuo's works,
Zhuang is a recognizable and namable type of character, for he is
nonetheless an "intellectual." Based on the different interpretations of
this central character, critics diverge in their evaluation of the book as a
daring effort to depict the moral reality of the current society or as uncrit-
ical, yielding general moral decay. Critics do not have to put this book in
a separate category, such as hoodlum literature, in order to understand it
or to believe that they can understand it. Wang Shuo's works deprive
critics of such certitude by forcing them to see the limitations of their
interpretive framework.

From Unitary Culture to Unitary Discourses

Wang Shuo's hoodlum literature not only challenges people's conventional and unquestioned expectations of literature by highlighting the
function of discursive ideology in regard to intertextual positioning, but
it also dislodges the unitary culture ensured by a homogeneous language.
Critics cannot categorize his literary language any more than they can
classify his characters or him as a writer because of his work's extraordinary linguistic irreverence. Jim Collins (1989) suggests the importance of
exploring the heterogeneity of culture through the heterogeneity of language, and his discussion is particularly illuminating for our understand-

ing of Wang Shuo's linguistic irreverence. Proceeding from Bakhtin's theory of heteroglossia, Collins seeks to find in language a new theoretical framework to account adequately for a culture's heterogeneity and explain how "nonliterary" languages in mass culture challenge the notion of unitary culture by subverting its unitary linguistic model. "Language," as Bakhtin sees it, "like the living, concrete environment in which the consciousness of the verbal artist lives, is never unitary. Actual social life and historical becoming create within an abstractly unitary national language a multitude of concrete worlds, a multitude of bounded verbal ideological and social belief systems" (1981, 288).

Bakhtin distinguishes two basic tendencies within this multitude of languages: the centripetal and the centrifugal. "Alongside the centripetal forces," Bakhtin says, "the centrifugal forces of language carry on their uninterrupted work; alongside verbal-ideological centralization and unification, the uninterrupted processes of decentralization and disunification go forward" (1981, 272). According to Bakhtin, the novel is fundamentally heteroglot because it embraces the diversity of languages and makes the differences among them explicit. Unlike poetry, which he considers the willful reduction of differences in pursuit of an artistic language, the novel creates a tension that cannot be resolved. The voice of the narrator is only one among many in the novel, but the voice of the poet is unitary and marked as a special type of language apart from everyday speech. Consequently, for Bakhtin the emergence of the novel as the dominant language of narrative signifies the victory of an egalitarian aesthetic over an aristocratic one. The novel becomes, then, the consummate popular art form, and only "literary" discourse, especially poetry, maintains its unitary quality. Jim Collins presses Bakhtin's conclusion one step further and points out that "in a world where the novel and its latter-day counterpart, the feature film, are radically subdivided and differentiated, the novel as a narrative mode is itself a tangle of competing languages" (1989, 66).

We find in Chinese fiction this diversity of languages, but we also find in it the assertion that certain types of literary languages are superior to others because they are believed to be more aesthetic, moral, or politically correct. As Jim Collins remarks, "If we can no longer take for granted the homogeneity of culture, neither can we continue to take for granted any kind of homogeneity in the languages produced within those cultures" (1989, 65). We need to pay attention not only to the function of discursive ideologies in regard to intertextual positions but also to their impact on "the 'semantic differentiation' in various narrative discourses." Wang Shuo's fiction appears to be an excellent example of the heteroglossia Bakhtin describes and of the "semantic differentiation" Jim Collins mentions. His fiction employs multiple narrators—not just one single type of *pizi* as they are often caricatured—who indicate distinct differences in their verbal-ideological perspectives. The preferred use of popular street language and raving chat style (known as *kan*) in Wang Shuo's works is a form of dramatic heteroglot that refuses to acknowledge any dominance of a literary/serious language or of an official party discourse. Geremie Barmé describes vividly the characteristics of Wang Shuo's language as follows:

> The language of Wang Shuo's fiction is extraordinarily rich in paradoxical humor. In early stories . . . there is only a hint of the linguistic irreverence that becomes a major feature of his later work. With the inflation of Party rhetoric and the deflation of ideological effectiveness and relevance—a widening, if not yawning gap between official language and social reality—increased linguistic dysfunction has developed in China with greater possibilities for political humor than ever. Wang is certainly the most artful and frequent user of such humor in his writing. "Historical irony" (*lishide fanfeng*) is spoken of as being a basic trait of Wang's fictional approach, and irony based on the use and abuse of the political codes of communist rule, combining as it so often does leaden and empty rhetoric with crass colloquialisms. It is a humour that has been criticized for being too narrowly based and one that relies on turning the elements of the Party's historical world into "linguistic toys" to be played with by Wang's heroes, ignorant and ill-educated disaffected youth. Yet . . . the *liumang* in Wang's fiction can be seen as belonging to a more venerable "underground" tradition, the modern-day bastard progeny of the knight-errant, urban tricksters armed with a caustic wit which they use to lunge and parry as they make their way in a mendacious world. Much of his humor is an expression of defiance, debunking as it does political piety; at other times it is a humor of cruelty with its object innocent (or pretentious and therefore not so innocent) young women, university students, intellectuals and writers. (1992, 57)

In Wang Shuo's fiction one does indeed find a preferred use of street language, but one also finds that this street language is set in conflicting relationships with other languages whose dominance is usually taken for granted or seldom seen as questionable. This is nowhere more obvious than in the opposition between the cynical townspeople's language, on the one side, and the stilted intellectual language and the pompous Party language, on the other. While the differences between these modes of language are used as means of humor and laughter, nonetheless a politically interesting tension exists between them, since both the intellectual language and the Party language are languages of authority within the discursive arrangements, but the townspeople's language is the language of transmission and, by extension, the language that invites readers to share. The townspeople's language is set in opposition to both the intellectual language and the Party language as a defiant subculture in opposition to a unitary culture, even though in that culture the intellectuals' discourse may appear like a counter-discourse to the dominant Party discourse. The complexity of such an interlanguage repositioning explains why Chinese intellectuals, as one critic suggests, often serve as handmaidens of the political *liumang* in power and are involved in the complicit relations between intellectual and political authorities as an abiding phenomenon, not just an aberration (Wang Yi 1991). Overturning the hierarchy and linguistic order of the arrogant intellectual speech and the pompous Party idiom at the same time, Wang Shuo's language appears to be marked by a cynical and black despair or even extreme alienation.

Wang Shuo's popularity indicates the increasing decentering of Chinese society and the decline of its cultural homogeneity and unitary authoritative discourses, a process that must be understood in China's postsocialist condition. The many significant changes involved in this process are yet to be coped with and understood by humanist intellectuals. Many of them have allowed their instinctive contempt for a market economy and mass culture to prevent them from appreciating new opportunities for freedom from integrated forces of party-state and state-run economy. It is too politically costly to blame the so-called moral decline on, and solely on, the market economy and to forget how the tight relationship between central government planning and an authoritarian political system helped to lead China to totalitarianism, a social system of total control. The extraordinary concentration of power in the state that sweeping government ownership and central planning require once plunged China into catastrophes such as the Great Leap Forward and the Cultural Revolution. We can be cautiously optimistic that some market control is necessary not only to ensure economic viability but also to help to bring about new opportunity for social decentralization and liberalization.

The market economy, however, is not a magic panacea for democratization; it cannot bring about democracy by itself. For modern community building and for democratization the debate is thus not about whether to embrace markets but about what kinds of markets to embrace. To invoke the market economy is a cheap shot in elite writers' diagnosis of problems China is facing today. Some of them have so dramatized their hostility to the market economy that they literally crusade against the corrupting invasion of commercialism. Zhang Chengzhi, a well-known serious writer, for instance, claims that religious faith is now the last resort for a conscientious writer to keep his moral integrity and his commitment to the transcendental value of literature. Adopting a martyr's attitude, he declares his commitment to redeeming the fallen world: "My little boat is going to sail against the tide of rampant human desire and greed, for no particular reason, because I am predestined to do so, to fill the vacuum. When you feel angry, when you feel justice is lost in this age of moral decline, when you miss other people's understanding, when you want to live cleanly even though that is difficult, remember, you have my literature."[18] We could consider this isolation, which is artistically constructed in a heroic and lonely voice, a charming desire for freedom from outside temptation, a hope of maintaining untroubled wisdom and faith in a world that allows too little for intellectual lucidity. We could also think of it as an example of unfounded naïveté and self-delusion. We might see it as the willingness of an arrogant intellectual to affirm, perhaps reluctantly, the social and institutional division that maintains the stratifications in the status quo culture. What is profoundly ironic, however, is that it is precisely Zhang's unique voice of a spiritual saint that has turned the writer himself into a unique and valuable commodity in the book market. As one critic has sarcastically pointed out, Zhang's books can now be found in any sidewalk bookstall, displayed in eye-catching places side by side with stories of movie stars (Xu Jilin 1996, 42).

The dichotomy of a spiritually pure serious literature and a commercially corrupted mass literature is as false as it is full of irony. The dichotomy of serious and vulgar literature as it is formulated in the post-1989 cultural discussion is outworn; the issues crammed in these concepts should be separated and analyzed in different terms and the dichotomy itself should be abandoned. The power of a categorical dichotomy, however, is not to be underestimated. The area of cultural discussion is strewn with dichotomies in terms of which questions have been formulated, theoretical energies riveted, and answers constrained. Take, for instance, many intellectuals' obsession with the cleavages between *ya* (good taste) and *su* (bad taste), enlightening art and cheap entertainment, the spiritual and the material, worldly need and ultimate concern, the elite and the mass, and so on (Zhou Xian 1995; Zhang Rulun 1994). Such categorical dichotomies are essential, in Pierre Bourdieu's words, for "regard[ing] taste in legitimate culture as a gift of nature," rather than seeking explanation for it in "an economy of cultural goods" and "its specific logic" (1984, 1).

The economy of cultural goods and its specific logic that Bourdieu has in mind include "the conditions in which the consumers of cultural goods, and their taste for them, are produced" and "[the consumers'] different ways of appropriating such of these objects as are regarded at a particular moment as works of art" (1984, 1). All these can reveal to us what the facile dichotomy of "vulgar" and "good" tastes has long concealed and mystified, that the definition of cultural nobility is a struggle that has gone on unceasingly between different social groups. What is at stake is not just cultural differences but social hierarchy and stratification as well. As Bourdieu says, "To the socially recognized hierarchy of the arts, and within each of them, of genres, schools or periods, corresponds a social hierarchy of the consumers. This predisposes tastes to function as markers of class" (2).

The notion of class, as Richard Curt Kraus (1981) indicates in his study of Chinese class configuration, imbricates two models of stratifications in China—the first is "stratification of class designation," and the second is "stratification of occupational rank." Both models of stratification have been declining in their influences since the late 1980s and, in order to maintain themselves, have been impelled to seek new forms of legitimacy, of which the distinction of taste or moral sense becomes a prominent one. Stratification of class designation is primarily political in nature. It used to serve as the basis of the Party's ideology of antagonism until it began to disintegrate after the Cultural Revolution. In its hierarchical scheme class designations specify "categories which were clearly bad, such as capitalist and landlord, through the intermediate designations of petty bourgeoisie and middle peasant, to the workers and poor peasants in whose name the revolution had been made" (20). The intellectuals, usually labeled as "petit bourgeoisie," are not high in this hierarchy. On the other hand, stratification of occupational rank is primarily social-cultural in nature, its central measures being income and educational levels. In the occupational hierarchy intellectuals, because of their special knowledge and skills, are much more highly placed than in the class hierarchy. It should be clear that these hierarchies are not the only stratifications of the Chinese populace. As Kraus points out, however, "Class designation and occupational rank assume special weight because they are both (at least superficially) economic stratification, and because they are both officially sanctioned" (35).

The interrelationship of these two models of social stratification forms an important aspect of the context within which the Chinese intellectuals seek to exert some influence in their society. They cannot aspire to compete with the governing Party elite, with its privileged role in the stratification of class designations, which has enabled it to claim absolute political authority. But they want to compete for cultural and moral authority based on the particular type of knowledge they have created, the professional and specialized scholarly knowledge. Yet any competition for cultural and moral authority has to take place through the institution of Party leadership, which is the structural foundation of most intellectual activities under the authoritarian rule. The institutional arrangements that bind the intellectuals to professional strata induce them to believe that, after all, they can still act freely and with sufficient authority in their nonpolitical realm. Under these circumstances the more these intellectuals insist on the differences of their taste, moral sense, and knowledge from the rest of the society, the better they serve the purpose of those institutional arrangements. They are forced into precisely the position that Russell Jacoby characterizes with such scorn: "This may be a paradox, but it recalls an inner contradiction of academic freedom— the institution neutralizes the freedom it guarantees. For many professors in many universities academic freedom meant nothing more than the freedom to be academic" (1987, 118–19).

Even the very intellectual identity is rooted in academic institutions, whose complicated relations to the party-state must also be closely examined. Academic institutions in China are patronized and controlled by the state at the same time. Academic institutions (universities and research academies of the humanities) are places intellectuals are put together for convenient centralized control as well as for mutual surveillance. They function as a mechanism to keep intelligence circulating harmlessly within the insular debates on professional issues and within traditional scholastic idealism. They guarantee that, even when the intellectuals are critical of the established order, they will keep their criticism within narrow grounds, safe from contact with the people in the streets or spillover into an adversarial relation to the state. An examination of the institutional basis of intellectual activity is necessary, in truth the only way, to break the impacted stratification that keeps the intellectuals not only aloof and superior but actually cut off from one another.

The hard work of intellectual criticism will not be possible until critical intellectuals seize cultural discussion as an act in the struggle against autocratic rule of the enormous institutions of stratifications (political, social, economic, and cultural) and the general coercion of these institutions' vested values. With such a focus on the role of intellectuals in the existing orders of stratification, the critics' central concern may well be the discrepancy between the cultural choice of the majority of people and the arrogance of those who are empowered by contemporary institutional arrangements, a discrepancy the intellectuals could lessen if they resisted power temptations in their own work and attitudes and opposed institutionalized arrogance of every sort. An awareness of the intellectuals' own role within the existing institutions may lead away from the insularity of elite culture to pose questions more accessible to the general populace—questions about loss of social and political consensus, about structural domination and violence, and about corruption resulting from increasing social inequality, abuse of power, and general skepticism and cynicism.

The Humanist Spirit and Its Ultimate Concern

The discussion of the humanist spirit has engaged not only those serious writers who see themselves as spiritual guardians against the threatening mass culture but also many humanist intellectuals who are particularly worried about the loss of *zhongji guanhuai* (the ultimate concern) in today's Chinese social life. The moral concern of these humanist intellectuals differs from the ordinary discussion of moral issues (corruption, profiteering, contagious selfishness, etc.) in that it seeks to avoid the inconsistency of ad hoc comments of current affairs by thinking more rationally, carefully, and consistently than people generally do. Several of the humanist intellectuals' collective deliberations have taken the form of group discussions, and, over and over again, they have come back to the central issue of the ultimate concern. The results of these discussion seminars were published, from March to July 1994, under the general title

"Reflections on 'The Humanist Spirit'," in five consecutive issues of *Dushu* (Reading), a journal very popular among students and intellectuals.[19] These seminars immediately received nationwide attention. The ultimate concern serves as a key notion that allows participants of these discussions to come up with one moral issue that will tie various questions together, answer them in some coherent way, and provide guidance on a wide range of specific intellectual and ethical issues. Their deliberations never really lead to a theory or even a generally accepted definition of the key notion "the ultimate concern." Yet precisely because they use this key notion as a catchword rather than as a specific term of a systematic moral theory or philosophy, they can articulate, in very loose terms, what they see as the hostile forces against moral integrity and the most fundamental and pressing problems in the current Chinese culture.

Most of the participants in these deliberations on the humanist spirit have emphasized the ultimate concern as a special issue of intellectual humanism and approached it in exclusive humanistic terms. Wang Xiaoming, one of the initiators of the discussion, remarks, "If we understand the ultimate concern as our inner need for some ultimate value and the effort we take to achieve this value, then the humanist spirit itself is the embodiment of this concern" (Zhang Rulun et al. 1994a, 10). Wang's linking of the ultimate concern with the humanist spirit is important for us to have a glimpse of how the humanist core of this ethical concern and the discussion of the humanist spirit relate to the interest in humanism in the 1980s. The basic meaning of *humanitas* carries the idea of humanity as a virtue. To be human in this sense means much more than being a member of the human race; it means to be moral in one's attitude and behavior toward other human beings. This meaning is contained in the Confucian virtue of *ren*, or "true humanness." Parallel terms in the Western Christian tradition include *humanitarian, humaneness*, and, more recently, *humanization* and, on the negative side, the phrase "man's inhumanity to man." All such meanings carry obvious moral and religious connotations.

Many post-1989 Chinese intellectuals evoke the ethical meaning of humanism or the humanist spirit as an antidote to what they see as the general moral erosion of their days and a possible resolution of the crises it imbricates. It is also their way of articulating and naming the redemptive moral force they believe is still available in today's China. As Chen Sihe, Li Tiangang, and other participants in the discussion of the humanist spirit note, contemporary Chinese people do not have a religion to rely on as a valuable resource of moral norms (Zhang Rulun et al. 1994a, 9; Gao Ruiquan et al. 1994, 74). Neither can the Chinese people effectively resort to traditional Confucian norms, since such norms have been discredited and damaged beyond repair by the radical cultural criticism of the May Fourth Movement tradition. Therefore, it becomes all the more important for intellectuals to "search for and reconstruct a humanist tradition" in order to fill the normative and ethical vacuum (Zhang Rulun et al. 1994a, 9). Many humanist intellectuals are keenly aware of the contradiction between the intellectuals' function and their individual existence, their intellectual universalism and their professional particularism. The intellectual is an agent of specified knowledge and situated self-interest, yet he is impelled to speak for the society as a whole. In the face of this dilemma Xu Jilin and others make a distinction among three kinds of traditions in the Chinese culture—the moral, the political, and the scholastic—and claim that the moral tradition is what intellectuals today must uphold because it is the highest of all the three (1994, 48). Moral tradition or morality in Xu Jilin's model is something inadvertent, marginal, and unaffiliated with the political and other institutions that have helped to create the highly repressive and stratified Chinese culture in the past. Wang Xiaoming, on the other hand, envisions retreat into a personal search for virtue as a possible remedy for the intellectual's basic dilemma. He is correctly cautious not to turn the search for the ultimate value into an intended or unintended means of self-empowerment in the name of general value or truth, but his way of presenting the project of search for the ultimate value as a blissfully uninvolved custodian of moral sense is dubious in its own way:

> Some people regard the interpreter of the ultimate concern as a representative and spiritual prophet of the society. They believe they are unquestionable spokesmen of some absolute truth which should be accepted by everyone else. Many horrible things are conducted in the name of such absolute truth. Therefore, when we talk about the ultimate concern, I want to emphasize its personal quality, and that is (1) you can only search for the ultimate value from your personal experience, (2) what you find is your own interpretation of what the ultimate value is, not the ultimate value itself, (3) your search is completely personal and none should monopolize the right of such a search. It is in this sense that I believe that what will emerge from works done by an intellectual of the humanities is his personal expe-

rience and reflection of the human existence. (Zhang Rulun et al. 1994a, 8)

There is a certain acivic tone to the choice of *person,* as though *social member* and *citizen* are not apt choices because their connotations are insufficiently privatized. There is also a fierce insistence on the primacy of personal predilection rather than universal value claim. Wang does not offer any account, narrative or otherwise, of the personal/collective (or private/public) distinction. Rather, he asserts that it is a "necessary" one, which suggests a hard-and-fast quality that widens the gap between the enlightened few, intellectuals in particular, and the public.[20] Failing to explore the tentative character of the shifting boundaries of and interdependencies between domains named as personal and public or to connect them in the framework of civil society reconstruction, Wang's solution to the tension experienced by many humanist intellectuals is apartheid—a separation between personal sublimation and public hope. Are intellectuals today destined to be those who can only enhance their private conscience but have nothing to tell us about our public goodness and responsibility? What, then, do they have to do with democracy, solidarity, and citizenship? The short answer is nothing. Nothing if we think that personal reflection on ethics entails nothing about our public goodness and responsibility.

This separation of the personal and public domains works against the humanist impulse of many intellectuals' own moral concern, which is, after all, not about the decline of professional norms, like that of the New Scholars I will discuss in chapter 2, but, rather, about the moral degeneracy of the present Chinese society as a whole. The remedy that humanist intellectuals prescribe for the social moral disease is not political change but improvement of personal conscience. It directs attention to the self rather than to the world. But our public norms as citizens are not the same as our private consciences as individuals. The public norm cannot be automatically derived from our private consciences. Indeed, it is not the sum of private virtues nor their highest common denominator nor even the total of enlightened intellectual selves. With its roots in personal conscience the notion of the ultimate concern turns out to be inappropriate to characterize the remedial public action, since public action is motivated not by a concern with the integrity of one's conscience but by a concern with the injustices taking place in the world. The ultimate concern is primarily moral, not political. It reminds us of what Hannah

Arendt remarked about the nature of conscience: "Conscience is unpolitical. It is not primarily interested in the world where the wrong is committed or in the consequences that the wrong will have for the future course of the world . . . [It just] trembles for the individual self and its integrity" (1972, 60–61). The rules of conscience are unpolitical; they concern the self's integrity in the world. Their concern is to avoid self-reproach, to avoid being implicated in something they consider wrong, rather than fighting for the redress of injustice. They say: "Beware of doing something that you will not be able to live with" (64). As such, their ultimate concern may be of some value during emergencies, but it cannot serve as a political standard. Their ultimate concern is too much bound up with themselves to serve as a basis for collective action aiming at the redress of injustice in the world. Acting as good persons is not the same as acting as good citizens. Paradoxically, people often become unusually eager to salve their conscience when they are disillusioned about possibilities to improve their society's polity or to establish standards of universal justice.[21]

The elevation of the ultimate concern signals an unfortunate transformation of humanism: the retreat from the socialist humanism of the 1980s to the spiritual and moral humanism of the 1990s. This change is, of course, not the result of the intellectuals' choice alone but, rather, is related to adversary sociopolitical conditions that have rendered it increasingly difficult for the intellectuals to intervene in social change. Keeping a deep suspicion of politics and trying to maintain their intellectual independence, many humanist intellectuals, most of whom participated in the cultural discussion of the 1980s, manage to hang onto their belief that cultural change is a conductive force toward real social changes. The erosion of the social fabric and the growing political apathy seem to be reflected, however, in the humanist intellectuals' new choice of priority; they shift their critical attention from elements of Chinese culture imbued with the residue of despotism to the visionary absence of some transcendental virtue. For understandable reasons they are reticent about the linked crises of collective identity, social ideals, and the legitimacy of the system, saying almost nothing about the problems for the general public caused by political disillusion and cynicism. Instead, they point the accusing finger at the obviously corrupting and demoralizing influence of commercialization and mass culture.

This is not to say that intellectuals in the 1990s should ignore moral problems arising from the new economic condition, since rebuilding the social fabric requires change in the economic order and mass culture. But, while alert to common phenomena of moral decay, the critical intellectuals must also spotlight institutionalized immorality rooted in China's political structure. The authoritarian control the party-state holds over the society, for instance, has created many forms of stark inequality, unscrupulous injustice, and official deprivation, just as it has enabled those who are associated with political power to become rich quickly and easily. A cynical public now has privileged so much about the powerful and the rich that they have become numb to scandals, immorality, and corruption. Can they be blamed for the disintegrating social morality or for their apathy toward empty rhetoric about "socialist morality"? Writing about the widespread dishonesty and corruption in China of the 1990s, Nicholas D. Kristof notes, "While small payoffs are common in many societies, corruption in China often takes strange forms and seems particularly institutionalized," and the problem of corruption is that it spreads: "at some point, the corruption reaches a critical mass and people begin to say: Everybody else is doing it, so why not me? It then accelerates and becomes almost impossible to uproot" (1995, 194). If this is true, then the first task for critical intellectuals is to extend the debate on values into a prolonged public examination of morality from the top in which the moral decline with the greatest impact on civil society is concentrated. The power holders are the principal source of the moral rot leeching into the rest of the society.

As things stand now, humanist intellectuals' moralistic language and sensibility do not seem to square fully with the ordinary Chinese, whose lives are built around different forms of concerns of daily survival and needs and who have to deal with all forms of bureaucratic and institutional abuse. This discrepancy underscores the intellectuals' aloofness and elitism. The irony is that this may not be a purposefully adopted attitude but one imposed on them by the undemocratic political situation, which makes it extremely difficult for caring intellectuals to link their concerns with the everyday life of the ordinary people. The many taboo areas of intellectual inquiry in China forbid the critical intellectuals to deal with the conditions of their own concerns, making it impossible for them to ask the question of how it comes about that their well-intended intellectual concerns have become so pathetically elitist in China today.

Although the humanistic intellectuals may have articulated cultural and moral issues that reverberate across the social spectrum, their words are not likely to move many outside their own circle due to the barriers between intellectuals and the masses. Less privileged Chinese, especially after the experience of 1989, have always been distrustful of the words of those who only talk. In addition to all the barriers of highbrow concept and program, a principal obstacle limiting the spread of the intellectuals' moral ideals is their derogatory view of the masses as mere subjects under the sway of self-interest or the consciousness industry and totally incapable of developing, on their own, critical consciousness and a sense of agency in their everyday life activities. The intellectuals' pride in their own freedom projects the alleged lack of freedom onto the masses. Following the Frankfurt School tradition, they have thus far conceptualized the common public only as "mass" in its most passive and uncreative sense.[22] Their analysis of the current popular culture has emphasized exclusively the numbing effect mass cultural products allegedly have had on the ordinary Chinese minds. According to the humanist intellectuals, mass culture only helps turn the ordinary people into dupes of the status quo because they can find great pleasure within it. They explain the construction of social subjectivity completely in terms of the victory of the dominant forces, the outcome of which is inevitably a relatively unified, singular social subject, unthinking and incapable of thinking. Their denial of cultural and political vitality in the masses of people and their condescending way of talking down to them and rendering them inert actually play a part in blocking democratization in today's China.

The 1990s humanistic ideal has so far served as a safety valve to the intellectuals' own frustration, rather than as a practico-ethical vision or framework of sociocultural critique. No other social stratum or class has tried so hard to distance itself from the mundane and imperfect society as the humanist intellectuals. Yet they have not sufficiently addressed the practical and often desperate problems of survival, lack of power, and vulnerability that ordinary Chinese (and, indeed, intellectuals themselves) confront in their everyday life.[23] They have refused to recognize the fact that these pressing problems often find their way into the current popular culture and receive expression in language and cultural forms that are relevant to the everyday life needs and experience of the common public. The suspicion and hostility shared by many humanistic intellectuals toward the popular culture in today's China have become a major obstacle limiting the connection of their critical concerns with the production and circulation of subversive meaning in the daily cultural activity of the ordinary Chinese. Chinese humanist intellectuals need yet to move from their studies to the homes and working places of common people, if they want to produce more than just empty talk.[24] The real test of any appeal to social reconstruction and moral redemption is whether it engages the hearts and minds of ordinary people. Thus, potentially one of the most powerful means by which the intellectuals could spread their ideal would be relating their own lifeworlds to those of the common people and thus helping to model a new social ethos that transcends the division of the elite and the popular. If the humanist intellectuals can finally wean themselves from their own addictions to career, ego, and status, they will certainly increase their ability not only to speak of their own deepest needs but to offer to others the embryo of a less self-centered and more democratic model of social morality.

Chapter 2

Retreating from the Public into the Profession

"The humanities," Charles Frankel says, "are a curious combination of involvement and detachment."[1] Fleshing out Frankel's observation on the general dilemma of humanist scholars, John Agresto and Peter Riesenberg comment on the difficult role of the humanities and humanist scholars in the public: "Too great an involvement in the present and the public soon converts the humanities into ideology and partisanship. Too high an expectation of the immediate uses of the humanities—or of humanist scholars—leads quickly to disappointment." Instead of trying to strike a perfect balance and put the humanities in their proper place between involvement and detachment, Agresto and Riesenberg lean toward involvement and insist that "the humanities are vital for life and that the imposition of too great a detachment reduces the humanities to a mere frill on the borders of human affairs, to pleasant ornamentation and irrelevance" (Agresto and Riesenberg 1981, vii).

Similarly, He Yi, a young Chinese critic, in his deliberation on the humanist intellectuals' dilemma of involvement and detachment, has no illusion about finding an easy resolution to this dilemma by avoiding too much involvement. Like Agresto and Riesenberg, He Yi (1995) emphasizes the humanist intellectuals' responsibility to the public, not just to their profession. Yet, unlike Agresto and Riesenberg, He Yi does not take a general and universal approach to the humanities' dilemma. Instead, he locates this dilemma in the specific Chinese social and political context of this century and explains how the country's reality underlies the professional decisions made by generations of Chinese intellectuals. He Yi treats these Chinese intellectuals as social beings who are molded not just by their intellectual status but, more important, by the concrete social and political circumstances in which they may or may not have the opportunity or will to function as involved intellectuals. In an article about the Chinese intellectuals' choice of public responsibility in the twentieth century, He Yi describes three major waves of "collective escapism" on the part of Chinese intellectuals, which resulted from a combination of an adverse environment and intellectuals' own lack of determination to be involved. The first wave happened after the May Fourth Movement, when iconoclastic intellectual leaders like Hu Shi shifted from radical cultural criticism to "reorganization of the national heritage." This shift of intellectual orientation provided a pretext to the conservatives to promote blind worship of the tradition in resistance to new ideas for modernizing China. The second wave occurred after the 1949 Communist takeover in mainland China, when a large number of Left or progressive intellectuals were silenced and de-radicalized by endless Communist political campaigns. Many of them disappeared from the public scene and became harmless specialists in separate and isolated academic fields. The third and the most recent wave of collective escapism has come in the 1990s, and its most remarkable representative is what is known as *xin guoxue* (new Chinese national studies or new Chinese scholarship). He Yi treated the post-1989 new Chinese scholarship as a notorious case of the intellectuals' retreat from the public into the profession (1995, 25–28). While basically agreeing with He Yi's evaluation of this new intellectual trend, I want to go one step further and emphasize the complexity of the public meaning of this retreat—both its conservative and potentially progressive meanings, rather than its lack of public meaning. Instead of condemning it as a blatant betrayal of intellectuals' faith, I want to approach it as a political-cultural phenomenon, probing its formation as well as examining its ambition and limitation.

The "Post-" Status of "New" Chinese National Studies

What is now known as *xin guoxue* is a collage of events, activities, publications, and theories surrounding studies of Chinese classical or modern texts as the national cultural heritage. Within the motley array, however, we can distinguish two main components. One component, appealing to the general populace, particularly to young students, is the rekindled interest in indigenous Chinese culture, especially in classical texts. The other is a more professional type of emphasis on theorizing proper research problems, methodologies, standards, and norms in order to pursue valid Chinese studies. Elements of both the renewed interest in Chinese traditional culture and the effort to form a proper theory of Chinese studies mingle with a crisis of national identity to become a general cultural phenomenon worth examining on its own.

Among the landmark events and activities registering the emergence of *guoxue* as a special post-1989 cultural phenomenon, the most noticeable is probably the appearance, in 1993, of *Guoxue yanjiu* (Chinese studies), an immense journal published by the Research Center of Chinese Cultural Tradition of Beijing University. The significance of this journal was reinforced and brought out by the popularity of a series of seminars on Chinese culture, which were offered in the same year on the campus of Beijing University. These campus events, due to the unusual reports by *Renmin Ribao* (People's daily), the prominent Party mouthpiece, soon drew national attention.[2]

Even before these highly publicized events, interest in indigenous Chinese culture had been growing. A dozen books of the *Guoxue congshu* (Series of Chinese studies) had been published by Liaoning Education Publishing House. *Guoxue dashi congshu* (Series of masters of Chinese studies) were then put out by Baihuazhou Literature and Art Publishing House of Jiangxi. Plans of publishing huge collections of Chinese classical texts, such as *Siku quanshu cunmu congshu* (Books with their titles mentioned in Siku Quanshu [Complete library in four divisions]), *Xuxiu siku quanshu* (Collection of books supplementary to Siku Quanshu), *Chuanshi cangshu* (Heritage library books), and *Dongfang dadian* (Encyclopedia of the East), were being made. Meanwhile, journals of Chinese cultural studies began to appear one after another, *Chuantong wenhua yu xiandaihua* (Traditional culture and modernization), *Zhongguo wenhua yanjiu* (Research of Chinese culture), *Zhanlue yu guanli* (Strategy and management), *Dongfang* (Orient), *Xungen* (Search for roots), and *Xueren* (Scholar, an irregularly published journal) being among the most well-known. The emergence of these journals during a short period of time seems to have signaled that something unusual was happening in the Chinese intellectual atmosphere. What is the nature of the newly revived interest in indigenous Chinese culture? Why did some local campus events suddenly become a big intellectual issue and phenomenal cultural fashion? Scholars have always studied Chinese culture and classical writers and texts—why did their scholarly interest and activities suddenly take on special national significance? Why at that moment? What specific social and political conditions led to this new fervor of *guoxue*? And, indeed, what, after all, does *guoxue* itself mean under post-1989 conditions?[3]

Zhang Dainian, a senior professor of Beijing University, defines *guoxue* as more than a newly reinstalled discipline or subject matter of study. Zhang makes two kinds of distinction in order to establish *guoxue* as a distinct post-1989 intellectual pursuit. First, *guoxue* is Chinese studies done by indigenous Chinese scholars: "'*Guo*' means native country, and '*guoxue*' means scholarship of one's own nation, and that is indigenous Chinese studies." Western scholars studying China or Chinese culture are "Sinologists," and what they produce is not *guoxue* although these scholars may be considered students of *guoxue*. Second, *guoxue* is not the same as "the old Chinese studies" done by non-Marxian Chinese scholars such as Hu Shi. This is how Zhang specifies the difference between the new Chinese studies and the old Chinese studies:

> To talk about *guoxue* today, we should remember "*guo*" means nation, and "*guoxue*" is not the same as scholarship in the past. "*Guo*" is a spatial rather than temporal conception. *Lu Xun's Life* and *Hu Shi's Life,* two books of the Series of Masters of Chinese Studies published by Baihuazhou Literature and Art Publishing House, have shown that *guoxue* is not confined to ancient time. Hu Shi made significant contribution to Chinese studies by advocating *zhengli guogu* (reorganization of the heritage). *Guogu* is composed of the six Confucian classical texts. What we call *guoxue* today is not the same as *guogu,* and Chinese studies today are not the old Chinese studies.

Zhang Dainian's definition of new Chinese studies in terms of the discipline's indigenous character and difference from the *zhengli guogu* model developed by liberal intellectuals is not just a nonchalant gesture to ensure official endorsement but, rather, a real manifesto of what is politically correct in present Chinese studies: "The new Chinese studies must be directed by the universal truth of Marxism . . . and aim at building a new socialist culture of Chinese character" (1995, 2). The sycophancy captured in this otherwise boring attempt to reinstate a bankrupt official ideology in the Chinese academic world can at least explain why the politically correct *guoxue,* a post-1989 academic platitude, succeeds in passing for intellectual innovation and why its local campus events are officially praised as a popular overflow of cultural patriotism.

Although Zhang Dainian's definition of new Chinese studies is convenient to give a general name to the various publications and events concerning Chinese culture and serves as a convenient propagandizing slogan, it is not very popular with those who have so far made the greatest contribution to put the so-called new Chinese studies on the intellectual map of the 1990s. These latter scholars want to form a distinctively new paradigm of Chinese studies by establishing exclusively professional standards. Since many of them participate in the symposium that helped to set the agenda of the *Scholar,* a lead journal of the new Chinese studies, I will refer to them, for the sake of convenience, as "the New Scholars." Their definition of new Chinese studies is much less servile and much more thoughtful than that exemplified by Zhang Dainian's and therefore worth our closer examination.

What the New Scholars understand as new Chinese studies is exactly what Zhang Dainian calls "old Chinese studies," which was associated with those non-Marxian scholars of the May Fourth generation, such as Hu Shi and Gu Jiegang. Instead of proving the "universal truth of Marxism," the New Scholars want to revisit the new Chinese studies which took shape in the 1920s and 1930s. What they are concerned about is not primarily how to establish a distinctive indigenous Chinese type of scholarly research but, rather, how to pursue scholarly research that will allow them (1) to define for themselves a worthy position in the "history of scholarly research" (*xueshushi*), (2) to assert their intellectual identity as professional scholars, and (3) to postulate professional norms and standards that can contribute to redeeming the dilapidated social morality.

The diametrically opposed views on what *new* means to new Chinese studies, as He Manzi notes in his article "The Collapse of 'Post-Chinese Studies'" (1995), point to a peculiar "post-" condition of 1990s *guoxue*. Post- denotes, in the scholarly form of Chinese studies, the wishful attempt to recuperate and justify the allegedly indigenous *guoxue* of the 1920s in a noncontextual way. The unfortunate fact is that *guoxue* has never "really" been a Chinese form of scholarship. First appearing as *zhengli guogu* in the 1920s and 1930s, *guoxue* acquired its identity as a reaction to the cultural iconoclasm of the May Fourth Movement.[4] From the very beginning *guoxue* is marked by epistemological and methodological characteristics (positivism, empiricism, philology, etc.) that are *not* rooted in a purely Chinese intellectual tradition. *Guoxue* is destined to lack the indigenous purity many of its advocates in the 1990s want to gain or maintain.[5] *Guoxue* had a hard time under the Communist regime, and it was almost completely wiped out during the Cultural Revolution. It is gradually rehabilitated after the Cultural Revolution and finally surges forth in the 1990s. The post–Cultural Revolution condition in which *guoxue* acquires a new life differs entirely, however, from that of its inception in the 1920s and defines 1990s *guoxue* as "post-*guoxue*."

He Manzi challenges the claim that *guoxue* can be an autonomous discipline based solely on its pure and interest-free scholarly values. The 1990s *guoxue*, He Manzi argues, is torn between the desire to transcend commercialism and the pull to be part of it. This contradiction adds to the complexity of the post- status of new Chinese studies. "The *guoxue* fervor [in the 1990s]," He Manzi notes, "is basically swayed by economic force. It is influenced more by the market than by cultural quest."[6] Advertising *guoxue* in the 1990s is politically harmless; it flatters the popular sense of China's prosperity; and it promises enormous commercial opportunity. *Guoxue* has joined and contributed actively to the omnipresence of commodities, the incorporation with global capitalism, and the embourgeoisement of the state bureaucracy. The state-controlled publication machine is eager to turn out book series of an enormous size partly because, as He Manzi reveals, "each book series of *Dongfang dadian, Chuanshi cangshu, Siku quanshu cunmu congshu,* and *Xuxiu siku quanshu* will be sold at tens or hundreds of thousands of yen" (1995, 60).

The more independent variety of *guoxue* in the 1990s tries to break away from the grand narrative of Marxist historiography that claims to "objective truth" and has long been a dictating discourse of modernity in the field, but it still adheres to the ideal of professional modernity and its grand narrative of objective truth. The contradiction in *guoxue*'s attitude to different grand narratives of modernity must be understood, although it does not have to be solved. Like its precursor of *zhengli guogu,* the scholarly ideal of *guoxue* in the 1990s privileges a certain kind of knowledge, the professional knowledge that derives its validity from proper epistemology and methodology. The standards of such professional knowledge are intrinsically bound up with the culturally specific presuppositions of modernity. For example, the separation of cognitive truths from moral and political knowledge and indeed the primacy of cognitive truth, the emphasis upon propositional knowledge, or the rationales for what counts as evidence or facts get their coherence from the modern empiricist and positivist tradition. In the 1920s, when scholars like Hu Shi applied new scientific methodology to studies of Chinese classics and antiquity, they were not just rekindling interest in Chinese culture, but, more important, they were pursuing intellectual renewal through critique and reconstruction. What we find missing from the 1990s *guoxue* is precisely this motif of renewal through critique and reconstruction because it takes for granted the validity of positivist and empiricist assumptions of modern professionalism. By ignoring later challenges to science as a privileged form of reason or the medium of truth, the modernist epistemological and methodological ideal of *guoxue* becomes an anachronism. We can further explore the epistemological and methodological ideal of *guoxue* and its limitation by approaching its three central tenets: self-positioning in the history of scholarly research, professional identity, and professional standardization.

Self-Positioning in the "History of Scholarly Research"

It is highly remarkable that the first issue of the *Scholar* began with a symposium on the "history of scholarly research," which is conceptualized by the New Scholars as consisting of the heritage, development, and changes in Chinese studies. Although all the participants in the symposium seem to agree on the importance of a scholar's knowledge of such a history, they diverge on the purpose of such knowledge and the use to which such knowledge is to be put. Wang Shouchang suggests that such a history "has only symbolic meaning today. It means a renewed commitment to careful study and solid scholarship of old fashion" (1991, 7). According to Wang, scholars may be able to trace the history of scholarly research into the past, but it is no longer possible for them to continue such a history, due to the cognitive and methodological rupture caused by Western academic influence. "'History of scholarly research,'" Wang contends, "is a term that doesn't exist in Western cultural vocabulary. It can only be understood against the background of Chinese cultural tradition. China used to have the tradition of 'men of wide knowledge' (*tongren*) or 'comprehensive scholar' (*tongru*) [those who mastered all the Chinese classics] . . . This tradition has been interrupted by the Westernized mode of knowledge specialization which began to influence the Chinese academic world since the end of Qing and the beginning of the Republic." Qian Wenzhong, on the other hand, believes that Chinese scholars do have much to learn from their own history of scholarship because this history also includes those great scholars of Chinese classics and history who have been influenced by Western methodology (1991, 12). Those great Chinese scholars who manage to combine the Chinese tradition and Western methodology, such as Chen Yinke, are new heroes in the Chinese history of scholarly research and are worth studying on their own.[7]

A third kind of opinion, which is what I want to examine in detail, suggests that the study of the history of scholarly research is necessary because it can serve the purpose of distancing 1990s scholars from their counterparts in the 1980s. Jin Dacheng, a very articulate advocate of this opinion, makes this point very clearly: "a reflection on the history of scholarly research is an important means to reevaluate the academic experience of the 1980s" (1991, 15). For Jin Dacheng the typical 1980s intellectual inquiry into Chinese culture and tradition was too radical and represented an "academic myth of antitraditionalism," and it is time now to bring Chinese studies back to the right track of professional scholarship. Jin Dacheng is not the only New Scholar who is critical of the intellectual activism of the 1980s. Chen Pingyuan, a leading New Scholar, himself an active participant in the cultural discussion of the 1980s, does not share the somewhat popular view that the 1980s intellectual activities were "intellectually rootless and shallow minded," but he agrees that it is time to replace the old paradigm of the 1980s with a new one (1991, 3). Xu Ming, another participant in the symposium, comments on the 1980s in a similar tone: "The 1980s was historically significant for the decade's role of emancipating people's minds. But that was also a time when weaknesses grew in the scholarly character of the younger generation, when in the humanities, opinions counted without having to be supported by learning and knowledge" (1991, 45).

The New Scholars' harsh evaluation of the 1980s cultural inquiry, though not completely biased, seems to be misleading, based as it is primarily on scholarly value rather than sociopolitical necessity and function. The fact is, however, that the cultural inquiry of the 1980s was primarily a sociopolitical event rather than a scholarly showing of force. In order to understand the 1980s cultural inquiry as a historically conditioned interaction of ideas and social milieu, it would be more proper to use *history,* or more precisely *intellectual history,* rather than *history of scholarly research,* as an illuminating framework. By positing history or intellectual history as the locus of the meaning and value of the 1980s intellectual activism, I do not mean to suggest that the value of intellectual action is independent of the kind and quality of ideas used to motivate or support it. On the contrary, I believe that the way ideas are constructed as reliable knowledge is important for their acceptance and effective influence. We do not restrict history to politics or public events, if for no other reason than that these cannot be understood without reference to the climate of opinion in which they take place or the kind of knowledge (ideas, theories, and discourses) that helps to legitimate or delegitimate them. For example, the 1980s intellectual maneuvers, such as the call for returning to humanist Marxism and overcoming alienation, the search for roots, the postulation of active subjectivity, were inextricably located in the historical context of the post-Mao era. The significance and value of these maneuvers cannot be understood apart from actual social forces involved in the shaping, construction, and appropriation of intertwined discourses and counter-discourses. The New Scholars' claim that intellectual works of the 1980s were motivated by extra-scholarly interest and therefore not "good scholarship" is objectionable not because this accusation is fallacious but because it is banal and trivial.

A better way of evaluating the 1980s intellectual trends is through intellectual history. The domain of intellectual history lies in "the interaction of historically important ideas with social milieu from which they emerge and which they in turn influence" (Stromberg 1975, 2). Intellectual history is not the same as the mere history of ideas of a specific field. The separate disciplines, such as philosophy, the sciences, as well as Chinese studies, insofar as they study their past ideas, tend to do so ahistorically, treating them substantially and as if they arose in a vacuum. It is not proper to equate intellectual history with the history of scholarly research, since the latter is often too rigidly construed in technical and methodological terms. A history of scholarly research, pursued historically, is itself part of intellectual history. As Roland N. Stromberg contends forcefully, few research methods, techniques, or alleged "scientific structures," if any, can stand the absolute test:

> The reason they appear and are adopted, become popular and influential, is related to factors other than the mere immanent laws of thought. These factors, it may be suggested, are historical and social; historical, in that ideas evolve in time as one generation hands down its thoughts to others who take them up and use them as points of departure—the endless dialectic of intellectual history; social, in that the selection of some ideas rather than others for emphasis and discussion has to do with the structure of social reality at a given time—the issues, atmosphere, and great events of the

day. Even genius must create with reference to the external social
world it finds at hand; it cannot create in a vacuum. (1975, 3)

Although the New Scholars are not completely unaware of the
imbrication of research methods in social and intellectual milieu, they
force an arbitrary distinction between the history of scholarly research
and intellectual history anyway in order to distance their professional
activity from the 1980s style of intellectual activism. Jin Dacheng, in a
deliberately drawn "outline of modern history of scholarly research,"
specifies the position he wants the New Scholars to identify with, the
position of scholarship for scholarship's sake as a counter-position to
that of scholarship for extra-scholarly purpose. He finds the archetypal
"objective scholars" in those new intellectuals of the May Fourth Movement generation, such as Hu Shi, Fu Sinian, and Gu Jiegang, who contributed to the project of "reorganizing of the Chinese heritage." *Reorganizing of the Chinese heritage (zhengli guogu)* is now used as a special
term to denote the modern development in the studies of Chinese classics.
According to Jin Dacheng, these model scholars have managed to combine a profound knowledge of Chinese classics and modern scientific
methodology and thereby successfully formed the paradigm of new Chinese studies. Jin Dacheng views the new Chinese studies as a model fundamentally different from that of the old Chinese studies, the kind of
Chinese studies done by scholars of an older generation, most of whom
were reformists of the late Qing Dynasty, with Kang Youwei, a leader of
the Hundred Days' Reforms (1898), as their paramount leader.

The particular distinction and polarization of the new and old Chinese studies allow Jin Dacheng to emphasize the difference between a
"pure" scholarship from an "extra-interested" one. Jin's opposition of
these two kinds of scholarship differs from Zhang Dainian's dichotomy
of Marxist/non-Marxist scholarship but is a dichotomy nonetheless. In
Jin's schema, on the one hand, is the old Chinese studies that cannot
stand free from "extrinsic" interest; on the other hand is the new Chinese
studies, which operates solely by its own "intrinsic" criteria. The old Chinese studies must be rejected because it is motivated by interest other
than pure research, and it is nowhere better exemplified than in the Chinese studies done by Kang Youwei. According to Jin Dacheng, what
Kang Youwei did to Chinese studies was exactly what many intellectuals
did to the humanities and cultural studies in the 1980s, and that is to use
scholarship as a political tactic for pushing reform. Kang Youwei, for

example, claimed that Confucius had actually been a reformer in anti-
quarian guise. Confucius wrote and revised, Kang maintained, the six
classics to support his own conception of reform. In order to bolster his
political movement Kang also wrote several books to prove that many of
the traditional Confucian classics were forgeries and that others, which
suited his reform campaign, were genuine. Kang's disciple Liang Qichao
carried Kang's skeptical spirit and approach still farther and expanded
their application in the field of Chinese historiography. This kind of
scholarship, Jin Dacheng avers, is short-lived because it is based on political expediency rather than genuine and testable knowledge.

Jin Dacheng tactfully quotes Liang Qichao to make the point that
Kang and Liang's old Chinese studies failed to achieve top scholarly quality (1991, 16). According to Jin Dacheng, Liang Qichao himself was
aware of the paradigmatic change in Chinese studies accelerated by the
introduction of the Western conception of science and scientific methodology, and that is why Liang confessed: "Both Kang Youwei and I were
confined by the enlightenment ideal of 'making use of knowledge' and we
dressed up our political opinions in the garb of scholarly research. Mis-
led from the right path of 'studying classics for the sake of studying classics,' we did not accomplish much in our scholarly research. It is now
time to follow the new path opened by Western thinking." The right new
path that Liang Qichao decided to follow, Jin Dacheng explains, is the
kind of studies of Chinese classics and history that is based on methodological principles developed in modern archaeology, sociology, and
mythology. Yet, Jin Dacheng remarks, the real master practitioners of
new techniques of scholastic research are later new scholars such as Hu
Shi and Gu Jiegang rather than Liang Qichao himself. Hu Shi's study of
ancient Chinese philosophy based on agnosticism and the genetic method
opened new possibilities for Chinese studies. Hu Shi's study of old Chinese vernacular novels such as *All Men Are Brothers* and *Dream of the
Red Chamber,* focusing on the verification of the authorship and evolution of the stories, provided young Chinese scholars with an example of
the application of a scientific method and attitude in textual criticism and
study. Gu Jiegang also based his study of ancient history on agnostic and
genetic methods. He traced the evolution of legends in different times,
comparing the ideas with current folklore and folk songs. Gu used these
methods to study the biographies of many historical figures, illustrating
how Chinese views on Confucius and the myths surrounding him
changed from time to time.

Jin Dacheng uses modern scholar icons, such as Hu Shi and Gu Jie-gang, to underscore the scientific and methodological aspects of the new Chinese studies. Jin Dacheng's view is typical of many New Scholars, who believe that the value of the new Chinese studies lies completely in its scientific approach and objective conclusions. The new model is taken to involve a faith in the possibility of scientific study of classics and history that shares epistemological status with that of natural science regarded as an ideal example of human knowledge. Such methodological and objective research aims at discovery of truth. Its truth or falsity depends exclusively on its logical relationships to the empirical data provided through unbiased observation. No other criteria are relevant. Academic research must be governed by the requirement of objectivity, of freedom from the distortions that result from the intrusion of any extra-scholarly purpose.

The quest for scholarly purity and disinterested objectivity may sound methodologically attractive. But the problem is that, in studies of Chinese classics and history, normative issues are not distinct from methodological ones. Hu Shi's experimentalist methodology, for example, was not a sudden happening in the history of scholarly research but a sociohistorically conditioned interaction of method and need of method. Hu Shi's scientific methodology, as Jerome B. Brieder observes, was a necessary complement to the skeptical intellect, which was in opposition to the bondage of traditional conformism of Hu Shi's time (1970, 113). The purpose of the logical process—the encounter with a problem, recognition of a problem, postulation of hypothetical solutions to it, examination of the probable consequences of these hypotheses, and, finally, careful evaluation of the results attained in practice—was, as Hu Shi explained in a detailed discussion of experimentalism, meant to enable men "to use their own intellectual powers to test and prove one by one the ideas and concepts gained from experience, and to maintain a critical attitude toward all institutions and customs, not using their ears instead of their eyes, nor muddleheadedly accepting the ideas of others as their own" (1921, 2:478).

The New Scholars' way of relating the technical meaning of scholarly research to its social meaning is questionable. They believe that scholarship itself should establish no more than preconditions about the consequential effect or use of its special knowledge and should not justify the goals of such effect and use. They do not seem to care whether this knowledge is used to advance oppositional criticism and cultural self-emancipation or to reinforce a politically repressive tradition and status quo. This is why He Yi (1995), in his criticism of the post-1989 new Chinese studies for being a "new wave of political conservatism," refuses to distinguish between propagandists of the new Chinese studies like Zhang Dainian and the professionally more sophisticated New Scholars. He Yi feels uneasy about the official enthusiasm in the recent fervor of Chinese national studies, no matter whether it is expressed in ideological or in professional terms. The new eulogy of Chinese national culture has fueled the official rhetoric of cultural patriotism and boosted its efforts to use cultural nationalism to gloss over the many disparate elements that the Chinese nation has fractured into: the new rich and the old poor, unequal classes and strata with conflicting political and economic interests, the cynical masses and their corrupted rulers, and so on. National culturalism has been particularly useful for pumping up political parochialism, which the governing elite employs as a major theoretical weapon against the general ideal of democracy. As long as the Chinese official ideology continues to use the uniqueness of Chinese culture and tradition to argue for its antidemocratic domestic policy, scholars of Chinese studies cannot properly drop vigilance regarding the state's imbrication in the making and employment of the knowledge about China and Chinese culture.

Criticism from deep within the profession of Chinese national studies, which is also self-criticism, is yet to emerge. Such criticism would introduce the much-needed perspective of the sociology of scholarship for the New Scholars to be aware of the psychic closing-off effect that their pure scholarship may have on themselves. Classical scholarship offers the New Scholars the luxury of believing that they can perform remote and unengaged scholarship. Paradoxically, the professional status of Chinese classical scholarship is enhanced by the deplorable situation of many other forms of contemporary scholarship in China. The paucity of new thoughts and ideologically straitjacketed writings in many humanities areas have made them scorned fields. In contrast, in the field of Chinese studies, the solidity of a five thousand–year history and the accumulated treasure of classical and historical writings seem to evoke a sense of lasting value and identity. Pure knowledge, a dream that is not conceivable in many other fields of contemporary scholarship, appears to be still possible in the fields of classics and ancient history. To hold onto this dream helps to mitigate the feeling of impotence many Chinese intellectuals feel in their academic work as well as in society in general. The ideal of pure knowledge becomes symptomatically therapeutic. Yet it is also symbolic of a crisis-laden situation of impoverished minds and a lack of political will, from which the most efficient way of escape for the New Scholars seems to be closing themselves off from contemporary politics and immersing themselves in remote scholarship.

Asserting a Distinctive Professional Identity

The replacement of intellectual history with a history of scholarly research as a framework of self-positioning has enabled the New Scholars not only to distance themselves from the more socially engaged intellectuals of the 1980s but also to emphasize their own professional identity as "scholars" rather than "intellectuals." Someone who sees himself as an intellectual is more likely than others to define his work as committed to critique of the existing social order and status quo. He is also more likely to see his function in society as inseparable from the duty of raising his voice against general complacency. All through the 1980s and, to a less extent maybe, into the 1990s, many Chinese intellectuals have been able to reconcile optimism about the intellectuals' oppositional role with an awareness of possible intellectual complicity with status quo. The newly emphasized professional identity for many New Scholars is not a rejection of the intellectual but, rather, a new effort to mark out where intellectual work stands today in China, or what they believe it can stand for.

The decline of intellectuals' influence after 1989 calls attention to the present difficulty of locating the specific character and contour of the context of cultural criticism. On which culture, for instance, should critics focus? Should they put the focus on the contemporary world of popular art forms, mass media, and the varieties of cultural phenomena or on the traditional academic practices with their standardized bodies of knowledge and well-defined fields of subject matter? Can these different emphases be so neatly separated after all? What are the relations between them? What is cultural criticism's specific object? Can it be thought to have one, or will intellectual work continue to intersect diverse textual fields and problems? Perhaps it is now necessary, if uncomfortable, to pursue a conflict-laden track that attempts to straddle disciplines, to link previously adjacent or discontinuous bodies of research, in order to locate the tactical advantages as well as the purely theoretical clarity of doing one's own professional business.

This is, unfortunately, not the track the New Scholars want to follow. Their newly adopted identity of "the scholar" indicates a sad retreat from the cultural criticism of the 1980s to the professionalism of the 1990s. For many of them the most important task is, as one New Scholar puts it, "to reconstruct a new disciplinary paradigm" and to establish "standards" and "norms" for that discipline (Chen Pingyuan 1991, 3). The New Scholars emphatically claim that their move is meant to overcome the commercial erosion of their profession. It is ironic, however, that the New Scholars' call for unitary standards of their profession comes at a time when a market economy, which is based on the ideals of profits and standardization, is not only influencing the shaping of the new fever of *guoxue* but also providing it with a normative model. Magali Sarfatti Larson's observation on the relationship between the standardization of knowledge and market control is particularly pertinent here: "The standardization or codification of professional knowledge is the basis on which a professional 'commodity' can be made distinct and recognizable to the potential publics" (1977, 40). We can certainly explore the economic conditions of the present booming of Chinese studies and the relationship between new Chinese studies and the particular kind of market economy in China (see the discussion by He Manzi 1995 and Chen Lai 1995). I will focus, however, on the cognitive aspect of group formation in the professional ideal of the new Chinese studies, for, as Larson notes, "cognitive commonality, however minimal, is indispensable if professionals are to coalesce into an effective group" (1977, 40).

In the case of the New Scholars what is at issue is a professional group whose members seek the common identity of scholars. For this professional group the ideal of normalization or standardization of Chinese studies is primarily not about the subject matter of knowledge but, rather, about a particular kind of knowledge that meets certain standards of acquisition and verification and therefore qualifies as reliable, truthful, and worthy of respect. In fact, the *Scholar* does not carry articles exclusively on Chinese subject matter but includes articles on Western subjects as well.[8] It is true that the object of the knowledge must be specific enough to impart distinctiveness to the professional products. What is even more important, however, is that the knowledge must be formalized or codified enough to allow standardization of the "product," which means, ultimately, standardization of the producer, the qualified New Scholar himself.

Forming a new paradigm of Chinese studies contains a special concept of change. Change must not be so rapid or so fragmentary that it precludes the possibility of socializing the aspiring scholars into a recognizable group. And change, to be legitimate, must be perceived by these scholars as progress. Were it not so, it could (and ultimately would) be perceived simply as aberration. For the New Scholars much of the 1980s scholarship aimed at radical criticism of traditional Chinese culture did not represent a "real change" in the history of scholarly research but, rather, merely a "scholarly myth of antitraditionalism," an aberration to be condemned and corrected (Jin Dacheng 1991, 19). Although it was a change, it was not an acceptable change; it was not only too radical but also too risky for the maintenance of the professional discipline itself.

The sociological content of Thomas S. Kuhn's approach to scientific production is relevant for the analysis of the New Scholars' view of professional progress (Crane 1972). An apparent tautology, which needs to be explained, sums up a central part of Kuhn's observation: science is inseparable from a perception of progress because it is the exclusive product of specialized communities of scientists. The perception of progress presupposes a tacit acceptance of what problems are worth solving or what goals are worth reaching. Scientific communities, says Kuhn, are characterized by sets of shared tacit understandings, which he calls scientific paradigms. A paradigm is not an abstract system of explicit rules but a *practice,* accessible through a long process of socialization. The guidelines of this practice are embodied in concrete examples of successful scientific inquiry. These examples are "concrete puzzle-solutions" that contain the promise that all the remaining problems proposed within a paradigm can, indeed, be solved. Because their shared definitions of reality are based on relatively uniform and standardized practices, scientists work toward and reach cumulative results: normal science consists of converging attempts to solve the same puzzles, to elaborate, articulate, and adjust to the same paradigm. "Once the reception of a common paradigm has freed the scientific community from the need constantly to reexamine its first principles," Kuhn writes, "the members of that community can concentrate exclusively upon the subtlest and most esoteric of the phenomena that concern it" (1970, 163–64). In the pages of the *Scholar* the paradigm formation of the new Chinese studies is clearly manifested. This journal provides a place where practice of the new Chinese scholarship can be displayed as a model and examples of such practice can be easily found, compared, and learned from. And, indeed, the paradigmatic meaning of such scholarship itself is contextualized by the place it appears or, to be more precise, exhibits itself. We can find many studies of Chinese classics and history that meet all the technical standards of the new Chinese scholarship but, nonetheless, are not recognized as such because they appear in different kinds of reference groups.

Liu Dong, a participant in the symposium on the history of scholarly research, warns his colleagues of the intellectual risk of posing prefixed norms and standards for the new Chinese studies. "Now we have scholars," Liu Dong says, "who read an academic work backward. If its cited works are not plenty enough, or if its sources of quotations are not authoritative or unfamiliar enough, they will reprimand it as 'shallow' and discard it as completely unworthy even though it may offer original insights into well-known materials" (1991, 25). Scholars of standardization do not seem to mind insulating themselves by defining the boundaries of correct practice, because after all they are working only for an audience of colleagues, an audience whose members share one another's values and beliefs. Therefore, they can take a single set of standards for granted.[9] At the limit such a professional community becomes its own world: professional scholars are simultaneously the producers and the main consumers of their products. Because their practice is relatively independent of all external factors, it *appears* to be solely determined by the norms of its own discipline and by its own internal tradition of research. This is why the construction of tradition is such an essential part in the New Scholars' efforts to theorize the new Chinese studies. If the New Scholars show how they fit into the history of scholarly research better than the practitioners of the Chinese studies of the 1980s, it is in the sense of T. S. Eliot's "Tradition and the Individual Talent," in which individual writers alter the whole of the preceding tradition in order to make their places in it. We can even say that, because they have the need to legitimate their idealized identity as scholars, the New Scholars must construct a history of scholarly research, with its monumental icons and heroes. Such a history of scholarly research, of course, involves more than mere heritage construction. Anything they say about the Chinese heritage is a product of the assumptions and the disciplined experience they bring to this heritage. They not only *find* models in a past and different era; they *put in* concepts of what they are to find and how they are to decode whatever they find there.

Professional Norms as Resistance to Moral Degeneration

The symbolic character of the new Chinese studies cannot be understood apart from its normative imperative. The New Scholars explain this normative initiative in different ways. Chen Pingyuan, for example, sees good scholarship as a means of self-discipline and personality cultivation: "to a genuine scholar, scholarly research is not just a matter of knowledge or profession, but more fundamentally, a form of life choice and value inquiry" (1991, 4). Wang Shouchang claims that returning to the classical model of the new Chinese studies is a symbolic attitude of criticism in the face of current "academic indecency," and he identifies this indecency in contemporary academic behaviors such as "making haughty comments in other people's fields" and "attacking other people's conclusions without paying attention to their arguments" (1991, 8). Jiang Yin suggests that "the history of scholarly research is fundamentally a form of study of man," since research always reflects the humanistic concerns of the researcher (1991, 41). Other New Scholars relate the normative function of research to the necessity of rules for defining argumentative terms, evaluating evidence, and analyzing and arriving at conclusions. They treat qualified scholarship not only as a pragmatic activity that guarantees valid research but also as a behavior model that has normative benefits for the profession as well.

In their enthusiasm in pushing for professional excellence, the New Scholars unfortunately tend to neglect that professional norms, expressed and experienced only as a matter of profession paradigm forming and as something irrelevant or beyond the laity of everyday life, are at most an elitist ideal. The professional elitism of the New Scholars is a retreat from the enlightenment position of the 1980s intellectuals in China. The basic distinction in the New Scholars' professional elitism is between "the professional" (with the moral connotation of goodness) and "the unprofessional" (with the opposite moral connotation). Professional elitism is an outlook that takes this distinction to be fundamental in understanding cultural activities and their social meanings. It elicits the elite as the only source of worthy knowledge and culture, the exclusive guardian of quality, the privileged preserver of standards, and the unquestionable locus of expertise and authority.

The problem with this professional elitism is not its somewhat esoteric object of study or its ideal of quality and excellence but, rather, its club spirit that circumscribes the extent of outreach of its ideal. As Abraham Edel and Elizabeth Flower point out, a subject matter of study is esoteric if it can be understood only by a professional in-group but not by a wider out-group. But the esoteric is relative to time and place. Whether in art or science or humanities, what is esoteric in one age may be much less so in another age. To be esoteric is not necessarily a permanent feature but a changing historical feature. The scholar with an esoteric interest need not be elitist, for elitism deals with a quite different dimension. The core of elitism is not the unusual values desired but the conviction that the few are the bearers of such values and that the people at large cannot or need not participate in or create these values and perhaps cannot even adequately appreciate them (Edel and Flower 1981, 141–42).

Elitism reflects a club spirit or small-establishment sentiment, and it is this spirit and sentiment that we need to take to task when considering the professional elitism of the 1990s new Chinese studies. The professional norms of the new Chinese studies, if not confined strictly to the narrow purpose of paradigm building but promulgated as a form of rational discourse of democratic potential, could have moral benefits for society at large. We can, for example, defend the ideal of collecting information and evaluating evidence, logical analysis, and reasonable argument for the same reason that we defend free speech, a free press, and transparency of public policy. In a civil environment that is independent from arbitrary state power, widespread literacy, training in thinking, and accessibility to information ultimately benefit all members of society, not only those who are the immediate beneficiaries of education, because only an informed citizenry can make responsible choices. One distinguished critic explains that "democracy depends on a citizenry that can reason for themselves, on men who know whether a case has been proved, or at least made probable."[10]

It is not too much to say that rational discourse is the very basis of democratic order and one of the basic social (not just intellectual) principles that oppositional cultural criticism must help to establish in China. In today's China coercion, which expresses itself in a number of reprehensible forms—censorship, prohibition of free speech, strict control over media and publication, and so on—is still the government's favored means of removing opposition to its established truth. The norms of rational discourse that are upheld and practiced in specific fields of humanities studies can thus play an important part in China's everyday life if they are also used as a decisive means to explore the prospect of social norms and politics based on critical and reflective discourse. Here the central aim of talking about rational norms is, of course, not just to build a scholarly paradigm, no matter how important it is, but, rather, to clarify the possibility and requisites of rational discourse in a society. Unfortunately, the New Scholars have not yet admitted this consideration into their preoccupation with professional excellence.

Against this background we can see the shift from "the intellectual" to "the scholar" and the retreat from "cultural criticism" to "scholarly research" as a counterproductive move made by the New Scholars in the 1990s. This shift of positions does not occur just in the field of Chinese studies but in other fields of the humanities as well, although scholars in most other fields are not as interested as the New Scholars in making a concordant effort to theorize and legitimate such a shift. By adopting a self-insulating academic position, the New Scholars unwittingly foreclose the intellectual influence they could have sought in society at large. In order to build a more constructive relationship between their profession and society and, indeed, advance self-understanding of the profession itself, they might want more efficiently to imagine their professional community as a social space. This space, small and precarious as it is, is the place from which intellectuals can expand not just "scholarly rules" or "professional norms" but, rather, what Alvin W. Gouldner (1979) called "the culture of critical discourse," the culture that marks the unique role of intellectuals in a modern society.

"The culture of critical discourse," Gouldner explains, "is a historically evolved set of rules, a grammar of discourse, which (1) is concerned to *justify* its assertions, but (2) whose *mode* of justification does not proceed by invoking authorities, and (3) prefers to elicit the *voluntary* consent of those addressed solely on the basis of arguments adduced . . . It is a culture of discourse in which there is nothing speakers will on principle permanently refuse to discuss or make problematic" (1979, 28). The professional community premises a sphere of autonomy in which speech and action are rule oriented rather than causally controlled by external forces. But this is not an Eden of pure reason or absolute consensus. Gouldner's study of intellectual culture admits the extent to which intellectual work is founded on a carefully nurtured sense of cultural detachment and on professional disagreements. At the heart of the intellectual enterprise is a fundamental uneasiness about what constitutes critical authority and scholarly expertise. In some sense one could say that authority itself is the central topic of concern for writers in every branch of knowledge, humanistic knowledge perhaps most of all, since the canonical documents and scholarly procedures that establish an academic discipline are always open to challenge. Underneath the contests that generate scholarship a set of rules and assumptions—all of those conceptions and practices that embody a field of study—relates the norms of discourse that allow someone to enter a particular intellectual community. The crucial factor in organized intellectual work thus is the "normalizing" of routines and questions, eventually of the texts and disciplinary standards, that collect into a recognizable rationality with its own rules and special language. These are the habits that allow intellectuals to perceive themselves historically as free agents whose self-defined activity is not attached to any vested authority or power beyond their own professional competence.

The positive aspects of this position should be obvious. Intellectuals, because of their self-regulating rationality, have been able to define their adopted positions as role models in society. The ideal of the New Scholars under discussion, for example, marks out a position that claims it is not political talk but solid scholarly research that will resolve confusion and bring certitude. Solid scholarly work would happen both through scientific method being applied to what were previously activities done by rules of expediency and appropriation and also by the general adoption of "scientific" ways of thinking. Although scholarly research seems to be above the vagaries of the day, in fact social imagery is extremely important in it. Scholarly research appears to possess an ethical quality that the self-interested party-state politics does not have. The ethic of devoting one's life to the impartial search for truth is one of its great attractions. This activity provides a metaphor for society and thus comes to play an unparalleled part in making the mold in which the society in general may be cast.

Intellectual culture, as Gouldner noted, is a critical discourse that proceeds "not by invoking authorities" but by advancing arguments that seek to authorize themselves without recourse to external social arrangements. This, at any rate, is the scholarly ideal. The wish to set intellectual self-authorization above the standpoint of common sense and of everyday life, however, generates a new dilemma that Gouldner articulates in a lucid passage in his "Prologue to a Theory of Revolutionary Intellectuals":

> The real crux of the historical problem of intellectuals and intelligentsia . . . [is] that they are *both* elitist and the bearers of an eman-

cipatory rationality; their rationality enables a critique of the institutionalized forms of domination, but it also contains the seeds of
new forms of domination. Their new rationality entails an escape
from the constraints of tradition but imposes new constraints on
expressivity, imagination, play, and insists on control rather than
openness as the key to truth, on a certain domination of nature,
including the self, rather than on a surrender to it. (1975–76, 20–21)

The intellectuals' culture, while undermining traditional authority and
inequality, constructs its own authority and its own standard of inequality: "to speak well and live with reflexive self-examination is better than
living an unexamined life" or "to do professional research is better than
amateurish interest in texts and history." "Thus even as the traditional
inequities are subverted," as Gouldner explained, "a new hierarchy of
the knowing, the knowledgeable, the reflexive, and insightful is silently
inaugurated. This is a central contradiction of emancipatory intellectuals—the new universal class in embryo—that brings a new darkness at
noon" (21).

    One of the most remarkable post-1989 phenomena is probably the
surge of intellectual elitism, expressed not only in the academics' growing
professionalism but also in their derogatory attitude toward mass culture
or the nonprofessional culture. It is painfully ironic that, after the 1989
pro-democracy movement that once brought together students, intellectuals, and citizens from all walks of life, intellectual elitism should come
to reinforce the official political elitism and join forces in a monopoly of
power (or division of power) over the common people. Political elitism in
China has always legitimized the ruling group to monopolize not only
power, glory, and benefits but also the authority of social ideals. Political
elites have treated social ideals as bases of manipulation rather than as
the articulation of common people's needs. Against this background
establishing an independent professional paradigm can be seen as seeking
an alternative authority to compete with the absolute political authority.
Such an alternative authority, if it were not confined to professional elitism, could have marked out a new position to empower the mass of people rather than to de-power them further. In establishing such an alternative authority, the New Scholars must de-idealize as far as possible the
notion of elite scholarship and show how their ideal of objective scholarship connects with the common people's need for social change. From

this perspective objective study is no longer a body of knowledge or a set of methods and techniques but, rather, organized social activity of men and women who are concerned with extending individuals' freedom from arbitrary, coercive, and authoritarian state control through these methods and techniques. The relationships among these people, guided by shared norms and standards, become the basis of a new political consciousness.

For the intellectual-scholar one way to achieve such a political consciousness is to resist the temptation for closure at work in the post-1989 Chinese academic world and to raise the issue of political apathy and intellectual irresolution. The moral perplexity of academic "neutrality" stifles needed dissent within the university and the society, dissent in particular against the misappropriation of knowledge and intellectual skills by the university-state arrangement that builds an integrated knowledge-power ideology. Resisting the ambition to describe the boundaries of knowledge and limits of thinking, the intellectual-scholar can redefine his or her specialized professional activity as a form of social activity and seek to broaden the contact between it and other everyday-life activities in opposition to domination, tyranny, and injustice. The stress on professional excellence of such everyday-life activities is not straitjacketed by club spirit but, rather, is oriented toward addressing social issues in connection with and benefiting democratization.

Abraham Edel and Elizabeth Flower, in an article entitled "Elitism and Culture" (1981), name several such possibilities, among which are the cultivation of quality and standards, the need for discipline and self-mastery, expanding the range of personal abilities, and access to knowledge-information and participation in its production and circulation. In breaking with the club spirit of the elitist concept, it is important not to lose any vital impulse it contains, particularly the insistence on quality and disciplined excellence and the emphasis on the range of abilities and the possibility of increasing participation. Functional democracy depends on a citizenry that seeks quality and disciplined excellence in everyday life. Common occupations, no less than specialized professions, are capable of nourishing the essential qualities for democracy. Self-discipline and self-mastery can be developed in all walks of life. It becomes necessary to avoid simplistically pitting the populist's romantic faith in the people against the elitist's view of the common herd. While the pessimistic elitist view operates to block experimentation, the romantic populist view underestimates the difficulties (Fiske 1989, 20–21). Critical cultural think-ing needs to avoid both extremes and link development of general human abilities to democratization of the social condition.

Revitalizing Intellectual Identity for Sociopolitical Intervention

Reflections on scholarly norms and professional perfection, like the debates on serious-vulgar literature or the humanist spirit, can serve to raise our understanding of scholarly, intellectual, and cultural crises in contemporary China. So far, however, such discussions and debates have skipped over the profound social and political causes of these crises. The intellectual identities favored by the post-1989 humanist and professional intellectuals—the self-styled scholars, serious writers, and spiritual humanists—are troublesome and flawed for supporting a theory of the unencumbered self and for presuming disembodied intellectual activities. The starting points for most of them lie outside the sociopolitical domain. This fundamental external relationship to the sociopolitical world—different in each case—contributes significantly to the limitations of their projects. It leads to misunderstanding the sociopolitical nature of intellectual activity and the intellectual's basic civic identity and his or her experience of citizenship. The result is that pure intellectual or pro-fessional theories are poorly prepared for revealing the nature of the post-1989 social and intellectual situation and for indicating how opposi-tional criticism may assist in its amelioration.

We have already discussed how the 1990s trend of new Chinese stud-ies touches on two important issues: the goal of scholarly devotion to tra-ditional culture and the proper role of intellectuals in contemporary China. For its advocates the answer is obvious. Professional and rigor-ously disciplinized studies of Chinese classics by Chinese scholars will emphasize the uniqueness of Chinese national culture and make China more competitive with the rest of the world in general, with the West in particular. Studies of Chinese philosophy and literature are supposed to contribute to the "reconstruction of Chinese national spirit and value system" (Chen Lai et al. 1994, 21).[11] But many writers and critics question the goal of establishing faith in Chinese exclusivity through the nation-ally homogeneous combination of Chinese materials and Chinese schol-arship. Some argue that such Chinese scholarship sets the Chinese cul-tural tradition apart from the contemporary modern world and can unwittingly reinforce Samuel Huntington's theory of "clashing civilizations" (Hu Xiaoming 1994). From a different perspective others argue that overenthusiasm in China's tradition can distract people from the present task of renewing and improving Chinese culture and society (Li Lianke 1995; Fan Qinlin 1995a, 1995b).

Still other reviewers find that what is at stake in the promotion of the new Chinese scholarship is not a methodological or academic issue but, rather, the intellectuals' desperate need for a satisfying self-image and identity. This self-image or identity becomes more and more precarious as political cynicism, moral nihilism, and philistinism, which permeate Chinese society of the 1990s, keep marginalizing the intellectuals' role in society. Anxiety about achieving a valuable and sustainable identity, as many articles on the current Chinese intellectual situation and problems indicate, has become a fin-de-siècle malaise haunting a large number of Chinese intellectuals in the 1990s. Most writers on the subject, however, seem to focus solely on the intellectuals' general dilemma about detachment and involvement and shy away from their particular post-1989 plight as thwarted critics under repressive political circumstances (Nan Fan et al. 1994; Tao Dongfeng 1994; Liu Jianjun 1993; Zhang Zhizhong 1994; You Xilin 1994; Zheng Ning 1994; Wang Yuechuan 1994; Wu Xuan et al. 1995). Most of the 1990s writings on intellectual issues, like the 1990s intellectuals themselves, are severely circumscribed by a political environment hostile to intellectual liberalism and activism.[12] It comes as no surprise that these writings frequently skirt the issue of the intellectuals' relationship to the one-party rule and the authoritarian political culture dictated by it.

The official ideological control has compelled liberal and humanistic intellectuals in the 1990s, more than in the 1980s, to hide their social and political concerns under the veil of professionalist requests, requests for self-perfection and authenticity, for academic purification and artistic freedom, and for the separation of intellectual activities from politics or commercial interests. They have to seek expression for their liberal-modernist and humanistic worldview or social vision in the so-called pure scholarship or the genuine spirit of literature and art. These intellectuals have to face two not easily reconcilable challenges: one, to cultivate their selves, watch over their intellect excellence, and thus hold the disturbing and contaminating influence of the outside world at bay; the other, to take responsibility for it. As the intellectuals face the encroaching influences of authoritarian politics and crass commercialism, too exclusive and intense a preoccupation with the salvation of their own integrity means surrendering the world to corrupting politics and commercialism. Too much eagerness to guide and to better the world leads to too much mixing with the unregenerate society, to the employment of all the instruments of power and wealth, the arcana imperii that erode the purity of the humanist spirit. The dilemma facing intellectuals in the 1990s and their efforts aiming at rebirth and purification are not just a matter of their existential raison d'être; it is aggravated by the repressive environment in which they have to struggle very hard in order to express their subjectivity and cast their identity.

The problems of subjectivity and identity—of the relationship between the thinking and acting subject and the larger sociopolitical setting—are significant ones, not only in the theoretical arena but also in the sociopolitical arena. These two arenas, of course, intersect. The notion "subject" is installed within a number of different areas of discourses of the human sciences today. But the subject is not just something set up in theoretical or philosophical terms. It is also, as Paul Smith puts it, "the complex but nonetheless unified locus of the constitution of the phenomenal world." The subject can and must be understood in political terms: "In different versions the 'subject' enters a dialectic with that world as either its product or its source, or both. In any case, the 'subject' is the bearer of a consciousness that will interact with whatever the world is taken to consist in" (1988, xxvii).

In the self-images of post-1989 New Scholars and literary humanists the subject's links to Chinese conditions and existing sociopolitical order are unclear. The New Scholars' history of scholarly research has an indeterminate relationship to China's historical and political traditions. The historical and political foundations of "serious literature" are similarly ambiguous. The ultimate concern is grounded in humanist spirit whose historical and institutional status is equally obscure. All these theories need to clarify the historical and political coordinates of the theorizing subject. In order to make their critical pertinence felt by the society at large, professional, moral, or spiritual intellectuals must also posit themselves as concretely situated "citizens."[13] The community in which they are located must shed its universalist veneer to reveal itself as a society related to a particular kind of state.

What many post-1989 New Scholars, advocates of serious literature and intellectual humanism, and crusaders against mass culture have in common is their suspicion of politics and reluctance to venture out of the safe professional enclosures into the sociopolitical domain. This political apathy and withdrawal has made it impossible for these intellectuals to develop a real conceptual framework of social criticism or to turn the professional, literary, or intellectual subject into a real sociopolitical agent. Articulate without urgency, lucid without politico-ethical designs, professional-humanist forms of cultural discussion have been captured by the myth of intellectual neutrality or of the intellectuals' role as a mere bystander. Their notion of the academic and professional space as the arena of effective social intervention presents severe shortcomings that can be superseded only if intellectuals rejoin the historically specific community where they are constituted as citizens and not just as scholarly researchers, writers, or humanists. They need yet to envision for their intellectual activities a mode of sociopolitical association larger than professional and literary circles. In order to be socially and politically effective they must not circumscribe their experience of citizenship, the form of identification that alone will allow them to become engaged intellectuals.

Citizenship, as Chantal Mouffe carefully explains in her discussion of radical democratic citizenship as an alternative political identity to the liberal individual, is not simply a legal status. It is an indispensable form of political identification. It allows one to be related to other people who, although engaged in many different purposive enterprises and with differing conceptions of good, accept the same submission to the formal relationship of community in terms of normative rules, not a substantive relation in terms of nationality or common ancestry. The rules that bind the members of a civic association together are sociopolitical norms and values that are both preexisting and contestable. These rules are contestable only from within that civic association: only members who have earned the rights to criticize by their sustained attentiveness and commitment to that civic association can effectively challenge these rules.

In China today the party-state controls the civic association in which the identity of citizen is formulated. The civic association in China is now defined by an ossified notion of common substantive purpose ("socialism") and national blood ties ("Chineseness"). While intellectuals must reject this officially defined concept of civic association and its undemocratic concept of citizenship, they must not jettison the political identity of the citizen itself. Indeed, it is precisely because citizenship is now defined in an essentialist framework that oppositional critic-intellectuals have a particularly important role to play in advancing a more constructive notion of citizenship that will endorse the individual citizen as active

"agent" rather than mere passive "subject." Such a reconceptualization
of citizenship is concomitant with an emphasis on "civil society," which,
as Mouffe explains, designates a common enterprise of agents who, "by
choice or circumstance, are related to one another so as to compose an
identifiable association of a certain sort. The tie which joins them, and in
respect of which each recognizes himself to be *socius,* is not that of an
engagement in an enterprise to pursue a common substantive purpose or
to promote a common interest, but that of loyalty to one another" (1991,
76).[14] Civil society is not a mode of relation defined by a prescribed "common purpose," but a relation in which participants are related to one
another in their knowledge of the authority of democratic conditions in
action. Such a relation is possible only in a society in which democracy,
not autocracy, reigns.

Democracy calls for its articulation as a question of community and
civic identity. Indeed, all questions of significant social transformation,
political authority, sovereignty, and citizenship return to the notion and
question of what kind of civic community we envisage and what part an
individual agent can and wants to play in it. Civil society that is not coer-
cively controlled by the state is a requisite condition for developing
democratic citizenship as well as for sociopolitically effective intellectual
work. To any present-day Chinese intellectual really committed to his or
her role in social democratization, democratic citizenship is not just one
identity among others, as in liberalism, or the dominant identity that
overrides all others, as in civic republicanism. Democratic citizenship is
"an articulating principle that affects the different subject positions of the
social agent . . . while allowing for a plurality of specific allegiances and
for the respect of individual liberty" (Mouffe 1991, 79).

Against this background Paul Smith's study of the subject as a political category and his constitution of "multifarious subject-positions" as
the locus of resistance must be seen as a major contribution to the task of
formulating a politically and ethically oriented theory of human agency
(Smith 1988, 150). Two aspects of Smith's theory of the subject are particularly worth examining here: his distinction between the subject and
the agent and the notion of multiple social identity and multiple subject-
positions.

Smith introduces an important distinction between the subject and
the agent. The subject is torn between being a self-projected opposite of
the object (subject as the source of conscious action) and something that
is subjected to dominant forces. The agent, on the other hand, marks the

idea of "a form of subjectivity where, by virtue of the contradictions and disturbances in and among subject-positions, the possibility (indeed, the actuality) of resistance to ideological pressure is allowed for" (1988, xxxv). The chief aim of this distinction, as John Mowitt explains in his foreword to Smith's study, is to criticize the theorizing of the self-generating subject as "at once enclosed by or set off from its enabling conditions and thereby marked as the bearer of an empowering legacy" without "rejecting the activating dynamic which the subject inadequately designates, namely agency." This distinction permits us to reassociate the activated subject (the agent) with his political resistance.[15] This distinction also allows us to break down the commonly used term *subject* and to reveal that what had been inaccurately described as an undivided, unified whole is actually "the series or the conglomeration of positions, subject-positions, provisional and not necessarily indefeasible, into which a person is called momentarily by the discourses and the world that he/she inhabits" (xxxv). We find that many post-1989 Chinese intellectuals are inconsistent in theorizing their own subjectivity as self-generating and the subjectivity of the "masses" as completely subjected to outside determinants. Their assumption that a human subject can be defined as an undivided and unified whole labeled as a scholar, a serious writer, or the opposite is also untenable.

This leads us to the second aspect of Paul Smith's theory of the subject: the multiple identity or multiple subject-positions. Smith's demystifying of the self-generating undivided subject owes more to the post-Marxist project of contextualizing subject constitution in antagonistic social relations than to the deconstructionist project of decentering the subject. The individual is seen as having positions within a social system, and attached to each of these positions is a set of interpersonal relations.[16] Smith's notion of multiple social positions owes much to that of Chantal Mouffe, who says, "With every society, each social agent is inscribed in a multiplicity of social relations—not only social relations of production but also the social relations, among others, of sex, race, nationality, and vicinity. All these social relations determine positionalities or subject positions and cannot be reduced to only one" (1988a, 89–90). New social movements, new relations of antagonism, and new forms of social conflict emerging in a society give rise to new forms of political subjectivity. By bringing an individual's multiplicity of social subject-positions to the fore, Paul Smith, like Mouffe, articulates a nontotalizing social theory, the central moment of which is to recognize that "what are often thought of as presignified social positions are the result of, and not the prerequisite to, political struggle and the negotiation of interests" (1991, 100–101).

From this perspective it is not difficult to understand that the intellectuals, like other members of a society, are actually engaged in diverse forms of political struggle. Their various forms of political struggles are always already inscribed in the presignified social positions of scholar, serious writer, intellectual humanist, or whatever. Far from being a natural or detached identity, the term *scholar, writer,* or *humanist* indicates what an individual intellectual has to mobilize in practical social struggles under conditions adverse to other forms of social identity. The particular form of political struggle or negotiation of interests that most fully occupies each individual makes one or several of his subject-positions or identities politically meaningful to him. Further, an individual is not just an "intellectual" but also a Chinese, a citizen, a man or woman, a member of a privileged class or an underdog, etc. His multiple functions as a social being must be understood in relation to the constitutive conditions of the sociopolitical community in which he is situated, and these functions together consist of the sociopolitical meaning of an individual's intellectual identity. This is why it is important to consider the political nature of intellectual identity and its intersections with other forms of identity.

Unfortunately, many Chinese intellectuals in the post-1989 years want to deny the political dimension of their intellectual identity and seek to redefine this identity exclusively in professional or moralistic terms. What they are yet unwilling to recognize is that the professionalist or moralistic redefinition of the intellectuals' identity is itself a political one. Such a definition suggests, in a rather politically subversive way, that public officials cannot be trusted to codify and enforce the distinction between the bogus and the genuine knowledge or between the moral and the immoral. The attempt made by many post-1989 Chinese intellectuals to distance themselves from politics and from the intellectual activism of the 1980s underscores deep disillusion and distrust of the current political life in China. It reflects the general sense that the political relevance of intellectual work has been obliterated by the dilapidated condition of politics in China, that intellectuals are left either to affirm the status quo or to snipe at it unproductively. Better, therefore, to ignore the difficult or impossible task of reanimating political consciousness by staying away within the safe confines of professional specialization, the development of personality and taste, and the cultivation of personal morality.

The efficacy of intellectual activity, however, does not lie solely in its methodological, aesthetic, or hermeneutic sophistication. It is a matter of the intellectuals' fundamental relationship to the possibility of knowing—of seeing or finding connections among meanings, texts, problems, issues, and the actual world in which they live. This fundamental relationship in the 1990s is not substantially different from that in which intellectual activism of the 1980s managed to operate and function with considerable sociopolitical effectiveness. Only many 1990s intellectuals seem to have succumbed to the dream of maintaining scholarly aloofness against risk-taking involvements that appear to compromise intellectual autonomy. The intellectual activism of the 1980s was situated in the midst of similar power—political power, institutional power, economic power, and cultural power—which offered distinct and limited choices that are still available to intellectuals of the 1990s. Such choices taken and emphasized can still define for the oppositional criticism of the 1990s the democratic changes in Chinese society.

Chapter 3

The Postmodern-Postcolonial Stimulus and the Rise of Chinese Post-ist Theory

One way to understand the complexity of postmodernism in China is to understand the contradictory legacy of modernity and its ideological implications that are revealed in political catastrophes such as the Cultural Revolution and the Tiananmen massacre and the trauma they cause to the nation. Postmodernism made its way to China in the mid-1980s, unfolding its aesthetic hedonism, its penchant for relativism, heterogeneity, and hybridity, its antiessentialism and its rejection of "grand narratives." In the post-Mao years prior to 1989, however, modernization was the predominant discourse that was used by both the government and most intellectuals to envision progress and development and to prevent the Cultural Revolution from happening again. The term *postmodernism,* in the context of rethinking what the Cultural Revolution represents, is one that elicits both anticipation and distrust—the former from the implications of being liberated from the dogmas of communist teleology, essentialism, and grand narratives; the latter from the concern about the postmodern disregard of different orientations of modernity and the conflict between central and peripheral, totalitarian and democratic, modes of modernity in China. The ongoing postmodernism debate in China is both a continuation and a transformation of the modernity debate of the 1980s, which was focused on "Four Modernizations" (industry, agriculture, science and technology, and military), and alternatives to this official rhetoric of modernity. The Chinese postmodernism debate emerges in the mid-1990s; it rekindles, from a new perspective, the incomplete modernity debate.

The postmodern sensibility in China, from the beginning, has been marked by a sense of belated modernity due to China's third-world status. Because of this desperate and seemingly unconscious desire to move into the future, postmodernism in China has shown a tendency to forget not only the violence of the Cultural Revolution but also the trauma of the Tiananmen incident of 1989, preferring instead to focus on the globalization of capitalism and Western cultural homogenization. The complexities of the postmodernism debate are thus compounded by other controversies, including such questions as: can we legitimately do postmodern theorizing in China without tackling its dominant mode of modernity, which is inherited from its totalitarian past and epitomized by the violence and brutality of the Cultural Revolution and the Tiananmen massacre? In order to understand such totalitarian modernity, how shall we approach China's uneven modernity and people's differentiated modes of participation in modernity there? From what political vantage shall we make sense of the interaction between the so-called global postmodernism and China's local "posts" (in particular postsocialism and posttotalitarianism)?

I want to address these complexities and concurring controversies in order to reveal how postmodern and postcolonial theories in China are not pure academic discourses but, rather, discursive spaces of cultural politics by which Chinese intellectuals resist or, unfortunately, implicitly help to reproduce a certain dominator-dominatee relationship in Chinese society. As Raymond Williams indicates in *Keywords* (1976), the more complexly and contradictorily nuanced a word is, the more likely it is to have constituted the focus of historically significant debates, to have occupied a semantic ground in which people imagine or find that something precious and important is embedded. The degree of semantic complexities and overloads surrounding terms such as *modernity* and *postmodernity* at the moment signals that people with conflicting interests and opinions feel that there is something sufficiently important at stake to be worth struggling and arguing about.

The Contradictory Legacy of Modernity in China

Arif Dirlik and Zhang Xudong, in their summary of Chinese postmodernism and of the debate on postmodernism in the 1990s, define the uniqueness of Chinese postmodernity as a reaction to modernity in general and to Chinese "socialist and revolutionary modernity" in particular (1997, 8). To them this socialist and revolutionary modernity represents not just one of a number of ideological and conceptual categories of Chinese modernity but Chinese modernity itself:

> Since the end of the nineteenth century, thinking about history and
> culture in China has been dominated by the categories of modernity
> and the Enlightenment. Chinese communism was arguably the most
> forceful, and ultimately the most successful expression of an ideo-
> logical commitment to modernity. (9)

Based on this abbreviated and formulaic view of Chinese modernity—
and, indeed, of Chinese revolution—they posit Chinese postmodernism
as reflecting China's moving beyond its revolutionary past and as an
emancipatory "cultural vision" that unveils the mythology of modernity.
What is left untouched by Dirlik and Zhang's modernity-postmodernity
pairing is the metamorphosis of modernity in China. The notion of
"modernity" or "modernization" in China is not an object of static
analysis and must be put in the context of change and contestation. It has
undergone many changes and is still changing. It has always been an
object of contestation. A proper understanding of Chinese postmodernism must include a careful consideration of the changing and contradictory nature of Chinese modernity.

Chinese modernity must first of all be understood in China's changing relationships to the West since China's failure of syncretism to meet
the nineteenth-century challenge of the West. Chinese socialist revolution
is indeed a forceful way to meet such challenge, but its legitimacy as a
modernity project, as the modernization debate of the 1980s indicates, is
not without question. This is no place to go into details of China's
encounter with modernity in the form of various impingements of the
West. Suffice it to say that China's early encounters with the West exper-
imented quite unsuccessfully with ad hoc measures. Recognition of the
need to borrow Western technology gave way in turn to intellectual
demand for Western institutions. When the effort to transplant institutions failed to produce the wealth and power that Chinese leaders saw in
the West, the search for new values and resistance to such a search were
simultaneously born. It was not until the times of the New Culture
Movement and the May Fourth Movement that "science" and "democracy" were formulated as essential paradigmatic themes of China's move
away from its traditional past and in the direction of a modern country.

What made the 1980s cultural discussion different from that of the
May Fourth period was a more focused emphasis on modernization as a
trope of change to replace "revolution," which had remained the master
trope influencing China's process of changes from the May Fourth Move-

ment to the end of the Cultural Revolution. Revolution had been favored as a means of national liberation, social rebuilding, and economic development. The revolutionary proposal implied a messianic and fundamental style of transformation, which carried in it a germ of essentialism and anti-intellectualism. Although modernization can be contained by the revolutionary rhetoric—as in Four Modernizations—it can also be an alternative to that rhetoric. Enlightenment modernization, for example, attempted to recast social change as an ongoing process of social-cultural self-education, not as revolutionary tutelage; it also strived to redefine modernity itself as an ever-changing condition of democratic social change.

The second, and even more essential, aspect of the notion of modernization is that it is not a homogeneous model of change but, rather, an arena in which different practical orientations and contending interpretations play out. The innovation of models of change or resistance to it cannot constitute by themselves a sociohistorical trend, for the latter by definition combines a reference to the goal of change with the consciousness of a social relation of domination. A model or trope of change may well have a social dimension, and ultimately always does: there is no such thing as a theoretical model in itself wholly independent of the mode of domination that is exerted upon it. In a purely theoretical conflict, such as that between notions of revolution and reform or revolution and modernization, there also lies the field occupied by social practices defined equally by their option for a new model and by internal conflict between different modes of social use of this new model. This field is what I am particularly concerned with, for a new model of change in itself does not automatically constitute progressive social change.

Modernization was the new model of change that official ideologues and critical intellectuals promoted in the 1980s, but they vied with one another to give it a specific social form and practical orientation. While the majority of intellectuals in the 1980s wanted to postulate modernization as an enlightenment ideal of emancipating people's minds, the official rhetoric confined modernization to technological terms and insisted that only its own interpretation of modernization was correct and legitimate. Since the official power holders monopolize the terms of modernization in China, the key issue is not just what new model of change was introduced in the 1980s but also who controlled the terms of this model upon which action was based. For the same reason the practice of modernization should be investigated not just as a matter of correct theorizing but also as a mode of cultural politics by which a certain dominator-dominatee relationship reproduces itself and maintains its legitimacy.

In the years immediately after the Mao era, when modernization was officially promoted as a slogan to rally national solidarity, its ideal was not yet so limited to the technological and economic areas as to become incompatible or contradictory with the ideal of democratization. As a matter of fact, it was the official argument that "four modernizations must be accompanied by political democratization" and that China would not be able to modernize economically without substantial institutional and judicial reforms.[1] In 1981, when the campaign of criticizing the writer Bai Hua seemed to signal the recurrence of another Cultural Revolution, the conception of modernization encountered its first challenge in the post-Mao era. The campaign revealed the limits of the Deng regime's modernization program. The regime would tolerate economic liberalism, or even a degree of artistic and academic pluralism, but would suppress any potentially threatening views that it believed challenged it politically. The campaign against "spiritual pollution" in 1983, in which Party elders made serious efforts to revive Mao's ideology, became a landmark moment when the distinction between modernization as a self-empowering official rhetoric and modernization as an enlightenment ideal came to the fore. The struggle over the definition of modernization itself became part of the process of China's modernization.

Containing modernization in China, which is manifest in the Four Modernizations, is expressed as a creed and a program that ensure that social change will take the course party-state authorities determine and that any change must satisfy the ends desired by these authorities, including the principal end of maintaining political stability in favor of the party-state power. At times political stability is indeed the condition necessary for economic development or technological innovations. At times it serves only as rhetorical praxis for the hegemony of power holders. Early in 1980, before the first undemocratic political campaign of the Deng era had dampened the ideal of modernization, the debate over whether democracy was a means or an end already pointed to the danger of containing modernization in China. Deng Xiaoping saw political reform as a means to a more efficiently run economy. Alternative views held democracy as an end in itself. An article in _Philosophy Research_ asked, "If socialist democracy were regarded merely as a means for realizing modernization and not as an end itself, what value would there be in achieving economic modernization?" The article warned that such an approach had already resulted in "great damage."[2]

The distinction between the official and the alternative concepts of modernization became absolutely inevitable after 1983, and it crystallized the debate over the very concept of modernity in general and Chinese modernity in particular. This distinction emphasized that the modernization advocated by many intellectuals differed significantly from the course of social change promoted, achieved, and labeled as modernization in the official rhetoric. Modernization, as the majority of intellectuals in China understood it then, means social growth and progress, not merely in material realms but also in human capabilities and the competency of members of a modern society. Implicit in their welcoming of the development of technology and science is a view of technology as a liberator of humanity and science as the successor to prejudice. Their understanding of the power of human beings—amplified by science and technology—caused them to be dissatisfied with anything less than improvements in the life chances of all people. This essential enlightenment ideal of modernization was articulated in much of the cultural discussion that began to build momentum in 1985, although it was certainly not shared by all intellectuals.

Some intellectuals were skeptical of the possibility and desirability of immediate democratic change and argued that a neo-authoritarian order was more suitable for China's process of modernity (Sautman 1992). The argument for neo-authoritarianism based on the economic experience of the Asian Dragons was part of China's modernity debate in the late 1980s. Although it provided one of the 1980s conceptions of modernity, it did not seem to take flight in the face of that decade's enlightenment passion for opening to the outside world and for forging a new path for the future of the country. The enormous popularity of the six-part series *He shang* (River Elegy) in 1988–89 indicated that people seemed to prefer a nontraditional modernity. The theme of *He shang* was that China's civilization (symbolized by the Yellow River) had declined. It advocated that China cast off the burden of its tradition, including the Confucian mentality and values, and open itself to the West (symbolized by the blue sea beyond).

It was more than coincidence that promotion of the enlightenment ideal of modernization by literary intellectuals and the demand for political and institutional reform and democratization by reformist intellectuals occurred at the same time in 1986. The former was articulated in discussions about humanism, subjectivity and human agency, and the desirability of modernity over premodernity (feudalism); the latter in the demand for political reform and democratization.[3] Both the political and the philosophical-literary approaches were alternatives to the official rhetoric of Four Modernizations, and together they necessitated some statement of relations between what modernity is and what it is not. What is not modern was at that time stated as the premodern. In such a statement what was at issue could not remain only at the philosophical or literary level but had to move into the social and political realms. In the social and political realms the premodern society was conceptualized as based on a traditional elite ruling by some mandate of heaven, and modern society was viewed as based on the broad participation of the masses, which did not accept any traditional legitimation of the rulers and insisted on holding these rulers accountable in terms of secular values and efficiency. Above all, premodern society was seen as bound by the cultural horizons set by its tradition, while a modern society was upheld as culturally dynamic and oriented toward change and innovation.

The contrast of the premodern and the modern carried an implied criticism of the absence of moral theory in the official program of the Four Modernizations. A moral theory of modernization is a set of ground rules that states the ethical limits beyond or in violation of which modernization does not count as authentic. In the 1980s for many reformist intellectuals this moral theory of modernization was expressed as democracy, while for many literary-philosophical intellectuals it was expressed as humanism, or the ideal of anthropocentric "culture." Neither humanism nor anthropocentric culture is nonpolitical, for they are directed against the dehumanizing force in orthodox Marxism, which treats the individual as a pawn, as an insignificant instrument in the general development of mankind or in some overriding mission of the nation-state.

From the perspective of the humanist, or the anthropocentric, ideal, modernization must have some rules other than "do it." Yet nowhere in the Four Modernizations can people find procedures for ensuring that it is the humanistic ethics and not the groups who claim to be the leaders, prophets, and guardians of the country's future that rule the working of modernization. Lacking in the officially defined Four Modernizations is the first principle of modernization modeling and practice, that is, a willingness to take its ideal seriously enough not to fix it beforehand or to reify it. This first principle of modernization is the principle of enlightenment.

The omission of humanist concern or ethics of democratization in the Four Modernizations matches well with the undemocratic nature of the party-state in China. Without a public check on whether or not the Four Modernizations play by moral rules or without some means of assuring that the democratic and humanistic ideals of modernization are treated with an appropriate degree of respect, neither the political nor the philosophical-literary approach to modernization can effectively continue when the party-state decides to stop such discussions, as was the case in the Campaign against Bourgeois Liberalization in 1987. And in really bad times, as in June 1989, the most horrendous crimes can be committed and justified in the name of the Four Modernizations, in complete violation of their core ideals.

That something like the Tiananmen incident could happen after the Cultural Revolution, when the crackdown on the popular protest of April 5, 1976, was still fresh in people's minds, pushed to the foreground the horrendous similarity of these two events and raised question about whether being "premodern" really explains China's political problems. Critique of the Cultural Revolution in the 1980s basically treated the Cultural Revolution as a lack of modernity and, in particular, as a return of feudalist despotism or tyranny. Conditioned by its own historicity, such a critique failed to realize and emphasize that the Cultural Revolution is not just a new form of old despotism but, rather, a particular form of *modern* despotism that must be understood in its own terms and called by its rightful name, totalitarianism. We can hardly blame the modernity debate in the 1980s for not getting ahead of its time and for not taking a postmodern view on itself. Only in hindsight can we now say that misidentifying the Cultural Revolution as a case of *premodern* despotism rather than *modern* totalitarianism cannot advance the post-Tiananmen criticism of the Cultural Revolution. The lack of exact precision with which phenomena of totalitarian modernity can be analyzed and the failure to posit an explanatory model capable of embracing the relevant data (such as totalist ideology, party-state terror and violence, fanatic mass movement, etc.) can imperil a differentiated critique of modernity and a historical view of China's specific modernity.

The basic perception of the Cultural Revolution as lacking modernity has left untouched its pernicious modern quality and its totalitarian operation. Hannah Arendt (1951) described totalitarianism and its mass movement as a uniquely twentieth-century occurrence and singled out the combination of terror, coercion, propaganda, and one-party dicta-

torship.[4] Very much to the point, she presented totalitarianism as a
demonic tale of modernization. What makes totalitarianism modern in
China and elsewhere is its reliance on a totalist ideology and its one-party
dictatorship. The Party's legitimacy is derived from an all-embracing ideology (Marxism-Leninism) that concentrates all activities on the achievement of ubiquitous forms of control and a "utopian" or allegedly "new"
society. This was exactly what the Cultural Revolution attempted and
claimed to achieve, and it was how the modern tyranny of the Cultural
Revolution distinguished itself from old-style tyranny. Discussing the
modern quality of totalitarianism, Irving Howe emphasizes its break
from, rather than continuity with, tradition:

> There have, of course, been unfree societies in the past, yet in most
> of them it was possible to find an oasis of freedom, if only because
> none had the resources to enforce total consent. But totalitarianism,
> which represents a decisive break from the Western tradition, aims
> to permit no such luxuries; it offers a total "solution" to the prob-
> lems of the twentieth century, that is, a total distortion of what
> might be a solution. (1963, 191)

As is proved by the Cultural Revolution and, unfortunately, once
again by the Tiananmen massacre, only a modern society has the technological and discursive resources (state apparatus, ideology, mass communications, police surveillance and control, governmental and grassroots
organizations, etc.) to achieve totalistic and monopolistic control. As Jeffrey Goldfarb points out, "Though traditional autocracies may sometimes be more unpleasant and brutal, human ontology is not undergoing
a conscious, politically enforced systematic redefinition" (1989, 4).[5] It was
the relentless efforts to enforce totalist and systematic redefinition of
human ontology by political means that marked the Cultural Revolution
and the Tiananmen massacre as prototypical occurrences of modern
totalitarianism. Theories that minimize or ignore the distinctive qualities
of modern tyranny lead not only to ignorance but also to the misformu-
lation of critical agenda. The tradition/modern, premodern/modern
dichotomies formulated in the cultural discussion of the 1980s, with feudalism as its object of criticism, did not adequately serve as a guide to
either the Cultural Revolution or the "rational totalitarianism" of the
Deng era itself.[6] A different theoretical formulation is called for. If intel-

lectual humanism in the 1980s was not up to this task, neither is post-modernism as it is practiced in the 1990s in China.

When, and How, Did Postmodernism Become Chinese?

Proponents of Chinese postmodernism tend to trace the beginnings of Chinese postmodernism back to the 1980s, construing a continuous history that erases its formative moment after the Tiananmen incident. It is true that Western writers and theorists now known as "postmodernists" were introduced in the 1980s, but they were part of the upsurge of Western names and -isms of that decade and enjoyed no special status (Goldman, Link, and Su Wei 1993).[7] Western theorists who are now identified as master postmodernists were then often introduced by other designations. Fredric Jameson was made known as a Marxist or neo-Marxist literary theorist; Michel Foucault a philosophical and cultural poststructuralist; Roland Barthes a textual strategist; and Jacques Derrida a deconstructionist (Wu Xiaoming and Meng Yue 1987; Li Hang 1987; Ge Hua 1987; Wang Ning 1987; Xu Ben 1989). Even in special studies of postmodernism and postmodern theorists, postmodernism was treated as a new aesthetic style or cultural sensibility that was remote to Chinese reality.[8]

There were a good number of Chinese scholars who wrote about postmodern writers, theorists, and theories in the 1980s but no self-conscious Chinese postmodernists, for it was not the purpose of these scholars to construct Chinese postmodernism. In the post-Mao years prior to 1989 Western theories, including postmodernism, were introduced in a borrowed frame of modernity, from which, paradoxically, even postmodernism acquired distinctive modern attributes. This articulating frame of modernity is now often falsely presented by Chinese postmodernists as "Chinese modernity." The historical fact is that the quest for modernity in the 1980s was not the same as Chinese modernity. On the contrary, it expressed a strong sense of China's lack of modernity. Chinese intellectuals' interest in Western ideas and theories was then motivated by a desire to move into modernity, not out of it.

Of those who participated in introducing Western postmodern theory in the 1980s, only a very few became self-conscious postmodernists in the 1990s. The main body of Chinese postmodernists come from a quite unexpected quarter. Most of them are young critics of contemporary Chinese literature or film, who are not familiar with original theoretical texts in Western languages (Wang Ning 1997b, 34). In their effort to form Chinese postmodernism they have to rely on Western theories introduced by other Chinese scholars for quite different purposes. The result is not just a poor match of theoretical understanding and practical purpose but also a dogmatic quality of Chinese postmodernism itself. In their hands postmodernism is more a mind-set than a theory, more a cluster of shared preconceptions than a closely argued system of thought. This, however, should be regarded as a theoretical character rather than a weakness, for, after all, most enthusiasts of postmodernism in China are not interested in doing postmodernist theory per se; their main preoccupation is in construing a nativist cultural theory by whatever convenient attitudes or themes they can glean from existing postmodernism.

Chinese postmodernism encountered the right time and the right atmosphere in which to take shape and grow in China after Deng Xiaoping's inspection tour to southern China in early 1992, which broke the stalemate of the dark period following the Tiananmen incident. First, with Deng Xiaoping's push for accelerating market reforms and order to stop debates on -isms,[9] the socialism/capitalism conflict was suspended in order to clear the way for China's export-oriented economic liberalization. This gave China an unprecedented chance to join the trend toward globalization and share its common condition of postmodernism. Second, the erosion of socialism/capitalism difference made it all the more important for the state to use nationalism to fill the ideological void. Immediately after the Tiananmen incident, nationalist rhetoric in China was basically deployed in a defensive manner to ward off criticism from outside as interference in China's internal affairs. After 1992 it began to draw strength from the nation's economic success and indigenous culture. This new, assertive nationalist feeling is central to Chinese post-ist theory; it also informs much of the post-ist theory's criticism of the May Fourth Movement. Although the May Fourth Movement was basically a patriotic movement, the nationalism that evolved from its tradition is essentially anti-mainstream. By contrast, the nationalist and nativist sentiments of the 1990s are pro-mainstream.

Postmodernism became a Chinese theory when it ceased to be merely a remote Western discourse and began to be deployed as a significant indicator of China's present condition. Of course, this did not happen all of a sudden. But some important moments in its formation can nonetheless be recognized. One of these moments is when the January 1993 issue of *Wenyi yanjiu* (Literary and art research) published seven articles in order to explore "how postmodern phenomena appear in literary and art areas in the wake of economic openness and development of the market economy and what are the characterizing features of postmodernism in China."[10] This forum is a landmark formative moment of Chinese postmodernism for two reasons. First, it was a collective action that for the first time treated postmodernism as part of China's own reality; it also exhibited some kind of intellectual consensus regarding Chinese postmodernism. Second, characteristic tendencies, themes, and attitudes of Chinese postmodernism—such as attention to mass culture, emphasis on a synchronous relationship between global postmodernism and the Chinese post–New Era, blanket hostility toward enlightenment, modernity, and universalism, and preoccupation with national history and identity—were clearly articulated in some of these articles. At the same time, differences and controversies regarding Chinese postmodernism also began to emerge.

Another important moment was in September 1993, when *Dushu* (Reading) published three articles on Edward Said's notions of Orientalism and cultural imperialism (Zhang Kuan 1993; Qian Jun 1993; Pan Shaomei 1993). Among responding works two pieces of seminar discussion caught much attention in the intellectual circle and greatly reinforced the feeling that some commonly shared intellectual interest in postcolonial theory was under way. The first is "Periphery, Center, East, and West," written by a group of five writers (Wang Yichuan et al. 1994), and the second is "Orientalism and Postcolonial Culture," written by four writers (Chen Xiaoming et al. 1994); both were published in early 1994. Said and his notion of Orientalism had been introduced in China earlier (Zhang Jingyuan 1990), but it was not until after 1993 that his work began to move into the center of Chinese intellectual discourse. The increasingly complicated interaction between local and global cultures in the 1990s and the resulting anxiety about national identity and native authenticity have played a big role in preparing the fertile ground for a warm reception of postmodern and postcolonial theories in China.

Chinese postmodernism is a post-Tiananmen phenomenon not only because it partakes in the general nationalist ethos after 1989 but also because it bears the mark of intellectuals' recovery from the dark period immediately after the Tiananmen incident. The period from summer 1989 to early 1992 was the most intellectually depressing time since the reform following the Cultural Revolution. With Deng's call to renew the Party's policy of openness, Party hard-liners, conspicuously offensive since the crackdown, pulled in their horns. The intellectual circle began to recover from the shock effect of the Tiananmen incident, but a new intellectual atmosphere had set in. There was a general intellectual cooling off of ideologically subversive ideas and politically sensitive issues. A new kind of realism, one that values political stability and orderly change, became prevalent. This political disenchantment differs from the humanist depoliticization of the 1980s, which was a disguised form of intellectual politics. What was suggested by humanist depoliticization was a counternotion of politics that restricted it to specific areas, taking away its omnipotence and freeing it from orthodox Party principles in order to make it less oppressive and less intervening in every corner of Chinese social life.

By contrast, the political disenchantment in the 1990s is much more reconciliatory to the existing order, institutions, and the status quo.[11] Chinese postmodern-postcolonialism reflects the political disenchantment of the post-Tiananmen era. What makes it stand out in this circle is that its political disenchantment is expressed as disappointment with modernity, which is again dressed up in the garb of a criticism of Western hegemony. It is too condescending to distinguish different modes of modernity in Chinese society, too impatient to ask what and whose modernity is in crisis, and too meek to take to task the actually existing authoritarian modernity. Striving to catch attention both in and out of China, Chinese postmodern-postcolonialism is now presenting itself in China as a defender of Chinese cultural interest and outside China, with the help of their advertisers, as a challenge to China's socialist and revolutionary modernity. The first claim is trivial, and the second is absurd. It may "creatively" use Western theory to defend the necessity of Chineseness, but it is certainly not critical of either Chinese socialism or Chinese revolution. The double strategy of thrust and parry should not be underestimated. It has rhetorical advantages. The built-in option between the two claims—one convincing but ironic and the other newsworthy but implausible—gives Chinese postmodern-postcolonialism great resilience and a capacity to succeed. By artfully shifting weight from one foot to another, it can claim both patriotism and intellectual resistance, taking maximum advantage of whatever audience is at hand.

In order to understand the unique character of Chinese postmodernism and how it differs from postmodernism commonly known in the West, we must move beyond its pretentious gestures and scrutinize its complicated "contrast-effect," David Scott's notion intended to underscore the relation between criticism and strategy. Contrast-effect allows us to grasp not merely the internal cognition of criticism but also the particular strategy criticism employs in order to construct a discursive space in which a particular target of criticism can emerge. Critical operation derives its force, in part at least, from the contrast-effect it produces: "when criticism enters a field it does so in relation to some target with the implicit or explicit self-understanding that that target is worth aiming at, and that it is worth aiming at because disabling it will have desired effects. One crucial way to produce contrast-effects is to bring new targets into view" (Scott 1996, 9). Postmodern criticism in China has brought into view the new target of modernism and its manifestation in China. Postmodernism in the West is a reaction against principal features of modernism: against the totalizing discourses of or metanarratives of history; against a teleological belief in science; against a view of progress and development as inevitable and linear; and against a belief in the unified subjectivity of the rational individual. When postmodernism becomes Chineseness, it modifies its reaction against modernism by emphasizing the Western affiliation of these principals. Therefore, Chinese postmodernism is logically intertwined with third-world concerns about Western hegemony and the asymmetrical power/knowledge relationship between the first world and the third world.

Chinese postmodernism does not operate by itself; it is always combined with particular Chinese postcolonial concerns. Chinese postmodern-postcolonialism is a nativist reaction against Western-centered metanarratives of history, Western teleology of development, and Western concepts of enlightenment, human subject, and social progress (democracy). This contrast-effect sets Chinese postmodern-postcolonial theory in the 1990s apart from whatever postmodern or postcolonial theories that were introduced into China in the 1980s. When postmodern and postcolonial theories were first brought to China during that decade, they were totally disconnected. Their contrast-effects were separate and not focused. Postmodernism remained for a long time a mere floating element in the nebulous zone of aesthetics, and postcolonialism was practically indistinguishable from an emotional expression of third-world passion for dignity and identity.[12] It was not until postmodernism joined forces with postcolonialism, redeploying the grandly all-embracing critique of modernity as a critical refusal of Western hegemony, that Chinese postmodern-postcolonialism began to find its own voice. This Chinese postmodern-postcolonialism—with its bifurcations of postindividualism, postrevolution, post-Enlightenment, post-elitism, post-Baihua, post-allegory, and post-criticism—has construed a particular Chinese post-ist discourse that does not comfortably fit the category postmodernism or postcolonialism. This is why it is now often simply referred to as Chinese post-ist theory.[13]

The contrast-effect of Chinese post-ist theory is complicated by its negative attitude toward notions of reason, social agency, enlightenment, democracy, and human rights. This negative attitude has led Chinese post-ist theory to targeting the pro-democracy and pro–human rights cultural criticism in China as its main object of attack. This is not just a rivalry between different theoretical discourses but, rather, a cultural-political conflict conditioned by two different kinds of intellectual-political zones in China. As Tang Tsou (1986, 3–66) and Merle Goldman (1996, 37) have observed, there exist in China side by side "zones of indifference" and "forbidden zones." The former are reserved for intellectuals who pursue their professional and artistic interests without disturbing the existing political order; the latter are erected to protect the state from "challenges to Leninist political structure, the Party or leadership," and into these zones "intellectuals entered at their peril" (Goldman 1996, 37). While post-ist theory is now practiced in zones of indifference, pro-democracy and pro–human rights cultural critique has to be done in forbidden zones.[14]

The conflict between intellectual activities in different kinds of ideological zones, as that between Chinese post-ist theory and pro-democracy cultural criticism, produces a subtle but important dimension of contrast-effect. The contrast-effect of Chinese post-ist theory can thus be discerned from two interrelated perspectives. On the one hand, it locks on to the undifferentiated modernity as its main target of criticism, denigrating social enlightenment, democracy, and human rights as ideas of insidious Western modernity or universalism and denying their urgency and relevance in the Chinese context. On the other hand, facing those who question post-ist theory's conservative political implication in China, post-ist theorists often picture the postmodern debate as a conflict between indigenous and Westernized intellectuals, displacing the political contrast-effect with that of national affinity (Zhang Yiwu 1995a; Liu Kang 1996b; Chen Xiaoming 1998). Such a displacement leaves out a key player involved in the apparently academic game: the party-state. The party-state not only participates in the game with its dominant ideology; it also dictates the rules of the game. The state allows post-ist theory to fare well, but it does not permit divergent voices on democracy or even on memories of the Cultural Revolution and the Tiananmen incident to have an outlet in the public forum. Post-ist theorists are the lucky ones in the Communist system of censorship, which used to tell people what to say but now advises them what not to say.[15] The official ideology in China still sets and maintains the limits of what can rightly be done in cultural theorizing, and, to a large extent, it gives shape and conviction to the arguments these fortunate post-ist theorists make.

Chinese postmodernism has a very short history. The contrast between this history in the 1990s and its prehistory in the 1980s is significant because it indicates not only the different emphases Chinese intellectuals put on "postmodern" ideas in these two decades but also the changed circumstances under which they view and appropriate postmodernism for quite different purposes. Diminishing this contrast can lead to desensitizing us to the significant rupture of intellectual commitment and critical agenda caused by the Tiananmen trauma in 1989, which most Chinese postmodernists sensibly eschew entirely. The change in intellectual sensibility and ethos at the turn of the decade did not happen, as some observers suggest, simply as a natural consequence of socioeconomic transformation. It is related to a certain historical event that until today remains a forbidden zone of public discussion in China. The absence of attention to this historical event conceals its own historicity. The alertness to ideological and political influence and restriction on Chinese postmodernism involves a political understanding of it. In fact, the ongoing debate on Chinese postmodernism has become one of the focal points of cultural-political controversy among Chinese intellectuals.

Nativist Formulation of Chinese Post-ist Theory

Postmodern-postcolonial theory in China emerged at the crucial moment when the rapid decay of socialist ideological beliefs and the devastating memory of the events of 1989 had led the authoritarian party-state to an increased reliance on nationalism as a new unifying ideology. This new ideology, though different from the old Maoist orthodoxy, is its continuation and supplement because, like the old ideology, it draws its strength from some fundamental conception of clash, conflict, and antagonism. An ideology of antagonism, in this case, can be understood as sociocultural preconditions for authoritarian rule and repressive state politics. It provides the state with a tremendous capacity to enlist the loyalty and self-sacrifice of the general populace. Class struggle used to serve as such

an ideology of antagonism; the Chinese party-state employed class struggle to legitimize its authoritarian rule and support its massive repression
of what it considers "class enemies." As an ideology of antagonism, class
struggle had been severely discredited but not completely incapacitated
by the Cultural Revolution. The vacuum left by the demise of class struggle is now filled by a new ideology of antagonism, the intensely affirmative and assertive nationalisms.

Allen S. Whiting, in his discussion of the official nationalist attitude
in Chinese foreign policy after Deng, suggests differentiating three types
of nationalism—the affirmative, assertive, and aggressive:

> Affirmative nationalism centers exclusively on "us" as a positive in-
> group referent with pride in attributes and achievements. Assertive
> nationalism adds "them" as a negative out-group referent that chal-
> lenges the in-group's interests and possibly its identity. Aggressive
> nationalism identifies a specific foreign enemy as a serious threat
> that requires action to defend vital interests. (1995, 295)

In the case of post-1989 China the affirmative and assertive nationalisms
have emerged as a new ideology of antagonism because unfavorable
domestic and external factors have combined to pose serious threats to
the ideological and political legitimacy of the state power: "Domestic
demonstrations challenged leadership legitimacy, Western criticism of
their forceful suppression placed China in a pariah status, and erosion of
Communist rule in Eastern Europe and the Soviet Union seemed to
threaten its survival in Asia." All these factors, converging all of a sudden, contributed to inducing "a siege mentality" that fueled official
nationalism (296).

Official nationalism has not completely replaced class struggle but,
rather, supplements it. The new ideology of antagonism differs from the
old one in that it places more weight on external factors, although that
does not mean it de-emphasizes internal factors. Throughout the second
half of 1989 mainland media reiterated Deng Xiaoping's explanation for
the April–June crisis: "This storm was bound to come sooner or later.
This was determined by the *major* international climate and China's own
minor climate."[16] Emphasizing external factors justified an assertive
nationalism directed against the foreign threat. But the official assertive
nationalism had a hard time finding new things to say about the outside
threat beyond bringing up China's past conflict with foreign powers.

Despite the delicate shifts between affirmative and assertive nationalisms expressed by the controlled media, two old themes can be discerned.[17] They are both articulated in terms of patriotism (*aiguozhuyi*).
Patriotism is a corollary to national pride and sovereignty. In the ideology of patriotism both the past history of Western antagonism and present hostility on the part of the West play a significant role. Immediately
after the Tiananmen massacre *Renmin ribao* published an article evoking
China's past humiliation by foreigners: "For a country to shake off foreign enslavement and become independent and self-reliant is the premise
for its development . . . Although China was a big country before liberation, it was slavishly dependent on others and could only be bullied by
them."[18] The next year the government ignored the Tiananmen anniversary by promoting patriotism through two other commemorations, both
pointing to China's past humiliations by Western powers: the May
Fourth Movement of 1919 and the 150th anniversary of the Opium War.
International criticism of the Tiananmen massacre was brushed aside as
being an excuse for the West to continue to bully China and a scheme for
the West to interfere in China's internal affairs.[19]

The official rhetoric of assertive nationalism, which appeals to populist emotion rather than intellectual understanding, is hardly capable of
going beyond its position of defending China's greatness and sovereignty.
In the early 1990s it found an unexpected ally in postcolonial theory,
which could help it not only to update its outworn language of patriotism
but also to specify better what a foreign threat may actually mean to
China in the post–Cold War era.[20] The foreign threat is against many different things that may be lumped together under the umbrella category of
"China": the ideological legitimacy of the Chinese Communist Party,
China's political stability, its social or economic system, its territorial
integrity, its sovereignty, Chinese history, Chinese tradition, the Chinese
way of life, Chinese values, and so on. Postcolonial discourse creates the
chance for the official ideology of assertive nationalism to present the
outside threat as not only being against the state or its representatives but
also, more fundamentally, as being against the Chinese way of life, essential Chinese values, Chinese perspectives and perceptions, Chinese history and cultural tradition—that is, the very core of Chineseness. It also
opens the door for the official ideology to present the threat as coming
not only from Western imperialism, foreign governments, and foreign
political forces but also from Western values, Western cultural heritage,
Western modes of knowledge, the Western vision of history—in other

words, from an absolutely incompatible, unchangeable, and alien Westernness. Moreover, the newly formulated concerns about the lack of fitness of Western values and the power differentiation between core and peripheral countries help China's repressive government to express its own anxiety of legitimacy as a heroic form of third-world resistance to the first world.

The ideology of antagonism once defined by class struggle has found a happy supplement in the notion of an inexorable West-East clash and first-world/third-world conflict. The combination of the two has greatly reinforced the ideological basis for the Chinese government's political repression in the name of safeguarding the "Chinese style" of development. The affirmative and assertive nationalisms resorted to by the leadership are used to impress on the population the importance and justice of the government's cause and the need for undemocratic measures: eliminating all opposition and dissent, repressing all activities that can be interpreted as demeaning or subverting the power of the party-state, and denying the people a free press, labor unions, the right to strike, the right to a fair trial and due process, and other civil liberties, in the name of defending the country from combined outside and inside threats. The notion of West-East conflict serves as a useful tool for shaping the people's sense of the imminent threat to their world. On the one hand, this ideology induces people to view cultural differences as irreconcilable. Often what they see as a genuine conflict of interests or as a threat from another country is the result of an "us" versus "them" differentiation, bias, and mistrust. On the other hand, because of the mistrust, conflicts will arise, and real conflicts will be magnified, as people often respond not to the issues at hand or to the people involved but, instead, to the stereotypes and negative images that they hold.

The general view of the China-West conflict in the 1990s is characterized by its post–Cold War complexion. There is a common elite and public consensus that the Cold War ideological opposition between communism and capitalism is now replaced by differences in tradition, values, and reality among nation-states. To a large extent this consensus, as one Chinese critic notes, is connected with many "negative stimuli" from the West (Xiao Gongqin 1996, 62). Popular national sentiments are stirred, on the one hand, by events such as the failure of China's Olympic bid in 1993, its repeated clash with the United States and the West on issues of MFN trading status, entry into the World Trade Organization, human rights, Taiwan, and Tibet. On the other hand, intellectuals' national feeling is sensitized not only by these events but also by the debate on the clash of civilizations. Many Chinese intellectuals have reacted strongly to Samuel P. Huntington's article "The Clash of Civilizations," which argues that geopolitical conflicts in the post–Cold War world are not ideologically motivated but are defined by different civilizations. Huntington's argument that the biggest threat to Western civilization is Islamic and Confucian culture, and thus the West should be alert to a Confucian and Islamic alliance, has considerably disillusioned many Chinese intellectuals who used to look to Western modern civilization for inspiration for China's modernization. The hostility conveyed by Huntington's argument makes them all the more sensitive to China's own values, national interests, and identity (Shi Zhong 1993; Wang Hui 1994; Wang Jisi 1995).

With an enhanced sense of national and cultural identity, some Chinese intellectuals try to balance China's national specificity and the world trend toward modernity (Liu Dong 1993; Wang Hui 1994; Qu Xuewei 1994; Li Shenzhi 1994, 1995). Others suspect that the West has a hidden agenda, using democracy and human rights to interfere in China's internal affairs and to maintain hegemony by slowing down China's prosperity and crippling its competitiveness (Song Qiang et al. 1996; Liu Kang et al. 1996). Criticism from the West about China's lack of democracy and poor human rights record has revived and released a deeply felt bitterness about colonization and colonialist assumptions on oriental tradition and culture. In the context of a reflection on Western influence on contemporary Chinese culture, some Chinese intellectuals voice their concern about the phenomena of "colonial culture" (zhimin wenhua) (Ji Xianlin et al. 1995; Wang Meng et al. 1995; Liu Fangping 1995; Zhao Yingyun 1995; Xu Jialu 1995; Du Yell 1997). In a more counteroffensive manner arguments against imperialism and cultural imperialism are turned into a frantic expression of hurt pride and bitter arrogance (Song Qiang et al. 1996; Liu Kang et al. 1996). For many Chinese intellectuals this has made national and cultural identity a salient issue and a problem for cultural discussion; national-cultural identity relates to a collective memory, through which the contemporary nation recognizes itself through a common past, heritage, and tradition. What has happened is that there has been a reemergence and revitalization of Chinese values. First, this reflects the new confidence of many Chinese as a result of their economic success and their sense of cultural identity. Second, it represent a reaction against the perceived attempt of the West to export its culture and values.

Variations and amalgams of post–Cold War national sentiments and concerns constitute a peculiar environment in which postcolonial theory travels from the West to China. Discussing the movement of ideas and theories from point to point, Edward Said emphasizes the need to "specify the kinds of movement that are possible, in order to ask whether by virtue of having moved from one place and time to another an idea or theory gains, or loses in strength, and whether a theory in one historical period and national culture becomes altogether different for another period or situation" (1983, 226). The traveling of postcolonial theory in China and its transformation into Chinese nativist post-ist theory represent an interesting case of how a theory's movement into a new environment "necessarily involves processes of representation and institutionalization different from those at the point of origin." Given China's postsocialist and posttotalitarian condition and the dominant role played by the official ideology of patriotism, the important questions seem to be: what oppositional edge should Chinese post-ist theory keep from the politically engaged and oppositional postcolonial theory? How should it resist co-optation by the official propaganda that claims the Party's absolute national authority as the ambit of what constitutes "patriotic" should become greatly expanded? What could be the political price of redefining intellectual debate in terms of Chineseness? What kind of intellectual opposition will it be if it attacks only one form of domination and repression (Orientalism, cultural imperialism), but apologizes for others (authoritarianism, totalitarianism)?

Because these questions are by no means clearly addressed by the nativist post-ist theory as it is now practiced in China, many Chinese intellectuals have expressed concern about its fitness and political implications in China. They share post-ist theorists' vigilance regarding Western hegemony and wish to emancipate previously submerged colonial histories and identities. They are deeply concerned, however, about the way in which post-ist theorists set about these tasks. One of the basic questions raised is a sociological one: why is postcolonial theory advocated primarily by intellectuals from third-world countries who are working in Western academic institutions? This question differs somewhat from the epistemological or political inquiry into the intellectual influence or moral imperative of postcolonial theory. Some critics suggest that intellectuals such as Edward Said who come from third-world countries are simultaneously entangled in and estranged by Western academic institutions and that their strongly expressed national affiliation should be seen as a sign of this situational tension. They indicate that Western-educated Chinese students, such as Zhang Kuan and Qian Jun, are attracted to postcolonial theory and try to introduce it into China because they personally are coping with the same situational tension (Wang Yichuan et al. 1994; Chen Yaohong 1994).

Others point out that writers of the younger generation have enthusiastically embraced postmodern and postcolonial theories because these theories provide them with a shortcut for distinguishing themselves from and competing with writers of previous generations. From this perspective cultural nativism has to do with current Chinese academic politics. The rise of cultural post-ist theory involves academic reciprocal positioning as well as ideologically circumstantial contingency. An awareness of the complexity of the social and academic conditions surrounding post-ist theory will lead us to suspect that the contemporary positions of anti-colonialism and Chineseness, while theoretically radical, do not tell the whole story. These proclamations must be seen as moves within the academic community that are also responses to the post-1989 reconfiguration of intellectual-state relations (Zhang Dexiang 1994; Tao Shuiping 1994a).

Another basic question often raised about Chinese post-ist theory has to do with its politico-ethical implication: should cultural criticism have a coherent politico-ethics that applies to intellectual resistance to tyranny, injustice, and domination in local as well as in international relations?[21] Critics of post-ist theory question whether it can be a genuine oppositional discourse because it shies away from basic norms such as freedom, equality, and justice and opts for Chineseness as its fundamental moral principle. Lei Yi is among the few writers in mainland China to point out that, by redefining oppositional criticism in the us-versus-them polarity, nativist disciples of postcolonial theory have forfeited their role as critics of the undemocratic order at home. In an article published in *Dushu* Lei Yi (1995) openly disputes the perfunctory reading of Edward Said as merely an anti-Western or anticolonialist critic. He insists that we should learn from Said not his apparently anti-Western posture but, rather, the oppositional stance he takes against the mainstream culture of the world in which he lives. If nativist-postcolonial critics really want to oppose and deconstruct hegemony, domination, universalism, and totalization, Lei Yi challenges, why don't they start their intellectual critique by resisting these repressive forces in their own society and in their own daily life?

Yet most critics who do raise questions about the political conservatism of post-ist theory are mindful of various political and social taboos in contemporary China, and, accordingly, they generally express themselves in an elliptical fashion. Instead of directly challenging the ideological orientation of post-ist theory and its complicity with the official patriotism and nationalism, opponents of post-ist theory usually point out its misuse of postmodern theory in the Chinese context. Like postcolonialism, postmodernism is frequently evoked by post-ist theory, but postmodernism's obvious lack of suitability for China makes postmodern theory an easier target than postcolonial theory. Zhang Dexiang, for instance, describes the forced grafting of Western postmodern theory onto the Chinese reality as "theoretical magic shows and cultural ravings." He writes angrily, "So long as hundreds of millions of Chinese peasants are still confined by a premodern agricultural economy, and so long as the majority of Chinese urban dwellers are still struggling for everyday bare survival . . . the so-called postmodern theory in the 1990s' Chinese academic circus stages only its own 'discursive escapism'" (1995).

Post-ist theory appropriates postmodern theory and the notion of postmodernism for a rather specific purpose, and that is to denigrate China's attempts at modernity, especially democratization. This narrow purpose often results in the fetishization and misrepresentation of postmodernist theory.[22] Post-ist theory's favorite China-West dichotomy lends itself to a caricature of democracy as a Western-modeled ideal of modernity. Accusations against democratic ideas of freedom, self-choice, and pluralism based on modern social and political values can be heard across the spectrum of humanities departments in Chinese academia in the 1990s. Usually what fuels these accusations is not free and public discussion of the social, political, or cultural agenda of change—such discussion is not allowed in the current political circumstances—but, rather, discussion of specific professional and academic topics. Yet, whenever these considerations deepen and expand to include the social and political implications of intellectual work, they inevitably cross and recross with the question of their own ethical norms and with the larger issues of justice, democracy, and human rights.[23]

To post-ist theorists who decry the asymmetrical relations between the first world and the third world, democratic values bear the ideological stigma of being "possessions" of the West and are therefore considered unfit for China's social and political progress. Zhang Kuan, one of the first to introduce postcolonial theory to China, for instance, has taken an increasingly strong anti-Western stance and has published a number of articles on radical Western theories to demonstrate that Western ideals of democracy, human rights, and civil liberties are criticized *even* in the West.[24] At the 1995 conference "Literature and Spiritual Civilization" sponsored by the Research Institute of Literature of the Chinese Academy of Social Sciences, attended by a large number of professors, scholars, and journalists from several leading universities and newspapers in Beijing, Zhang Kuan sharply reprimanded those participants who "fail to take a critical attitude toward Western discourses." He went further than most critics of modernity by asserting: "There are people who have been harping on concepts such as liberty, democracy, pluralism, and writers' independence for many years, embracing these capitalist ideas without ever considering the differences of [Western and Chinese] historical conditions" (1995b).

Through the incorporation of avant-garde Western theories with China's officially endorsed antidemocratic stand, theorists like Zhang Kuan have arrived at what Said calls the final stage of traveling theory: "the now full (or partly) accommodated (or incorporated) idea is to some extent transformed by its new uses, its new position in a new time and place" (1983, 227). Postmodern and postcolonial theories have undergone a particularly drastic transformation in China and are now adapted for the sole purpose of rejecting Western thought (sociocultural as well as political) as colonizing, imperialist, and altogether unsuited to Chinese realities. Chinese post-ist theory is conveniently used to affirm the value of local and traditional elements and even the cultural and political status quo. All this is done in the name of enhancing Chinese cultural subjectivity.

But what is Chinese cultural subjectivity? How should it be conceptualized? Given that traditional Chinese culture was so badly disparaged by China's own iconoclast intellectuals in their effort to achieve a new culture and social system, how is it to be revindicated? All of these may be questions for which there are no answers, although they must be somehow addressed if Chinese cultural subjectivity is to be conceptualized at all. It is from this perspective that we can best understand the usefulness of contemporary postcolonial theory to Chinese nativist cultural thinking. Postcolonial theory is extremely efficient at finding cultural subjectivity in the absence of any clear answers to these questions. Moreover, postcolonial discourse, due to its sensitivity to trauma of national identity and national history, provides a convenient and powerful tool with which Chinese cultural subjectivity can be conceived of not in terms of what it wants to achieve (a positive ideal) but, rather, in terms of what it has been prevented from achieving by the influence of alien Western culture (a might-have-been ideal). In nativist-postcolonial discourse the focus falls on the *wounds* others inflicted on China by cutting short the nation's "autonomous" and "natural" process of evolution, though that supposedly indigenous and natural process is never clearly explained. As Isaiah Berlin has pointed out, the "infliction of a wound on the collective feelings of socicty or at least on its spiritual leaders, may be a necessary condition for the birth of nationalism" (1979, 350). China's identity is, as the identities of individuals often are, defined by its past hurt, pain, or injury.

These conditions tend to create both shaky self-esteem and an anxious desire to protect and enhance the nation economically and to maintain or increase its power, prestige, and cultural purity. In Chinese postist theory both such self-esteem and desire are frequently expressed. An illustrative example can be found in an article entitled "From 'Modernity' to 'Chineseness',", a manifesto coauthored by three Beijing based professors, Zhang Fa, Zhang Yiwu, and Wang Yichuan (1994). It seeks to turn "cultural China" into a totalizing conceptual framework in which Chineseness can be established once and for all as a unique indigenous model of knowledge, a register of a historically new epoch, and a distinctive quality of cultural experience.

"From 'Modernity' to 'Chineseness'"

Chineseness: A New Model of Knowledge and a New Epoch

"From 'Modernity' to 'Chineseness'" bears a significant subtitle, "Inquiry into a New Model of Knowledge." Its authors set out first of all to describe the distinctive quality of Chineseness as a model of knowledge, which is different from that of modernity. They make a fundamental distinction between two different models of knowledge, which they call modernity and Chineseness, designating, respectively, two distinct temporal spans in modern Chinese history. Modernity is used to refer to a particular model of knowledge established under Western influence, which, according to the authors, remained unchallenged during the one and a half centuries between the beginning of the first Opium War, in 1840, and 1989. They allege that during this historical era China was reduced to the status of the Other of the West because it accepted the West's idea of modernity as a means of survival and progress. They divide the period of modernity in China into five phases: 1840–95, 1896–1919, 1919–30s, 1930s–76, and 1976–89.

The first phase they call "the technology-centered period"; during this phase, as a consequence of its defeat in the wars with the Western powers, China wanted to empower itself by borrowing modern, especially military, technology from the West. The second phase is "the period of political institutions"; it was marked by the drive for dynastic reform and by the reaction to China's defeat by Japan in 1895. During the "Hundred Days' Reforms," in 1898, governmental institutions were revamped, and modern institutions (such as bureaus of commerce, industry, and agriculture) were established to emulate Western institutional efficacy, if not Western political systems. The third phase, "the scientific period," arrived when the modern concept of science became one of the two leading banners of the New Cultural Movement and the May Fourth Movement. Here the authors' deliberate omission of the other banner, democracy, is remarkable. The scientific movement resulted in national efforts to create a new national character, which, it was thought, would lead to curing all kinds of diseases that were afflicting Chinese society, politics, and culture. The fourth phase, the "phase of sovereignty," began when China faced aggression by Japanese imperialism and includes the period when, after the success of the Communist revolution, China faced its two arch-enemies, the United States and the Soviet Union. The fifth phase is called "the New Era"; it suggests both continuity and discontinuity with the Maoist regime. These three authors recognize the fifth phase as being marked by Chinese culture's "total collapse into the status of 'the Other' [of the West]" in its effort at reform and self-change because China's drive to modernize was stimulated by the nation's abrupt exposure to the developments of Western civilization after its self-seclusion during the Cultural Revolution (Zhang Fa, Zhang Yiwu, and Wang Yichuan 1994, 13).

Such a picture of China's victimization by the idea of modernity is meant to set up a promising new model of knowledge and a new epoch of national authenticity, both based on the notion of Chineseness. According to the article's three authors, the rise of the new model of knowledge, Chineseness, must be understood in the historical context of what they call the post–New Era, which began in 1990, apparently all of a sudden. Chineseness, through which consciousness of the new epoch is expressed, becomes the criterion of the newness for this historical era, because, these three theorists tell us, the post–New Era is an age in which "[China] makes the decisive effort to move beyond her status as 'the Other' [of the West] and to reevaluate the idea of 'modernity.'" Chineseness implies a qualitative claim about the newness of the times in China's own terms, in the sense of the times being completely Other, and better, than what has gone before. The arrival of the post–New Era "designates the end of the idealism and cultural fever of the New Era, and the beginning of new possibilities for a third-world nation with a developing market economy" (14).

"Social Features of 'Chineseness'"

The authors of "From 'Modernity' to 'Chineseness'" list three social features that serve as registers of the new paradigm of knowledge they refer to as Chineseness. Those social features are the Chinese-style market economy, Chinese popular culture, and Chinese diversified values. First, they use Deng Xiaoping's concept of *xiaokang* (literally meaning "comparatively well-off") as a Chinese concept for economic and cultural development that is indigenously configured without resorting to the Western or Russian models and therefore "opens a new avenue for national self-identity and self-discovery" (15). While enthusiastically embracing Deng's domestication of development and modernization, they accept willingly and without question the ideological implications of this policy-saturated definition.

Second, they see in the rise of popular culture a positive expression of Chinese society's turning away from the enlightenment ideals of the 1980s. New trends in literature, such as New Realism, that turn to current daily life for subject matter and artistic inspiration are cited by the three authors as denoting a salutary change on the part of writer-intellectuals who, in the face of the Chinese status quo, are giving up their classical critical and enlightenment stance and adopting, instead, a "realistic" attitude of acceptance (16).

Third, they point to the diversifying of cultural discourse, manifested in the coexistence of different trends in intellectual stances, of which the major varieties are new conservatism, new pragmatism, and new enlightenment. While posing as a metatheory surveying the diversified fields of contemporary currents, post-ist theory nonetheless identifies itself with one of these specific trends, namely, new conservatism. The three authors praise new conservatism as "a cultural reorientation of the 1990s" that is significantly different from the modernization drive of the 1980s. "Adopting non-Western strategies to ensure political and economic development, social stability, and consensus of social values," they contend, "[new conservatism] takes a strong critical and negative attitude toward Western culture" in an effort to "recentralize the Chinese state and nation" in cultural thinking. Both new pragmatism and new enlightenment are mentioned only as foils for or negative opposites of new conservatism. New pragmatism, they say, represents a yielding attitude toward consumer culture and individualist needs, and new enlightenment represents a hangover from and diehard habit of intellectual modernism and elitism inherited from the now obsolete radical tradition of the May Fourth Movement (17).

The Components and the Center of Chineseness

In addition to the three social features that signify the new paradigm of knowledge and the new epoch of Chineseness, the three authors investigate a number of characterizing components of Chineseness. These components include the following: an indigenous conception of development based on a firm rejection of Western-modeled "modernity"; the aim of contributing to world culture in, and only in, a unique Chinese manner; and the establishment of the rim of Chinese culture. The last is by far the most important and therefore deserves the most detailed explanation.

The three post-ist theorists expand the concept of the rim of Chinese culture—which is facilitated by both the economic miracle of the four small dragons in Asia and the emergence of New Confucian theories outside China—into five separate but intertwined aspects. They are the Asian-Chinese economy, Chinese ethics, the "Han language" (the Chinese language), the Chinese aesthetic style, and the Chinese way of thinking and reasoning. Three of the five aspects of the rim of Chinese culture—ethics, aesthetic style, and thinking—are marked by the thrust of absolute cultural relativism because they are described as completely culturally distinctive and as sharing little common ground with other cultures of the world. The ambitiously constructed theory of the rim of Chinese culture is reminiscent of the traditional Chinese system of tributary relations. Although it is carefully couched in the language of cultural relativism rather than the language of a supreme civilization enshrined in Confucian doctrine, the rim of Chinese culture strikes a pathetic note, echoing the dream of restoring the lost hierarchy of a China-centered order. The rim of Chinese culture, we are told, should be composed of four layers, with mainland China as its core; Taiwan, Hong Kong, and Macao as its second layer; all overseas Chinese as its third layer; and "East Asians and Southeast Asians under Chinese cultural influence" as its fourth and outside layer (18). With the rapid economic development in Taiwan, Hong Kong, Singapore, and, lately, in mainland China, the idea of a "community of Chinese" (*Zhongguoren gongtongti*) has frequently arisen in regard to cooperation in this region, especially in economic matters. The *rim of Chinese culture* is reminiscent of the term *Pacific Rim,* but it is far more ideologically hegemonic and culturally homogeneous.

What Does the Grand Theory of Chineseness Deliver?

In the ambitiously constructed theory of Chineseness, the new model of knowledge of Chineseness represents an epochal climax or great moment of arrival in China's self-liberating history of cultural transformation. Such a theory of cultural transformation has emphasized broad unidirectional patterns. This unidirectional model of cultural change is seriously circumscribed. One of its chief limitations is its large time periods, which lump together and distort significant short-term changes and developments. For example, the fourth phase of modernity, the phase of sovereignty, includes an odd mixture of China's Others—Japan, America, and Russia—and contributes little toward an understanding of China's changing role in the world or comparing one Other to another. A second limitation is the lack of attention paid to concrete mechanisms of cultural change, such as ideological movements, military conflicts, or polarization of social classes. The unidirectional history assumes only two mutually exclusive categories, modernity and Chineseness. It treats modernity and Chineseness as two fixed models, two articles of faith, rather than as testable hypotheses. Seldom are detailed historical studies conducted with an eye toward testing or modifying these models. Only unidirectional change between these two models is emphasized, the progress implied being a value judgment that may or may not be warranted. Its unidirectionality causes it to concentrate on some kinds of change but to ignore ideological continuity and the importance of countercurrents that arise in opposition to presumably dominant cultural tendencies.

The grand theory of Chineseness is beset with other more serious problems than just its simplistic, unidirectional historical pattern. We are told that modernity must be rejected because it inscribes the will of Western hegemony. We are invited to see the post-ist critique of orientalist and other forms of privileged knowledge as an emancipatory act, to commend its concern with relations of domination and its efforts to unlock and release national history, culture, and identity, which have been frozen by the Western notion of progress. This not only implies that every culture can and should represent itself on the basis of its uniqueness but also suggests that such self-representation eventuates in forms of knowledge that are emancipatory, transcending relations of domination. The problem is that these assumptions are not consonant with the post-ist attempt to install China as the center of the so-called rim of Chinese culture and to replace the authority of modernity with that of Chineseness in this China-centered zone of influence. As Shao Jian, a staunch critic of cultural nativism, points out, the post-ist blueprint for Chineseness reflects a dangerous dream of a new cultural hegemony, which is disguised as a struggle for cultural independence and a counter to the old Western hegemony (1994, 16).

Shao Jian makes a useful distinction between two major groups of intellectuals in China who are particularly concerned with the national culture: cultural traditionalists and cultural nativists. The feelings of belonging to a native culture in China, Shao Jian claims, need to be differentiated according to the intellectuals' corresponding attitudes toward modernity or modernization. Cultural traditionalists are primarily concerned with modernization or, more exactly, with the kind of modernization that will not jeopardize the Chinese tradition. Cultural nativists, on the other hand, are concerned with problems of modernity while ignoring problems of modernization: "Cultural traditionalists want to move toward the modern without leaving behind the traditional, whereas cultural nativists want to move beyond the modern and into the postmodern, the former fostering a conservative posture, the latter promoting rash advance" (1995, 25). Traditionalists seek to install the *Chinese* historical and cultural coordinates of modernity; but nativists, treating modernity as an essentially *Western* concept of homogenization, remove from the concept all Chinese social and temporal determinacy and rob it of any possible indigenous specificity and pertinence.

Unlike cultural traditionalists, who identify strongly with the Chinese cultural tradition, cultural nativists rally under the banner of nation.

Therefore, Shao Jian (1994) argues, cultural nativism is a particularly pernicious and aggressive form of "national culturalism." In an article entitled "The Fallacy of the Orient" Shao Jian relates this particular form of national culturalism firmly to a "new form of 'orientalism'" in China, which, ironically, is empowered by the postcolonial critique of Western Orientalism. Nowhere can we find this "Chinese orientalism" articulated more blatantly, Shao Jian notes, than in the nativist dream of a China-centered rim of Chinese culture.

Shao Jian's distinction between cultural traditionalism and cultural nativism can help us to accommodate a range of variations that are otherwise obscured by the single concept of cultural nationalism or cultural nativism. It is fair to say that there may be significant psychological and political distinctions to be made among different post-1989 forms of national and cultural identification. These include dedication to tradition or traditional culture (e.g., New Chinese Studies), riding the crest of official rhetoric of patriotism and national pride (e.g., xenophobic cultural nativism), dissatisfaction with current imported forms of culture (e.g., resistance to commercialized mass culture), or sensing "at homeness" or return from another country (e.g., the nationalistic feelings of Western-educated Chinese students). Shao Jian's analysis helps to tidy up these experiences and needs in regard to cultural nationalism or national culturalism. To this extent his emphasis on modernity or modernization as a clarifying element in analyzing these issues is particularly valuable.

Shao Jian's criticism of the theory of Chineseness strikes at, although sometimes only partially hits, what I consider both the main problem with post-ist theory and the source of its appealing strength—namely, its use of postcolonial and third-world theory in advocating cultural independence and its preaching at the same time about culture and civilization clashes. The key to the matter seems to lie in the relations between two meanings of Chineseness—Chineseness as a distinctive, fixed form or quality of cultural experience, the historical value of which is automatically guaranteed, and Chineseness as an incomplete project whose historical content is to be continuously constructed and worked out. Post-ist cultural theory does touch on some general features of postcolonial or third-world conditions found in China. Yet, because it remains only on the level of doctrinaire abstraction and antagonistic binary, what it tells us about its capacity for solving China's problems is basically unconvincing.

The New Epochalism of Nativist Post-ist Theory

Postmodernism and postcolonialism push their way forward in China, as elsewhere in the world, "because they are large categories: they make claims to fix the present moment in the most general, historicizing terms possible. They offer the promise of self-representation. That is the basis of their seductiveness" (During 1985, 366). Rey Chow suggests that the two leading themes of postcolonial politics do not apply to China very well (1992, 159). The first is "the ownership of particular geographical areas, an ownership whose ramifications go beyond geography to include political representation as well as sovereignty over ethnic and cultural history." And the second is "reclaim[ing] native cultural traditions that were systematically distorted by the colonial powers in the process of exploitation." China does not perfectly fit into these themes for a variety of reasons. First, except for marginal areas such as Hong Kong, China was not territorially occupied by the European colonial powers. Second, even when China faced foreign incursions, it retained primary use of its own language, which continued to be the language used for writing and historiography; China thus preserved its cultural tradition in forms that are not easily supplanted by the West. Third, China, under the Communist regime, has shaped its international identity primarily in relation to socialist countries. Its acceptance of third-world status remains lukewarm, ambivalent, and opportunistic (Kim 1989, 1991, 1992). Last but not least, the anti-imperialist and anticolonialist arguments of Marxism that postcolonial criticism mobilizes so forcefully have long been part of the dominant ideology in China. Theoretically at least, China has already been thoroughly decolonized, thus preempting the problems of postcolonialism.

In China post-ist theorists use postcolonialism in a particular, domestic sense, which makes its intersection with its usage elsewhere in the world obscure. The key to understanding how the notion is used lies less in its special "Chinese" definition than in the particular Chinese historical or temporal framework to which it is subjected. The Chinese postcolonialism has a completely *Chinese* temporal framework, the so-called post–New Era. Post-ist critics describe the post–New Era as a new epoch of national consciousness marked by China's awareness of its own third-world mode of thinking.

The notion post–New Era is advanced by those who are in one way or another associated with the rise of post-ist theory in China. They use this notion to refer to the years after 1989 as a chronologically new epoch and as a stage of linear progress. Even when they assume the postures and categories of historical thinking, their assumptions are purely technical and stylistic. Post-ist theorists use the notion post–New Era to rewrite the real-world changes before and after 1989 as textual changes rather than changes affected by political atmosphere, social structure, and governmental measures. They reduce the historical rupture in 1989 to changes in literary techniques, writing techniques, and aesthetic sensitivities.[25] Following the logic of the official naming of the post–Cultural Revolution era as the New Era, the naming of the post–New Era emphasizes China's readiness, in the 1990s, to move into another, historically newer and better epoch. Those who coined the name *post–New Era* tell us that the era is characterized by immense intellectual buoyancy, unprecedented cultural diversity and creative possibilities, and a new national consciousness. They call these new developments postmodern phenomena, reading into them indications that China has finally broken the spell of modernity and entered an age of "post-" emancipation, free from being subjected to Western historicity (Zhang Yiwu 1992, 1994a; Wang Ning 1992, 1994, 1995; Zhang Yiwu, Wang Ning, and Liu Kang 1994).

In the rosy picture of the temporal advance from New Era to post–New Era we find a self-congratulatory process of national maturing that purposefully leaves out any possible historical reverse and, in particular, omits what happened to China in June 1989. It not only keeps silent about party-state repression after 1989 but also actually helps to erase the originary relation inscribed in the event of June 4, 1989, precluding the necessity for alternative historical interpretations of that event in the face of the official one.[26] The New Era / post–New Era periodization is characterized by a strategy of avoidance that replaces interrogation with explanation and treats the symptomatic as the real and by a political nominalism that uses radical rhetoric of cultural transformation to depoliticize intellectual critique. The smug rhetoric of historical progress after 1989 serves as the best defense for the political tyranny exemplified by the Tiananmen massacre and the consequent tightening of ideological and political control. In the post-1989 circumstances post-ist theory's overemphasis on Chinese particularism, its anti-enlightenment stance, its moral parochialism, and its lauding of the post–New Era run a particularly high risk of working against the basic interests of the people post-ist theorists claim to represent.

My charge here goes beyond criticizing post-1989 post-ist theory for its hypocritical complicity in maintaining the status quo. I am concerned with its implied model of postmodern politics in China. Post-ist theory now masquerades as political sensitivity and radical action, so much so that politics has in effect been absorbed by its theory and reduced to abstract mockeries of real social conflict. Post-ist theory defines oppression and domination in terms of the binary of China versus the West, removing these issues from the structures of everyday life and disengaging them from the concrete domestic context. It subsumes oppositional practice into nativist affiliation and disguises its political withdrawal and escapism as engagement. It consciously takes on the function of identity politics *as if,* for the radicalization of thought and social change, what really matters is not the position it takes in relation to the party-state and its domination over society but what it says about its own cultural affiliation and its own cultural opponents. The political features of post-ist theory should be included less in the context of a critique of modernity than as a consequence of the peculiar form of Chinese modernity, which has tended precisely in the direction of a political impasse.

The New Epochalist discourse about the post–New Era defines not only what intellectuals can do politically in a rhetoric-as-politics age but also what post-ist theorists take to be the general outlines of the history of our time and, in particular, the overall direction and significance of that history. The overall direction of history delineated by post-ist theorists is that of postmodernism, which allows them to take lightheartedly China's setbacks in social and political modernization, especially in the areas of democracy and civil rights, and to view those setbacks as a triumphant move toward China's postmodernity. Post-ist theory stresses points of intersection between China's post–New Era and the postmodern age outside China in order to prove the universal demise of modernity. In its special usage *modernity* cobbles together two remote meanings—a Western meaning and a general, third-world meaning—in order to discredit a third meaning, one inherent in the Chinese context. In this usage *modernity* denotes a cluster of issues classified under the rubric of Western postmodern theory: the loss of faith in history, the crisis of truth, representation, and reason, and the disappearance of subject. It also stands for the Western hegemonic discourses on modernity, enlightenment, and democracy. But it omits what modernity means to China, whose process of modernization has been cut short by events such as the Cultural Revolution and the Tiananmen massacre. Post-ist theory uses the two remote meanings of modernity to override the pressing need for modernization, in particular social and political modernization, in China. Post-ist theory's appeal to postmodernism to understand China's problems of modernization and the detours after June 4, 1989, tends to blur the diverse social and political interests of different Chinese people, obscuring rather than illuminating the condition of modernity in contemporary China.[27]

The connection of Chinese post-ist theory with postmodernism reveals the latter to be a master discourse and the former to be the lagging partner. Post-ist theory rejects modernity, parroting the postmodernist debunking of reason, history, and subject and, by a sleight of hand, posing this as opposition to *Western* reason, *Western* history, and *Western* subjectivity. Yet no theoretical framework has been established to explain exactly how post-ist theory as an oppositional critique is to be integrated with the apocalyptic vision of the death of reason, history, and the subject. The paradox in which post-ist theory finds itself seems to be that, while it regards Western discourse as fiction, it nevertheless proceeds as if its own position, based on the exclusive model of Chineseness, reveals the truth. How, then, is post-ist theory to legitimate and sustain its own critique of Western discourse once it recognizes the existence of a more general legitimacy crisis, which questions the grounding and authority of all forms of knowledge? How is post-ist theory to account for the postmodern skepticism of epistemological and ethical norms, which echoes in and potentially undermines its critique of the Western model of knowledge and subjectivity? How can post-ist theory challenge Western subjectivity and its claims of neutrality and at the same time manifest faith in its own autonomous and authentic subjectivity? Is the post-ist subjectivity really free from its domestic material determination and completely in control of its "true" political meaning? How are post-ist theory's own discursive attachments and ideological ambivalences to be understood? What are its continuing claims of Chineseness and representation of the nation?

Post-ist theory in China has rarely paused to consider these questions and has chosen to ignore them in its enthusiasm to advance an anti-modernist and anti-Western stance. Its oversimplified view of China versus the West has led many post-ist theorists to the predictable rhetoric of unmasking hidden Orientalism as the critics' only job. The characteristic gesture of "unmasking" has turned into a smug ritual, since its attention remains fixed on the mask instead of the emancipatory purpose of the

action of unmasking. These theorists define the main effort of oppositional criticism as being directed at the asymmetrical first-world/third-
world relationship rather than at the very essence of domination, violence, and tyranny that is revealed beneath such a relationship. They not
only retreat from the actual conditions of social life and the existing
political horrors of their time but also take a hostile attitude toward
other critics or writers who tackle these issues.[28] The post-ist theory of
cultural critique has channeled its energy to seek a particular form of
knowledge (Chineseness) that can claim certainty and a particular form
of agency (the universal and amorphous native Chinese) that is determined to deny its own domestic ideological construction. This wishful
designing of cultural critique privileges a notion of authentic national
subjectivity as the domain in which the true meaning of all cultural activities are supposed to be constructed. Such national subjectivity remains
abstract because it is idealistically homogeneous. It is neither embedded
in any concrete civic order nor defined by actual conflicting social, political, and economic interests. Far from being an intervening force on the
domestic scene, this national subjectivity is incompatible with any collective movement for democratic social change and is easily co-opted by
authoritarian power. It obscures the imminent reality of oppression, cru-
elty, corruption, and gross inequality in China, leaving intellectual critics
without the vision or the will to act upon their world as citizen-agents,
unable to function as a vital force in China's incomplete project of modernization and democratization.

Toward a Democratic Postcolonial Criticism

A significant democratic theme that has evolved within postcolonial criticism has been its recognition of the emancipatory value of national independence and self-realization. It is in this sense that national liberation
movements in the peripheries of the world system are the main features
of the most essential democratic change in our modern world, even
though democracy does not often fare well later in many postindepen-
dent countries. Together, these struggles, actual or potential, inaugurate
the "postimperial" or "postcolonial" age. At its best postcolonial criticism reinforces its democratic themes by linking its struggle against colonialism and imperialism with struggles against other forms of domination and injustice. It demands to break out of a simplistic nationalist
outlook, realizing that it takes a very particular perspective—that of

postcolonial critique—to render visible the contradictory status of the colonizer and the colonized, the dominating and the dominated. From this perspective *the colonized* becomes an idiom to express the experience of the third world. *The colonized* does not simply refer to a historical group of Western colonies that has won national sovereignty and has therefore disbanded but to a category that includes literally all the inhabitants of non-Western countries. The history of colonialism, as Edward Said puts it, has left the colonized with a lingering and traumatized identity: "'the colonized' has since expanded considerably to include women, subjugated and oppressed classes, national minorities, and even marginalized or incorporated academic subspecialities" (1989, 207). The experience of the colonized is thus paradigmatic of the dreadful secondariness of people who are subalterns of all kinds.

The postcolonial, as Helen Tiffin suggests, can be conceived of as a set of "discursive practices"—theories and writings—"prominent among which is *resistance* to colonialism, colonialist ideologies, and their contemporary forms and subjectificatory legacies" (Adam and Tiffin 1990, vii). Such a conception of the postcolonial, however, leaves unanswered some important questions: what is the difference between the postcolonial critique and the anticolonial critique or the anti-neocolonial critique, since the latter two share the commitment of resistance to colonialism? While *anticolonial* and *anti-neocolonial* imply both resistance and the kind of oppression against which it functions, why do we still need the concept of the postcolonial? Is the postcolonial, after all, as Ella Shohat suspects, a concept of political emptiness (1992, 107)? Is it true that the term, because it seems to transcend such dichotomies as colonizer/colonized and neocolonizer/neocolonized, "posits no clear domination, and calls for no clear opposition"?

What I want to suggest here is that the most important difference between traditional anticolonialist theory and postcolonial theory lies in the fact that, while the former, due to the Manichaean terms in which it is framed, takes its function of resistance for granted, the latter has to develop a theory of domination and liberation in order to understand and legitimate its self-constructed function of resistance. In other words, it is not in the binary opposition of colonizer/colonized but, rather, in the theoretical domain of liberation that postcolonial critics must find their telos of resistance and intellectual opposition. It is not something intrinsic to the object of its opposition (the West, the nation-state, universalism, etc.) that marks out a discursive practice as the postcolonial but the oppositional way in which that practice is deployed. The significance of postcolonial critique can only be fully comprehended by specifying its oppositional and liberating character in specific sociohistorical formation, namely, where its challenge to the structures of domination is most sharply articulated. Therefore, the postcolonial perspective cannot be solely found in the reworking of one single paradigm. It consists, rather, in the implementation of a variety of active revisions that register the historical, social, and ideological changes and specificities in each third-world country. Deprived of its natural object of resistance and constantly measuring its political urgency, and indeed relevance, against the priority among a plurality of changing forms of dominance, postcolonial critique must include a theory of domination.

Johan Galtung's works on peace research illustrate how such a theory of domination can be conceived in terms of the common structures and the interpenetration of intranational and international forms of violence. Galtung defines violence as "*anything* that interferes with human beings so that their 'actual somatic and mental realizations are below their potential realizations'" (1980, 409). Galtung's definition of violence was first concerned with both direct violence and structural violence; he expanded it to include "cultural violence" in his later studies.

Direct violence, in the form of killing, maiming, torture, and detention, and its use in establishing and protecting various patterns of dominance are often obvious. It takes more critical insights to reveal the expression and nature of structural violence. Galtung identifies four basic components in structural violence: exploitation, penetration, fragmentation, and marginalization, all defined around the central notion of dominance. Exploitation is "an asymmetric pattern of division of labor" that favors one party over the other; penetration is a pattern whereby "the dominant party controls the center of the dominated, by controlling an elite among the dominated or by controlling the mind of the dominated person"; fragmentation is a pattern whereby "the dominated are split and kept apart from each other whereas the dominant interact with each other dealing with the dominated one at the time"; marginalization is a pattern whereby the dominant keep the dominated outside or on the periphery (Galtung 1980, 406). Either direct or structural violence, in order to acquire social legitimacy, depends on the support of cultural violence, which Galtung defines as "those aspects of culture, the symbolic sphere of our existence—exemplified by religion and ideology, language and art, empirical science and formal science (logic, mathematics)—that can be used to justify or legitimize direct or structural violence" (1990, 291–92).

What characterizes the modern forms of intranational and international domination is the interpenetration of different components of structural violence both within and across national borders. Many forms of intranational and international domination can be seen in these terms, from imperialism, colonialism, totalitarianism, to the political, social, cultural, communicative patterns known as hegemony, supremacy, and repression. Galtung suggests that imperialism can be conceived in terms of the structural violence it inflicts on its target, "as a configuration where all these structural components, or at least some of them, are found across the board—in economic, political, military, social, cultural and communicative relations. In capitalist imperialism the economic factor is basic, in social imperialism the social factor." The same perspective should allow us to recognize in the four components of structural domination some fundamental features of the undemocratic or totalitarian state. These features, Galtung tells us, include "a strict division of political labor between rulers and ruled, making out of politics an in-group game, often violent, always filled with intrigues and quarrels because it is hidden from the marginalized *and* fragmented masses, combined with the type of penetration of minds obtainable under conditions of control of all means of expression and impression" (Galtung 1980, 406, 409).

The theory of dominance and violence becomes a meeting point between anticolonial and antitotalitarian cultural critique and between them and other problem-oriented critical activities, each using its own concrete definitions of the concept of domination and violence as conceptual bridges to new problems areas. Due to this departure, the oppositions posed by critical intellectuals to the intranational and international problems they discern in today's world have one thing in common: all these oppositions have to do with the moral idea of human self-realization, and they hold to a principle about human potential that commands our moral admiration. Postcolonial criticism, owing to its vantage, which washes away the border lines between intranational and international politics, is no longer only on the receiving end of other critical theories, such as Marxism, poststructuralism, and postmodernism. It itself becomes a producer of a paradigm for the critical tasks of third-world intellectuals and for linking them with other oppositional critics. To realize the paradigmatic value of the postcolonial perspective is to recognize that it plays an important role in the theory debate and connection between those who analyze contemporary culture and society from either a first-world or a third-world position. It is thus understandable why for the third-world position the postcolonial is such an irresistible category in spite of all its ambiguity, problems, and internal tensions.

Unlike traditional anticolonial or nationalist discourses, postcolonial cultural critique, as a new paradigm of resistance to domination, is more sensitive to what Lester Edwin J. Ruiz, in his discussion of the Filipino quest for democracy, has called "the interstructuration of domination," that is, "the irreducibility of history to forces, factors, elements, and variables, that can be and need to be isolated in order to be understood" (1991, 174). It is no longer interesting, nor is it possible, to understand domination in the third world as simply the inevitable consequences of the colonial past. In Joel S. Migdal's words, "Western imperial powers were not only the cubête noires in the transition from colony to statehood, but they were also models to be emulated" (1988, 4). What calls for our attention is that certain Chinese experiences of domination—like patriarchy, suffocation of free thought and speech, abuses of authority, and witch-hunts for "class enemies"—which have their own origins and trajectories apart from colonialism, have intersected with the modern nation-state of a particular sort (the totalitarian or authoritarian party-state) and made interstructuration of domination a particularly pressing issue. Recognizing the interstructuration of domination in postcolonial and postrevolutionary China, like in other third-world countries, is not the same as denying general frameworks of domination but, rather, constitutes a strategic rejection of the logic of "grand narratives" and the tendency toward homogeneity and univocality in these frameworks of analysis. The logic of grand narratives, such as "China's history of anti-imperialism," "the Communist revolutionary cause," or "socialism with a Chinese character," has long rendered it difficult for intellectuals to understand new forms of domination, antagonism, and resistance in China or to come to terms with the plurality of actors that inhabit China's postcolonial space.

A theory of contemporary forms of domination and cultural violence can contribute to the reconstruction of third-world critical theory in China. Such a third-world critical theory, located within the context of domination and within the present conjuncture of world history, is not only a part of anticolonial or anti-imperialist struggle but also a part of a wider terrain of transformation that may well be termed *democratization*. It presumes and calls for the participation of the common people, and it stresses the democratic value of China's anticolonial, anti-imperialist, and nationalist struggles in the past. Decolonization and self-determination, and indeed nationalism itself in the anticolonial struggles of the third world, as Yoshikazu Sakamoto says, "can be considered to be the pursuit of international democracy as far as it is oriented to the equality of nations." Yet, as Sakamoto also points out, true democracy must not limit itself to a mere stage of national development; it "cannot exist in any context except that of the world-system." To transform the inequitable structure of first-world and third-world countries, democracy has to be globalized "and to globalize democracy, this inequitable structure has to be transformed" (1991, 126, 127). A theory of international and intranational domination and violence is a first step toward involving China's third-world cultural critique in the emerging framework of globalizing democracy.

Chapter 4

The Anxiety of Cross-Cultural Theorizing

With the advance of postmodern and postcolonial theories in China, nativist and post-ist theorists are able to form a broad united front in divergent academic areas. They are able to rely on post-ist perspectives and not merely on pragmatic considerations. These perspectives, which combine the binarism of indigenous culture versus foreign culture, the conflict between first- and third-world interests, and pride in Chinese identity, have constituted an amalgam of theoretical discourses in which the West serves as a central reference point of cross-cultural thinking. The relevance of the West as an essential reference point differs in various fields of academic studies. For some, such as studies of foreign literature and theory, the encounter with the West as their natural object of study is so much a given that the issue of Chineseness has seldom been seriously raised. For others, such as studies of Chinese classical literature, poetry, and philosophy, the lack of obvious foreign reference makes the issue of Western influence secondary at most. Because the united front covers a broad spectrum of academic areas and is informed by diverse intellectual interests, its insistence on indigenous authenticity and an anti-Western stance has by and large remained at the level of a metatheoretical faith.[1] And yet there is one unifying and coherent concern that stands out saliently from the divergent issues, and that is how to craft a new cultural politics capable of revealing the asymmetrical China-West relationship in cross-cultural exchanges.

This cultural politics is bifocal in nature, supposedly responding to the two basic roles involved in the cultural exchange at the global level: the sender and the receiver. The bitterness of the new cultural politics rests on a twofold discovery: first, the discovery of China as a servile and prostrate "producer" (or "sender" or "source") of exotic scenery for the West; and, second, the discovery of China as a passive and submissive "consumer" (or "receiver" or "target") of hegemonic Western culture. In each case China is seen as a helpless victim and the West an all-powerful victimizer. The combination of the two discoveries accounts for the intensity with which nativist theorists react to "Orientalism" and "Western hegemony." At the very moment that they become aware of China's cultural conflict with the West, they become aware of each other and come to see themselves as belonging to the same united front.

The discovery that others are fighting the same fight against Western hegemony and Orientalism, the discovery that one has after all taken part in a general awakening, that one's struggle is part of the struggles of sensitive people everywhere, endows the moment with a sense of endless possibilities. It suggests hidden treasures of aspiration, yet unfathomed, lying beneath the surface of an outwardly peaceful but actually contentious global cultural order. The awareness of their own emancipation makes these nativist intellectuals see what may be accomplished by the liberation of the repressed energies of all their fellow intellectuals. Yet, where expectations run so high, disappointment is sure to follow, and anxiety rather than exhilaration becomes the dominant mode. It is through this anxiety that I will approach the nativist cultural politics.

I will examine two different cases of such anxiety; each illustrates one of the double aspects about China's alleged victim status: as a servile producer of distorted third-world culture and a submissive consumer of superior Western culture. I select the first case from some critics' attack on *Farewell My Concubine,* a well-known Fifth Generation film, and the second from a professor's proposal to develop an indigenous Chinese theory of foreign literature. Critics of *Farewell My Concubine* go after this film as a typical producer of Chinese ugliness for the Western voyeur, or gazer. The advocate of an indigenous Chinese approach in the field of foreign literature studies deplores the discipline's role as a passive consumer of Western discourse or a cultural comprador. The question I want to raise about both cases of nativist anxiety is whether cross-cultural thinking in terms of "native informant" or "cultural comprador" has really tapped the problems that have to be faced or whether it distorts the argument over significant cultural and political issues.

It is my belief that the vague rhetoric of nativist fervor obscures many important issues, such as human agency, construction of cultural and national identities, cultural politics, and intellectual opposition and its moral imperative. These issues should be separated and analyzed in different terms. My discussion of the nativist anxiety and its twofold fear of China's victim status will thus expand to a wide set of concerns in an effort to examine the premises and characteristics of nativist views regarding particularism and universalism, literary and conceptual translation, and cultural and social reconstruction.

The Fear of Being Watched

The Nativist-Postcolonial Attack on Chen Kaige's *Farewell My Concubine*

It comes as no surprise that Chen Kaige's film *Farewell My Concubine* arouses suspicion and animosity among certain Chinese critics. Winning awards for Best Foreign Film and the Palme d'Or at Cannes in 1993, the film suddenly acquired stardom at the crossroads of East-West cultural exchange. A particular group of avant-garde and nativist theorists balk every time such a thing happens. To them, although the apparently West-ern-bestowed fame and success do not prove a film's merit, they certainly provide the essential, if not the sole, reason to scrutinize the film as a sus-picious piece of cultural sellout. They see the very production of *Farewell My Concubine,* which involves the Taiwanese capital, Hong Kong writ-ers, a Chinese director, and Western critical approval, as a hybrid cul-tural commodity for Western consumption.[2] Condemning the film for its "purposeful invitation of Western cultural baptism" and pandering to a Western audience, critics such as Dai Jinhua, Zhang Yiwu, and Chen Xiaoming assert that the film functions as a cultural courtesan who offers herself promiscuously to any admirer and sells herself as a commodity that takes its place wherever its value as fetish will be confirmed (Chen Xiaoming et al. 1994, 127).

Adopting a culturally patriotic stance, these critics make a point of differentiating their critical position from, on the one hand, the Western liberal ideal of cultural pluralism and, on the other, from the postcolonial criticism situated in the West. They recognize the cultural relationship between the first and third worlds as one of asymmetrical power. "The current cultural mutual penetration," Chen Xiaoming emphasizes, "is not one of equal relationship, those developed countries with economical advantage also often occupy a culturally dominant position in this rela-tionship" (1994, 126). They do not see those first world–trained "third-world" critics, such as Edward Said and Gayatri Spivak, as their equal partners. They see "Western Left and progressive" theories as "embody-

ing the Western cultural hegemony" and as part of the oppressive forces
that make the indigenous Chinese critics unable to articulate their own
native cultural agenda (127). In their effort to define an independent position for themselves, these nativist critics find themselves caught in a
dilemma, which Dai Jinhua summarizes: they are yet incapable of invent-
ing a new critical discourse that they can claim as their own. Even if they
could, it probably would not do them much good because of its third-
world status (127). Their need to define a nativist position is thus more
real than the nativist position they can define. Such a stance is laden with
ambivalence and confusion, entrapped as it is by the desire to recover an
"authentic" native voice.

It is this insistence on the "native" in spite of the irreversible loss of
precolonial innocence that underlies the nativist critics' readings of the
Fifth Generation films by Chen Kaige and Zhang Yimou. These critics'
most serious allegation against Zhang Yimou and Chen Kaige is that they
willfully submit to Western cultural hegemony. Films by Zhang and
Chen, according to those nativist critics, consist of "a postcolonial cultural phenomenon" that is not helplessly marked by imposed Western
penetration but, rather, by its purposeful invitation of "label" and "cultural baptism" by the West. They accuse these Chinese filmmakers of
"actively and consciously seeking identification with the Western cultural
hegemony" and coaxing Western recognition (Chen Xiaoming et al.
1994, 138). Chen Xiaoming and Zhang Yiwu assert that, like *Red
Sorghum, Ju Dou,* and *Raise the Red Lantern* by Zhang Yimou, Chen
Kaige's *Farewell My Concubine* is but a humble "article of tribute" (*wenhua gongpin*) and a showy and stereotypical "piece of curiosity" (*minsu
qiwen*) that the postcolonial Chinese artists put before the West (138,
139). Chen Xiaoming harshly criticizes Zhang Yimou, the leader of Fifth
Generation filmmakers, for obsequiously selling Chinese stories to the
West by manipulating adultery, promiscuity, and concubinage as commercial gimmicks: "Zhang knows too well how to mix commercial and
national factors in a dexterous way." Chen also taunts the Western audience for accepting Zhang's works as Chinese "national films" and examples of "oriental art" (139). Dai Jinhua challenges Zhang's creation of
Chinese myth and assaults "the new national myth" created by Zhang in
Red Sorghum as not only false and shoddy but also absolutely "foreign
to the Chinese reality and national culture in the East" (141). Dai Jinhua,
Chen Xiaoming, and Zhang Yiwu all agree that, following Zhang
Yimou's misguided lead, Chen Kaige, in spite of his "cultural commit-

ment" in his previous films (*The King of Children* and *Life on the String*, in particular), has come step by step to *Farewell My Concubine*, in which he consciously shapes his film according to the "Bible of West/East polarity" and "effectively codes his story according to orientalist strategies" (142–43). Keeping the difference and incompatibility between Chinese and Western receptions as a central analytic concept, Zhang Yiwu even pronounces that Fifth Generation filmmaking is "an aberration from the Chinese tradition" and "a curious phenomenon outside the history of Chinese film" (139).

The dismissal of *Farewell My Concubine* as a work stigmatized by a lack of authenticity and infidelity to its native obligation raises a number of problematic theoretical questions. What is "national film" in the Chinese context? How shall Chinese critics conceptualize the indigenous history of Chinese film? Has there ever been such a thing as an uncontaminated national film in China? Can Western cultural hegemony be resisted only by retreating into a vision of precolonial innocence? How might the film text be read differently within different national or historical locations? What conceptual framework do we need to develop in order to understand that different audiences read films differently? These and many other such issues have remained marginal, if not completely absent, from nativist film criticism.

Chinese film never possessed the "uncontaminated" native quality the nativist critics want to glorify, simply because in China film is by nature "third world" in its status. It displays the tensions between the forces of the indigenous and the nonindigenous to a particularly intense degree. Unlike printed literature, film does not rely solely on the Chinese language, which becomes the essential force sustaining the native quality of Chinese literature.[3] The "language" of film is to a great degree a transnationalized language, invented in the West. All of those who have to use this language are also people who have to some extent lost their roots. "A filmmaker, a radio or television producer," Roy Armes notes, "will be using a Western technology" (1987, 24). A Chinese writer can still use his own language, but a Chinese filmmaker is like a writer who has to employ the former colonizer's language, and, like a writer without his native language, "he will almost certainly be using formal structures derived from a foreign source," for the basic forms of filmic narrative are imported.

The evocation of "the history of Chinese film" by nativist criticism in ostracizing *Farewell My Concubine* shows the centrality of history in the imagining of "the native" and the defining of "the national."[4] The conceptualization of the genuine native depends on the idea of an "authentic" tradition and history. Evoking history as an anchor of certainty for evaluating the representation of film, nativist criticism fails to see that history itself is a representation that is produced in the encounter between interpretation of the past and the present field of social action, which is symbolically constituted. What the official history in China tends to conceal is precisely the representational nature of history, occluding the process of interpretation and the conditions of its production, and re-representing history as an objective and transparent "given." Before the emergence of the Fifth Generation films, almost all Chinese films, as government-sponsored projects of mass education and propaganda, had to function as footnotes to official historiography about China's ascent to socialism and to Party power, which is officially equated with the triumphal process of nation building. Whatever national authenticity is revealed in a history construed from the tradition of such films is already conditioned by the official definition of the nation and the correct meaning of loyalty to it (the same as loyalty to the Party). Since such films are themselves ideological products of partisan interest and integral to the project of the party-state, can we still regard them as setting an objective national tradition? Can we still treat their "tradition" as if it were a wholly unified and independently achieved domain, capable of sustaining its purity and authenticity in pristine isolation from official representations of the past, reality, and the truth?[5]

Against this background it is not difficult to see that *Farewell My Concubine* challenges the official historiography by suggesting an alternative narrative of history, a self-described "logic of disintegration." The film's narrative of history contradicts the orthodox Marxist philosophy of history, which is basically progressivist. According to the philosophy of history implied in the narrative of the film, "progress" becomes tantamount to progress in domination: mastery of the self, extended to mastery over other persons (embodied in the power of the opera master, the eunuch, and Master Yuan), and then, ultimately, to the absolutist project of the remodeling of human nature undertaken by the Cultural Revolution. The concept of Chinese history as a triumphal progression of its cultural achievements, enlisted by official nationalism after the Cultural Revolution, is at once suggested and subverted by *Farewell My Concubine*. Critics who simplistically interpret this counter-representation of Chinese history as an attempt to "please the West" or as a distortion of the native do not seem to be at all embarrassed by the cynicism of the official version of history.

Nativist film critics in China are concerned about the capital investment from abroad in the making of *Farewell My Concubine*. They believe that this kind of economic and commercial influence and leverage lures Chinese filmmakers and Chinese writers to tell stories the Western audience wants to hear (Chen Xiaoming et al. 1994, 143). What they fail to see are the positive effects that may result from such changes in the mechanism of the Chinese film industry. In the past monopolization of the Chinese economy by the state allowed the state to have absolute control over filmmaking. Indeed, the state still controls radio and television, using these major tools to restrict public opinion and communication. The economic leverage independent filmmaking now has in loosening the ossified structure of the state-sponsored propaganda apparatus should be welcome as an important part of the burgeoning civil society and public sphere in China. Encouraged by the new economic mechanism of production and dissemination, new films in China are gradually being freed from the propagandistic functions they used to serve. As they gain autonomy, new films increasingly tend to defy the orthodoxly unifying strategies of spectator positioning and to disregard official censorious control over their distribution and exhibition.

The transformation of filmmaking into a free enterprise has provided new films with unprecedented opportunities to create multiple levels of textuality and to appeal to audiences of diverse interests (in China and overseas). It is true that the rise of new films corresponds to the emergence of new transnational corporate networks that circulate films and videos along with music, food, fashion, information, and communication technologies. It would be misleading to assume, however, that globalization always means homogenization. Rather, while systems of distribution and exchange are interconnected and organized on a global scale, this process is characterized by a burgeoning diversification of products: "new forms and genres of diasporic and indigenous mass culture have emerged, at once syncretistic and original" (Hansen 1993, 199).[6] *Farewell My Concubine* is not merely a cultural commodity meant for a globalized market. Rather, it conveys a critical edge that is galling to the dominant ideology in China, as testified by the very hostile official attitude toward it. While the government turns a cold shoulder to new films such as *Farewell My Concubine,* it allows the showing of highly commercialized imported films to a mass audience. These products are generally the

cheapest and shoddiest available, reaching the very outer limit of whatever the state censors will allow with regard to the depiction of sex. Such
films fare far more comfortably with official censorship because they do
not touch on sensitive social issues or historical events in the way that
many Fifth Generation films do. Even though they are not part of the old
stable diet of "films of socialist values," the Chinese government tolerates
them, since they are "innocent," "pure" commercial products posing no
threatening alternative cultural values or national representation.

Film and the Public Sphere in China

In thinking of the film's relationship to the state apparatus, we need to go
beyond the state/market conceptual framework, which tends to stultify
any discussion of film's relation to its viewers. A third term, "the public
sphere," is called for. The public sphere is a space for informed and rational cultural activity distinct (though not completely separate) from the
economic realm and the state. In film criticism, especially in the Chinese
context, we can use the term *public* in a rather broad sense, denoting "a
discursive matrix or process through which social experience is articulated, interpreted, negotiated and contested in an intersubjective, potentially collective and oppositional form" (Hansen 1993, 201). Despite its
original conceptual root in the Habermasian "public sphere," this concept of the public involves two major modifications proposed by Oskar
Negt and Alexander Kluge (1993; Kluge 1981–82, 1988). First, this concept
of the public de-emphasizes its connection with *institutional,* or establishment, activities (the nonstate force, the press, independent organization, etc.) and stresses, instead, its normative function as a "general social
horizon of experience." The public not only denotes the formal conditions of communication (free speech, equal participation, etc.) but, more
important, includes "the context of living" (*Lebenszusammenhang*),
which "has to do with everyone and which only realizes itself in the
heads of human beings, a dimension of their consciousness." Second, the
public as a sphere of autonomous social action, a realm that resists both
assimilation to the sphere of economic interests and the fully ritualized
logics of existing institutionalized politics (the party system, the state),
does not exist above or separate from the marketplace (Hansen 1993,
203–4).
    Given the absence of institutional public spheres and the weakness
of civil society in China, as well as the role of economic reform in social

transformation, a modified concept of the public becomes all the more important for understanding Chinese film and mass media. For Habermas (1989b) the "structural transformation of the public sphere" is a story about the changing capacity of modern citizens to govern themselves on the basis of political institutions legitimized from below, by informed discussion and reasoned argument. It is a story with a hopeful beginning but, so far in the twentieth century, an unhappy ending. Although written about the history of the modern West, Habermas's work on the public sphere, as Richard Madsen (1990, 186) suggests in a different context, can be relevant to the study of contemporary China, "if it is used at the proper level of abstraction." I would suggest that this "proper level of abstraction" should be measured by the urgently felt need of the Chinese public to explore the prospect of a politics based on critical and reflective discourse. It is at this level that we can begin clarifying the possibility and requisites of rational discourse in a more democratic Chinese society as well as assessing the constructing features of its public sphere.

Three such features need to be mentioned. First, the stress is shifted from Habermas's emphasis on the set of *institutions* that facilitate widespread public discussion to the *norms* the public discussion should be about, the norms that must govern public affairs as well as public discussion itself. It is from the norms and not just the institutions that we may appreciate the democratic nature of public discussion that brings together people of widely varying social backgrounds. Second, public discussion in China has to struggle for a noncoercive environment rather than take it for granted. Only when public discussion is free from state domination can it be based not on social status or political authority but on appeals to reason. The drive for anticoercion is important because in China public discussion is still restrained, if not completely controlled, by state power. Third, owing to the ideological control of the party-state in China, public discussion often takes a roundabout route, combining public issues with entertainment and appearing in artistic forms such as literature, fine arts, or film and in various forms of popular culture. These cultural forms play a larger part in shaping public opinion in China than in the West, and the distinctions between high and mass culture that they represent are not as clear. Media in China at this historical moment cannot be defined by the technology employed or by any presumed effect on popular taste. They do not involve a fixed manner of reception that is predetermined by a built-in ideological content.

Moreover, media in China, instead of being a monolithic system, constitute a contesting ground of different forms of "mediation," ranging from those under direct government control to those that have managed, to different degrees, to circumvent such control. As a significant part of mass media, Chinese film is itself a ground of contestation in terms of each film's relation to government control. Given such complications, our understanding of Chinese film should not be based on the Western model of mass media, as though film's relationship with a particular society were inherent in the media themselves. The different circumstances under which mass media function give rise to crucial differences. Whereas film may be treated as a typical form of mass culture, it also takes on some of the aura of high culture and influences the public accordingly, because of its comparatively autonomous status, especially if a film, such as *Farewell My Concubine*, is intended to be serious art.

To emphasize the aforementioned features of the public sphere in China does not signify surrender of its struggle for autonomy in the face of state control. The focus on the moral and cultural dimensions of social transformation rather than on immediate institutional shake-up may be, in its intent and consequences, more effective in shaping a public space than is a direct encounter with the state. The public sphere is still very weak in China. Yet, because of post-Mao period reforms, especially those in the economic area, there have arisen a variety of social relations within Chinese society that are at least partially autonomous from the state. The significance of these new social relations as the emerging public sphere must not be understood as analogous to the classical bourgeois-liberal model in the West, as a presumably autonomous sphere *above* the marketplace and economic interests. Their contours as public sphere must be traced to the new industrial-commercial publics that no longer pretend to have such a separate, independent status. It is in view of the economically related public spheres in China that I find the concept of "new public spheres of production" proposed by Negt and Kluge particularly useful (1993, 12 ff.), not only in explaining the specific dynamics of the new state-society relationship in China but also in assessing non-state-sponsored filmmaking there.

The new public spheres of production include a variety of contexts, such as spaces of commerce and consumption, artist and producer groups, and, of course, independently financed filmmaking, publication, and mass communication. Most of these elements are still very weak and are exploring strategies to circumvent authoritarian state control. They constitute a small and precarious social space, with hardly any institutional support to expand freedom and to win rights. But their importance cannot be overestimated, even if they "only" provide an opportunity or point out a direction of future evolution. In today's China they represent what Raymond Williams calls the "emerging culture," in contrast to the "residual" and the "dominant" cultures (1977, 121–27). Since this emerging cultural model is now playing a valuable emancipatory role in social transformation, it would be theoretically counterproductive and politically conservative to assert, as nativist critics tend to do, that money from abroad and international prizes, which are indeed commercial motivation, serve only to lure Chinese filmmaking from the right path, whatever that may be. I would suggest instead seeing these factors as signs of the changes that have assailed the state-controlled institution of filmmaking over the past decade. For cultural criticism the struggle for indigenous development of culture is inseparable from the task of creating and maintaining a domestic public space in which the terms of understanding of this culture can be deliberated and advanced. Nativist critics' one-sided emphasis on cultural authenticity and avoidance of overseas commercial connections dehistoricizes the multiple and heterogeneous factors in China's social transformation, removing them from historical conjunctures in which they are mobilized and appropriated. It also devalues the radical cultural critique whose opposition to *all* forms of domination must be enacted on both the international and domestic fronts.

The concept of a public sphere as a normative space for cultural deliberation and for creating and circulating cultural meanings can be mobilized to address a number of key concerns of film and cultural studies in China. In general terms thinking of film in terms of the public allows us to combine textual readings with inquiries into reception mechanisms, rather than opposing these to each other. This is what Miriam Hansen describes as "the dual focus" of the public sphere of the cinema: "the cinema functions both as a public sphere of its own, defined by specific relations of representation and reception, and as part of a larger social horizon, defined by the media, by overlapping local, national, and global, face-to-face and deterritorialized structures of public life" (1993, 206). As an immediate horizon of experience, the film text does not work unidirectionally to construct, interpellate, and reproduce passive viewers or solicit them to identify with and through ideologically marked positions of subjectivity. We need to make a distinction between the social subjectivity of a viewer and the textual subjectivity the film makes possible for him. For a viewer the experience of reading a film text is an encounter and a negotiation between the two. In practice there are very few perfectly dominant or purely oppositional readings, and consequently viewing film is typically a process of negotiation between the text and its variously socially situated readers.[7] By activating this process (without assuming that all film texts have the same potential of being activated), a viewer can produce a negotiated reading. Indeed, the ability of a film and a viewing situation to trigger active reading is a measure of their quality as public sphere.

In a larger horizon of experience defined by overlapping local, national, and global structures of public life, thinking of film in terms of the public means reconstructing a horizon of reception not merely in terms of national or territorial determinants but also in terms of collective memory, intertextual association, and situated experience, which initiate and prompt historically conditioned interpretation, cultural reflection, and social criticism. The empirical division of Western audience versus Chinese audience, which hinges on a hypothetical geopolitically monolithic spectator, misses out on the lifeworld parameters of subjectivity that structure and enable our engagement with the film. Audience members, assumed to be receivers of meaning, are actually active collaborators. They respond to the film not as an isolated event but as a reminder of other filmic or cultural discourses, of their own social experience and private lives. These parameters of subjectivity, in the case of *Farewell My Concubine,* include, for instance, the particular content that set off viewers' memories (the Peking Opera,[8] wars and suffering, the Cultural Revolution, the nameless everyday tyranny and brutality); the intertextual associations that locate the film in relation or contrast to other filmic forms (the official socialist formulas of realism, shoddy entertainment films, etc.); the particular style that makes implicit comment and criticism on linguistic or discursive practices the Chinese viewers are familiar with (the stilted drama-oriented language, the political jargon, empty nationalist rhetoric, etc.); and the particular filmic diegesis that upsets the certainty and complacency incubated by political orthodoxy (the priority of nation building over social criticism, the infallibility of the Party, blaming the "Gang of Four" for the Cultural Revolution, etc.).[9]

These and other factors structure the horizon of experience Chinese viewers carry around with them, stimulating them, and allowing them the opportunity, to reflect upon their collective memory and lifeworld situation. It is from the historical and social coordinates of this reflection that we draw the intragroup cultural status of film and its relevance as social criticism. Social criticism must be understood as an important by-product of the artistic activity that involves cultural elaboration and reflection. This is the work of writers and historians, artists and filmmakers, intellectuals and critics. The possibility of criticism exists with these people not because they constitute a permanently subversive "new class" or because they are the carriers of an "adversary culture." They carry the common culture in such a way that the conditions of their community's collective life can be considered. The concept of the public allows us to envision artists and writers as members of an interpretive community in general. These people—though perhaps the most rigorous among readers—are only intermediary readers of a common culture. The interpretation of culture and society is aimed at all men and women who participate in that culture—the members of what we might call a community, or horizon of experience.

A Film of Cultural Self-Reflection

It is in view of the social criticism implied by *Farewell My Concubine* as a cultural reflection-from-within that I find it highly necessary to argue for its artistic sophistication and its positive political meanings to the Chinese public. In order to appreciate this film as a serious effort of cultural self-reflection, we need to locate it in the arena of Chinese domestic cultural politics. This is not a film that Western audiences are naturally more disposed to grasp than Chinese audiences because it wins prizes in the West. To assert that *Farewell My Concubine* necessarily fares better with Western audiences is another way to say that Western audiences naturally have better film literacy and are naturally more attuned to intelligent interpretation than their Chinese counterparts. Western audiences may view this film as being about the turmoil in Chinese society. That, however, is a very obvious and perhaps the least satisfactory way to see the film—as a mirror of the age. What is more revealing, though harder to ascertain, is the significance of its persisting themes, images, legends, and style, which give the film its force, vitality, and relevance to the Chinese social horizon of experience. Because *Farewell My Concubine* is rich in these kinds of themes, images, and legends, it contains unspoken messages left to the tacit understanding of the Chinese audience in particular.

One such message of tacit understanding for the Chinese audience can be found in the film's probing of the deterioration of political order and its effect on human life. In opposition to the official teleology of communist revolution, the film delineates modern Chinese history as a sad trajectory of disintegration, presenting the changing scenes of succeeding political and military powers in relation to the Peking Opera. The age of traditional China, which, ironically, was dominated by the figure of a hideous eunuch, passed into the period of Japanese occupation. The Sino-Japanese War complicated but did not subvert the artistic prestige of the Peking Opera. The Japanese officer who mercilessly conducted cold-blooded murders of innocent Chinese people was nonetheless a Peking Opera fan. The ill-disciplined Chinese KMT soldiers ruined the decorum and elegance of Peking Opera performance in a way that "even the Japanese would not do to it." Yet the KMT general knew better than his soldiers. He was a lover of Peking Opera. Only the Communists, the saviors of the nation, and the Red Guards during the Cultural Revolution fell so low in the ladder of civility that they turned their backs on the good old Peking Opera. Thus, the apparently innocent rhetorical question of the old Opera Master—"Have you ever seen any human being who does not like Peking Opera?"—takes on a sarcastic tone, suggesting the gradual falling of humanity to animality under brutal political regimes.

Farewell My Concubine is neither a collection of Chinese curiosities nor a disquisition on the politics of blame. The film is not principally about child abuse, prostitution, homosexuality, communist brutality, or oriental despotism, though obviously the filmmaker is not above noticing such things. Its principle concern is with the barbarity contained in a civilization that has not only bred the Cultural Revolution but also created women like Juxian the prostitute, used them, poured contempt on them, and finally killed them.

The theme of prostitution in the film brings together theater and life, legend and reality, past and present, individual sufferings and collective reflection, in a large context of symbolism and representation. Charles Bernheimer, in his study of the literary and artistic representations of prostitution in nineteenth-century France, recognizes an innate linkage between art and prostitution, with its etymological roots in the idea of setting forth (Latin: *statuere*) and placing in public (*pro*): "When Baudelaire wrote that art is prostitution, he may have had this etymology in mind, for indeed art is the making public of private fantasies, the public exposition of one's imaginary creation" (1989, 1). Yu Ji, the legendary companion *and* entertaining female of Xiang Yu, the king of Chu, is his concubine. In the film she becomes an aesthetic figure of the affinity of prostitution and the Peking Opera, which evolves through the intriguing relationships among the film's three major characters. Juxian (the prostitute) and Dieyi (the male actor who plays the female role) are both attached to Xiaolou, who plays the part of Xiang Yu, and they, like the tragic courtesan, both finally bid farewell by committing suicide.

Dieyi's relation to the figure of the prostitute embodied in Juxian is complex, involving both repulsion and identification. Dieyi not only plays the part of Yu Ji, the legendary concubine, but also actively identifies with her in his relation to Xiaolou, competing with Juxian for his attention. What makes his acting art particularly prostitutional is his willingness to give himself to any admirer: the Japanese major, the KMT general, or the Communists, if they would only appreciate the genuine Peking Opera. Dieyi offers himself promiscuously to all regardless of national or ideological difference, and his dedication to art emphasizes the prostitutional nature of art.

Dieyi's opera role of a female figure is covered over with cultural signs, whose artificiality and abstraction are the focus of fetishistic fascination for the eunuch, Master Yuan the Fourth, and probably also for the Japanese major and the KMT general. What fascinates them is the myth of the prostitute, artfully constructed as a montage of accessories that obscures the carnal body. Onstage Dieyi becomes the incarnation of the idea of female beauty, which involves "a sublime deformation of nature, or rather a permanent and successive attempt to reform nature" (Baudelaire 1961; qtd. in Bernheimer 1989, 97). As an artistic creation, Dieyi is a female more perfect than nature can ever produce. By making himself up to resemble a work of art, enveloping his body in shimmering silk and gauze, and by decorating himself with sparkling jewels and tassels, the female figure on the stage becomes a ritualized image, a cultural idol. This idol has all the marks of publicly available femininity—dress, jewels, makeup, and so on—but without the prostitute's carnal sins and sordidness.

Dieyi's rejection of Juxian is motivated not only by his rivalry with her but also by an unconscious rejection of his own natural self. His mother was a prostitute, and, when he was ridiculed by other students in the opera school, he burned his mother's garment as a reminder of her shame. It is notable that a particular ambiguity exists in the nature of Dieyi's affection for Xiaolou. At stake here, however, is something more than the question of Dieyi's homosexuality. It is not through oversight or prudery that the film leaves the reader in doubt about whether or not Dieyi has sexual relations with Master Yuan the Fourth. The question then becomes what is the representational function of Dieyi's (homo)sexuality.

Roland Barthes's discussion of the representational meaning of "the Oriental transvestite" can help us to understand the circulation value of Dieyi's "femininity." The Oriental transvestite, Barthes writes, "does not copy Woman but signifies her: not bogged down to the model, but detached from its signified. Femininity is presented to read, not to see: translation, not transgression" (1982, 53). Dieyi, playing the role of Yu Ji and identifying with her as a female of fidelity, is exactly such a signifier that not only is detached from the signified but also projects the signified as its opposite. Submerging life to acting (*ren xi bu fen*), Dieyi the actor-female is a cultural invention, an image that claims its distance and difference from life. Although Dieyi's acting is prostitutional, he can still turn Juxian into his contrary, because as a woman of inert carnality, as a prostitute, her circulation value lies only in her corporeality. The Peking Opera does not just give a new gender identity to Dieyi; it functions to de-realize his sexuality, making it into an imaginary role, so as to escape the horror of the prostitute's impure and implacable flesh. Defined as the opposite of both Dieyi's spiritual femininity and social norms of female chastity, Juxian is a prostitute in the worst sense of the term. She is an abominable creature of nature. She represents a female animality that must elicit horror. She is savagery within civilization, her beauty devoid of spirituality and dangerously seductive. She is doomed to be contaminated and contaminating, a disfiguring sexual threat regardless of whether or not she is a dedicated wife to Xiaolou.

Thus, the film works with and against the social presentation of prostitution as an irreversible descent into degradation and the prostitute as irreparably fallen. Chinese stories about prostitutes rarely have happy endings. Juxian's final humiliation and suicide seem to confirm this narrative pattern. Serving as the contrary to Dieyi's metaphorical femininity, however, Juxian's feminine naturalism reasserts its claims. Although she is a prostitute, Juxian manages to buy her own freedom and successfully cheats Xiaolou into marrying her by offering him the chance of playing his favorite protective role. She plays with and even takes advantage of society's Janus-faced sexual ideology regarding the prostitute—moral condemnation coexisting with acceptance so long as the male-determined terms of the game are not challenged. She is a mother figure in the film, even though hers is a barren motherhood. Despite Dieyi's hostility to her, no other person seems to understand Dieyi better than Juxian. It is Juxian who successfully persuades the reluctant Master Yuan the Fourth to help Dieyi when he is awaiting trial, takes care of him when he is undergoing drug treatment, and shows sympathy to him when his role is taken by his own student, putting a cape on his shoulders—a gesture he rejects as he did his own mother's garment. Juxian's effort to rescue Dieyi's sword from the fire and her shocked and reprimanding glance at her husband as he pours accusing words on Dieyi fail to earn from Dieyi the recognition she deserves. Instead of understanding her sympathy, Dieyi humiliates her in public, an action that thematically repeats his burning of his mother's garment in front of his roommates. The film consciously transforms the theme of social ostracism into an alternative story of tragic human misunderstanding. It assimilates artistic acting and prostitution and reproduces them in a deliberately transfiguring situation that entails the conflicting forces of civilization and barbarity, idealism and prejudice, and the social and the personal. All this makes the film stand out from other Chinese cultural treatments of opera or prostitution.

By making a plea for a less rigid and moralistic judgment of Juxian, *Farewell My Concubine* begs to be judged accordingly and not to be condemned as ideologically prostitutional because of its success beyond the territorial boundary of China. What emerges from the film as truly unforgettable is not so much the prevalence of social injustice as a deep sense of the guilt of civilization, which probes the quintessence of tyranny, violence, and injustice, on the one hand, and representation, role-playing, and history, on the other. The film compels not only more Chinese but also more Western people to be concerned with the indifference, resignation, and confusion in which people live. An important dimension of the film's argument is that, as long as the Chinese continue to think in ways mandated by their own cultural tradition, they will be unable to deal effectively with their problems. But this is a problem that confronts people in other cultures, too. Because of the peculiar way in which *Farewell My Concubine* has forcefully raised issues quintessential to our understanding of ourselves regardless of racial and national differences, it merits the world's appreciation. The film is not just China's bygone past construed for the Western gaze. It is informed by a sense of the past, the meaning of which is yet to be interpreted and understood by the Chinese themselves. This past should, of course, include China's past as a third-world country and its position as a dependent in global relations. Yet "real independence," as Raymond Williams puts it, "is a time of new and active creation: people sure enough of themselves to discard their own baggage; knowing the past as past, as a shaping history, but with a confident sense of the present and of the future, where the decisive meanings and values will be made" (1989, 103). If we don't want to be "fixated on the past" (again to borrow a phrase from Raymond Williams), we should place this film in its own cultural location and social horizon of experience, approaching it with a sensitivity that is able to deal with Chinese culture not simply as an assertion of the non-Western but as a human creation that must be made and remade.

Abdicating the Role of "Translator"

The Nativist-Postcolonial Attack on "Colonized Foreign Literature Studies"

The arrival of the terms of *colonial* and *postcolonial* on the scene of foreign literature studies must surely be one of the most interesting developments in Chinese literary theory in the 1990s. Once these terms are introduced by Chinese post-ist theory in confrontational ways, critical attentions shift, and other considerations come to the fore. Recent colonial and postcolonial considerations in the field of foreign literature studies have found an articulating voice in the article "Beyond the Cultural Dilemma of Colonial Literature" (1994) by Yi Dan, a professor at the United University of Sichuan.[10] Taking "foreign literature research" as his immediate object of observation, Yi Dan examines what he calls the "colonial situation" of literary studies in China. Although he uses the term *foreign literature research,* given the limited scope of the "foreign" in his observation, what he really means is "research of Western literature." This is the starting point from which he asserts that foreign literature studies in China have been playing the "ridiculous role" of the "chief agent of colonial literature." According to Yi Dan, the whole discursive system in the field of China's foreign literature studies is alien to China: its object of study is foreign literature, its methodology and terminology imported from the West, its result of research predetermined by Western terms, and its "cultural position" doomed to be not Chinese (114). This is how he described the dire situation:

> The role foreign literature research has played in our literature and culture is "colonial literature" or "colonial culture." What we do in

this field is not different from those foreign missionaries. We are even doing a far better job than those missionaries because we have a better knowledge of our culture, our people's psychology, and our language. With no exaggeration I can say that everywhere in China there are people propagating foreign literature and culture. We have become perfect propagators of foreign culture and excellent salesmen of the "colonial literature." (112)

Defining "the colonial" from a cultural perspective—the term refers to "the domination and conquering of a weak civilization by a strong civilization" (112)—and understanding literature basically as "rhetorical narratives of cultural ideas and people's reaction to their surroundings," Yi Dan makes it clear that his concern is not just with literature but with culture, and culture clash in particular: "As a discipline situated between different cultures . . . foreign literature research must face the important issues of cultural differences and cultural confrontation." Cultural confrontation, Yi Dan tells us, covers a wide range of issues, from "international politics or economic strategy" to "social ethics and values" and from "definitions of 'human rights' and 'democracy'" to the "assertion of tradition and cultural uniqueness" (111).

Once the issues of culture clash or cultural confrontation are taken on board, the whole enterprise of comparative literature and cultural comparison, as well as its necessity, becomes questionable. Cultural comparison is a major part of the Chinese cultural discussions in the May Fourth Movement period (the 1910s and 1920s) and in the 1980s.[11] Cultural comparison in China is a necessity, since, to a great extent, it results from the cultural contact and confrontation between China and the West. However difficult, painful, and confusing such contacts may have been, the Chinese do not live entirely locked up in a cultural solipsism. This is perhaps why cultural comparison has always been an essential part of cultural discussions aiming at social and cultural changes in China. This kind of cultural comparison is often based on the notion of a cultural "gap" that the person doing the critique must "bridge" in order to make the comparison happen. This basic assumption rests on the basic incommensurability of *different* cultures, but it is also geared toward the reality of practical cultural comparison people make anyway. Therefore, we can define what might have been thought of as a "gap" first of all as a "relationship," that is, as the bringing together of two or more cultures through the *event* of comparison.

Parallel cultural comparison has declined in significance in China since 1989, although comparative practice is alive and well and thriving under other nomenclature. The nativist theory is based on a comparative practice that seems to conclude that Chinese and Western cultures are not only totally different but also locked in an antagonistic relationship. Ironically, this "indigenous" Chinese view is based almost completely on the Western anthropological principle of liberal cultural relativism. According to this principle, at the level of primary, basic interpretation of reality, all cultures are equally meaningful. There is no higher or lower culture, there is no right or wrong way, there is no better or worse way for a basic understanding of human life, social and political norms, our relations to the physical universe around us, and so on. If China wants to increase production, Western technology may help it, but, as such, a modern scientific worldview is not at all a challenge to any of its traditional values, worldview, or habits of perception.

The most perturbing and deliberately ignored problem of such a cultural relativism is that, if two cultures involved in the comparison are so antagonistically different that influence from one cannot but implicate its hegemony or control of the other, how does the person who compares account for his or her own knowledge of the alien culture, which by definition is cognitively contaminating? How does such a "knower" of two cultures situate him- or herself if the gap between them is so unsurmountable? What is the purpose of bringing together these two cultures except to prove the already predictable conclusion that they are different? The person who compares is a faithful defender of his or her own threatened culture rather than someone going between two cultures. Do normative, comparative, or systematic judgments apply to this knowledge and under what conditions? Is the knowledge of the difference and antagonism between Chinese and Western cultures the end product of the comparing process or only one aspect of the complex cross-cultural interaction that involves the person who compares as an interpreter? Does the comparing process aim at producing through trial and error one and only one conclusion? These questions have either remained unasked or been completely ignored by the nativist theory.

In order to unpack these questions and break the deadlock of cultural clash theory, we need to think of the person who compares different cultures not in absolute binary terms of foreign-indigenous, colonized-uncolonized, etc., but, rather, as a translator, both literally and as a figure of mediation. Zhang Hong (1994), in his criticism of Yi Dan's nativist theory, makes a point in this direction by arguing that, first of all, translators do not just do translation; they do translation with a consciously and actively adopted purpose; and, second, doing translation, they do not simply transplant a discursive system from one culture to another; they appropriate it and remake it into something new. Zhang Hong invites Yi Dan to recall how literature of translation, during the May Fourth Movement period, introduced new concepts, ideas, and values to China that have ever since played an important role in China's social modernization, establishing individual dignity, liberating women from the patriarchy, justifying working-class consciousness, discrediting despotism and tyranny, and so on. Even notions such as postmodernist and postcolonial criticisms, which are essential to Yi Dan's own nativist theory, are indebted to translation from non-Chinese texts. What really matters, Zhang says, is not what is the original source of new ideas but, rather, "their intended purpose and [practical] effect" (123).

The Translator as Mediator

The figure of mediator, of course, cannot be derived from the practice of translation automatically but instead involves what Lance Hewson and Jacky Martin (1991) call "redefining translation" itself. Hewson and Martin's efforts at redefining translation concentrate on moving translation beyond a matter of reusable techniques of converting a source text into a target text. It is their purpose to probe a variety of "conversion strategies" that are to be assessed in relation to the comparative requirements of the two "language cultures" involved: "Translation is not an *instrumental* but a *comparative* and *adjustable* process" (7). Of the sources of inspiration for such a strategic change of emphasis of translation theory, Hewson and Martin mention in particular George Steiner and Henri Meschonnic, who break philosophical new ground for a more dynamic theory of translation. Both Steiner (1975) and Meschonnic (1973) consider translation as a particularly consistent example of human consciousness in the process of understanding through hermeneutic exploration. Hermeneutic translation, or translation as hermeneutics, is the experience of the contradiction between two cultural worlds, the experience that at the same time causes the translator to question his or her own preconceptions and assimilate what is foreign to him- or herself. Seen from this point of view, translation acts as a *converting operator* between cultures: "A culture is a sequence of translations and transformations of constants" (Steiner 1975, 426). The role of the translator is not simply that of an interpreter but that of mediator. The consequences of a translator's activity, as Henri Meschonnic has clearly shown, are cultural changes, be they of the expansive, regressive, or conservative type.

The theories of Steiner and Meschonnic are particularly valuable for our consideration of the role of a person who compares cultures in cross-cultural interaction. For my own purpose of defining translation as a figure or trope of mediation in cultural comparison, I want to mention two particular parameters of translation discussed by Hewson and Martin: the translation "initiator" and the "intervention" of a translator in the capacity of a mediator (chaps. 6–7). In order to lay the cornerstone of their translation theory, Hewson and Martin pursue a systematic conceptual definition of translation and its major parameters, which I cannot outline here. The theoretical thrust of their discussion is what is important to my discussion: the translator does not just transfer meanings from one language to another using the same set of notions but, rather, mediates between two different "linguistic universes," which in many fields do not touch. The translator's role as mediator derives from the nature of translation itself, which, according to Hewson and Martin, cannot be anything but a mediating activity.

What Zhang Hong calls the "intended purpose" of translation can illustrate the fundamental role of the "translation initiator" from the premise that translation does not just "happen" but results from a need or an order. The controversy between Zhang Hong and Yi Dan is basically about what kind of translation initiator cultural critics should consider of social significance and will pay special attention to. Yi Dan asserts that the initiator for Chinese translators is a matter of personal need: "their endless readings and comments are tools to earn jobs for themselves, to play intellect or discursive games, or to insure academic promotion" (112). While this may be true for many translators, it does not have to be the only kind of initiator available to Chinese translators. Zhang Hong and other critics of Yi Dan suggest, instead, that it is essential to see that the translation is carried out not just within the framework set by the translator himself but, rather, within a social set of conditions. This can have an important effect not only on the way a translator works but also on the choices he makes in his translation. The particular kinds of literary works translated during the New Cultural Movement and May Fourth Movement period and at the time of the 1980s Culture Fever bear abundant proof to the significance of historical and social initiators to translators.[12]

Translations were undertaken on an unusually large scale in China during the early decades of the May Fourth Movement period and the 1980s Culture Fever. Itamar Evan-Zohar (1978) suggests that certain conditions determine high translation activity in a culture. He identifies three major cases: when a literature is in an early stage of development; when a literature perceives itself to be peripheral or "weak" or both; and when there are turning points or crises or literary vacuums. The huge wave of literature of translation came in China during the May Fourth Movement period, when new vernacular literature (*baihua* literature) was in an early formative stage. *Baihua* literature needed inspiration from outside and was far from being reified, making it susceptible to outside influence. The new vernacular literature was peripheral to the established Chinese classical literature and was assigned to an inferior status, which the new intellectuals fought to change. Compared with modern literatures in other countries, *baihua* literature in the early decades of the century was burgeoning but weak. It represented a turning point for Chinese literature in the modern age and underscored the cultural and identity crises faced by the Chinese classical tradition. The shift from classical to modern literature—a shift that was termed one of "style" in shorthand manner—involved changes in larger elements such as genre and discursive choice, new subject matter, character typologies, new structures of narrative, rhetorical devices of argument, and new humanistic concepts and values. This transition also involved a profound shift from literati ethos to new intellectual codes and the celebration of individualism, social evolution, intellectual criticism, and so on.

Yi Dan is not the only one who denigrates the importance of literature of translation during the May Fourth Movement period and its positive influences on modern Chinese literature and change of social values. The paranoid and conspiratorial view of cross-cultural interaction of literature often leads to trashing the May Fourth Movement legacy. Nativist critics in the field of modern Chinese literature attack the *baihua* movement as unduly influenced by Western literature. Zheng Min (1993), for example, claims that the May Fourth intellectuals' effort to "modernize" Chinese language and literature has only resulted in deterioration of the quality of Chinese poetry. Zhang Yiwu asserts that "the incursion of Western discourse" has contributed to a false sense of modernity "at the price of devaluating the indigenous culture and turning the Chinese subject into the Other of the West." According to Zhang Yiwu, the only solution to the *baihua* problem lies in constructing the "post-*baihua*," which is defined by him as a "new strategy of Sinicizing in the realm of language." The post-*baihua* promises to become the linguistic means by which Chinese subjectivity will be transformed from its current state of "the Other [of the West]" to "the Other of the Other" and will finally "resurrect the Chinese culture" (1994c, 109, 111, 113; also see Zhang Yiwu et al. 1994). Like Yi Dan's polarization of China and the West, arguments against the *baihua* movement rely on shaky dichotomies (literary versus vernacular, classical versus modern, Chinese tradition versus Western incursion, etc.) that dissolve as soon as we reflect on them. It is more productive to see change from literary to vernacular style or from classical to modern literature as a mediated intracultural transformation through the trope of translation rather than as the result of a zero-sum "revolution." Translation as a trope of mediation is as useful for understanding intracultural restructuring as it is necessary for understanding the intercultural resetting of meaning coordinates and systems. In both cases "translation" functions as an operator of coherence rather than as an operator of separation.

There exists, for instance, a remarkable dynamic relationship between the dual translations—intracultural and intercultural translations—that underscores the transformation to new literature in the May Fourth Movement period. Intracultural translation, which at that time mediated the changes of style, conceptual system, vocabulary, poetical and rhetoric conventions, genres, etc., within the Chinese culture, was then a necessity because of the crisis of existing means of meaning production and circulation. The intracultural transformation depends on a translational function that helps to differentiate new literary phenomena from old ones without separating them completely. Differences then become a form of linkage. Intracultural translation makes the intercultural one play a supportive role, which is of course not necessarily secondary in status. Intercultural translation is not only a catalytic and shaping force in the new literature but also a primary manipulative and alternate textual strategy for installing a new system of meaning in China.

This notion of Chinese literature or culture as a polysystem—that is, as a multiple and dynamic "'conglomerate of systems' characterized by internal opposition and continual shifts"—draws validity from the "polysystem theory" of translation first advanced by Itamar Evan-Zohar and followed by other literary critics. The conception of literature as a system, as a hierarchically structured set of elements, goes back to formalist and structuralist literary theories but certainly is flexible and inclusive enough to adapt itself to different contexts and situations, such as cultural comparison and cross-cultural interaction. As Theo Hermans explains:

> Among the oppositions are those between "primary" (or innovatory) and "secondary" (or conservative) models and types, between the center of the system and its periphery, between canonized and non-canonized strata, between the more or less strongly codified forms, between the various genres, etc. The dynamic aspect results from the tensions and conflicts generated by these multiple oppositions, so that the polysystem as a whole, and its constituent systems and subsystems, are in a state of perpetual flux, forever unstable. Since the literary polysystem is correlated with other cultural systems and embedded in the ideological and socio-economic structures of society, its dynamism is far from mechanistic. (1985, 11)

The theory of polysystem sees intercultural literary translation as "one element among many in the constant struggle for domination between system's various layers and subdivisions." Translation does not just introduce "foreign," or "alien," literature into a different culture or situation of communication. Translation is a social and cultural event in another actual communication situation and, once it occurs, cannot but acquire some newly contextualized significance, depending on the conditions in which it is done. As we have shown in the discussion of "translation initiator" in intercultural translation, from the point of view of the target literature, all translation implies a degree of manipulation of the source text for a certain purpose, or, as Hermans puts it:

> In a given literature, translations may at certain times constitute a separate subsystem, with its own characteristics and models, or be more or less fully integrated into the indigenous system; they may form part of the system's prestigious center or remain a peripheral phenomenon; they may be used as "primary" polemic weapons to challenge the dominant poetics, or they may shore up and reinforce the prevailing conventions. (11)

In the May Fourth Movement period and, for that matter, in the 1980s as well, Chinese translation of Western literary and other works represented a crucial instance of intellectual shoveling and challenging of the established literary and cultural polysystemic order of hierarchy at home. Since notions of interference, functional transformation, and code switching are essential aspects of the polysystem theory, this theory can provide valuable clues to study translation as a force of mediating interference and as an operator of strategic manipulation. Interference and manipulation of translation often manifest themselves in a uniquely integrative and intensive or "dramatic" manner, both in the intracultural transformation and in the intercultural cultural interaction during times of cultural crises and reconstruction.

The radical implications of the polysystem theory to cultural reconstruction in terms of conceptual and nominal innovation are immediately clear. All kinds of questions can now be asked that used to seem not to be related or raised in inappropriate terms: how are intracultural or intercultural resources used for social and cultural reconstruction? How are new concepts and values, especially those closely related to public life, formed through the mechanism of intracultural and intercultural translation borrowing? What is the status of those "texts" in the source or the target system? What do Chinese translators know about translation conventions and feasibilities at given moments, and how do they assess translation as an innovatory and progressive force? Many important public life concepts and values we have today—such as democracy, human rights, justice, individuality, the people, freedom, equality, socialism, liberalism, state, nation, etc.—are results of translation of one or the other kind, or both. Some of them are resisted, suspected, or proclaimed as unfit for China because of their Western origins. The polysystem theory of translation can help us to reestimate their Chinese elements and pertinence and to understand how they become essential parts of the language of Chinese public life, regardless of unwarranted prejudice. Terms such as *modernity, democracy, freedom,* and *human rights,* as Lydia Liu notes, are not just translations of metropolitan European theories. More important, they are mediated forms of expression that the twentieth-century Chinese new intellectuals use to talk about their differences from whatever contingent identities they perceive as existing before their own (1995).[13]

Wittgenstein made famous the dictum: "The limits of our language are the limits of our world." This could mean that human consciousness comes to maturity within a given culture in which the whole structure of a language is perfectly in place. But this does not have to mean that such a human consciousness is bound entirely by that language. As a matter of fact, language itself can be enriched, expanded, and even restructured if the human consciousness plays an active role in cross-cultural encounter and expands the limits of its world. Robert Schreiter, in his landmark work, *Constructing Local Theologies*, speaks of "listening to a culture." He describes some tools we can use to make a cultural analysis. He opts for a "semiotic study of culture." Through description and perspective and by a study of culture's texts he searches for an inner identity to a culture or to its root metaphor. Such a study results in a "semiotic domain":

> The root metaphor of the dominant semiotic domain often provides the major linkage between the sign systems of a culture. They become the language "which everyone understands." They reflect the cultural ideal. In investigating a culture, one needs to try to seek out those metaphors governing semiotic domains, and especially those that aid in linking the domains together to create a cultural whole. (1985, 70)

Paul Ricoeur calls this kind of innermost cultural metaphor the ethico-mythical nucleus of a culture (1965, 70). Those aforementioned public life concepts (democracy, freedom, equality, rights, etc.) are precisely the ethical nucleus in terms of which we can learn about the contemporary Chinese culture. They become central concepts to talk about and think about China and Chinese society in a way that is not possible and not predetermined by the old concepts of Confucian or authoritarian ethics. The new concepts do not simply replace the old ones, but they disrupt the old structure of values around which the old society and the old worldview were constructed. Of course, the new concepts by themselves do not construct a new society or a new worldview by simply rejecting and replacing the old concepts. Yet these new concepts open up the avenue to innovating existing values by deconstructing the old values and their limits as stratified ones. The "newness" of "neologisms" is *implicit* in ongoing social practices and can be made explicit only in history. Old and new ethical terms about public life do not consist of mutually exclusive cultural systems but, rather, coexist and are related to one another in a dialectic relationship of productive tension.

Translation and Cross-Cultural Interaction

The anxiety of translation expressed by the Chinese nativist critique of foreign literature research reflects a deep-rooted worry about cultural or national identity that is eroded or betrayed in the process of cross-cultural interaction. In contrast to this essentialist notion of cultural identity, we may properly remember the suggestion by L. Sciolla (1983, 14; qtd. in Schlesinger 1987, 234–35) that there is also the possibility of conceiving cultural identity as a result of complex processes, "that is as constituted by an autonomous drawing up of boundaries and construction of symbols which nevertheless interacts with the expectations and projections of given culture and with which it might also come into conflict," in a sort of unstable equilibrium whose outcomes could be either the modification of the cultural identity or the modification of the relationship of the cultures involved. Underlying the various arguments for cultural identity defense is one central agreement: that importation of foreign cultural ideas and thoughts, concepts, and values can damage or even destroy indigenous identities. This view, which I want to challenge, naturally presupposes that we know a great deal about the effects of cross-cultural interaction. Moreover, the remedy—to develop and use only the indigenous thoughts, concepts, values—relies upon exactly the same premise.

Underlying this are unexplored assumptions about cultures and how their borders are constituted, reproduced, and modified and assumptions about the nature of the relationship between the "original" and "borrowed" ideas. And, indeed, the dichotomized way of naming these ideas as original and borrowed already makes it impossible to proceed to further exploration of their relationship. Obviously, we need to begin from renaming the two parties involved in the intercultural relationship. We need to turn around the terms of conventional thinking, not to start with cultural borrowing and its supposed effect on Chinese identity and culture but, rather, to begin by posing the problem of cross-cultural interaction itself, to ask how it might be analyzed and what important role translation (rather than borrowing) might play in its constitution. This will in turn call on us to examine, in the case under discussion, how translation is termed, what figurative language is used by translators to legitimize their work as valid and Chinese focused, and how the way the translators (and their critics) name and present their work reflects their thinking about the role and status of translation in their own time.

The way the two sides involved in cross-cultural interaction are usually termed reflects deep-rooted assumptions about their respective role
and status in this relationship. We can consider this from two perspectives, each perspective allowing both a positive and a negative attitude
toward the transfer of ideas. The first perspective is by far the more common of the two. It is target culture focused—in this case, Chinese
focused. The positive attitude toward the intercultural relationship is
reflected in the neutral or even positive words used to describe the transfer of ideas as a purposeful borrowing, or "use," while the negative attitude is reflected in terms such as *imitate* or *copy*, which not only suggests
servile and captive-minded activity but also presumes the possibility of
dogmas of faithfulness to the original idea.

The second perspective is source culture focused—in this case, Western focused. It has become an often adopted perspective in the Chinese
postcolonial or indigenous theories of the 1990s and usually conveys a negative attitude, as manifested in such referential words as *domination, penetration,* and *hegemony*. These words suggest that it is the "intention" of
the Western culture to spread itself in the world in order to control other
cultures, even though people who welcome some kind of Western influence
might see it as "help" or "support." Different as these presentations are,
they all suggest the relationship between a donor and a receiver.[14]

Susan Bassnet, in her study of comparative literature and translation
theories, challenges this assumed donor-receiver relationship. She
describes how some Brazilian translators and critics manage to present
an alternative view of the source/target pairing, which takes into account
the unequal relationships between European and Brazilian cultures and
at the same time emphasizes the Brazilian resource of subverting and
reverting this relationship. In the 1920s Brazilian modernism proposed a
revaluation of the ultimate European taboo: cannibalism. Oswald de
Andrade's article "Manifesto Antropófago" considered the case of a Por-
tuguese bishop, eaten in a cannibalistic ritual by Brazilian Indians in
1554, and pointed out that there are two entirely different ways of understanding this event. From the European perspective it was an abomina-
tion and an act against the principle of civilization. But from some non-
European perspectives the act of eating a person one respects is to absorb
his or her strength or virtues and is therefore perfectly acceptable. The
Antropófagista Movement saw in this dual perspective a metaphor for
the relationship between European and Brazilian cultures. As Randall
Johnson puts it:

Metaphorically speaking, it represents a new attitude towards cultural relationships with hegemonic powers. Imitation and influence
in the traditional sense of the word are no longer possible. The
antropófagos do not want to copy European culture, but rather to
devour it, taking advantage of its positive aspects, rejecting the negative, and creating an original, national culture that would be a
source of artistic expression rather than a receptacle for forms of
cultural expression elaborated elsewhere. (1989; qtd. in Bassnett
1993, 154)

The *antropófagos* suggested that the European models should be
devoured, so that their virtues would then pass into the works of Brazilian writers. The physical metaphor of cannibalism transforms the power
relationship between European and Brazilian cultures in a constructive
way. The Brazilian writer is not an imitator, not subservient in any way
to the European tradition, nor does protest involve a rejection of that tradition altogether. Rather, the Brazilian writer interacts with the source
culture, drawing upon it for nourishment but creating something new.

Similar figurative language has also been used by Chinese critics
deliberately to erase boundaries between source and target systems and to
conceptualize "cultural borrowing" not as a one-way flow from the
source to the target culture but as a two-way transcultural enterprise. The
neologism *grapism* coined by Lu Xun (1973, 6:47) in 1934 is now used
widely as a classical expression of the various physical metaphors that
present cultural borrowing as transfusion of new blood (*xinxian xueye*) or
as the human body digesting and absorbing the nourishment and excret-
ing the waste (*tugu naxin,* which literally means discarding the dross and
selecting the essence). These figurative ways of presenting the transcultural enterprise of using through learning and learning in order to use put
emphasis on the presence of the user as a goal- and purpose-informed
agent. To argue that this transcultural enterprise leaves no room for any
active choice and results only in new bondage for the user's colonized
mind is another way to maintain the power hierarchy that privileges the
source text and relegates the translator (user) to a secondary role.

The awareness of a power hierarchy between the first-world and the
third-world cultures is valid to the extent that it recognizes that the transfer of meaning never takes place in an ideological vacuum but, rather,
carries ideological implications that need to be unpacked. The awareness
of hierarchical relations in transcultural transfer of meaning firmly posi-

tions the parties involved as source and target cultures, a relationship that is phrased in linguistic terms (source and target languages) in most translation theory. This differentiation between a source culture, which is primary and an original donor, and a target culture, which is secondary and a passive receptor, gives rise to what Priscilla Weeks (1990) calls the "'new dependency' theory," which informs and motivates many post-colonial theorists to challenge Western "grand theories" in various fields of humanities studies. New dependency theorists criticize the international hierarchical relationship, which fosters the third-world theoretical dependence on the first world. Some call for indigenizing literary and cultural theories in third-world countries, believing only indigenous theories can provide needed information, explanation, and analysis of indigenous life. This critique is basically what is informing the Chinese nativist literary and cultural theories. Variously labeled as "deconstructive," "self-reflective," or "postcolonial," these cultural theories call for replacing "borrowed" theories with indigenously constructed ones because the borrowed ones are Western-born theories and therefore, from the perspective of the receptor, either unfit or contaminated by the power difference between source (or "core") and target (or "peripheral") cultures.

While sharing the third-world concern with maintaining an independent theoretical position and approach, we must also be aware of the limitation of the new dependency theory, especially if it is based on the assumptions of unerasable boundaries between the source and the target cultures and if it sees their interaction as possible only in the form of a process of direct and unmediated transfer of models from the stronger to the weaker. Such a new dependency theory could then echo the two basic presumptions of the old translation theory and become nothing more than the extension of that obsolete translation theory in the cultural realm. The two basic presumptions of old translation theory can be summarized as, first, the art of translation is a subsidiary art and derivative, and on this account it should not be granted the dignity and worth of the original work; and, second, translation between languages is possible because of the prior existence of a notional equivalence between linguistic (conceptual and experiential) systems, and translation is a transfer of meaning in the manner of a bilingual dictionary (Bassnett 1993, 145).

I have already touched on the fallacy of the first presumption of the old translation theory while discussing how new translation theories take the traditional presumption to task, starting from erasing the boundaries between the source text and the target text and reconceptualizing the translator as a constructive agent and his or her work as dynamic rewriting in new circumstances. This idea of translation as manipulative textual strategies aiming at accelerating changes in a home system has been widely accepted by translation theorists since the rediscovery of Walter Benjamin's now famous introduction to the German translation of Baudelaire's *Tableux Parisiens* (1923) and Derrida's elaboration of his ideas in the 1980s. Derrida's reading of Benjamin plays with ideas of the original and translation and with the problem of where meaning is located. Derrida (1985) suggests a further radical attack on the idea of the primacy of the original. The source text, according to Derrida, is not an original at all; it is the elaboration of an idea, of a meaning. In short, it is itself a translation. The logical consequences of Derrida's thinking about translation would be the abolition of the dichotomy between original and translation, between source and copy, and hence an end to the view that relegates translation to a secondary position. From a theological point of view Walter Benjamin proclaims the life-enhancing role of translation as a transformative process: "a translation comes later than the original, and since the important works of world literature never find their chosen translators at the time of their origin, their translation marks their stage of continued life" (1973, 69–83). Translation is therefore a particularly special activity, since it enables a text to continue life in another context, and the translated text becomes an original by virtue of its continued existence in that new context.

Some explanation is needed for the second presumption of the old translation theory, that a notional equivalence exists between different linguistic systems. Although the old translation theory has been refuted by the Sapir-Whorf hypothesis, which argues that "no two languages are ever sufficiently similar to be considered as representing the same social reality" and that "the worlds in which different societies live are distinct worlds, not merely the same world with different labels attached," many translators still want to believe in equivalence (Sapir 1956, 69). Disciples of the old translation theory have sought to define equivalence in terms of sameness, sometimes arguing that sameness can be interpreted in different ways and is open to negotiation but nevertheless is possible (Bassnett 1993, 145). New translation theories challenge this assumption of possible notional sameness from one culture to another by emphasizing the lack of neutrality or an interest-free position on the part of the translator. Hewson and Martin's translation theory provides an example of how a new translation theory stresses elements left out by the old translation theory, such as different and unequal systems of representation, situations of communication, and the anchoredness of the translator. The new stress on the situatedness of the translator as a social being as well as a language user is immensely illustrative of the daunting task of bridging the incommensurability of language worlds and the translator's role "as a mediator between two language cultures and as a regulator of the conflicting forces that are necessarily induced by bringing together of two cultural systems" (Hewson and Martin, 134).

Given a translator's unequal linguistic competence in two languages and his or her greater invested interest in one language culture than the other, he or she will not be able to claim a position in which to move comfortably from one system of representation to another, matching and comparing their complex conceptual and experiential areas, as though they were symmetrically structured, albeit different in content. The presumption that anyone can transfer, in the sense of "transplant," certain ideas from one culture (e.g., Western politico-ethical concepts such as "democracy" or "modernity") to another without having these ideas first "de-contextualized" and then "re-contextualized" or without disturbing the logical relations of its existing notions is completely unfounded.[15] The cognitive position of the translator is, after all, also a socially and politically situated one, which makes the act of translation also an act of sociopolitical intervention.

It seems that foreign literature studies and the cultural discussion in China today need a new translation theory that will help them to overcome the shortcomings of the two basic presumptions carried by old translation theory. Such a new translation theory should be sufficiently inclusive and adaptable to stimulate research in a variety of fields, not least those of comparative literature and cultural comparison. This theory, of course, is not meant just to provide guidelines for textual translation but, rather, to enable critics and translators to examine various translation activities within a framework that allows for using translation as a significant epistemological strategy for conceptual innovation and change of language cultures. Hewson and Martin, like Meschonnic (1973, 307 ff.), show how translation can change both language cultures involved in the transfer of meaning. Translation first "decenters" a language culture, that is, pulls it toward a second language culture, "until the second language culture develops and is redefined to include what were originally the foreign elements":

> One can see how, during different historical periods, translation has helped a [language culture] to develop, rather than to become stultified in some splendid isolation. A diachronic perspective is essential here, for, as Foucault never tired of pointing out, all cannot be said at any one time in any one culture. The point here is then that translation can be an *enriching* factor in the development of a culture—and not, as is often maintained, a dangerous external influence "polluting" the [language culture]. (Hewson and Martin, 128.)

The immediate implication of such a positive view of translation for the Chinese cultural discussion to rethink first-third world cultural interaction is obvious. The result of this approach to translation is, on the one hand, a considerable widening of the horizon, since any and all phenomena relating to translation, in the broadest sense, become objects of study; and, on the other hand, it provides a more coherent and goal-directed type of investigation, because it operates with more than just a professional purpose and begins to take account of the interplay of intellectual work and social change.

Chapter 5

Remembering Intellectual Activism in the Postsocialist-Postcolonial Condition

Memory, Forgetting, and New Cultural Conservatism

Many Chinese academics, pondering the intellectual situation and options of the 1990s, reflect on the previous decade and use it as a contrast to the present. Some even generate theories about that decade by analyzing its events and happenings with various descriptive or normative discourses. But theorizing and memory are not always the same. To remember—not merely in the sense of retaining impressions, theoretical introspection, or disembodied recollection but in the active sense of reinvigorating something to address a present need—is to endow knowledge with meaning and theorizing with a purpose. Having an active memory means having an ability to maintain a purpose over a period of time and return to it after interruptions. The active memory is a memory of will. In order to maintain purpose in this manner, individuals and societies alike must be able to control the lessons they want to draw from history and define the importance they attach to historical possibilities realized or not realized. History thus remembered is history active on the present stage of action. Although we may know about the happenings of the 1980s and the Culture Fever of that decade or we may continue to study and explain these things, unless we remember them in a way that reasserts their pro-democracy vision and their intellectual activism, we have already begun to forget them.

Memory of the Cultural Revolution as an atrocity against humanity prompted the discussions of humanism of the late 1970s and the 1980s and consisted of the pro-enlightenment and pro-democracy core of the 1980s Culture Fever. This memory differs from the official theorizing about the Cultural Revolution as a mere political miscalculation of Mao or the conspiracy of the Gang of Four as an unfortunate incident that became "history" and must be buried in the past. Memory and history, as Pierre Nora observes, are not synonymous but, rather, are often opposed: "Memory is life, always embodied in living societies and as such in permanent evolution, subject to the dialectic of remembering and forgetting . . . History, on the other hand, is the reconstruction, always problematic and incomplete, of what is no longer" (1992, 3). Memory is always a phenomenon of the present, history a distancing and defamiliarizing force unless actively remembered. The sometimes lenient political atmosphere of the late 1970s and the 1980s provided memory of the Cultural Revolution with a public forum and thus allowed it to be displaced from the individual realm into what Maurice Halbwachs (1992) called "social frames" and to become a collective memory. This collective memory bound the majority of the post–Cultural Revolution intellectual community together and allowed them to create social identities denied under the Mao regime, particularly those of sociocultural critic and concerned, engaged, and politically relevant intellectual.

In contrast to this memory of the Cultural Revolution, no collective memory can be formed about the crackdown of the 1989 pro-democracy movement due to the nonexistence of a public forum. The general silence about and lack of memory of the 1989 Tiananmen incident are symptomatic of the difficult situation many Chinese intellectuals find themselves in. On the one hand, the party-state remains repressive in the ideological and political realms and continues to limit intellectuals' engagement and interference. On the other hand, it has adopted a pragmatic orientation quite unlike Mao's heavy-handed cultural policy. In the cultural realm forces of commercialization and commodification have loosened the control of the state; they have also further marginalized the intellectuals and minimized their influence. A deep sense of powerlessness, irrelevance, and confusion among intellectuals has prevented them from formulating a coherent response; it has also resulted in widespread political disenchantment and apathy.

This is not to say that on an individual level academicians are not responding to the challenge. As a matter of fact, many of them are in a productive mood and are looking in various new directions, being particularly reflective about moral and professional matters, as in the cases of the humanist-spirit discussion and the new Chinese national studies. Yet these new directions, because they draw away from political issues, serve further to erase the memory of what happened to China politically in 1989.

Erasing memory is not all about forgetting; erasing memory contains its own mode of memorizing. Walter Adamson (1985) has developed a very illuminating distinction among what he calls modes of "memorizing," "memory," and "remembering." Adamson associates the mode of *memorizing* with the idea of a mental "faculty," or memory through which individuals seek to recall or capture a factual record of historical events "as they really were." Memorizing is a kind of realism that considers the historical past to be something that already exists as a sociocultural artifact, waiting to be discovered. In memorizing "history is fundamentally a process of discovering realities that lie 'out there,' rather than a reconstructing by conceptual thought." The mode of *memory* is quite different. It is associated by Adamson with idealism, which asserts that, while memory may not be able to provide an accurate, or "factual," account of history, it can, nevertheless, provide individuals with an interpretive account of the past that is "better than the past understood itself" (232–33).

Remembering, according to Adamson, is the most significant mode around which one can establish an emancipatory political project. "To remember," Adamson argues, "is to seek not the most accurate or the 'best' interpretation but the one most 'powerful' for the purpose of illuminating our projects for the future" (234). Whereas memorizing tries to recall what was and memory dreams of discovering the master code with which to uncover the best interpretation of the past, remembering is a critical and redemptive mode that attempts to "understand [the past] differently, and each time again differently." This emancipatory mode seeks not to establish our radical difference with the past but, rather, "to restore our relation to it." It is a critical mode in the sense that "it recognizes that we are always operating within a changing horizon—of expectations, problems, needs—that leads us to ask different historical questions and to be offered different answers" (233).

Emancipatory remembering does not conceive of history as a linear succession of events in which hindsight automatically provides better understanding, in which we can always feel complacent in the present moment with our wise-after-the-event criticism. Rather, remembering compels us to engage history as a living discourse that underscores the irreplaceable uniqueness of the present. The history of remembering "has no single necessary logic, nor does it assume historical continuity" (233). It provides us with a vantage point not for recovering or discovering the past but for entering a dialogue with it. Remembering in this sense conceives of history not as a constraint on the present but, rather, as a compelling moment for crucial viewpoints to be constructed for critical purpose. History, therefore, becomes a source of imaginative power, as remembering invites us to recall in a problem-posing way so as to comprehend our present social and political situation and problems.

In the years after the 1989 crackdown on the pro-democracy movement, memory works about the 1980s have been marked either by a harsh and often hostile mode of memorizing, depicting the 1980s as an abhorrent period of utopianism, political romanticism, irrational radicalism, and reckless Westernization, or by a pathetic and quixotic mode of memory, in which the 1980s are seen as a golden age of elitist achievement and freedom from commercial mass culture. In the meantime the present-oriented mode of remembering, especially that of the intellectual activism of the 1980s, is often overlooked. The abrupt change of political atmosphere and its after-effect have produced a collective fear of remembering. This retreat from remembering, in which intellectual consciousness seeks not to preserve its integral relation with past experience but to protect itself from being overstimulated by it, has become a very notable phenomenon of the post-1989 condition.

The fear of remembering and the proclivity to forget as an after-effect of the 1989 Tiananmen incident remind us of what Ian Gambles calls "forgetting recent history," which is also purposeful "un-remembering." Gambles distinguishes two different but interrelated forms of forgetting: the conscious state forgetting and the unconscious social forgetting. State forgetting is the deliberate silencing of a particular part of the past for political purposes. The state can also act as an initiator and facilitator of social forgetting: "a gradual, collective loss of interest in a part of the past that conveys an undesired self-image" (Gambles 1995, 26).

Much of the post-1989 recollection and reevaluation of the pro-enlightenment and pro-democracy cultural discussion of the 1980s demonstrates how unconscious social forgetting is at work among a large number of Chinese intellectuals. Such recollection and reevaluation of the 1980s are often done in terms of a new pairing of radicalism and conservatism. They are often characterized by condemnation of the 1980s cultural criticism and its intellectual activism, which are seen as too "radical," and celebration of the demise of intellectual radicalism in the 1990s. Not all cultural discussion in the 1980s was politically engaged and critical, but it did contain a significant body of thought and action that was motivated by democratic inquiry. By denying the legacy and the legitimacy of this body of thought and action and by eliminating it as a central point of reference in the march of time from the past to the present, such recollection and reevaluation participate in the state forgetting the true impulse of Chinese people for democratic change and its eruption in 1989.

The 1990s concepts of radicalism and antiradicalism are dramatic because they propose nothing less than a contest between right and wrong. Predictably, they have become hot topics in the cultural discussion of the 1990s. Antiradicalism, however, is not simply a subject of discussion among Chinese intellectuals who reflect on past events and trends; it has become a crucial element in some of their changing intellectual positions in the 1990s. Unlike the conservative/liberal contrast in the West, it is the conservative/radical contrast that defines the conceptual frame of "new conservatism" in China. Liberalism is not a practical contrast of conservatism in China because it does not even have a public forum to express and justify itself as a valid body of thoughts, much less as social practice. Unlike liberalism, radicalism conveniently conjures up a unity of ideas that does not exist in fact but is useful to label any practical or even attitudinal noncompliance or dissent regarding the status quo.

For new conservatives adopting the antiradical, rather than antiliberal, posture has several advantages. First, antiradicalism gives their conservative discourses a distinctive Chinese character and valuable indigenous legitimacy. Second, it allows them to keep a safe but respectful distance from the official antiliberal rhetoric and maintain some degree of intellectual independence. Third, it helps to induce even some liberals to embrace conservative ideas. If conservatism is to be successful in reaching those outside its traditional foundations, it has to develop new slogans and symbols. Conservatism in China had a more negative tone in the past, carping about erosion of China's tradition and cultural heritage but offering few alternatives. New conservatism has taken on a more positive cast with an agenda of attacking radicalism and political romanticism, emphasizing Chinese values as a resource of social change, and rebuilding national identity. Antiradicalism as a slogan and a sociocultural agenda gives energy to the new conservative legions.

Xiao Gongqin, arguably the most articulate advocate of new authoritarianism in the 1980s and new conservatism in the 1990s, describes Chinese new conservatism in this way:

New conservatism in the twentieth century is in fact a conservatism
that is oriented by modernization and transformation. It is essentially different from the traditional fundamentalist conservatism,
which respectfully regarded the traditional sociocultural order as
"unalterable" and opposed any change as heresy. On the contrary,
new conservatism sees tradition as national collective experience
and wants to establish this collective experience as a basis of gradual
social transformation. New conservatism emerges as a reaction
against radicalism in China's process of modernization. (1997, 128)

The social transformation to which new conservatives like Xiao Gongqin
give their blessing is basically an economic one. The fast economic development is deeply felt in the Chinese conscience. To many Chinese
identification with the Deng-Jiang policy of combined political authoritarianism and economic marketization is equivalent to adopting a popular cause, one that is changing the way people think about the governmental authority and its role in their lives. The post–Cold War global
market economy has played a big role in transforming the character of
conservatism in China.[1] The most powerful conservative voice no longer
comes from those who aim to roll back Deng's market reforms in order
to maintain China's socialist purity but from those who promote the
political legitimacy of the undemocratic authority by embracing its new
economic policy. Fear of social chaos, political instability, and economic
setback resulting from the weakening of authoritarian government—as is
the case of the dissolution of the Soviet Union and regime changes in
some Eastern European countries after 1989—has prompted the popular
view that for the sake of stability and economic growth it is worthwhile
to sacrifice greater political freedom.

New conservative thought is different from the popular fear of chaos
and instability in its explicit efforts to legitimate a strong political authority and its hegemonic order as necessary and sufficient conditions of evolutionary transformation in the direction of a wholesome civil society
(Xiao Gongqin 1997, 134). Moving away from an authoritarian order
ironically aims to retain authoritarian principles. How this ironic logic
works can be perceived in Xiao Gongqin's evocation of Burkean conservatism. Using Peter Viereck's differentiation of Burkean and Maistrian
conservatism, Xiao Gongqin argues that, while Edmund Burke represented "evolutionary conservatism," Joseph de Maistre represented
"reactionary conservatism" (1997, 126–27). Based on this distinction,

Xiao presents Chinese new conservatism as a politicocultural thought that makes serious efforts to draw useful elements from the first and has nothing to do with the second. Unlike Maistrian conservatism, Xiao contends, Chinese new conservatism has no objection to social transformation and does not want to go backward toward better days in the past; it wants to see transformation take place in China in an "evolutionary" and "natural" manner without the interference of utopian ideologies.

Xiao Gongqin manipulates Viereck's definition of Maistrian conservatism in a peculiar way. Viereck regards Maistrian conservatism not only "reactionary" but also "authoritarian" and asserts that it is reactionary because it is authoritarian (1978, 11). Viereck considers authoritarian conservatives extreme in their emphasis upon political control as contrasted with the traditional, or Burkean, conservatives' emphasis upon liberties. It is not only the desire to move backward in time but also the primacy of political authority that is at the heart of the difference between authoritarian (Maistrian) and traditional (Burkean) conservatism. Xiao isolates the Maistrian desire to move backward from the Maistrian primacy of political authority and ties the latter to the Burkean idea of social evolution within tested traditions and institutions. The traditions and institutions Burke relied on were based on liberal values and an autonomous civil society. Given the authoritarian tradition and reality (system, institutions, and political culture) in China, Chinese new conservatism is caught in a dilemma: the harder it tries to be Burkean, the more inevitably it becomes Maistrian.

Ostensibly following the Burkean tradition, Xiao Gongqin (1997), in his consideration of the valid resource of social transformation, resorts to the binary opposition between what he calls "collective experience" and "political romanticism" (utopian ideology). The problems is, in a society in which the public forum is controlled by the party-state, who dictates what counts as collective experience and what should be condemned as political romanticism? Xiao Gongqin is aware of the difference between Burke's England and contemporary China. "When Chinese conservatism attempts to counter radicalism with Burkean thought," he acknowledges, "it does not have the latter's material and spiritual resources based on civil society." But Xiao believes that in China a real civil society can be "gradually achieved through the forming of an enlightened authority" only if this evolutionary course is not disturbed by troublesome political utopianism (1997, 134). What Xiao remains evasive about is by what the Chinese authority is to be enlightened and the fact that the current authority in China is established and legitimated precisely by a certain political utopianism, that of communism and socialism.

As is exemplified by Xiao Gongqin, what is problematic about Chinese new conservative thinking is not its attack on political utopianism but its overlooking the real dominant utopian ideology in China that has so relentlessly attempted to remake society and humans in the image of some ideal. To a large extent, the 1990s Chinese conservative anti-utopianism is triggered by a disillusionment with the promises and experiments of the 1980s pro-democracy intellectual activism. It mistargets the sociocultural critique of this intellectual engagement as the object of its assault on utopian ideology. Pro-democracy cultural critique is not the same as utopian ideology in its dynamics and social goal. While pro-democracy intellectuals cherish diversity, the authoritarian ideologues prize uniformity. The official ideologues view men as instruments to be manipulated in the interest of obtaining a uniformity of practice. By contrast, pro-democracy intellectuals value variety, complexity, difference, and dissent. Pluralism and free thinking, the benchmarks of enlightenment for the pro-democracy advocates, are the embodiment of those values. They insist that the individual learn standards and norms of acceptable behavior more through dialogue, discussion, deliberation, and collective reflection, and through community institutions like school, public forum, civil society, and voluntary associations, than through laws and regulations imposed by government and the party-state. In this sense pro-democracy cultural discussion is against utopian ideology and its radical embodiment in Chinese society.

Without China's absolute authorities and the always ill-fated challenges to them, there would be no articulate Chinese new conservatism. In the eyes of conservatives, the ideal of a human existence liberated from the intolerant existing order seldom brought freedom and never spawned social improvement. The conservative anti-utopian and antiradical rhetoric masks important questions that new conservatives are reluctant to face: why has the radicalism/conservatism debate become so important at this particular time, and what contending interests does it involve? What political and ideological role does antiradicalism or anti-utopianism play in the contest to define the terms of intellectual engagement and cultural critique? What are the prospects for the ascendency of moderate and pragmatic thinking in shaping the intellectuals' and the public's mentality with regard to democratic social change within the authoritarian order?

Antiradicalism and Realistic Thinking

As a key component of Chinese new conservatism, new cultural conservatism is an intellectual position that is constructed first of all as an overcoming of the alleged radicalism, utopianism, and political romanticism of 1980s cultural criticism. By depicting the intellectual scene of the 1980s as a state of grave disorder, proponents of new cultural conservatism cast themselves as therapists for that decade's sick theories and for a hapless intellectual community infected by unwholesome ideas. Meng Fanhua, a critic from Beijing, puts it this way:

> New cultural conservatism has taken shape without a manifesto since the beginning of the 1990s. New cultural conservatism has three characterizing features. First, it rejects the radical critical spirit and opts for moderate and steady discursive practice. Second, it gives up anxiety, concern, and questioning of the collective situation, and turns its attention to the personal situation; third, it declines the quest for ultimate value, goal, or faith, and is concerned with solutions to local problems. This is obviously a major paradigmatic change of cultural temperament and we are clearly aware of its happening now. (1994, 53)

New cultural conservatism needs its 1980s "other" of radicalism to constitute or to frame its own narrative or referential fracture. This contrast of self and other has enabled Zhang Yiwu, a leading postmodern-postcolonial theorist in China, to propose new cultural conservatism as an audacious protest against many fallacies shared by Chinese intellectuals in the 1980s and as an initiator of a genuine critical spirit that cannot be resisted:

> In the 1990s, profound changes are happening to the culture of mainland China . . . People can no longer ignore this cultural reality, a new cultural conservatism is on the rise. [New cultural conservatism] has surpassed the cultural discourses we were familiar with in the 1980s and enjoys increasing influence in the new environment . . . This [new conservative] cultural trend involves critical reflection on cultural movements in the 1980s and on the radical discourses since the May Fourth Movement. Its development is related to the new post–Cold War global structure, and is a reaction to it. The neo-

conservative spirit has successfully penetrated into every cultural area and acquired different forms of expression in different cultural spaces. (1994b, 55)

The elevation of the present moment of intellectual conservatism requires that conservative thinkers sketch a history that catches hold of "disastrous" moments of radicalism, which are often counted backward from the 1980s Culture Fever to the Cultural Revolution and then to the May Fourth Movement.

Proponents of new cultural conservatism can be divided into three major components formed by three different groups of intellectuals (Yang Chunshi 1996). The first group is composed of scholars who take a parochial view of Chinese learning and values, scholars who are influenced by various cultural traditionalists and have adopted a hardline antiradical position.[2] The second group has in its ranks young intellectuals who are known as post-ist theorists. These young theorists employ postmodern and postcolonial theory to defend Chinese identity and authenticity in the face of Western hegemony that exerts its influence through notions of modernity, democracy, and human rights. The third group is made up by some old-generation intellectuals who played an important role in the 1980s Culture Fever but have modified their position after 1989 and put more emphasis on creating change within the existing order. Each of these components of new cultural conservatism has its own characterizing origins, themes, attitudes, and concerns, but they resonate with one another in their particular ways of memorizing China's alleged tradition of radicalism in the past and in their attempts to construct out of the renunciative, antiradical stance a superior model of intellectual sensibility and reasoning: realistic thinking.

Realistic thinking is characterized by its recognition of the status quo. And China's reality in the 1990s does not seem to encourage people to think otherwise. Not only is the combined force of a Leninist party-state and a rampant market economy too powerful to allow for effective intellectual opposition or resistance, but also the reality is too full of incongruities to allow for imagining focused social change and for creating critical initiatives to appeal to the public. The party-state still maintains its monopoly of power, but it is less coercive and less intrusive in ordinary people's lives; it still persecutes political dissidents, but it allows greater individual freedom to ordinary citizens; it still maintains a tight control over the media and publication, but it leaves intellectuals alone as long as they do not challenge the party and leadership directly; it still uses communist ideology as a whip over the society and individuals, but it does not bother to tame the apparently uncontrolled mass culture; the Chinese system of market economy is ridden with problems, runaway skulduggery, monetized graft, and gross inequality, but it is raising people's standard of living; commercialization corrupts and invites extortionalist grotesqueries of all sorts that eviscerate the social organism, but it is providing people with more goods than ever before.

The 1990s-style realistic thinking in China stresses the *limits* imposed by this new political-economic order—by its historical density and weight—and thus positions itself as a "calm" and "moderate" force in relation to this existing order. It shifts its focus from critique to understanding: attention is given to the social forces that have shaped thinking, not to the question of how people have shown a commitment to change. As Wang Desheng, one of the proponents of new cultural conservatism, makes clear, the new intellectual mentality is marked by a deliberate shift away from political romanticism and idealism to realism and pragmatism: "after a brief period of silence, Chinese intellectuals in the 1990s have become calm and moderate, replacing radical sociopolitical critiques with academic critiques and scholarly inquiry in order to understand China from political, economic, and cultural dimensions." "The cultural rupture after 1989," Wang asserts, is characterized by "the dysfunction of radical cultural critique and enlightenment" and by "the reargarde function of cultural conservatism" (1994, 56).

Realistic thinking has become prevalent in the three groups of new cultural conservatives via different routes. For cultural traditionalists it is a transformation from the philosophical, often nostalgic, speculation of Chinese cultural tradition before the 1980s; it is now an on-the-spot thinking about "China-specific modernity" and about its dynamics of Chinese values (or Asian values). For post-ist theorists realistic thinking is a transformation of Western-born postmodern and postcolonial theories; its primary task is to demystify the modernity project in China and to celebrate China's postmodern reality. For previous pro-enlightenment intellectuals realistic thinking is a transformation from their exploratory thinking within a Marxist frame in the 1980s; it now holds a progressivist and evolutionist view of social change, assuming that political transformation will automatically occur once the economic conditions are created.

In order to describe the contours of realistic thinking in China in the

1990s, it is necessary to make an analytical distinction between what it is and what it is not. Realistic thinking is different from critical thinking, although the two are not necessarily opposed to each other. First, realistic thinking and critical thinking differ in their views of history. Realistic thinking searches out firm phenomena and patterns that recur and which are presumably intelligible by themselves. Critical thinking stresses a historicism that emphasizes social fluidity and change, a kind of organicism calling for the contextual interpretation of events. Realistic thinking sees history as composed of objective facts. Critical thinking sees history as a text that different people read for different purposes. Therefore, realistic thinking and critical thinking differ in their most basic background assumptions with respect to the role of *xue* (knowledge, understanding) as against *yong* (application, critique). Because of their different views of history, realistic thinking emphasizes the similarities between radical movements—the May Fourth Movement, the Cultural Revolution, and the Culture Fever of the 1980s—while critical thinking emphasizes their differences.

Second, realistic and critical thinkings differ in their concepts of change: one is gradualistic and evolutionary, the other more discontinuous and abrupt. Since realistic thinking accents the objectivity and the weight of history, it sees the social world as difficult to deflect in its course and thus as unchangeable by "mere will." Indeed, realistic thinking sees the social world as imposing itself on persons, rather than being a fluid medium open to human intervention. On the other hand, critical thinking refuses to submit to "what is" or to wait interminably until the right conditions of change come into being in the course of history. It is convinced that there is always some way to exert pressure against the status quo. In terms of social change, realistic thinking and critical thinking differ also in that the first view is object centered, addressing the changes in economics, technology, and science, while the second also involves the activity of the knowing subject and his or her sense of value. These two concepts of change underlie the difference between the "Four Modernizations" and the "modernization of man" and the difference between economic and democratic priorities of social change in China.

Third, realistic thinking and critical thinking differ also in their politics. Realistic thinking and critical thinking have different political strength. Realistic thinking stresses necessary material conditions of social change, the careful appraisal of these conditions for what they are, not confusing them with what people would like them to be. Critical thinking, on the other hand, is alert to the dangers of political exhaustion, apathy, and undue reliance upon circumstantial forces. Realistic thinking and critical thinking differ in their notion of what constitutes "change" in China today and how it is made and, vitally, in their vision of what is to be brought into existence. Critical thinking is much more explicit and emphatic than realistic thinking in positing democracy as a worthy goal of social change in China. This difference is linked to realistic thinking's stress upon instrumental measures and to critical thinking's concern with ultimate values. The political expression of this is found in realistic thinking's great commitment to the nation, to Chineseness, to socialism, and so on. On the other hand, critical thinking makes its deepest commitment to humanistic values, to a conception of sociopolitical consciousness, and to certain ethical qualities that make social change desirable at all.

Variations of New Cultural Conservatism

Cultural Traditionalism

How the antiradical memory work operates in China in the 1990s to constitute a conservative position and how it is related to the prevalent realistic thinking can be seen in a seminal article, "Radicalism of the Twentieth-Century Cultural Movements," by Chen Lai, a philosophy professor at Beijing University and an articulate cultural traditionalist. This article, written in 1991 and published in 1993, proclaims the need for reevaluating and rejecting "the Chinese tradition of radicalism" so that China can move safely into the next century. According to Chen Lai: "Cultural radicalism has played a predominant role from the May Fourth Movement, through the Cultural Revolution, to the Culture Fever [in the 1980s] . . . All cultural movements [in China] throughout the twentieth century have been dominated by radicalism" and have led to "political radicalism" (revolutionism). Radicalism in China, Chen tells us, is characterized by its confusion of politics with culture, by the intellectuals' unwillingness to separate their political role from their intellectual role (1993, 73).

Chen may be right about possible devastating social effects of radicalism, but his argument contains two unexamined assumptions. First, to be radical is not the same as to be political. Neither is antiradicalism the same as depoliticalization. Politics ranges from radical to conservative. Second, instead of assuming the natural homogeneity between cultural radicalism and revolutionism, Chen needs to explain what exactly are the particular Chinese conditions that frequently subjugated cultural radicalism to revolutionism and how cultural radicalism can assert its democratic ideal by resisting co-optation by dominant political interests that claim legitimacy in the name of revolution.

The prototypic case of pernicious radicalism in Chen's discussion is the Cultural Revolution. Few people in China would want to see the Cultural Revolution happen again, but this does not justify Chen's use of the Cultural Revolution as a scare tactic against radicalism. Again, if Chen wants to tell us what is wrong with the Cultural Revolution, he needs to do more than just label it radical. He needs to tell us at least in what sense the Cultural Revolution is a case of bad radicalism. Failing to do that, Chen puts in the same category of radicalism the Cultural Revolution and the pro-democracy critique of its authoritarianism in the 1980s. What makes Chen's argument politically counterproductive is that he suggests there is no difference at all between bad radicalism and radicalism that opposes bad radicalism by a worthy principle. To recognize that there is a need to distinguish, to choose between different elements in radicalism, and indeed between radicalism and conservatism, requires recognition of the preeminent role of a critical principle.

Failing to construe and posit such a principle of distinction, the central argument Chen makes against radicalism is based on the empirically observed features shared by the May Fourth Movement, the Cultural Revolution, and the 1980s Culture Fever—particularly their destructive effects on traditional Chinese culture. The May Fourth Movement, Chen contends, wanted to find a shortcut to national wealth and power through Western-born democracy and science; the Cultural Revolution attempted to construct a completely new socialist culture by destroying everything that was deemed old and obsolete; and the Culture Fever dreamt of modernizing China by importing Western ideas wholesale (1993, 41). By taking these historical events out of their contexts and by ignoring their very different sociocultural impacts and political orientations, Chen Lai creates a Chinese genealogy of radicalism with increasing intensity.[3] Here Chen speaks as a realistic-thinking historian who empirically searches out historical patterns that are presumably intelligible in themselves and pays no attention to their deep-level differences.

Chen Lai's realistic thinking is also reflected in his consideration of a China-specific modernity, which would not necessarily be a conservative move in itself if it had not become exclusive and parochial in envisioning possible resources of China's modernity. There has been a growing confidence in China in the 1990s, buoyed by substantial economic successes since the late 1980s, that Chinese values and tradition have served Chinese modernity well. And this makes it possible for cultural traditionalism to change from a more or less philosophical speculation about China's past glory to realistic thinking about its actual economic achievement. Defense of Chinese traditional culture is not new in the 1990s. Previous defenders of Chinese cultural tradition include *Kongjiao pai* (the Confucian School) represented by Kang Youwei, *Guocui pai* (the Chinese Essence School) represented by Zhang Taiyan and Liu Shipei, *Xueheng pai* (the Critical Review School) represented by Mei Guangdi and Wu Mian in the 1920s, *Dongfang wenhua pai* (the Oriental Culture School) represented by Du Yaquan and Zhang Shizhao in the 1920s, *Zhongguo benwei wenhua pai* (the Indigenous Chinese Culture School) represented by Tao Xisheng and nine other professors in the 1930s, and *Xin rujia xuepai* (the New Confucian School) represented by famous Confucian scholars such as Liang Shumin, Xiong Shili, Feng Youlan, Tang Junyi, and Mu Zongsan. What is new to China's cultural traditionalism since the 1980s and explicitly in the 1990s is that it finds itself in the unprecedented position of defending Chinese cultural values not just as a unique and therefore worthy model of civilization but also as a tested form of praxis of modernity. It can now point to the economic successes of the Four Mini-Dragons (Hong Kong, Singapore, South Korea, and Taiwan) and argue that traditional values do not necessarily impede the process of modernization, and, as a matter of fact, they can even contribute to accelerating this process.

This replacement of tradition by modernity as a central thesis of cultural traditionalism can be seen in Chen Lai's article "Confucian Ideas and Modern East-Asian World" (1994). In this article Chen argues that the contrast of tradition and modernity has been made obsolete by the economic reality of "Asian miracles" and therefore must be replaced by a new contrast, Asian (basically Chinese-Confucian) values versus Western values; both sets of values have benefited modernization in their own ways in different parts of the world. Chen Lai contends that the two basic Confucian values, "harmony" (*he*) and "humanity" (*ren*), are the driving force of Asian modernity. Chen's ideas of immutable and impervious Chinese values and the actual or potential benefits of these values to modernization constitute an essential part of his antiradical logic: if radical movements, such as the May Fourth Movement, the Cultural Revolution, and the 1980s Culture Fever, had not destructed these basic Chinese values and interrupted China's natural course of development, modernization would probably have come about sooner in China.[4]

Nativist Postmodern-Postcolonial Theory

Along with cultural traditionalism, Chinese nativist postmodern-postcolonial theory is another mainstay of new cultural conservatism in the 1990s (Ye Wen 1997). Unlike cultural traditionalism, Chinese nativist post-ist theory has rather radical origins. Indeed, it is a prima facie unlikely union of Western postmodern, postcolonial theories and Chinese concerns about national authenticity and identity. As Wang Hui observes, the nativist inclination of Chinese post-ist theory binds it to the mainstream and official culture in China and endows it with a conservative complexion in spite of its radical origins (1994, 17–18). Although Chinese post-ist theory may seem to be related to the radical postcolonial criticism in the West, the difference between the two is far more significant than their superficial similarity. While the latter is characterized by its oppositional stance against the Western mainstream culture in which it is situated, the former does not have such an oppositional function with regard to its own mainstream culture. On the contrary, Chinese post-ist theory conforms itself to and reinforces the Chinese mainstream culture, especially its prevalent patriotic-nationalist propaganda and ideology. The assertive nationalist feeling that is central to Chinese post-ist theory informs much of its attack on the May Fourth Movement. Although the May Fourth Movement was basically a patriotic movement, the nationalism that evolved from its tradition is essentially anti-mainstream. By contrast, the 1990s post-ist nationalist sentiment is pro-mainstream.

Chinese post-ist theorists have little interest in Chinese values (such as the Confucian harmony and humanity) or Asian values (respect for authority, strong family ties, frugality, hard work, saving, and sacrifice, etc.), which appeal to many cultural traditionalists. They are primarily concerned with Chineseness, which is often constructed from primordial qualities such as language, ethnicity, ancestry, indigenous life, and empirically conceived history and identity. What makes Chinese post-ist theory conservative in China today, as Lei Yi analyzes in his article, "What Is Conservatism? Who Opposes Democracy" (1997), is its repudiation of basic democratic ideals and values of social change that were introduced by the May Fourth Movement and its denigration of the May Fourth Movement as a dangerous initiator of radicalism in modern China. Proponents of Chinese post-ist theory, such as Zhang Yiwu (1994a, 1995a) and Zhang Kuan (1995b, 1996), assail democracy as an empty and hypocritical ideal of Western liberalism; they accuse pro-enlightenment thinking of generating the social chaos of the Cultural Revolution and the 1989 pro-democracy movement; and they disparage China's modernity project as subjugation to Western hegemony. By inculcating a nihilistic and cynical attitude toward democratic change, citizen enlightenment, and social modernization, post-ist theorists reduce the substantial critical agenda to cultural dilettantism and political quietism.

Wang Hui calls into question the political implication of Chinese post-ist theory, especially its posture on the issue of enlightenment. The post-ist anti-enlightenment stance poses as deconstruction of the arrogant discourse of modernity. According to most post-ist theorists, enlightenment represents nothing more than the arrogance of Western influenced intellectuals, and, as a project of social change, it is no longer relevant to China's reality today. Wang Hui challenges this reality claim by post-ist theorists: "Ridiculing enlightenment in China, [post-ist theorists] declare that enlightenment as a historical process and social practice is out of date because we have already entered a 'postmodern' society of commodified mass culture and commercialization" (1997, 142–43). The post-ist total denigration of enlightenment, Wang Hui contends, is ahistorical, because it ignores the historical conditions that have attracted generations of Chinese intellectuals to the ideal of enlightenment. Instead of being intellectual arrogance itself, enlightenment in China is a limits-of-reason tradition. Arrogance is more justly ascribed to political authorities presuming to tell individuals how to think than intellectuals practicing independent thinking. Although many of China's political disasters came after the enlightenment, they had other causes than the enlightenment's alleged success. They may even have resulted from the failure of enlightenment to take root. The post-ist theory calls on people to be emancipated from enlightenment, but it has no positive vision of what is to be brought into existence in the post-enlightenment age.

New Social Evolutionist Thinking

Enlightenment was a central ideal of Chinese cultural criticism in the 1980s, but it has become a major target of neoconservative disparagement in the 1990s. Even some previous pro-enlightenment intellectuals, such as Li Zehou and Wang Yuanhua, have begun to retreat from their former position and have adopted an evolutionist attitude toward social change. Basically working within the Marxist frame, these intellectuals played an important role in the 1980s enlightenment movement. Their reflections on the relationship between politics and literature, on Chinese history, on the role of Chinese intellectuals, and on human subjectivity, needs, and potential appealed to a wide range of people who were disappointed by orthodox Marxism. These pro-enlightenment intellectuals were outspoken about the importance of critical initiatives and were reluctant to wait for objective conditions spontaneously to produce social change. But they have changed to an antiradical tone after 1989, arguing for a realistic and gradualistic approach to social change and warning against a premature lunge toward social and political democratization. According to them, democratic change depends on objective economic conditions, and, unless it is made in an evolutionary way that is tolerable to the existing political authority, it will produce nothing short of social chaos and cultural rupture (Wang Yuanhua 1993, 1995c; Li Zehou 1994, 1995).

In his writings in the 1990s Li Zehou has repeatedly expressed his worry about radical social change. In an attempt to discredit radicalism Li Zehou contrasts "violent revolution," which is shorthand for radicalism, to "peaceful reform," which he poses as the ideal of conservatism. Such a contrast calls into question why anyone of goodwill could ever advocate the former alternative.[5] Basing his criticism of radicalism on a categorical rejection of revolution, Li proclaims:

> I believe the 1911 Revolution was a bad one. It was caused by radical thinking. Although the monarchical system of the Qing Dynasty was rotten, it still had its value as a political system. It would be much better to pursue moderate change [than to stage a revolution]. The reform plan suggested by Constitutionalists would have been more efficient [than the revolution] to compel the system to modernize and save the nation. The revolution messed it up by seeking total change and the result was prolonged fightings among warlords. We have had endless revolutions ever since the 1911 Revolution— "Second Revolution" [led by Sun Yat-sen against Yuan Shikai, 1913], "Defending the Country" [*huguo,* the military campaign against Yuan Shikai led by General Cai E and others, December 1915–June 1916], "Defending the Constitution" [*hufa,* the military

campaign against Northern warlords, led by Sun Yat-sen, July 1917–May 1918], "Northern Expedition," the 1949 revolution, and Mao's continuous revolution. "Revolution" is an honorable word even today, while "reform" is still a bad word. We must reverse the order and make it clear that "revolution" does not have to be a good thing in China. (Li Zehou and Wang Desheng 1994, 71)

By recontextualizing the 1911 revolution in a revolution-versus-reform framework, Li obscures its original appeal and multiplicity of differentiations, such as Han and Manchu nationalities, monarchy and the republic, feudal and modern political cultures, etc. Even if revolution is about vast and rapid change, men who are equally convinced that revolutionary changes are urgently needed can differ sharply about priorities and directions. In the case of the 1911 revolution some wanted greater emphasis placed on certain social and economic goals; some cared little if at all about anything other than driving the Manchus from power. Some wanted a republic, and some did not. In the case of the 1949 revolution some wanted to initiate democratic politics; some wanted to seek power for Communists and revenge on Nationalists; some wanted to have a share in the newly acquired state power, caring little about what kind of power it was. The list of differences is almost endless. Critical thinking of either the 1911 or the 1949 revolution would have entailed the obligation not to embrace or reject the revolutionary program itself but, rather, to examine the underlying social, political, and cultural issues and to ensure the right kind of social changes by clarifying its basic values. From such a critical perspective what many revolutionary radicals have lost is not their way in the revolutionary labyrinth but their original commitment to democratic values. Li Zehou is hesitant to go back to these basic values; instead, he is hopeful that conservatism can do what radicalism cannot do in China.

Revolution is a central issue raised by Li Zehou and Liu Zaifu in their coauthored *Farewell to Revolution: Reflection on Twentieth-Century China* (1995). This work continues the thesis of "national salvation suppresses enlightenment" advanced by Li Zehou (1986, 236–80) in the 1980s, which contends that the inherent defect of Chinese revolutions is the lack of an enlightenment dimension. What is ironic about Li Zehou's reiteration of the revolution thesis in the 1990s is the shift in emphasis from a call for enlightenment to an attack on radicalism. The two authors of *Farewell to Revolution* delineate a four-stage agenda for

China's modernization: economic development, personal freedom, social justice, and democratic reform.[6] They establish economic development as a fundamental condition of any other form of social change. By arguing for putting economic development before the other three stages, the authors unwittingly retreat from their pro-enlightenment position in the 1980s, prioritizing national interest over enlightenment ideals of freedom, justice, and democracy. This economic determinism, as a critic of Li Zehou's antirevolution argument, Gu Xin, suggests, is a form of "historical determinism," which contradicts Li's own emphasis on "human subjectivity" and "historical contingency" in the 1980s (1996, 88). The change in thinking of Li Zehou and his like-minded peers from their pro-enlightenment position in the 1980s to a meek social evolutionism in the 1990s should not be seen simply as a conservative gesture of endorsing the official policy of delaying democracy in China. This change can be more properly understood as a tension-ridden effort to reconcile their frustrated intellectual ideal with reality—that is, to keep alive the ideal of personal freedom, social justice, and democracy by suspending it as an untimely and vulnerable agenda of social change.

The Pseudo-Binary of Conservatism versus Radicalism

It is important to recognize that pointing out the realistic thinking of various forms of new cultural conservatism does not deny that fundamental changes have indeed taken place in China's social and political reality. If it were not for the new reality in China, antiradicalism might be set aside as irrelevant. The antiradical rhetoric of neoconservative arguments should be seen, therefore, not so much in terms of its relevance as an explanation of the need for intellectual moderate thinking but as an ideology integral to post-1989 reality. The distinction between radicalism and conservatism thus becomes secondary to an analysis of the origins and the dynamics of antiradicalism and political realism.

The pseudo-binary of conservatism versus radicalism disguises more substantial differences in Chinese society, especially different attitudes toward the authoritarian status quo and toward democracy as a means and a goal of changing this status quo. Radical/conservative debate is far from being a focused one in China's political condition, "because [the] supposed rival of [neoconservative viewpoint]—liberal democratic views—has been silenced" (Chen Feng 1997, 592). In the absence of a democratic principle of distinction much of the current rhetoric of antiradicalism has skewed the mangled usage of neoconservatism into inanity. Some use this term to explain the logic of the evolution from radicalism to antiradicalism (Chen Xiaoming 1994a). Some use it to designate the fall of literary avant-gardism or pure intellectual inquiry under the influence of mass culture (Zhao Yiheng 1995). Some assert that neoconservatism represents a new awareness of China's history and identity, which was distorted by the 1980s frenzy of Westernization-modernization (Zhang Fa, Zhang Yiwu, and Wang Yichuan 1994). Some insist that neoconservatism offers a better name than anything else for intellectual criticism that "supports a market economy" and "does not give up hope for democracy" (Tao Dongfeng 1996b). Some interpret neoconservatism as a new intellectual strategy in the 1990s that, as far as its "critical attitude" is concerned, is not so different from the radical social and political criticism of the 1980s (Li Zehou and Wang Desheng 1994, 70).

When open and explicit criticism of the status quo and its dominant ideology—that is what intellectual radicalism is usually associated with—is prohibited, the conventional distinction between radicalism and conservatism loses much of its transparency. Under such circumstances a forced radical-conservative distinction serves only to obscure subtle shades of intellectual-political coloring. It is excessively simplistic to suggest that intellectuals living in a repressive environment can still choose to be a radical or a conservative. The radical-conservative distinction becomes impossible where everyday intellectual activity has to combine calculated submission, a low ideological profile, and deliberate evasiveness on politically sensitive topics. As one Chinese critic observes, people in China actually do not live by the choice of conservatism or radicalism but, rather, in "the narrow cultural space between conservatism and radicalism." They often find that "radicalism is convincing but not pleasing, conservatism is pleasing but not convincing" (Ji Guangmao 1995, 19).

New cultural conservatism resonates with certain tendencies and attitudes of post-1989 official ideology. In both there is a view of democracy as unsuitable and impractical in China today, a denigration of liberal values as being the products of "Westernization," a narrowing of the definition of political stability to the absence of dissent, and an adherence to certain forms of cultural nationalism. This may partly explain why certain new conservative views are favored in official forums. New cultural conservatism and official ideology are not always compatible, however, in terms of theoretical origins, discursive orientations, or political interests. Li Zehou's neoconservative position on revolution, for example, has become a major target of criticism of many Marxist critics who want to defend the legitimacy of revolution, especially the Communist Revolution. Fang Keli, director of the graduate program of the China's Academy of Social Science, questions the "ideological intention" of Li's argument against revolution and accuses it of subverting Marxist ideology and the regime that rules in its name (1995, 62). Fang's view is widely shared among orthodox theorists (Ai Nong 1996; Sha Jiansun 1996; Jin Chongzhi, Hu Shengwu, and Lin Huaguo 1996; Gong Shuduo 1996; Xing Bensi 1996).

Another notable example of the rivalry-complicity relationship between new cultural conservatism and official ideology can be found in the official attitude toward traditional Chinese culture. Cultural traditionalists' emphasis on Chinese tradition and culture in thinking of contemporary change makes them potential new fellow travelers of the Party in post-1989 circumstances. After the Tiananmen incident and facing international accusation, the Party has increased its efforts to acquire nationalist authority and to present itself as the sole legitimate representative of national history, identity, and cultural ethos. This is why elements of the Party's propaganda apparatus warmly endorsed the fever of Chinese studies when it emerged in 1993. Yet insistence on the ultimate authority of Chinese tradition and culture may potentially threaten the authority of the orthodox revolutionary tradition because the latter also grounds its validity in the infallibility of Marxism, which does not have national origins and therefore can be defined as alien to, and unwelcome in, the Chinese tradition. This explains why the fever of Chinese studies and its professed neoconservatism later became a target of repeated official and semiofficial assaults. The rivalry-complicity relations between the old and new traditions have greatly complicated the attitude toward tradition as a conventional measure of the radical or conservative distinction in China.[7]

Radicalism, Conservatism, and Intellectual Activism

Radical-conservative pairing may not help us to chart accurately the intellectual field of the 1980s and 1990s, but it does provide an incentive to do so. Moreover, it points out a curiosity that needs explaining: at the same time that rhetorical assaults on radicalism are on the rise, there is an embarrassing absence of radical thinking and a forced silence of radical voices in the intellectual arena. Although neoconservatives insist that

Chinese intellectuals in the 1990s have advanced sufficiently to reject radicalism by separating their action and values from politics, it is political conditions that make up the deeper background to this radical-conservative pairing; this goes partway toward explaining both the rise of neoconservatism and the reasons why at another level radicalism remains compelling.

Current controversies over radicalism and conservatism can give us an inkling of the usage of these terms within the Chinese context. The expressions of antiradicalism in China entail a number of basic issues that Chinese cultural criticism is concerned with. These issues include the process of change, its desirable speed and cultural resources, modernization and progress, the relationship between politics and cultural activities, and the role of intellectuals, among others. Any effort at critical analyses of these issues will be confused if the analyst forgets that these are not new issues but were in fact constituted at the turn of this century. The historical dimension of the analysis is particularly indispensable because Chinese radicalism itself is a modern phenomenon. As an intellectual mode or political attitude, radicalism itself was formed at the same time as those aforementioned issues took recognizable shape.

Discussing the birth of modern Chinese radicalism, which prepared for and played a big role in the Revolution of 1911, Michael Gasster proposes to consider Chinese *radicalism* alongside other controversial terms, such as *moderate, revolution, modernization,* and *intellectuals* (1969, xx). Radicalism, in regard to promoting change, is a modern phenomenon, one unknown in China until the period 1895–1905. The urgency of change in modern China, as Gasster notes, was unique for being propelled by foreign might and guided by foreign influence:

> Change in earlier periods may have rivaled the speed of recent change, and there may have been a time (such as Ch'in-Han) when China shifted direction as sharply, but never before had change in China been so fast, so sharp, and at the same time so much directed toward borrowing from foreigners as in the last century. It is the concurrence of all three factors—speed of change, sharpness of change, and the degree of foreign influence—that is unprecedented in Chinese history. (xix)

Of the three factors of change mentioned by Gasster, the degree of foreign influence—or, by implication, what role Chinese resources can play in national reconstruction—is crucially important. The issue of change in China has ever since inevitably been tied to China's relations to the West.

If change in China is frequently informed by the country's awareness of its lagging behind modern Western countries, it was also informed simultaneously by two different tropes of transformation, "modernization" and "revolution." The needs of modernization and the needs of revolution have not been so incongruent as to be incompatible. Yet there exists profound conflict and tension between these two different kinds of needs. Not all Chinese revolutionaries were modernizers, and not all Chinese modernizers were revolutionaries. The disputes between generations of revolutionaries and modernizers have raised questions about the *nature* of revolution and the relation between revolution and modernization. In a revolutionary age change tends to be rapid, deep, and extensive. But these characteristics can be even more pronounced in late-modernizing societies. In their drive to modernize many third-world societies are trying to compress centuries into decades. Modernization in these societies tends to be as radical as revolution.

It is not in change per se but the purposes, priorities, principles, and basic values with which change is pursued and justified that we must look for the differences between modernization and revolution and, indeed, between different shadings of radicalism, modernization, or revolutionary changes. In our consideration of radicalism, in particular, we are concerned not only with its attitude toward change (whether or not it welcomes change, how fast the change should occur, etc.) but with other factors as well. We need to specify the sensibilities and styles of thought that a radical movement assumes as a means of mobilizing its emotional energy—whether its goal is to release individual potential or to establish some binding collective will. We need to explain the ethical and normative posture that movement adopts as a means of negating prevailing sentiments that sustain the existing order—whether to assert freedom and equality or to establish another absolute authority or order. We need also to analyze the historical phenomena that account for the counter-concepts that radical thinkers attempt to overcome. The problem of context or the situation of change is intractable and not profitably resolved by a hasty resort to a prescribed formula of radicalism.

Neither the change from the 1980s to the 1990s nor the different intellectual positions of today can be reduced to the difference between radicalism and conservatism. The issue at stake is not whether radicalism or conservatism is preferable as a categorical ethical stance or as a generally reliable guidance of intellectual action but, rather, how to preserve the dynamic of social critique and intellectual activism and prevent it from being abstracted into a doctrine. The ideal of intellectual activism implies a certain set of democratic values: justice, freedom, equality, and critical reason. The values of intellectual activism derive neither from the virtues of its practitioners nor from the finger-wagging codes of conduct by which every profession reminds itself to be good. The values have grown out of the practice of intellectual activism itself, because they are the inescapable conditions for its practice. These democratic values emphasize a sensitivity to the human significance in society, a vital concern with the human condition, intellectual independence, open-mindedness, and broad vision.

Contemporary Chinese intellectual activism can be traced back to the May Fourth Movement, although it is certainly not everything about that movement. The humanistic impulse compelled many intellectuals of the May Fourth Movement and their heirs in the 1980s to reveal, resist, and root out various forms of oppression and exploitation of humans by humans and to be committed as much as possible to improving the conditions under which people live. This tradition of intellectual activism nourishes critical motivation in terms of human needs, not grandiose political programs. Unlike violent, party-oriented revolution, intellectual activism encourages selective commitments, rather than consecration of a totalitarian faith. Criticism committed to seeing through social and cultural facades, unmasking and debunking existing systems, is an important feature of intellectual radicalism in China.

Intellectual activism calls into question not only the familiar social and cultural landscape that is the target of cultural criticism but also the subject of critical activity. Intellectual criticism probes the roots of critics' personal situations and prompts them toward an ongoing reflection on the dilemma of their own oppositional engagement—the position of the knower, the assumptions that govern the shape of his discourse, that provide certain unexamined suppositions about the world, about intellectual activities, and about the relation between intellectual activities and the world. Tom Hayden describes this relentless nature of intellectual activism as a kind of radicalism that "involves penetration of a social problem to its roots" and "finds no rest in conclusions; answers are seen as provisional, to be discarded in the face of new evidence or changed conditions" (1967, 6).

Humanistic, critical, and reflexive commitments serve to measure the differences between two kinds of radicalism in China: intellectual radicalism and enforced radicalism, with their respective characteristic expressions of "critique" and "revolution." They do not have to be mutually exclusive, though their long-term alliance has been proven unlikely in China. The organized radicalism of revolution has frequently attracted radical intellectuals and lured intellectual radicalism to join forces with it. Yet revolution has always treated individual persons as cellular parts and has in the end alienated critical intellectuals. In all of China's officially organized radical campaigns after 1949—the Anti-Rightist Campaign, the Great Leap Forward, the repeated campaigns of class struggle, and the Cultural Revolution—revolution is determined to turn the intellectuals, like the rest of the society, into mere symbols of the faceless "people" or "members" in the grandiose revolutionary cause. As individuals, intellectuals have no choice but to be fixed in the revolutionary machine and to become tools to implement its grand narratives.

To understand how all the revolutions of the twentieth century—communist, socialist, nationalist—have been able to use in one way or another the concept of revolutionary cause, we must examine some peculiarities of its structure. First of all, the revolutionary cause bears testimony to the instrumental rationality, which leads to a new structure of domination. It is within this configuration that Adorno and Horkheimer's reconstruction of the historical dialect of reason is relevant. Revolutionary rationality originated as the tool for mastery of man's national, social, and political environment, but, being intimately connected with self-renunciation, it has turned "against the thinking subject himself" (Horkheimer and Adorno 1972, 26). Second, the revolutionary cause is the will of an enforced community. It is not the will of all or the will of the majority or the consensus of interacting wills of groups and individuals but, rather, the will that all would share if they knew what was really good for them. This leads to the third feature of the revolutionary cause: it serves as a historical justification of a particularly repressive form of enlightenment, one that curtails and tames rather than empowers and liberates its objects of education. If separated from democracy, intellectual radicalism could itself become a form of enforced enlightenment. The rationale of the revolutionary cause forbids persons from actually being individual human beings, free thinking and uncontrolled. There is no place in the conspectus of the revolutionary cause for intellectual radicalism because intellectual radicalism must exist as resistance to unquestioning obedience.

Democratic intellectual radicalism seeks change through noncoercive reasoning, while the enforced radicalism of the revolutionary cause relies on violence as the chief agent of political transformation. The conflict between democratic intellectual radicalism and enforced radicalism accounts for much of the tension between modernization and revolution and between democracy and revolution in China. Michael Gasster's observation on the 1911 Nationalist Revolution applies equally well to the 1949 Communist Revolution. In both instances the process by which radical ideas so swiftly gained ascendancy in Chinese thought and politics raises questions about the relationships between democracy and revolution and between revolution and modernization. We can even say that, given the vast proportions of these revolutions, at their early stages, the needs of revolution and the needs of democracy may have temporarily crossed. Yet,

> when the changes sought are so great and the hatred generated so intense, and when violence is relied upon as the chief agent of political change by the very same leaders who preach democratic ideals, it proves impossible simultaneously to create a belief in orderly processes, the rule of law, a legal and loyal opposition, peaceful transference of power, and similar accoutrement of popular rule. Furthermore, violent revolutions attract men with very different motives and aspirations, not only men whose long-range goals preclude postrevolutionary cooperation but men who seek only personal aggrandizement and adventure. The Chinese revolution attracted many who subverted its principles, and even among its most prominent leaders the disagreements were substantial enough to interfere with the revolution itself. (Gasster 1969, 245)

Because of its violent nature, life-and-death struggle, and zero-sum strategy, it would be unreasonable to expect revolution to breed "a more noble or more determined and conscious effort than [its leaders] made to understand the principles of democracy and plan a transition to a democratic form of government" (Gasster 1969, 246). Successful modernization by means of revolution may be unlikely for similar reasons. Many liberal-minded Chinese intellectuals have believed that modernization should include democracy. Not all modern societies are democratic, of course, but, as the focus of the 1980s cultural criticism shows, these intellectuals would not have considered an undemocratic China a truly modern China.

The fundamental differences on issues of democracy and modernization, which defined the contest over concepts of political and social reform in the 1980s, make it highly improper to label the decade as a homogeneously radical one. Although it may not be improper to view the critical intellectuals' quest for democracy as radical, it is highly questionable to see the official opposition to democracy as equally radical. Even with a careful differentiation between intellectual radicalism and enforced radicalism, it still could be misleading and confusing to define radicalism as the absolute opposite of conservatism. In fact, although the official drive for technical and economic modernization is a form of enforced radicalism, it is very different from the enforced radicalism of the Communist Revolution, because the rebel radicals before 1949 had long been power holders by the 1980s. So far as power and status are concerned, the Communist power holders have more at stake to conserve than to risk by wholeheartedly embracing fundamental change. At least in their attitude toward democratic change in China, they are new conservatives more than new radicals.

The dread of a democratic principle for measuring ideological positions characterizes much of the antiradical and neoconservative rhetoric in the 1990s and reflects the crippling situation and the impasse in which neoconservative thinking is caught. However different various attempts at defining and justifying neoconservatism may be, the rhetoric is bound, from the beginning, with a disillusionment with and suspicion of radicalism understood as a dangerous form of intellectual activism that has become impossible in China in the 1990s. The current debates turn not only on issues of tradition, modernization, and national identity but also on questions of labeling, the outcome depending to a considerable degree on the success with which a neoconservative is able to depict the other, especially the 1980s intellectual activism and its predecessor, the May Fourth Movement, as "intemperate," "frantic," or "irrational." Hence, neoconservatism, like other creeds in fashion, is not a program but a language. It survives because it is a convenient substitute for real political choice, which is almost nonexistent in China. The "choice" between radicalism and conservatism is a matter not of proposing substantial social change but of theorizing intellectuals' temperament or state of mind. Yet most of those who use the radical-conservative dichotomy insist on talking as if it were a matter of intellectual action as well, as if it reflected the intellectuals' available political choices. The actual differences between the two attitudinal positions, in any case, are hardly clear-cut; but the act of "choosing" encourages people to exaggerate them and, in particular, to exaggerate the freedom of intellectual-political positioning in post-1989 China.

Democracy in the Postsocialist-Postcolonial Condition

Politically related terminology is a treacherous form of intellectual statement, and it is, as we have seen in the case of radicalism or conservatism, all the more so in China not only because correctly defining social and cultural phenomena is intrinsically difficult but also because the act of naming is restricted by existing political conditions. When we reflect on the historical specificity of democracy in China using *postcolonial* and *postsocialist* as designative and analytical terms, we have to encounter exactly the same conceptual precariousness. In the notion of the post-colonial as a concept of the present conjuncture of world history the notion's limits and scope of critical application come into view. The concept of a conjunctural view of world history is illustrated in Louis Althusser's elaboration of the Marxist view of history as alternative to either the "everyday" (empiricist) concept of history or the historical logic of Hegelianism. The conjunctural concept of history is constructed "on the basis of the Marxist conception of the social totality." Such a conjunctural view of history is different from the Hegelian "expressive totality" in that it is a whole of "complex structural unity," the level or instances of which are "articulated with one another according to specific determinations, fixed in the last instance by the level or instance of the economy" (Althusser and Balibar 1970, 97).

Such a contemporary structure of world history is termed by Masao Miyoshi, for instance, as "transnational corporatism," in the form of which, even in the absence of administrative and occupational colonialism, "colonialism is even more active" and "transformation and persistence in the neocolonial practice of displacement and ascendency" are taking place (1991, 728). In a similar vein Gayatri Spivak asserts that "postcoloniality" is "precisely the trajectory which has brought us to the planetary transnational capitalism, the break-up of space-based imperialisms" (1990a, 94). The problem we face now is how to understand today's global configuration of power and culture that is both similar to and different from the historical metropolitan-colonial paradigm.

Spivak approaches the problem by evoking the Marxian conception of the totality of today's world system (1990a, 94–95). She justifies the postcolonial as a category for a conjunctural analysis of what she calls "the planetary capitalism" because "even this trajectory of non-metro-politan transnational capitalism is a postcolonial phenomenon." The notion of postcoloniality comes to provide a standpoint for historical totalization. What is at stake in this notion is Western capitalism, which was born out of European colonialism and which, since the heydays of colonialism, has been the medium for the development of a specific world system and world history. World history, as Marx reminds us, "has not always existed; history as world history [is] a result" (1973, 109), and it is a result, primarily, of capitalism. As a concept of the present conjuncture of world history, the postcolonial is not just a question of periodization but, rather, a mode of present experience of irrevocable loss of precolonial innocence. Postcolonial critics, as Edward Said sees it, are "oppositional critics, not only in their work about the past, but also in the conclusions their work pulls into the present" (1988, ix).

The postcolonial, of course, is not the only categorical designation of the contemporary global conjuncture of capitalism. If the postcolonial is such a designation, it is such from the third-world perspective. From the first-world perspective the current historical conjuncture of global capitalism is often represented as the postmodern. The postmodern designates the first-world view of the categorical constellation of global capitalism, both in cultural and political-economical terms. Moreover, as Simon During points out, postmodernism is itself "a concomitant of consumer capitalism, which itself primarily generates demand (desire), in order to produce and sell commodities with no 'natural' use-value." *Concomitance* needs to be further defined in this context. As During explains, "if not merely a reflection of late capitalism, postmodernism remains a mode which functions in its service, operating against the last sites of bourgeois resistance to capitalism: high culture and critique." Postmodernism envisions its world as fragmented or deterritorialized; the venerable notions of center, periphery, margins, no longer wield their influence in the postmodern thought. Paradoxically, it is precisely the postmodernist notion of "decentering" that becomes the foundation of a first-world-centered or Western-centered conception of totalizing global configuration:

Modern consumer capitalism is not in itself a fragmented apparatus. It is global, it moves from the neo-colonial centres outward, blanketing the world. Nothing more totalising than its erasure of cultural difference, nothing more appropriative than what Jameson calls its logic may be imagined. So how must one think of the decentring it achieves? As a decentring from *within* a centre so expanded, so powerful, that it has no other, no outside by which it can be identified as a centre. Lyotard thinks of the discursive fragmentation of the "postmodern condition" as a breakdown, as apotheosis of negativity; but it can also be thought of as the apotheosis of cultural confidence and of economic strength. Power has become so centered, so organised that it no longer needs notions of organic totality. (During 1985, 368)

By contrast, the postcolonial helps form an alternative perspective on the global structure that will recognize postmodernism not as decentered but as centered, and Western-centered at that. It wishes to name and disclaim Western-centered postmodernism as derivative of, and heir to, colonialism in the present. And it does so by accepting and using those practices and concepts that such postmodernism most strenuously denies, in particular history, representation, and center/periphery and dominator/dominated contrasts. The postcolonial expresses a third-world sense of historical conjuncture defined not in terms of the first-world self-representation but in terms of the third world itself. As During remarks, the postcolonial as a third-world self-representation "operates in modes similar to what Derrida in his early work on Husserl called 'pure auto-affection': 'the operation of hearing oneself speak'" (1985, 369).

The need and operation of hearing oneself speak as a third-world country are beset with complications and confusion in China, for China derives its identity not just from its third-world status but from its commitment to socialism. Here we need to make a distinction between socialism as a governmental project and socialism as an ideology in the sense of apologia for that project. These two aspects of socialism used to be more or less integrally combined under Mao, but they have increasingly drifted apart as the country's economy shifts drastically in the capitalist direction and becomes more and more imbricated in the global system of capitalism. This change has been interpreted as signaling the end of socialism and the superiority of capitalism. The most triumphalist version of this representation of change incorporates it into the global story of the End of History, according to which the greater part of humanity have finally come to realize that the capitalist order is the only feasible economic ideal and the capitalist open-market economy will automatically lead to democracy.

The End of History is an easy target, and I will not spend time on it except to note that it is little more than a pretentious elaboration on the political implication of global capitalism and the alleged "death of socialism" in China. Chinese socialism represents no simple counter-concept of capitalism, being originally founded on a combination of asceticism, egalitarianism, and statism. Not all of these three key elements have remained intact and relevant in the process of China's incorporation into the post–Cold War global economic order, a process that has brought profound changes in former Chinese socialist values. The substantial change of Chinese socialism makes it necessary to replace the contrast of socialism and capitalism with a more appropriate framework of global constellation in our understanding of China's third-world position.

Chinese socialism used to be marked by its asceticism. Asceticism had as its central value the idealization of the poor, the propertyless, or the so-called spirit of the poor (*qiong bangzi jingshen*). This idealization of poverty was crystalized in the unwritten dictum "the poorer the more glorious" (*yu qiong yu guangrong*). The social objective, in its ascetic guise, did not mean simply the alleviation of the pressing need of the poor; it also represented a profound suspicion of wealth. Egalitarianism used to be another element of Chinese socialism. Of course, this does not mean everyone was really equal to everyone else. The socialist order was grounded on two basic models of stratification—class designations and professional ranks (Kraus 1981, chap. 2). Egalitarianism in Chinese socialism was used in a limited sense, primarily meaning equality of property. But it contributed more than any other element of Chinese socialism to appealing to the general populace and proving socialism's moral superiority to capitalism. The egalitarian practices used to include treating the wealth of the nation as common property that could supply the needs of the people; removing food and other essentials like housing from the sphere of free trade; instituting laws to guarantee job security, social insurance, compensation for victims of misfortune, infirmity, old age; and so on. When egalitarian values are jeopardized, socialism becomes empty rhetoric and the butt of cynicism. The Party's new policy of encouraging a few people to become rich first by whatever means they have and withdrawing the governmental responsibility for job security and social welfare, while tightening control over media, public opinion, and political speech, has destroyed the ties that united the original elements of Chinese socialism.[8] Of the three major elements statism is the only one that remains.

The statist dimension of Chinese socialism expresses itself in the belief that socialism is desirable because it is the only valid road to national wealth and power. The ascetic and egalitarian dimensions of Chinese socialism, which are attached to the idea of common people, were in practice determined by and subordinate to the statist goal. Socialism is the goal the Party introduces to the people for their own good. Society, ironically, is a social construct. It does not exist before the ideal of the socialist objective. Society must be regulated by its connection with the state through one-party leadership. Society must be administrated society. Such a view of society implies mistrust of "the people"—suspicious of their lack of sacrifice, lack of assertiveness, and political consciousness. What is needed is a vanguard party—courageous, clear-sighted, self-sacrificing, standing for moral values and probity, which would usher in an epoch of equality and would fight corruption, bureaucracy, and abuse of power. This could even, in a semantic sleight of hand, be squared with the idea of "socialist democracy," which is interpreted as the process of restituting what has been extracted from the poor by the rich, a process of elevating the poor, the "common people." Socialist democracy is thus pictured as gaining domination by the people over "the people's enemy," as "the people's democratic dictatorship." Central to the statist view of socialism is the idea not just of society but of a Party-run society, because for the administration of society only the tightly organized Party can exhibit the promptness of decision, unity of command, and strictness of discipline typical of the administrative spirit.

The disintegration of the original components of Chinese socialism makes it necessary for us to seek an alternative to the framework of socialism. I have suggested in chapter 1, in my discussion of the post-1989 legitimacy crisis, that we consider using a framework that might be called postsocialist. In my use *postsocialism* refers to the demise and disintegration of the socialist vision and its becoming something different, rather than a promising new stage or new model of socialist project. Here I would like to move one step further and suggest that we use the postsocialist as a complement to the postcolonial in order to understand the historical conjuncture of contemporary China.

The notion of postsocialism, as it is used by either Arif Dirlik or Paul G. Pickowicz, relates in one way or another to the notion of postmodernism rather than to that of the postcolonial. As Dirlik himself explains:

My use of "postsocialism" is inspired by an analogous term that has acquired currency in recent years in cultural studies, postmodernism. J. F. Lyotard has described as the prominent feature of postmodernism an "incredulity towards metanarratives." I would suggest by analogy that the characteristic of socialism at present is a loss of faith in socialism as a social and political metatheory with a coherent present and a certain future. (1989, 374)

In Dirlik's usage Chinese postsocialism is socialism in the postmodern present, when socialism with Chinese characteristics asserts incredulity toward the metanarratives of socialism "envisioned in the classical texts of socialism—Marxist, anarchist, or otherwise" (374).

Pickowicz adopts the notion of postsocialism as an alternative category to socialism, modernism, and postmodernism in order to provide a more adequate framework for understanding and analyzing "the dominant tendencies in mainland Chinese culture in the 1980s" (1994, 59). Although Pickowicz provides a definition of *postsocialism* that is different from that of Dirlik's, like Dirlik, he also recognizes a somewhat analogous relationship between postmodernism and postsocialism: "Postsocialism, the ideological counterpart of postmodernism, refers to a cultural crisis that is unique to societies that have undergone decades of Leninist-Stalinist (i.e., what I call traditional socialist) development" (80). Just as postmodernism underscores the crises of history, reason, and subjectivity inherited in modernism, so does postsocialism reveal the anomies rooted deeply in the Leninist-Stalinist system and the single-party dictatorship of socialism.[9] The analogous relationship between postsocialism and postmodernism, illuminating as it is, does not tell us sufficiently about China's particular postsocialist condition unless it takes into consideration China's semicolonial experience and the special postcolonial problems China faces regarding modernization, socialist project, national independence, and development. What is absent from the analogous relationship between postsocialism and postmodernism is the symbiotic context of Chinese socialism and China's third-world status.

Without fully considering China's third-world status, the concept of postsocialism alone cannot sufficiently illustrate the discrepancy between socialism and democracy in China. From the turn of the century socialism has been employed as a political project for decolonizing and empowering China in the face of intrusion and interference by foreign, especial Western powers. In its own way socialism has been China's route to modernization. Projects of socialism and modernization have managed an uneasy cooperation, a coordination that breaks down when specific issues highlight the consequences in priorities and strategies of their frequently incompatible fundamental analyses of Chinese society. Modernization, especially when it calls for democratization, has been resisted when these fundamental differences have become central to political strategy. The respective emphases on the primacy of democracy or the Leninist party's monopoly on power have been the major cause of the profound postsocialist legitimacy crisis, which is characterized by the general sense that socialist ideology that has justified the single-party hegemony for decades is inherently incapable of providing the social vision necessary for reform in the direction of democracy. The consideration of the postsocialist crisis will not be sufficient if it does not also include consideration of possible different responses to this crisis. As Pickowicz observes: "Postsocialism, in brief, involves a massive loss of faith. Some of the alienation, frustration, and anger it engenders leads to a politically healthy search for alternatives to traditional socialism, but some of that disaffection . . . produces self-destructive social and psychological behavior" (1994, 83). We can certainly regard the quest for democracy as a healthy form of search for an alternative to existing socialism. For this reason we must see the intellectuals' political apathy and avoidance of social intervention as self-destructive choices.

The concept of postsocialism does not suggest that socialism and democracy are inherently incompatible. And it certainly does not deny that even with the failure of existing socialist systems, socialism may still represent for many people a worthy alternative vision to the existing capitalist system, with all its domestic and international antidemocratic elements. Postsocialism, in the Chinese context, emphasizes the sober awareness of the shattered dream of socialist democracy that once served as a significant inspiration for revolutionary social change. The deterioration of socialism to its bare statist expression of single-party dictatorship has reduced socialism to a mere ideological disguise to suppress fundamental social and political problems that have become apparent after 1989. This makes it all the more important to differentiate socialism as a long-term outlook and project and socialism as an apologia for the absolute and demoralizing control of society by the party-state.

As a long-term outlook and project, Chinese socialism was once an example of what Samir Amin calls the "revolutions [that] entail delinking from the logic of worldwide capitalist expansion." Yet, as Amin implies, Chinese socialism fell short of the ideal of third-world democracy, because it relied on "'dictatorship of the proletariat' envisaged in the Marxist tradition." Its implementation of social change did not suppose "power based on 'national and popular' social hegemony that acknowledges a conflictual mix of aspirations of both a socialist and capitalist sort." Chinese socialism only "began to create the necessary conditions to eradicate the legacy of peripheralization produced by capitalism, by abandoning criteria of capitalist rationality and proceeding to internal social revolutions that had tremendous impact" (1991, 85). Although this rejection of capitalist peripheralization emphasized the socialism/capitalism contrast, it failed to produce a democracy better than the kind of liberal democracy in practice in capitalist countries.

There is no internal connection between socialism and democracy, just as there is no imminent, no internal, connection between liberalism and democracy. The connection had to be argued for, fought for, and the condition under which such connection was or is going to form becomes an essential part of our understanding of its historical dimension.[10] Amin suggests that a country's third-world status—especially when this status is defined in the "world system" of capitalism, which is different from capitalism as "a mode of production taken at its highest level of abstraction"—is often not congenial to democracy. Amin writes:

> If the third world countries have almost never seen their political systems develop in a genuinely democratic manner (on the lines of the developed capitalist countries of the West—since 1945 at least) this is neither an accident nor a holdover from their "traditional culture." Democracy here is incompatible with the demand of capitalist expansion. (1991, 85)

Although Amin is too hasty to conclude that "the absence of democracy from the periphery of the world capitalist system is *not* a residual of [a third-world country's] earlier eras," he is certainly right in perceiving that "international polarization inherent in [the capitalist expansion] brings in turn a manifold internal social polarizing: growing inequality in income distribution, widespread unemployment, marginalization, etc." (91; my emph.). The erosion of the egalitarian ideal of distributive socialism in post-1989 China, which has accelerated since the late 1980s, has greatly exacerbated various forms of gross inequality and deepened the crisis of democracy. New forms of undemocratic practices—hierarchy, domination, and repression—have added to the anguish of the old ones imbricated in statist socialism. Democratic postcolonial criticism, with its global view of domination and repression, must bring to the forefront these new undemocratic factors, since they have been either underestimated or ignored by most post-1989 forms of social and cultural criticism in China.

Democratic postcolonial criticism in China today must represent a new mode of experience informed by a new awareness that structural domination and repression cannot be fully apprehended either in the Manichaean terms of China versus the imperialist West or as a consequence of the continuing conflict between tradition and modernity. Democratic postcolonial criticism must point to a new locus of cultural politics. It must map out the territory of interpenetrated intranational and international domination and opposition and come up with feasible strategies for critical interference in it. Given China's economically dependent status in the world economy and its willful exploitation by transnational capital—not to mention the sub-transnational capital from Taiwan and Hong Kong, "the West" as an ideological and political presence asserts itself with such a density of indigenous institutions, discourses, and practices that its identity as "Western" is refracted and not always salient. In China today it is not the boot of imperialism that is felt as an identifiable weight upon one's neck. The pressure one feels compelled to resist is rather that of the nation-state, dominant social and political institutions, and oppressive policies of various kinds. No doubt, the activities of the nation-state are themselves related in complex ways to regional and global geopolitical trends, but it is the local face of this international phenomenon against which one is moved to fight. This is why third-world critics in China must not hesitate to insist that the political dimension of postcolonial cultural critique be expressed primarily in an engagement with repression and tyranny at home. Their major task is to expose the authoritarian parameters within which the governing elites employ anti-imperialist and anti-Western rhetoric to block domestic demands for democracy and human rights.

Decolonization in third-world countries does not bring emancipation automatically. As Edward Said points out, the great transformation of which Frantz Fanon spoke, that after liberation, nationalist consciousness must convert itself into a new social consciousness, has not often taken place. For democratic postcolonial criticism Fanon's observation still maps out a crucial step it needs to take, "because more dramatically and decisively than anyone . . . [Fanon] expresses the immense cultural shift from the terrain of nationalist independence to the theoretical domain of liberation" (1993, 208). This shift of critical consciousness cannot be realized until postcolonial critics focus their attention on those new states that are ideologically in thrall either to their former colonial masters or to the undemocratic practices of former imperial and colonial powers. The postcolonial critique has reached a point where it must learn to take more seriously the post-liberation oppressive systems in which many third-world people now live. These systems not only oppress in the way older colonial systems did—by openly legitimizing violence, domination, and repression. They also tap the first-world/third-world conflict and the colonial/anticolonial contrast to maintain social and political orders that are unjust, expropriatory, and violent in the name of national autonomy and anti-imperialism. And the result is often what Ashis Nandy calls the "uncomfortable" fact

> that the Third World societies usually maintain within their borders exactly the same violent, exploitative, ethnocidal systems which they confront in the larger world: the same center and periphery, the same myth that the sacrifices made by people in the short run will lead to the beatitude of development and scientific advancement in the long run, the same story of over-consuming elites fattening themselves to early death at the center, and starvation, victimhood and slow death at the periphery. (1983, xii)

The post-liberation (post-1949) record of democracy and human rights in China provides a realistic background for us to see how important it is to develop critical sensitivity to domestic problems in a new and authoritarian state. In the absence of such critical sensitivity the authoritarian state becomes all the more capable of using the official anti-imperialist and anti-Western stance to immunize itself from postcolonial critique or even make it its ideological ally.

To recognize the postcolonial dimension and quality of quest for democracy in China as a third-world country is to take into account both the history of Chinese democracy as a response to and consequence of Western impact and its never-ending move beyond the parameters of Western liberal democracy. The postcolonial cultural politics of democracy recognizes the inevitable presence of the West and the futility of seeking precolonial innocence. The modern West, as Ashis Nandy tells us, is less a geographical or temporal category than a psychological space: "The West is now everywhere, within the West and outside: in structures and in minds" (1983, xii). Once absorbed into the space of chronopolitics with the West and the conjuncture of world history with the West as its central figure, China cannot reclaim autonomy and seclusion as if its recent semicolonial past had never left a print on its history. In Masao Miyoshi's words, "once dragged out of their precolonial state, the indigenes of peripheries have to deal with the knowledge of the outside world, irrespective of their own wishes and inclinations" (1991, 730). The postcolonial quest for democracy in China must understand itself in terms of the present conjuncture of world history, that is, in terms of international centers, of a colonial past, and at the same time, in terms of China's particular kind of colonial past, of its own historicosocial formation in which its present struggle for democracy is located. Since the postcolonial effect is specific to each third-world country, Chinese intellectuals from a particular socialist background must rediscover the specificity of their experience, especially that of oppression and domination and of resistance and liberation in the postcolonial and postsocialist condition.

Notes

Introduction

1. The term *post-ist studies* was coined by Zhao Yiheng (1995, 1997).
2. See comments by Jonathan Arac (1997b, 273) on this point.
3. The same definition of Chinese postmodernity can be found in Zhang Fa 1997.
4. Issues of a constitutional ideal and the deficiencies of Chinese constitutional politics have recently been raised. See the special June 1998 issue of *Ershiyi shiji* (Twenty-first century) on constitutionalism and constitutional problems in China.
5. Classified Chinese Communist Party document issued by the Politburo on February 20, 1992; excerpted in *Shijie ribao* (World journal), March 2, 1992, 3; and cited by Minxin Pei 1994, 47.
6. *Statism* here denotes what Edward Friedman (1994, 86) refers to as "statist Jacobin-Leninism." Statist Jacobin-Leninism privileges the state's absolute legitimacy that "predisposed bureaucrats, intellectuals and the mass of the people to accept the notion that the state should take the leading role in mobilizing the resources of society and was entitled to carry out any changes it considered appropriate to that end, whatever the human cost" (qtd. by Friedman from Geoffrey Hosking, "Heirs of the Tsarist Empire," *Times Literary Supplement*, November 6, 1992, 8).
7. Specifically since the Third National Symposium on Confucius, in 1983, Confucian studies by scholars in mainland China began to encounter New Confucianism propagated by overseas and diaspora Chinese scholars directly. Although these two branches of Confucian studies remained quite different in their political orientations, together they worked out two major shifts in Confucian scholarship in the 1980s: first, the term *Confucian* expanded from its specific meaning (texts written by Confucius and his disciples) to a more general one (a system of ideas founded on Confucian values that are quintessentially Chinese); second, Confucian values moved from a negative to a positive complexion with regard to modernity. The first shift helped to form a notion of Chinese core culture; the second shift reversed the embarrassing Weberian observation about the deleterious effects of Confucian values on China's economic development as compared with the effects of the Protestant work ethic on the West. The economic performances of Japan and the Four Mini-Dragons of East Asia serve as successful examples of the linking of

Confucian values and modernity and push the theme of "Asia-specific modernity" or "China-specific modernity" into the discussion of cultural traditionalism.

8. I borrow the concepts of "time lag" and "belatedness" from Homi Bhabha (1991, 211).

9. While we can understand the "interstructuration of domination" as logical connections between intranational and international forms of domination, this concept also points to the irreducibility of history to forces, factors, elements, and variables that can and need to be isolated in order to be understood. As Ruiz suggests, it is no longer interesting, nor is it possible, for example, to understand domination as simply "the inexorable march of capitalism," orientalism, despotism, or whatever. "What is interesting," Ruiz notes, "is that other experiences of domination—like patriarchy or racism—which have their own origins and trajectories apart from capitalism, have converged with capitalist accumulation as a form of domination in the present" (1991, 174).

10. Slavoj Žižek (1991, 193–94), drawing from the political ideas of Claude Lefort (1986) and Ernesto Laclau (1990), makes an important distinction between "politics" and "the political." Politics is a "separate social complex, a positively determined sub-system of social relations in interaction with other sub-systems (economy, forms of culture . . .)." The political, on the other hand, refers to "the moment of openness, of undecidability, when the very structuring principle of society, the fundamental form of the social pact, is called into question—in short, the moment of global crisis overcome by the act of founding a new harmony." This distinction can help us to understand the political dimension of cultural criticism and the intellectual identity involved with it. Cultural criticism is not the same as politics because the former is rooted in a subsystem that can be distinguished from politics. This distinction—based on differences of subsystems—is not easy to maintain, however, because politics is "doubly inscribed": "[politics] is a moment of the social Whole, one among its sub-systems, *and* the very terrain in which the fate of the Whole is decided—in which the new Pact is designed and concluded" (193). It is no accident that violent revolution forces the political to become absolute. The crucial fact is that, to the revolutionaries, "the political dimension was not one sub-system among many but designated the emergence of a radical negativity rendering possible a new foundation of the social fabric" (194).

Cultural criticism, especially of the democratic type, must oppose any tendency of absolutizing politics the subsystem. This opposition will not be possible if critics fail to insist on their own role in the political and if they allot politics as the special province of politicians. Official politics in China has long dictated that intellectuals either become servants of power ("both 'red' and 'expert'") or "develop their specialized skills to the benefit of the state" (Meisner 1977, 171–72). It is essential for Chinese intellectuals to break this imposed dilemma and search for some tenable third position independent of both. This new position will redefine culture as fundamental to the construction of new political subjectivity and the new identity of intellectual-citizen. It will theorize cultural knowledge and its truth as a politics of representation. In this third position intellectuals would speak up as citizens, and citizens would assert themselves as intellectuals.

Addressing the political dimension of the intellectual work, we can ask, as Žižek does, "Why is truth always political?" and we can also ask, "Why are values and norms always political?" In the 1980s Chinese intellectuals raised many issues concerning cultural and intellectual values, the dignity of human creation and imagination, the necessity of independent thinking, the inviolability of individual freedom, the morality of tolerance, and the inevitability of change. They also condemned the Cultural Revolution for being immoral, inhumane, and barbaric. This kind of discussion is inevitably political because it entails the obligation to identify violations of these human needs as violations of *human rights*—rights to free speech, freedom from torture, freedom from arbitrary arrest, and due process, etc. There are, in China today, few issues that are as political as human rights and the need of democracy to improve the existing political condition.

Chapter 1

1. For more detailed discussion of Dirlik's work and notion of postsocialism, see Pickowicz 1990.
2. Using this term before the violent crisis of spring 1989 exploded in China, Dirlik (1989) emphasized the flexibility of Chinese socialist ideology and its promise of future success. Dirlik finds "postsocialism" a useful concept because it allows him to recognize the vitality of socialism with Chinese characteristics and to stress the promising future of this socialism. Dirlik remarks, "[Postsocialism] allows us to recognize the seriousness of Chinese socialism without falling into the teleological utopianism that is implicit in the word 'socialism,' which by itself refers not only to a present state of affairs as postsocialist, for without an immanent vision of the future, socialist societies may make claims upon the present but not upon the future" (377). According to Dirlik, Chinese socialism is a successful social vision because it has always contained some postsocialist elements: "In a sense, one could suggest that Chinese socialism was 'postsocialist' from its origins" (375).
3. By *postsocialism* Dirlik (1989) refers to "the condition of socialism in a historical situation" in which socialism's articulation with capitalism becomes a salient issue. Dirlik mentions three aspects of this postsocialist condition. The first is that "socialism has lost its coherence as a metatheory of politics because of the attenuation of the socialist vision" and partly because "socialist states . . . articulate 'actually existing socialism' to the demands of a capitalist world order." The second is that "the articulation of socialism to capitalism is conditioned by the structure of 'actually existing socialism.'" The third is that the process of such articulation ensures that "it does not result in

the restoration of capitalism" (364). For Dirlik postsocialism is made necessary by capitalism, or, more exactly, by postcapitalism, rather than by the
metamorphosis of the party-state's governing ideology. "Postsocialism," Dirlik asserts, "is of necessity also postcapitalism." I would like to say, instead,
that postsocialism in China is of necessity also posttotalitarian.

4. Other Chinese critics have also used the concept of "posttotalitarian" to refer
to the post-1989 condition in China. Tang Xiaodu, e.g., defines the posttotalitarian condition as one in which political control no longer relies exclusively
on fear and naked brutality. While still maintaining its domination over society, the posttotalitarian regime develops a certain degree of "ambiguity" in
its domination. This ambiguity is crucial to the effectiveness of the posttotalitarian domination because "it makes those who are dominated feel that they
can act out of their own free choice" (cited by Fang Zizhou 1996, 40). Ye Wen
(1997, 136) argues that the measurement of political conservatism in China
today is its apologetic attitude toward China's "existing posttotalitarian system." Major features of posttotalitarianism include the make-believe effect of
ideology, the transition from mass terror into civilized violence, the increasing social differentiation of the official language (Newspeak), greater tolerance of the unorthodox, and resorting to legal code rather than "supreme
instructions" for social control (Havel 1986; Goldfarb 1989).

5. As is shown by the famous song "East Is Red," Mao's image as a life-giving
father figure, the sun, was established in the years after the Long March.
After the success of the Communist revolution, Mao's image as a kind, caring father was reinforced. Mao himself certainly encouraged the making of
this image. The famous role model Mao recommended that all the Chinese
people learn from, Lei Feng, was an orphan who needed and found his par-
ents in the Communist Party and Chairman Mao. Learning from Lei Feng
again became the Party's slogan after 1989.

6. For discussion of how these principles have helped in developing and sustaining modern individual identity, see Taylor 1985, 255–60.

7. For instance, the official campaign picked the Goddess of Democracy as its
target and tried hard to discredit the pro-democracy movement by stressing
the statue's allusion to the Statue of Liberty of the United States. The Party
hard-liners also made all kinds of efforts to reestablish the authority of orthodox ideology. Yet neither the slogan banner "Socialism Is Good" put up near
Tiananmen Square nor the call to "Learn from Lei Feng" could regain much
justifying dynamic, though both might have conveyed the residual orthodoxy. See the photograph taken of such a government banner, which was put
up near Tiananmen Square after the violence in Beijing in 1989, in Lull 1991,
202.

8. Wen Liping (1995), e.g., provides a detailed collection of various kinds of
opinions, both pro and con, on the humanist spirit controversy. This collection, entitled *A Synthetic Summary of Discussion on "the Humanist Spirit,"*
includes quotations from over forty writers and critics, organized around
seven topics: (1) "What is 'the Humanist Spirit'" (various definitions of the

notion of the humanist spirit); (2) "The Universal, Particular, and Practical Characters of the Humanist Spirit" (human spirit as a universal quality, as a national feature, or as a character actualized in praxis); (3) "The Crisis of the Humanist Spirit" (the present social and moral crises as caused by the fundamental crisis of the humanist spirit); (4) "The Possibility and Necessity of Reestablishing the Humanist Spirit" (especially why and how humanist spirit is possible in the lack of religion); (5) "How to Reestablish the Humanist Spirit" (what heritage is available, the role of the intellectual, and the difficulty caused by a free-market economy, whose religion of self-interest relentlessly chips away all forms of social norms); (6) "How to Use Chinese Traditional Culture for the Task" (whether traditional Chinese moral norms and concepts are compatible with those of modern society and how the traditional can be used as a resource for rebuilding national culture); and (7) "The Humanist Spirit and the Ultimate Concern" (the ultimate concern as the foundation and core of the humanist spirit, in which the ultimate concern can be defined in either religious, secular humanist, or intellectual terms).

Wenyi lilun (Theory of literature and art), a monthly journal published by the National Center of Periodicals and Newspapers of the People's University in Beijing and distributed nationwide, which regularly reprints important articles in the field of literary and art theories, made the unusual decision to devote its July 1995 issue exclusively to articles on the humanist spirit. In its August and September 1995 issues more articles about the humanist spirit were collected. Many of the articles have also been included in Wang Xiaoming 1996 and in Ding Dong and Sun Min 1996.

9. Wang Meng's article "Avoiding Nobility" evoked many attacks; see, e.g., Yu Xinjiao 1995; Qi Shuyu 1995.

10. Wang Shuo's works give the readers the pictures of not just a particular kind of "indecent people" (liumang). They pinpoint a general social and political malaise far more serious than that created by social misfits, cultural rowdies, and ex-cons. As suggested by Yi Shuihan, "This liumang mentality has already insinuated its way into some Party and state organs, companies and industries . . . Acting as though one's workplace is a piece of turf in some mafia network, doing whatever you please, and ignoring all laws and principles are all part of liumang mentality" (cited by Barmé 1992, 30).

11. Zhonghua dushu bao (Chinese reading bulletin) published three sessions of a discussion on "Can Literature Give Up Its Ideals?" on May 3, May 24, and June 14, 1995. Both Xie Mian and Hong Zicheng were participants at the first meeting. Presentations made in these discussions include Zhang Huimin 1995; Zang Li 1995; Meng Fanhua 1995; and Wang Jiaxin 1995.

12. Many other critics are concerned with the effect of a market economy on literature and culture. See, e.g., Wang Shenzhi 1994; Zhuang Sihui 1994; Sun Zhanguo 1994; Wang Meng 1994a; Fu Kuiyang 1994; and Li Jiefei et al. 1995.

13. It is not Wang Meng's purpose to idealize the market economy. Refusing to take the market economy as a romantic or heroic phenomenon, Wang Meng (1994b, 47) says, "[Compared with the planning economy], the market econ-

omy operates more openly and therefore is less capable of hiding its own flaws and the weakness and vice of those who are involved in it. But the market economy is closer to the rules of human economic life, and more liable to human motivation and norms. It is the market, not the planning economy, that recognizes man's unique function and active role in society."

14. The Chinese language makes it hard to render the distinction between *popular culture* and *mass culture*. Both are frequently expressed in the convenient term *dazhong wenhua*. Popular culture in China is easy to identify yet hard to define. It is easily identifiable in the immediate reality of such things as popular periodicals, newspapers, songs, TV, and films as well as traditional varieties of local operas, performances, storytelling, and singing and dance. The most popular forms of popular culture, of course, depend on modern mass media (TV in particular) for their popularity. The problem lies in the fact that, when these objects and practices are placed in their larger context, the distinction of their category becomes more difficult to define. Certain TV programs, e.g., can be seen as "serious art" despite their popular form. Besides, popular culture can be the culture of the subaltern classes, thus carrying an implied opposition to dominant culture. But it can also be trendy entertainment or merely a replica of ruling ideology.

15. See, e.g., Zhang Wei 1994a. In this talk Zhang Wei, a well-known writer, pours contempt on "the uncivilized minds of those who are never exposed to great literature." According to him, the kind of literature loved by those people is "ugly," "vulgar," "destructive," and "must never be tolerated" (89–90). A similar view is expressed by Zhou Xian (1995). Other critics take a more positive view of the mass culture. For arguments for a more balanced understanding of the legitimacy of popular taste, see, e.g., Nie Zhenbin 1994; Sun Yongmeng 1994.

16. The writer characters in Wang Shuo's fiction are often boring hypocrites. See, e.g., Wang Shuo 1989.

17. A comment made by Song Chong, the former head of the Beijing Film Studio, quoted by Zhong Chengxiang (1989) in an official seminar on *Samsara* (a film made from Wang Shuo's short story). See *Dianying yishu cankao ziliao* (References of film art) 197 (1): 13.

18. Zhang Chengzhi (1994b, afterword). Another writer who also frequently expresses such haughty and elitist sentiment is Zhang Wei. Critical controversies over Zhang Chengzhi and Zhang Wei often expand to discussions of broader issues, such as the nature of serious literature and the role of the intellectual. These controversies are also a part of the general discussion on the humanist spirit. See, e.g., Shao Yanjun 1994; Zhang Yiwu 1995b, 1995c; Yin Changlong 1995; Gao Yuanbao 1995; Wang Binbin 1995. Zhang Chengzhi and Zhang Wei also participate actively in the discussion. For their views, see, e.g., Zhang Wei 1994, 1995; Zhang Chengzhi 1993, 1994.

19. The generic discussion on the humanist spirit, or, more exactly, on the loss of the humanist spirit, took shape in 1994, although this was by no means the first time contemporary Chinese critics had expressed such sentiments.

Dushu played an important role in staging this discussion by publishing these five "reflections on the humanist spirit." These discussion seminars appeared as Zhang Rulun et al. 1994a; Gao Ruiquan et al. 1994; Xu Jilin et al. 1994; Wu Xuan et al. 1994; Zhang Rulun et al. 1994b.

20. Indeed, Chen Sihe, another leader of the discussion of the humanist spirit and a close friend of Wang Xiaoming, makes it abundantly clear: "The humanist spirit should be daily-life norms of intellectuals" (Zhang Rulun et al. 1994a, 11).

21. Arendt believed that the morality of conscience was not appropriate to serve as a valid standard for political action, since it is often formulated in terms of absolute principles, which make it vulnerable to distortion and manipulation when introduced into the public realm. In place of conscience she advocated the political principle of active citizenship. To be sure, Arendt (1978, 1984) did not dismiss the role of conscience altogether: she argued that conscience, as the inner dialogue of me and myself, can prevent individuals from committing or participating in atrocities. We have many cases, e.g., during the Cultural Revolution, in which people listened to their conscience and did their best to protect the innocent and the persecuted. Yet, as is also proved by numerous cases from the Cultural Revolution, conscience cannot be taken for granted—many people lack it or are unable to feel self-reproach. It cannot be generalized either—what one person cannot live with may not bother another person's conscience.

22. Tao Dongfeng (1996a, 28), in a recent article, provides a critical analysis of why the Frankfurt School cultural theory has played a central role in the onslaught of popular and mass culture by the humanist intellectuals in China. His analysis is all the more interesting because it is meant to be self-criticism as well. Tao tells us that he also "once mechanically used the Frankfurt School theory" in his own discussions of popular and mass culture. Tao Dongfeng makes it very clear that now he realizes that the Frankfurt School theory is popular among the Chinese humanist intellectuals "*not* because it is applicable to the practical Chinese problems." Its popularity is, rather, accounted for by four other reasons. First, the Frankfurt School theory attracts the Chinese intellectuals with its antiscientist and humanist attitude. Second, its aesthetic and psychological approach and utopian ethos meet the intellectual needs of many Chinese humanists. Third, its vision of social reform through cultural radicalism is appealing to politically disempowered intellectuals. Fourth, its negative attitude toward commercialism and consumerism fits well with the derogatory view of commerce and industry, which is part of the tradition of Chinese literati.

23. I have elsewhere discussed how humanist and professional concerns can involve developing democratic ethics from common people's everyday life (Xu Ben 1998, 47–54, 67–72, 107–10).

24. This is, of course, not an easy task, given the government's strategy to make sure that academics do not mix with workers and peasants. This can be seen in the punitive measures the government took after June 4, 1989. On the one

hand, the government harshly punished those workers who joined the pro-democracy movement. On the other hand, it made those intellectuals who left university campuses to mobilize common people primary targets of persecution. The rigid boundaries between intellectuals and the masses, and between intellectuals of different academic specializations, have produced a whole gamut of self-serving attitudes and timid provincialism. Such boundaries are an extension of the social and political institutions that decree the principle of "divide-and-rule."

Chapter 2

1. Charles Frankel made his observation in his speech "Why the Humanities?" This speech is reprinted in Agresto and Riesenberg 1981.
2. These reports include "Guoxue, zai yanyuan qiaoran xingqi" (Chinese scholarship, quietly rising from Beijing University), *RMRB*, August 16, 1993; "Jiu wei le, 'guoxue'" (Welcome, "Chinese scholarship"), *RMRB*, August 17, 1993; "Beida xiaoyuan de 'guoxue re'" ("Fever of Chinese scholarship" on the campus of Beijing University), *RMRB*, May 4, 1994.
3. Some of these questions have been raised and addressed by commentators on the emergence of new Chinese national studies. Wang Yuechuan (1995), e.g., lists four reasons for what he calls the "shift from 'fever of Western studies' to 'fever of Chinese studies'" in the 1990s. First, "after the failure of [intellectual] radicalism, people began to turn to national traditional resources"; second, in the 1990s the scholarly paradigm "changes from macrostudies to microstudies," and this leads to more emphasis on "disciplinary rules and norms, professionalism, and scholarly tradition"; third, facing the threat from commercialism and moneymaking, academic and scholarly activities must affirm their own "spiritual values"; fourth, Chinese studies done by Chinese-American scholars, such as Tu Weiming, Yu Yinshi, and Lin Yusheng, began to attract Chinese scholars and act as catalysts as they attempted to establish a globally recognizable Chinese scholarship. Other explanations for the rise of new Chinese national studies in the 1990s include disillusion with the trend of Westernization of the 1980s, the economic prosperity of the Pacific Rim area, and rejection of intellectual radicalism. See, e.g., Zhou Suyuan 1995; Li Lianke 1995.
4. Chen Lai (1995) also traces *guoxue* back to the 1920s. He further suggests that the concept of Chinese *guoxue* may have been influenced by that of Japanese national studies, which was formed in the eighteenth century. *Guoxue* in China, Chen Lai points out, is a modern phenomenon. It carries two different but interrelated meanings: one is "[China's] traditional cultural system," and the other is "modernized studies of [Chinese] traditional culture" (25).
5. Like He Manzi, Chen Lai (1995) believes that *guoxue* is not the same as traditional Chinese studies; *guoxue* has never really been indigenous in China, since it privileges Western epistemology and methodology, and it depends on a Western-originated educational system. "From its inception," Chen Lai argues, "*guoxue* bears the stigma of a weak and marginal culture" (25).

6. This view is also shared by Chen Lai (1995). Chen observes that the fever of Chinese studies is generated by a crazy commodity-consumer economy unleashed by Deng Xiaoping's inspection tour to southern China in early 1992: "The propagation of 'fever of Chinese studies' in the second half of 1993 has its background in the irrationally active market economy and a culture that has lost its norms under the influence of commercialization" (28).

7. Chen Yinke (1890–1969) was a famous scholar of Chinese classical studies. He was regarded, together with Liang Qichao, Wang Guowei, and Zhao Yuanren, as one of the "four great teachers of Qinghua University" in the 1920s. He was professor of history at Zhongshan University in Guangzhou from 1949 until he died, during the Cultural Revolution. Chen Yinke is now actively remembered by many Chinese intellectuals as a prototypic scholar. For discussion of Chinese intellectuals' interest in Chen Yinke after 1989, see Su Wei 1996b.

8. See, e.g., Wang Wei 1992, Zhu Xueqin 1993, and Zhang Qiqun 1994.

9. This certainly bears testimony to what Kuhn (1970, 164) has said about the insulation of the specialists' community. The forming of an academic paradigm and special community, as Kuhn makes clear, is related to the specialist's insulation from the demands of the laity and of everyday life: "Just because he is working only for an audience of colleagues, an audience that shares his own values and beliefs, the scientist can take a single set of standards for granted . . . Even more important, the insulation of the scientific community from society permits the individual scientist to concentrate his attention upon problems that he has good reason to believe he will be able to solve."

10. Wayne C. Booth, "Boring from Within: The Art of the Freshman Essay," adapted from a speech delivered to the Illinois Council of College Teachers of English in May 1963; quoted by Annette T. Rottenberg, Elements of Argument (Boston: Bedford Books, 1994), 7.

11. Also see Zhang Dainian 1995; Deng Shaoji 1995.

12. Intellectual liberalism, as an essential but politically sensitive issue associated with the intellectuals' role in social and political criticism, is raised in oblique esoteric code common to Chinese cultural discussion. It is discussed, e.g., in the pages of Dushu through evaluation of Chen Yinke's intellectual career and achievement. See Ge Zhaoguang 1993; Lu Peng 1993; Xie Yong 1993; Ma Chenghua 1993; Yang Yuxi 1993. Many articles touched on the issue of intellectual freedom. The Chinese language uses the same word ziyou to denote "freedom" and "liberty." Liberalism (ziyouzhuyi), in the Chinese language, is a term that collides with the traditional value of self-submission and self-restraint. As Young-tsu Wong (1993, 457) points out, the Chinese term for liberty, ziyou, borrowed from a poem of Liu Zhongyan (773–819), connotes unrestrained freedom and therefore often causes misunderstanding of the notion "liberty."

13. One of the very few Chinese critics who do touch on the intellectuals' identity of citizen is Wang Yuanhua (1995a, 1995b), a senior Shanghai-based literary theorist.

14. Here Mouffe is quoting from Oakeshott 1975, 201.
15. See John Mowitt's discussion on the point in his foreword to Smith 1988, "The Resistance in Theory," x.
16. This is also a core concept of Ernesto Laclau and Chantal Mouffe, whose work *Hegemony and Socialist Strategy,* as Paul Smith tells us, has been of particular relevance to his work on the categories of "subject" and "agent" in human sciences (1991, 99).

Chapter 3

1. Quoted by Goldman (1994, 35). Goldman has provided other official and semiofficial documents on the necessity of democracy (34–35, 70).
2. Lu Zhichao, "Democracy Is Both a Means and an End," *Zhexue yanjiu,* December 25, 1980, 6–12; quoted by Goldman (1994, 70).
3. Representatives of the first group include Wang Ruoshui, Liu Zaifu, Li Zehou, and Gan Yang. The reformist intellectuals, on the other hand, were individuals who were associated at one time or another with Hu Yaobang, the former Party secretary-general who was ousted in 1987's Campaign against Bourgeois Liberalization. Among these reformist intellectuals the most well-known were Su Shaozhi, Yan Jiaqi, Sun Changjiang, Chen Yizi, Yu Haocheng, and Yu Guangyuan. Most of these intellectuals became targets of official criticism behind closed doors in the Campaign against Bourgeois Liberalization, and many of them fled the country after June 4, 1989. See the discussion of reformist intellectuals in the 1980s by Bonnin and Chevrier (1991).
4. Another well-known description of totalitarianism is made by Friedrich and Brzezinski (1956). It is known as the six-point definition. The six-point definition was modified by C. J. Friedrich (Friedrich, Curtis, and Barber 1969, 126) during the Chinese Cultural Revolution: a totalist official ideology, a single party committed to this ideology and usually led by one man, the dictator, a fully developed secret police, and three kinds of monopolistic control—namely, that of mass communications, operational weapons, and all organizations.
5. Even when Michael Curtis suggested giving up *totalitarian* as an inadequate description for the Soviet Union and Eastern European countries, witnessing the evolution of the Cultural Revolution in the late 1960s, he acknowledged the relevance of the term in the Chinese context: "Only in China has there been a consistent attempt to change human behavior and transform particularist loyalties to the family, class, or village into loyalty to the country or the party [Chairman Mao]. Chinese attempts to control behavior have embraced a variety of methods; control over communication, through reform, personal manipulation, confession, self-criticism, group study, debasement of language, public denunciation, and people's control correspondents who were known to be informers. In recent years, the attempt to control behavior has been illustrated in the extraordinary fashion by the Cultural Revolution, aimed at the transformation of social relationships and at the undermining of

those entrenched in power in the party and the state" (Friedrich, Curtis, and Barber 1969, 73). Also see C. Johnson 1968, 1–15.

6. The post–Cultural Revolution "rational totalitarianism" in China, as Maria Hsia Chang (1987, 162–63) observes, is characterized by "the government's continuing capacity and will to wield total power whenever it so chooses. The exercise of that fearsome power is made possible because the control apparatus of the single party state remains in place, always ready for implement." Chang's observation, made in 1987, unfortunately prophesied what happened in June 1989.

7. A barometer of interest in Western theories of 1980s intellectuals can be found in *Cultural Consciousness of Contemporary China* (1989) edited by Gan Yang, one of the leaders of the Culture Fever of the 1980s. In an effort to summarize the achievement of 1980s cultural discussion, Gan Yang put together a collection of what he saw as representative articles of that period, covering subjects from Chinese literature, art, and culture to Western literary and cultural theories. Among the nine Western theorists introduced there—Theodor Adorno, Daniel Bell, Walter Benjamin, Michel Foucault, Erich Fromm, Martin Heidegger, Herbert Marcuse, Lev Shestov, and Max Weber—only Foucault is a postmodernist. What is noticeable is that Fredric Jameson, who visited China in 1985 and whose work was translated into Chinese in 1987, was not on the list. Gan Yang's selection may not be the last word on the Culture Fever, but the publication date of his book is significant. This book was published in May 1989 and therefore was not influenced by the backlash against the Culture Fever after June 1989 or by the postmodern hindsight in the 1990s.

8. Wang Yuechuan, a leading scholar on postmodernism, contends that postmodernism is the product of Western historical legacy and reality and that, therefore, "we must face it and not blindly join it" (Wang Yuechuan and Shang Shui 1992, 43). Also see Wang Yuechuan 1992.

9. Deng Xiaoping, "Zai Wuchang, Shenzhen, Zhuhai, and Shanghai dengdi de tanhua yaodian" (The key points of the talk in Wuchang, Shenzhen, Zhuhai, and Shanghai), *Deng Xiaoping wenxuan* (Selected works of Deng Xiaoping) (Beijing: Renmin chubanshe, 1993), 372–73.

10. Editorial introduction to this issue of *Literary and Art Research*, 37. This group of articles appeared under the general title "Tuozhan lilun siwei, cujin lilun fanrong" (Open theoretical thought, promote prosperity of theory). Contributors include Wang Yichuan, Zhang Yiwu, Wang Yuechuan, Chen Xiaoming, Wang Ning, Wang Desheng, and Tao Dongfeng. Not all of them are now regarded as Chinese postmodernists, but Wang Yichuan, Zhang Yiwu, Wang Ning, and Chen Xiaoming are.

11. Here I am concerned with political disenchantment of sociocultural criticism rather than that of popular culture, although these two are related. Merle Goldman (1996) observes that popular culture in post-1989 China is tolerated "because it does not directly deal with political issues." She recognizes two seemingly contradictory aspects of popular culture's political withdrawal, its

escapism and potential subversiveness: "In fact, its escapist quality not only reflects the Party's desire for an apolitical rather than a politically engaged public, it also reflects the overwhelming desire of the population after 4 June [1989] to stay away from politics. Nevertheless, this widespread new culture indirectly subverts the Party because it promotes values that are alien to the mainstream tradition of Chinese and Marxist-Leninist emphasis on obedience and conformity." At the same time, Goldman suggests that political quietism is more harmful to Chinese intellectuals and that their subservient relationship to the political leadership is not likely to come to an end unless they themselves reject the limits of the arbitrarily set "limited zones of freedom" (50–51).

12. A typical example of this kind of third-world expressionism can be found in Zhang Yiwu 1993a. The appendices of this book include three of his articles or dialogues on China's third-world culture and identity, all published between 1990 and 1992.

13. These bifurcated *post*s were largely the coinage of Chen Xiaoming (1994c) and Zhang Yiwu (1994c). The two leading figures of Chinese post-ist theory are now called by the titles of Post-Master Chen [Chen houzhu] and Post-Master Zhang [Zhang houzhu].

14. Reflection on the Tiananmen incident is one of the newest of these forbidden zones. After 1989 the galling memory of the Tiananmen massacre has unwittingly turned the memory of the Cultural Revolution into another new forbidden zone. The officially controlled media prohibits discussion not only of the Tiananmen massacre but also of the Cultural Revolution for fear of dangerous associations. These historical events have become special objects of state forgetting. Post-ist theory in China, due to its parochial notion of "Chineseness" and rhetoric of neo-epochalism (the so-called post–New Era) seems to be helping exactly this sort of state forgetting.

    The official censorship on critical reflection on the Cultural Revolution has left a remarkable trace, e.g., in the contents of the June 1996 issue of *Dongfang* (*Orient*), which was planned as a special issue of the thirtieth anniversary of the Cultural Revolution. The editors were forced to replace the original group of articles on the Cultural Revolution with another group of articles on environmental protection. The two versions of the journal's contents, in Chinese and in English, do not match. The English version has four articles that do not appear in the published volume.

15. As György Konrad suggests in a different context, this is the difference between aggressive and defensive censorship, censorship with or without a dictator: "Under Stalin, censorship was both positive and aggressive; nowadays it is negative and defensive." Quoted by Rupnik 1989, 238.

16. Deng Xiaoping's speech of June 9, in *Jiefangjun bao*, June 28, 1989, 1.

17. Allen S. Whiting (1995) has documented the delicate shifts between affirmative and assertive nationalisms in China's controlled media during the four years after June 4, 1989. Further quotes regarding China's official patriotism are documented in Whiting's article; the translations are his.

18. "Zhiyou shehuizhuyi cai neng jiu zhongguo" (Only socialism can save China), editorial, *RMRB*, July 22, 1989, 1.

19. In the spring of 1990 the magazine *Ban yue tan* (Biweekly) sponsored a lecture series on patriotism that linked the past history of foreign antagonism to the present-day foreign threat: first, "the United States . . . mustered forces almost simultaneously from three sides—Korea, Taiwan, and Indochina—. . . to 'strangle' independent China 'in its infancy'"; then, "in the late 1950s, the Soviet leaders . . . flagrantly interfered in China's construction program so as to force it to agree with their model" by withdrawing experts, contracts, and plans; finally, "following the 4 June incident last year, some Western countries, led by the United States," imposed sanctions and interfered in China's internal affairs, but the "anti-China tide" was repulsed ("Independence—a Foundation for the Prosperity and Strength of the Motherland," *Ban yue tan*, no. 9 [May 10, 1990], 19–21). A PLA newspaper article asserted, "Since [the Opium War] Western capitalism has never stopped its aggression against China and its plundering of China. After the founding of New China, they first imposed embargoes and blockades and made armed threats . . . even spread the flames of war to the banks of the Yalu River in an attempt to throttle New China in its cradle" (Zhang Zongxian, "Fayang aiguozhuyi jingshen, jianchi shehuizhuyi xinnian" [Carry forward patriotic spirit, keep firm conviction in socialism], *Jiefangjun bao* June 5, 1990, 3).

20. The relationship between nativist-postcolonial theory and the official nationalist rhetoric must not be sought on a superficial level. No matter how unmistakable the semantic similarities between them may be—in their shared vocabulary, such as the words *imperialism, colonialism, hegemony,* and so on—the differences are obvious. Each of them has its own paradigmatic jargon and discursive authority. An analytical way to approach their relationship is to examine how the sentiment, tone, and argument of nativist-postcolonial style are recognizable in official discursive practices, such as the government's apologia for its record on human rights. Such an apologia is based on three different but interrelated (nativist-postcolonial) themes: Western cultural hegemony, the intentions for political domination and control, and cultural relativism. First, human rights represent an attempt by ethnocentric Westerners to impose their cultural values and institutions on the rest of the world. Second, human rights are a form of neo-imperialism and neo-colonialism. What Western powers want in seeking out alleged violations of human rights in China is a pretext for interfering in China's internal affairs and infringing on its sovereignty. Third, Chinese cultural tradition and reality define the kind of human rights suitable for China. In China human rights mean solving the pressing problems of feeding and housing a huge and growing population, and the unchallengeable authority of the central government over diverse peoples is the only guarantee of this solution. For the official apologia of China's human rights record, see Zhao Yao and Wang Zhengping 1994.

21. Explicit criticism of post-ist theory's collaboration with the repressive

authoritarian ideology can only be published outside mainland China. For criticism of post-ist theory's conservative politics and its complicity with the authoritarian order in China, see, e.g., Xu Ben 1994, 1995, 1996d; Guo Jian 1996; and Zhang Longxi 1996.

22. This is also where post-ist theorists often differ from those who have introduced the postmodernist theory to China. Those who have introduced the postmodernist theory to China are not necessarily postmodernists themselves.

23. Examples of specific academic debates that have led to controversy over the ideas of democracy and human rights can be found in several fields of the humanities. In the field of foreign literary studies, e.g., see Yi Dan 1994. The debate on Chinese post-ist studies also leads its defenders to accusing their critics of yielding to Western ideas of democracy and human rights or even of being "anti-Chinese and anticommunist." See Zhang Yiwu 1996; Liu Kang 1996b.

24. See, e.g., Zhang Kuan 1994. This article provides a simplified version of a number of politically correct ideas prevalent on American campuses. It should be noted that Zhang's introduction of both Edward Said and American-style political correctness were published by *Dushu,* a liberal monthly. The difference between "liberal" and the "conservative," however, can be paper thin in China. Zhang Kuan's article on Said, the "antiimperialist" and "anti-Western" theorist, was also published in official journals. His article "Said's 'Orientalism' and the Western Sinology" (1995a) was published by *Liaowang* (Lookout), one of the principal Chinese Communist Party theoretical journals. Some Chinese critics see Zhang Kuan as a typical example of intellectual "selling out" in the 1990s (Su Wei 1996a; Fang Zizhou 1994; Zhang Longxi 1994).

25. Examples of literary and cultural trends that allegedly characterize the emerging of the post–New Era include New Realism (*xin xieshi*) or New Condition (*xin zhuangtai*). For discussion of this, see Xu Ben 1996e. Zhang Yiwu and Wang Ning have probably contributed more than anyone else to establishing a theoretical relationship between these new literary trends and the post–New Era. A number of other critics either use the term *post–New Era* loosely or talk about these new trends without going as far as Zhang Yiwu and Wang Ning. For such treatment of the post–New Era, see, e.g., Chen Xiaoming 1994b; Wang Guangdong 1994.

26. The importance of events in history cannot be overemphasized. I borrow the concept "originary relation" from Dick Howard. Howard suggests differentiating the genetic and the normative dimensions of a significant historical event (1988, xxv–xxvi). In discussing the significance of modernity, he stresses the genetic and normative moments of events such as the American Revolution and the French Revolution: "The redefinition of the revolution as originary is not simply a methodological proposal; it has practical consequences. The genetic corollary to the normative political moment institutionalized in the republican state is democracy. The American Revolution must stand alongside the French as the modern political model."

Any historical event, such as that of June 4, 1989, is never a homogeneous moment but, rather, consists of many events or meaningful moments. To identify or stress one such moment as particularly meaningful is already adding a normative dimension to it, and to interpret a historical event as a normative moment implies the task of recognizing or even constructing meaningful events in history. Cultural criticism with historical consciousness and social commitment must be constantly involved in the politics of interpreting history so that it can be used to influence present and future social change. Cultural criticism will not be up to this task unless it addresses the issues associated with real historical events and their inscribed originary relations. Post-ist theorists in China, by positing the 1990s as post–New Era and by avoiding commenting on the post–New Era's relations to the official definition of the genetic and normative moments of June 4, 1989, acquiesce to the official definition of this event as "counterrevolutionary turmoil."

27. Critics in China and abroad have noted the paradox and irony of using Western postmodern themes to advance a so called indigenous Chinese cultural theory (Xu Jilin 1994; Nan Fan 1994; Zhang Longxi 1996; Guo Jian 1996; Lei Yi 1997).

28. Those who examine and criticize China's domestic structural violence and domination, institutionalized corruption, and antidemocratic cultural elements become native "informants" to the West. This view is expressed most strongly by Zhang Yiwu (1995a) and Liu Kang (1996b).

Chapter 4

1. As Jonathan Arac (1997, 143) suggests, disciples of postmodern and postcolonial theories in China tend to simplify and reduce Said's concretely pursued case-study of Orientalism into an abstract and unsituated "theory," or as I prefer to call it, "metatheory." Wang Ning (1997a), e.g., in a piece on the notion of Orientalism, accepts the Western-defined category of the Orient as a term of his own self-positioning, while Said's original purpose is to challenge and refute this category. "Wang points to the 'geographical limitation' that restricts the scope of Said's 'theory,'" Arac writes, "it seems he would rather be part of the 'Confucian-Islamic' threat conjured by Samuel Huntington than be 'overlooked' by Said." The point is that to accept the identity of the Orient and take an agnostic attitude toward the West as thus projected is itself a form of essentialist Orientalism.

2. Chen Xiaoming et al. 1994, 143. This article resulted from a seminar discussion. I use it as a representative piece of nativist criticism of Fifth Generation films in China. A similar stance is taken by Zhang Yiwu and Meng Fanhua (1993). Nativist criticism of film and TV draws its favorite subject matter from Chinese cultural works about first-/third-world cross-cultural experience, such as the TV series "Beijingren zai niuyue" (A native of Beijing in New York) or of fame in the West (such as Fifth Generation films).

3. The inextricable link between definitions of language and national identity is not a new topic. As Richard M. Morse (1979, 28) points out: "In nineteenth-

century Europe the linguistic concerns of the intelligentsia gave predominance to the languages of that continent and how they revealed the 'genius' of nations considered to be world-historical. The identification of 'language' and 'nation' became so strong as to shape the self-image of peoples, ambitions of leaders, and political demarcations of the continent." In recent years nativist critics in China have made efforts to anchor Chinese national identity in the Han language. See, e.g., Zhang Yiwu 1993a, chap. 3.

4. As Esther C. M. Yau analyzes in her article, "International Fantasy and the 'New Chinese Cinema,'" important Fifth Generation films, such as *Yellow Earth* and *Red Sorghum,* have a rather complicated relationship to what is being debated as the question of "the national" in China (1993, 97–98). Far from being a pure theoretical argument, the debate on the question of the national has become the locus and meeting place of domestic politics and geopolitics. Chen Kaige uses compelling tropes of Chinese civilization in his films (the Shanbei plateau, the Yellow River, the peasants, and, indeed, the Peking Opera). These may be construed as verifying a nationalist interest. His inclusion, however, of both domestic and overseas spectators as his potential audience suggests strongly his transnational vision. Zhang Yimou, in his film *Red Sorghum,* e.g., "impropriated national pride in the diegesis, only to criticize more harshly the repressive mechanisms at work that twisted the national psyche." The power base of the twisting force of the national psyche in China today is that of the party-state, even though the Communist Party has to a great extent fulfilled China's long-cherished dream of nation building. Identifying with such a twisting and repressive force, the hard-line officials have repeatedly accused Fifth Generation films of shameless exhibitionism and catering to Westerners, an accusation echoed now by the nativist critics, who, however, are often critical of literary orthodoxy in China. The official anticolonial and anti-Western attitude, itself a valid one, is nevertheless a pretext for the hard-liners to maintain their internal domination as representative of the nation's views. It is thus a co-opting force any politically conscious cultural critic must be wary of.

5. As Ma Ning has pointed out, film in China has always been ideological representation and political discourse rather than mere narrative (1987, 63).

6. Along with the current tendency of diversification of products, Miriam Hansen also emphasizes the accompanying trend of an increased privatization of the models and venues of consumption. Increasing literature on these developments includes Appadurai 1990; Featherstone 1990; Robins 1991; Mattelart 1988.

7. For a discussion of the relationship of the "socially produced subject" and the "textually produced subject," see Fiske 1987a, chap. 5, "Active Audience." Also see Hall 1980, 128–39.

8. That the music of the Peking Opera may not sound meaningful in terms of collective memory and aesthetic reception to many Western viewers is indicated by John Simon's comment on the film: "How you will respond to *Farewell My Concubine* may also depend on your tolerance for Peking Opera

. . . it is, I'm sorry to confess, not music to my ears" ("Chinoiserie," *National Review,* November 15, 1993, 63).

9. For many Western viewers the parameters of subjectivity may be quite different. The film, for instance, may trigger not the memory of personal experience in the Cultural Revolution but, rather, what they have heard about China and its Communist regime. Intertextual associations may be different as well. Instead of comparing this film with films of ossified socialist realism, they may compare it with European art cinema of the 1960s and 1970s and see it as only an exotic version of a canonized form, missing much of the form's political implication. These and similar associations will make the film a "foreign" rather than a "native" one to them.

How important the Cultural Revolution context is to the Chinese audience can be seen in actual on-the-spot interpretations like that provided by Hu Bin. Hu Bin (1993) sees in Dieyi "a lonely and tragic figure" who reflects "the destiny of many modern Chinese intellectuals": "[Dieyi] could have died under the persecution by the Red Guards during the Cultural Revolution. But the film must let him die on the stage after the Cultural Revolution so that he can die with [faith in his artistic dream]. This is the only possible dramatic situation because Dieyi was forced away from his stage during the Cultural Revolution." According to Hu, Dieyi's death after the Cultural Revolution is crucial to the film's logic of narrative and comprehension, making the Cultural Revolution an essential setting without which the film's story cannot even be told, not to mention be properly understood.

10. Responding articles to Yi Dan's article include Zhang Hong 1994; Huang Baosheng 1994; Zhao Yanqiu 1995; Wu Yuanmai 1995.

11. The cultural comparison prior to and following the May Fourth Movement (from 1915 to 1927) is also known as "debates on East and West cultures." It can be divided into three stages, each with its own major focus. *New Youth,* edited by Chen Duxiu, started the first stage of the debate, focusing on whether Eastern or Western culture is more preferable in the modern age. The second stage of the debate began with the May Fourth Movement, focusing on whether Eastern and Western cultures could be integrated or were simply contradictory in nature. The third stage of the debate, which began in the early 1960s, centered around whether China should stick to its own cultural tradition or be Westernized—i.e., which road China should take for its future development. See Chen Song 1989.

12. As Hu Shi, a leader of the May Fourth Movement, pointed out, the translation of modern Western literature in China was committed to developing the consciousness of self-choice (or "individualism," as it was often called) that was missing in the traditional Chinese culture. Translation of works by Western humanist writers like Ibsen was purposefully incorporated with advancing new Chinese literature written in *baihua,* or vernacular language. "After *New Youth* was resurrected in January 1918," Hu Shi wrote, "we were determined to make two moves. The first was to reject the classical writing and write exclusively in vernacular Chinese; the second was to devote ourselves to

translating modern literary works from the West. In June of the same year, *New Youth* was able to bring out a 'Special Issue on Ibsen,' which included a full translation of the play *Nora [A Doll's House]* that I had done in collaboration with Mr. Luo Jialun, as well as Mr. Tao Lugong's translation of another play entitled *Public Enemy*" (qtd. in Lydia Liu 1995, 79).

Translated writers in the post-Mao era, especially during the time of the Culture Fever of the 1980s, cover a wide range, from Latin American writer Gabriel García Marquez to French "new fiction" writer Alain Robbe-Grillet, from stream-of-conscious writers like James Joyce to existentialists like Jean-Paul Sartre and Albert Camus (Goldman et al. 1993). As a whole, the translated literature in that period may be seen as a counter-literature in relation to the abiding and officially endorsed socialist realist literature.

13. Lydia Liu uses the term *translated modernity,* which she borrows from Leo Oufan Lee, to refer to the history of translingual practice between China and the West through which new questions about "modernity" can be raised. These questions include: "How do twentieth-century Chinese name the condition of their existence? What kind of language do they use in talking about their differences from whatever contingent identities they perceive as existing before their own time or being imposed from the outside? What rhetorical strategies, discursive formations, naming practices, legitimizing processes, tropes, and narrative modes impinge upon the historical conditions of the Chinese experience of the modern?" (1995, 28).

14. Lydia Liu suggests that the *source/target* division is inappropriate and even misleading: "The idea of source language often relies on concepts of authenticity, origin, influence, and so on . . . On the other hand, the notion of target language implies a teleological goal, a distance to be crossed in order to reach the plenitude of meaning." For this purpose she suggests replacing the *source/guest* pairing with that of *host/guest,* and in this case *host* means China (Lydia Liu 1995, 26–27). Without neglecting its ideological implications, I will still use the *source/target* pairing simply because it is more commonly used.

15. As Hewson and Martin point out, the middle ground an "objective" translator seeks to occupy "is never one fixed and 'comfortable' area, but an obscure no-man's-land whose boundaries, language culture 1 and language culture 2, seem constantly to draw nearer and to recede, to change shape and size, as the language cultures evolve independently, and as the practice of translation itself evolves *within and between* language cultures, both influencing and being influenced by the independent development of the language cultures" (1991, 134).

Chapter 5

1. The picture of social progress by the force of market economy rather than by ideas of good society and good government, which the post–Cold War global capitalism offers to the so-called age of the death of ideology, has inspired

much of the global revival of conservative thinking. It thus has links with the antirationalist tradition of Edmund Burke. It completely rejects the notion that the intellectuals can form a critical and oppositional force in society. "On this account of social change," as Richard Rorty sarcastically remarks, "there is no way for the citizens of *Brave New World* to work their way out from their happy slavery by theory" (1991, 168).

2. Cultural traditionalism is not necessarily politically conservative. It can be politically liberal, as in overseas New Confucianism, which seeks points of compatibility between Confucian and liberal values or stresses the Confucian tradition of concerned, engaged, and political relevant intellectuals. It can be politically ambiguous, as in mainland Chinese New Confucian studies, which pledges to help promote "socialist spiritual civilization." It can also be politically conservative, as in certain "Asian Values" or "Chinese Values" theories that are mobilized by authoritarian regimes as ideological statements of their interests.

3. This genealogy of radicalism is the most often criticized idea of Chen Lai's conservative argument. Chen Shaoming (1996, 86–87), e.g., writes: "It is superficial and formalistic to use radicalism to associate the May Fourth Movement with the Cultural Revolution. Such an association obscures the substantial differences [between these two historical events]. The antitraditionalism of the May Fourth Movement was based on liberal values, and meant to drastically transform Chinese culture in the liberal direction. On the other hand, the Cultural Revolution was characterized by its anticultural nature. It was against all cultures, accusing them of being 'feudalist, capitalist, or revisionist.' We should never forget that . . . the social ideals cherished by the May Fourth Movement were rejected by the Cultural Revolution. It is not difficult to decide whether the Cultural Revolution was caused by cultural antitraditionalism or by special political condition. If we agree that the Cultural Revolution had its own social and political causes, cultural radicalism becomes an issue that is of little relevance." For further criticism of Chen Lai, see, e.g., Cai Zhongde 1996; Zhang Enhe 1995.

4. The parochial view of a China-specific model of development links cultural traditionalism to the neoconservative political thought of the 1990s, which goes back to neo-authoritarianism in the 1980s; both draw strength of argument from economic successes in Asian countries that appear to justify the Asia-specific modernity, which puts economical development first and gives priority to order, stability, and central authority (the "strong state"). There is a significant difference, however, between cultural traditionalism and neo-authoritarian or neoconservative political thought. The former is primarily concerned with how to prove the relevance and desirability of China's cultural tradition in the present, the latter with how to bolster the existing political authority in the face of its legitimacy crisis. To the latter, the usefulness of traditional resources is only secondary in importance. See Xiao Gongqin 1994, 21–23; Wang Shan 1994; Ong Jieming et al. 1996.

Many other Chinese intellectuals are also interested in the notion of "Asian values," or, more specifically, "Chinese values." They challenge the cultural traditionalist understanding of these values as static and impervious. Liu Junning (1993), e.g., argues in his discussion of the modern culture of Singapore that Asian values have functioned in Singapore's process of modernization precisely because that society has borrowed, adopted, and adapted liberal values. Also see Liu Dong 1993; Li Shenzhi 1994, 1995.

5. See Chen Jianhua's (1997) comparison and criticism of Li Zehou's sweeping rejection of revolution and Zhang Yiwu's total rejection of modernity as related neoconservative cultural phenomena in the 1990s.

6. This theory of four-stage development is criticized by Su Wen and Bian Wu for implicitly forfeiting consideration of social justice as the ethical imperative of sociopolitical transformation (1998, 160).

7. In an interview by Min Huiquan, Tang Yijie (1996) suggests differentiating the feudalist cultural tradition, which is embedded in the general Chinese cultural tradition, and the ultra-leftist doctrinaire tradition, which forms under the Communist regime after 1949. According to Tang, to defend either tradition is a sure sign of conservatism. A similar distinction between the old and new traditions is made by Xu Youyu (1997).

8. Maurice Meisner discusses the disintegration of the socialist egalitarian tradition in China and points out that, while new forms of inequalities may be seen and justified as temporary phenomena, as the necessary and immediate price of economic progress in a situation in which the rapid development of the productive forces is the overriding priority, their future disappearance can by no means be guaranteed (1989, 353).

9. Pickowicz's reluctance to go beyond this analogous postmodernism-postsocialism relationship and his rejection of the postmodern framework in his consideration of Huang Jianxin's postsocialist films have caused an uneasy feeling among critics who want to see an even more substantial relationship between postmodernism and postsocialism. Chris Berry and Mary Ann Farquhar, e.g., suggest that in Pickowicz's consideration of postsocialism, "What remains to be fully explored is the homology between this term [*postsocialist*] and 'postmodernist,' from which it is clearly derived." They propose to see postsocialism "as a complement to postmodernism" (1994, 84).

10. Peter Murphy succinctly delineates the historical conjunctures of liberal-democracy and socialist-democracy as follows: "The idea of a relatively autonomous, dynamic commercial economic sphere was crucial to liberalism's eventual acceptance of democracy. In the end, liberals came to believe that democracy was the form of government that most accommodated a dynamic economic order. Like liberalism, socialism was not, in its beginning, especially attracted to the idea of democracy. Liberalism made its peace with democracy in the wake of the French Revolution. Jacobinism's terrorist pursuit of liberal ideas—and the self-destruction of them—was sacrificing enough to push liberals into a reconciliation with democracy. Likewise, the defeat of the 1848 Revolution, and the evident failure of the insurrectionary mentality, was the springboard for the emergence of a social, as opposed to

liberal, kind of democracy. By the turn of the 20th century, the intellectual foundations for the Great Reconciliation of socialism and democracy had been securely laid. A key to this reconciliation was the preparedness of political thinkers, like Eduard Bernstein, to take up the key themes of the *social* thought of the nineteenth century, but to argue for reformist and democratic, rather than insurrectionary or revolutionary, i.e., despotic, political means for obtaining those social project" (1990, 59). Obviously, the Western historical conditions of the connections between liberalism and democracy and between socialism and democracy did not repeat themselves in China. Therefore, the issue of democracy must be understood as a matter of a different historical conjuncture.

Bibliography

Adam, Ian, and Helen Tiffin, eds. 1990. *Past the Last Post: Theorizing Post-Colonialism and Post-Modernism*. Calgary: University of Calgary Press.

Adamson, Walter. 1985. *Marx and the Disillusionment of Marxism*. Berkeley: University of California Press.

Agresto, John, and Peter Riesenberg, eds. 1981. *The Humanist as Citizen*. Chapel Hill, NC: National Humanities Center.

Ahmad, Aijaz. 1987. "Jameson's Rhetoric of Otherness and the 'National Allegory.'" *Social Text* 17:3–25.

Ai Nong. 1996. "Guanyu 'wenhua re' de jidian sikao" (Some notes on "culture fever"). *WYLYP* 1:50 55.

Althusser, Louis, and Etienne Balibar. 1970. *Reading Capital*. Trans. Ben Brewster. London: Verso.

Amin, Samir. 1990. *Delinking: Towards a Polycentric World*. Trans. Michael Wolfers. London: Zed Books.

Amin, Samir. 1990. *Transforming the Revolution*. New York: Monthly Review Press.

Amin, Samir. 1991. "The Issue of Democracy in the Contemporary Third World." *Socialism and Democracy* 12 (January): 83–104.

Anagnost, Ann. 1992. "Socialist Ethics and the Legal System." In Wasserstrom and Perry 1992.

Anderson, Benedict. 1983. *Imagined Communities*. London: Verso.

Appadurai, Arjun. 1990. "Disjuncture and Difference in the Global Cultural Economy." *Public Culture* 2:1–24.

Arac, Jonathan. 1997a. "Postmodernism and Postmodernity in China: An Agenda for Inquiry." *New Historical History* 28 (1): 135–45.

Arac, Jonathan. 1997b. "Chinese Postmodernism toward a Global Context." *Boundary* 2 24 (3): 261–75.

Arendt, Hannah. 1951. *The Origins of Totalitarianism*. New York: Harcourt Brace Jovanovich.

Arendt, Hannah. 1972. *Crises of the Republic*. New York: Harcourt Brace Jovanovich.

Arendt, Hannah. 1978. *The Life of the Mind*. New York: Harcourt Brace Jovanovich.

Arendt, Hannah. 1984. "Thinking and Moral Considerations." *Social Research* 51 (1): 7–37.

Armes, Roy. 1987. *Third World Filmmaking and the West.* Berkeley: University of California Press.

Aronowitz, Stanley, and Henry A. Giroux. 1991. *Postmodern Education: Politics, Culture, and Social Criticism.* Minneapolis: University of Minnesota Press.

Aronowitz, Stanley. 1987. "Postmodernism and Politics." *Social Text* 18:99–115.

Asad, Talal. 1986. "The Concept of Cultural Translation in British Social Anthropology." In James Clifford and George E. Marcus, eds., *Writing Culture: Poetics and Politics of Ethnography.* Berkeley: University of California Press.

Ashcroft, Bill, Gareth Griffiths, and Helen Tiffin. 1989. *The Empire Writes Back: Theory and Practice in Post-colonial Literature.* London: Routledge.

Ashley, Richard K. 1987. "The Geopolitics of Geopolitical Space: Toward a Critical Social Theory of International Politics." *Alternatives* 12 (4): 403–34.

Bakhtin, Mikhail. 1981. "Discourse in the Novel." In Michael Holquist, ed., *The Dialogic Imagination.* Austin: University of Texas Press.

Barmé, Geremie. 1992. "Wang Shuo and Liumang (Hooligan) Culture." *Australian Journal of Chinese Affairs* 28:23–64.

Barnett, A. Doak, and Ralph N. Clough, eds. 1986. *Modernizing China: Post-Mao Reform and Development.* Boulder, CO: Westview Press.

Barthes, Roland. 1977. "Writers, Intellectuals, Teachers." *Image-Music-Text,* trans. Stephen Heath. New York: Hill and Wang.

Barthes, Roland. 1982. *Empire of Signs.* Trans. Richard Howard. New York: Hill and Wang.

Bassnett, Susan, and André Lefevere, eds. 1990. *Translation, History and Culture.* London: Pinter Publishers.

Bassnett, Susan. 1993. *Comparative Literature: A Critical Introduction.* Oxford: Blackwell.

Baudelaire, Charles. 1961. *Oeuvres complètes.* Paris: Pléiade.

Befu, Harumi, ed. 1993. *Cultural Nationalism in East Asia: Representation and Identity.* Berkeley: Institute of East Asian Studies, University of California.

Benda, Julien. 1969. *The Treason of the Intellectuals.* Trans. Richard Aldington. New York: W. W. Norton.

Benjamin, Andrew. 1989. *Translation and the Nature of Philosophy.* London: Routledge.

Benjamin, Walter. 1973. "The Task of the Translator." *Illuminations.* London: Fontana.

Berlin, Isaiah. 1979. "Nationalism: Past Neglect and Present Power." *Partisan Review* 46 (3): 337–58.

Berman, Russell A. 1989. *Modern Culture and Critical Theory.* Madison: University of Wisconsin Press.

Bernheimer, Charles. 1989. *Figures of Ill Repute: Representing Prostitution in Nineteenth-Century France.* Cambridge: Harvard University Press.

Bernstein, Thomas P. 1967. "Leadership and Mass Mobilisation in the Soviet and Chinese Collectivisation Campaigns of 1929–1930 and 1955–1956." *China Quarterly* 31:1–42.

Berry, Chris, and Mary Ann Farquhar. 1994. "Post-Socialist Strategies: An Analysis of Yellow Earth and Black Cannon Incident." In Linda C. Ehrlick and David Desser, eds., *Cinematic Landscapes*. Austin: University of Texas Press.

Best, Steven, and Douglas Kellner. 1991. *Postmodern Theory: Critical Interrogations*. New York: Guilford Press.

Beverley, John, and José Oviedo. 1995. *The Postmodernism Debate in Latin America*. Durham, NC: Duke University Press.

Bhabha, Homi K. 1991. "'Race,' Time and the Revision of Modernity." *Oxford Literary Review* 13 (1–2): 193–219.

Bhabha, Homi K. 1994. *The Location of Culture*. London: Routledge.

Blundell, Valda, John Shepherd, and Ian Taylor, eds. 1993. *Relocating Cultural Studies*. London: Routledge.

Bonnin, Michel, and Yves Chevrier. 1991. "The Intellectual and the State: Social Dynamics of Intellectuals Autonomy during the Post-Mao Era." *China Quarterly* 126:569–93.

Bourdieu, Pierre. 1984. *Distinction: A Social Critique of the Judgement of Taste*. Trans. Richard Nice. Cambridge, MA: Harvard University Press.

Bourdieu, Pierre. 1993. *The Field of Cultural Production*. Ed. Randal Johnson. New York: Columbia University Press.

Brieder, Jerome B. 1970. *Hu Shih and the Chinese Renaissance: Liberalism in the Chinese Revolution, 1917–1937*. Cambridge: Harvard University Press.

Brunner, José Joaquin. 1995. "Notes on Modernity and Postmodernity in Latin American Culture." In Beverley, Aronna, and Oviedo 1995.

Buell, Frederick. 1994. *National Culture and the New Global System*. Baltimore: Johns Hopkins University Press.

Cai Zhongde. 1996. "'Wusi' de chonggu yu zhongguo wenhua de weilai" (Reevaluation of the "May Fourth Movement" and the future of Chinese culture). *Dongfang wenhua* (Eastern culture) 3:7–24.

Certeau, M. de. 1984. *The Practice of Everyday Life*. Berkeley: University of California Press.

Chang Qie. 1996. "Xinbaoshouzhuyi fanqi de beijing" (Background of the spreading of neoconservatism). *HZSFXB* 5:3–4.

Chang, Maria Hsia. 1987. "Totalitarianism and China: The Limits of Reform." *Global Affairs* 2 (4): 149–67.

Chatterjee, Partha. 1993. *The Nation and Its Fragments: Colonial and Postcolonial Histories*. Princeton, NJ: Princeton University Press.

Chen Baiming. 1997. "Jinnianlai guonei dui wenhua jijinzhuyi de pipan zongshu" (Survey of criticism of cultural radicalism in China in recent years). *WYLYP* 1:128–41.

Chen Feng. 1997. "Order and Stability in Social Transition: Neoconservative Political Thought in Post-1989 China." *China Quarterly* 151 (September): 592–613.

Chen Jianhua. 1997. "Guanyu 'geming' he 'xiandaixing' de yiyi he shiyong"

(Meanings and applications of "revolution" and "modernity"). *Zhongguo yanjiu yuekan* (China research monthly), April, 14–22.

Chen Lai. 1993. "Ershi shiji wenhua yundong zhong de jijinzhuyi" (Radicalism of the twentieth-century cultural movements). *Dongfang* 1:38–44.

Chen Lai. 1994. "Rujia sixiang yu xiandai dongya shijie" (Confucian ideas and the modern East-Asian world). *Dongfang* 3:10–13.

Chen Lai. 1995. "Jiushi niandai bulu weijian de 'guoxue yanjiu'" (The difficult "Chinese studies" of the 1990s). *Dongfang* 2:24–28.

Chen Lai, et al. 1994. "Quan fangwei tuozhan zhexue yanjiu, chongjian minzu jingshen he jiazhi tixi" (Expanding philosophy studies in all dimensions and reconstructing national spirit and value system). *XHWZ* 8:21–24.

Chen Pingyuan. 1991. "Xueshushi yanjiu suixiang" (Thoughts on research of scholarship history). *Xueren* 1:2–6.

Chen Shaoming. 1996. "Didiao yixie—xiang wenhua baoshouzhuyi jinyan" (Key down a little—advice to cultural conservatism). *Dongfang* 3:86–88.

Chen Song, ed. 1989. *Wusi qianhou dongxi wenhua wenti lunzhan wenxuan* (Selected essays on debates over Eastern-Western cultural issues before and after the May Fourth Movement). Beijing: China's Social Science Press.

Chen Xiaoming. 1993. "Lishi zhuanxing yu houxiandaizhuyi de xingqi" (Historical transition and the rise of postmodernism). *Huacheng* 2:192–207.

Chen Xiaoming. 1994a. "Fan jijin yu dangdai zhishifenzi de lishi jingyu" (Anti-radicalism and the historical situation of contemporary intellectuals). *Dongfang* 1:11–15.

Chen Xiaoming. 1994b. "Mianqiang de jiefang: Houxinshiqi nuxing xiaoshuo gailun" (Reluctant liberation: feminist fiction in the post–new era). *DDZJPL* 3:28–39.

Chen Xiaoming. 1994c. "Tianping honggou, huaqing jiexian: 'jingying' yu 'dazhong' shutu tonggui de dangdai chaoliu" (Filling up the gap and drawing the dividing line: contemporary trend of converging "elite" and "masses [cultures]"). *WYYJ* 1:42–55.

Chen Xiaoming. 1998. "Houxiandaizhuyi bushi yiduanxieshuo" (Postmodernism is not heresy). *Mingbao yuekan* 2 (February): 61–66.

Chen Xiaoming, et al. 1993. "Jingshen tuifei de kuangwu" (The wild dance of the spiritually decadent). *Zhongshan* 6:142–62.

Chen Xiaoming, et al. 1994. "Dongfangzhuyi yu houzhimin wenhua" (Orientalism and postcolonial culture). *Zhongshan* 1:126–48.

Chen Yaohong. 1994. "Houzhimin zhihou de jiyu yu xuanze" (Situation and choice after postcolonialism). *WYB*, September 17.

Chen, Xiaomei. 1995. *Occidentalism: A Theory of Counter-Discourse in Post-Mao China*. New York: Oxford University Press.

Chow, Rey. 1992. "Between Colonizers: Hong Kong's Postcolonial Self-Writing in the 1990s." *Diaspora* 2 (2): 151–70.

Chow, Rey. 1993. *Writing Diaspora: Tactics of Intervention in Contemporary Cultural Studies*. Bloomington: Indiana University Press.

Collins, Jim. 1989. *Uncommon Cultures: Popular Culture and Postmodernism*. New York: Routledge.

Collins, Peter. 1992. *Ideology after the Fall of Communism*. London: Boyards/Bowerdean.

Connerton, Paul. 1989. *How Societies Remember*. Cambridge: Cambridge University Press.

Crane, Diana. 1972. *Invisible Colleges*. Chicago: University of Chicago Press.

Curtis, Michael. 1969. "Retreat from Totalitarianism." In Friedrich, Curtis, and Barber 1969.

Dai Jinhua. 1994. "Tuwei biaoyan: jiushi niandai wenhua miaoshu zhiyi" (Breaking out of an encirclement: a description of the 1990s culture). *Zhongshan* 6:97–104.

Dallmayr, Fred R. 1984. *Polis and Praxis: Exercises in Contemporary Political Theory*. Cambridge: MIT Press.

Darnovsky, Marcy, et al., eds. 1995. *Cultural Politics and Social Movements*. Philadelphia: Temple University Press.

Deng Shaoji. 1995. "Wo guan 'guoxue re' " (My view of "fever of Chinese scholarship"). *Zhongguo shehui kexueyuan yanjiushengyuan xuebao* (Journal of Graduate School of China Academy of Social Science) 5:3–5.

Deng Xiaomang. 1996. "Lu Xun jingshen yu xinpipanzhuyi" (The spirit of Lu Xun and new criticism). *HZSFXB* 5;7–8.

Derber, Charles, et al. 1995. *What's Left? Radical Politics in the Postcommunist Era*. Amherst: University of Massachusetts Press.

Derrida, Jacques. 1972. *La Dissemination*. Paris: Edition du Seuil.

Derrida, Jacques. 1985. "Des Tours de Babel." In Joseph F. Graham, ed., *Difference in Translation*. Ithaca, NY: Cornell University Press.

Dhareshwar, Vivek. 1989. "Detours: Theory, Narrative, and the Inventions of Post-Colonial Identity." Ph.D. diss., University of California, Santa Cruz.

Ding Dong, and Sun Min, eds. 1996. *Shiji zhijiao de chongzhuang: Wang Meng xianxiang zhengming lu* (Encounters at the end of the century: controversy on Wang Meng phenomenon). Beijing: Guangming ribao chubanshe.

Dirlik, Arif. 1989. "Post-Socialism? Reflections on 'Socialism with Chinese Characteristics.' " In Dirlik and Meisner 1989.

Dirlik, Arif. 1994a. "The Postcolonial Aura: Third World Criticism in the Age of Global Capitalism." *Critical Inquiry* 20 (2): 328–56.

Dirlik, Arif. 1994b. *After the Revolution: Waking to Global Capitalism*. Hanover and London: Wesleyan University Press.

Dirlik, Arif, and Maurice Meisner, eds. 1989. *Marxism and the Chinese Experience*. Armonk, NY: Sharpe.

Dirlik, Arif, and Zhang Xudong. 1997. "Introduction: Postmodernism and China." *Boundary* 2 24 (3): 1–18.

Dittmer, Lowell. 1983. "The Study of Chinese Political Culture." In Amy Wilson et al., eds., *Methodological Issues in Chinese Studies*. New York: Praeger.

Dittmer, Lowell, and Samuel S. Kim. 1993. "In Search of a Theory of National Identity." In Dittmer and Kim 1993.

Dittmer, Lowell, and Samuel S. Kim, eds. 1993. *China's Quest for National Identity*. Ithaca, NY: Cornell University Press.

Dong Zhilin. 1995. "'Renwen jingshen' taolun shulue" (A summary of "the humanist spirit" controversy). *GMRB,* June 21.

Du Yeli. 1997. "'Zhimin wenhua' taolun zongshu" (A survey of discussion of "colonial culture"). *XHWZ* 7:160–62.

During, Simon. 1985. "Postmodernism or Postcolonialism?" *Landfall* 39 (3): 366–80.

Edel, Abraham, and Elizabeth Flower. 1981. "Elitism and Culture." In John Agresto and Peter Riesenberg, eds., *The Humanist as Citizen.* Chapel Hill, NC: National Humanities Center. Distributed by the University of North Carolina.

Evan-Zohar, Itamar. 1978. "The Position of Translated Literature within the Literary Polysystem." *Papers in Historical Poetics.* Tel Aviv: Porter Institute for Poetics and Semiotics.

Fan Qinlin. 1995a. "Shiji zhijiao de wenxue jueze yu 'jiushi niandai xinfuguzhuyi'" (Literature's choice at the turn of the century and "the 1990s doctrine of back to the ancients"). *Nantong shizhuan xuebao* (Journal of Nantong Teachers College) 2:7–11.

Fan Qinlin. 1995b. "Minzu zizun de wuqu yu xiandai wenhua de xuanze" (The blind zone of national dignity and the choice of modern culture). *WYZM* 2:33–36.

Fang Keli. 1987. "Ping 'zhongti xiyong' he 'xiti zhongyong'" ("Chinese substance and Western application" and "Western substance and Chinese application"). *Zhexue yanjiu* (Philosophical studies) 9:29–35.

Fang Keli. 1995. "Ping dierci wenhuare de 'huayu zhuanhuan'" ("Discursive change" in the second culture fever). *Gaoxiao lilun zhanxian* (Theoretical front of higher education) 5:61–62.

Fang Keli. 1996. "Yao zhuyi yanjiu jiushi niandai chuxian de wenhua baoshouzhuyi sichao" (Attention to cultural conservative thoughts in the 1990s). *Gaoxiao lilun zhanxian* 2:30–36.

Fang Zizhou. 1996. "Xunzhao xiezuo ziyou de yipian tiankong" (In search of free space for writing). *Mingbao yuekan* 5:37–41.

Featherstone, Mike, ed. 1990. *Theory, Culture and Society.* Special issue on global culture, 7 (1–2).

Feher, Ferenc, and Agnes Heller. 1983. "Class, Democracy, Modernity." *Theory and Society* 12 (2): 211–44.

Ferguson, Russell, et al., eds. 1990. *Out There: Marginalization and Contemporary Cultures.* Cambridge: MIT Press.

Fiske, John. 1987a. *Television Culture.* London: Methuen.

Fiske, John. 1987b. "British Cultural Studies and Television." In Robert Allen, ed., *Channels of Discourse.* Chapel Hill: University of North Carolina Press.

Fiske, John. 1989. *Understanding Popular Culture.* Boston: Unwin Hyman.

Fiske, John. 1992. "Cultural Studies and the Culture of Everyday Life." In Grossberg, Nelson, and Treichler 1992.

Foucault, Michel. 1977. *Language, Counter-Memory, Practice: Selected Essays and Interviews.* Ed. D. F. Bouchard. Oxford: Blackwell.

Foucault, Michel. 1980. *Power/Knowledge: Selected Interviews and Other Writings.* Ed. Colin Gordon. New York: Pantheon Books.

Friedman, Edward. 1994. "Democracy and 'Mao Fever.'" *Journal of Contemporary China* 6 (Summer): 84–95.

Friedrich, Carl J., Michael Curtis, and Benjamin R. Barber. 1969. *Totalitarianism in Perspective: Three Views.* New York: Praeger Publishers.

Fu Kuiyang. 1994. "Zhongyaode, quebei yiwang: guanyu 93 zuojia 'xiahai' remen huati xiaoyi" (The important that is forgotten: on the hot issue of writers doing business ("going out to sea") in 1993). *WYB*, April 16.

Galtung, Johan. 1980. *Peace Problem: Some Case Studies, Essays in Peace Research,* vol. 5. Copenhagen: Christian Ejlers.

Galtung, Johan. 1990. "Cultural Violence." *Journal of Peace Research* 2(3): 291–305.

Gambles, Ian. 1995. "Lost Time: The Forgetting of the Cold War." *National Interest* (Fall): 26–35.

Gan Yang, ed. 1989. *Zhongguo dangdai wenhua yishi* (The cultural consciousness of contemporary China). Hong Kong: Sanlian chubanshe.

Gao Ruiquan, et al. 1994. "Renwen jingshen xunzong—renwen jingshen xunsilu zhiwr" (Tracing back the humanist spirit—reflections on the humanist spirit, II). *Dushu* 4:73–81.

Gao Yuanbao. 1995. "Zhang Wei de fenji, tuique he kunjing" (Zhang Wei's anger, retreat, and plight). *Zuojia bao* (Writers' news), May 27.

Gasster, Michael. 1969. *Chinese Intellectuals and the Revolution of 1911: The Birth of Modern Chinese Radicalism.* Seattle: University of Washington Press.

Ge Hua. 1987. "Luolan Bate de benwen lilun" (Textual theory of Roland Barthes). *WXPL* 5:163–68.

Ge Zhaoguang. 1993. "Zui shi wenren bu ziyou" (The least free is the intellectual). *Dushu* 5:3–12.

Giroux, Henry. 1992. *Border Crossings: Cultural Workers and the Politics of Education.* New York: Routledge.

Goldfarb, Jeffrey C. 1989. *Beyond Glasnost: The Post-Totalitarian Mind.* Chicago: University of Chicago Press.

Goldman, Merle. 1994. *Sowing the Seeds of Democracy in China.* Cambridge: Harvard University Press.

Goldman, Merle. 1996. "Politically-Engaged Intellectuals in the Deng-Jiang Era: A Changing Relationship with the Party-State." *China Quarterly* 145 (March): 36–52.

Goldman, Merle, Perry Link, and Su Wei. 1993. "China's Intellectuals in Deng Era: Loss of Identity with the State." In Dittmer and Kim 1993.

Goldman, Merle, et al., eds. 1987. *Chinese Intellectuals and the State.* Cambridge: Harvard University Press.

Gong Shuduo. 1996. "Jianchi yi makesizhuyi zhidao shixue yanjiu" (Uphold Marxism as a guide for historical research). *RMRB*, August 27.

Gouldner, Alvin W. 1975–76. "Prologue to a Theory of Revolutionary Intellectuals." *Telos* 36:3–36.

Gouldner, Alvin W. 1979. *The Future of Intellectuals and the Rise of the New Class.* New York: Oxford University Press.

Goulet, Denis. 1992. "International Ethics and Human Rights." *Alternative* 17 (2): 231–46.

Grossberg, Lawrence, Cary Nelson, and Paula Treichler, eds. 1992. *Cultural Studies.* New York: Routledge.

Grossberg, Lawrence. 1993. "Cultural Studies and/in New Worlds." In Cameron McCarthy and Warren Crichlow, eds., *Race Identity and Representation in Education.* London: Routledge.

Gu Xin. 1996. "Ziyou minzhuzhuyi, haishi Heigeer shi makesizhuyi" (Liberal democratism or Hegelian Marxism?). *Beijing zhi chun* (Beijing's spring) 7:85–90.

Guo Jian. 1996. "Wenge sichao yu 'houxue' " (The ideology of cultural revolution and "postism"). *ESYSJ* 35:116–22.

Guo Qiyong. 1990. "Shilun baoshouzhuyi sichao" (Trends of cultural conservatism). *Xuexi yu tansuo* (Study and discussion) 1:4–14.

Guo Sujian. 1995. "Totalitarianism: An Outdated Paradigm for Post-Mao China?" *Journal of Northeast Asian Studies* 14 (2): 62–89.

Guo Youpeng. 1990. "Ping 'wenhua re' yanjiu zhong de fei lixinghua qingxiang" (The irrational orientation of the "culture fever"). *Shehui kexue* (Social sciences) 10:40–48.

Habermas, Jürgen. 1975. *Legitimation Crisis.* Trans. Thomas McCarthy. Boston: Beacon Press.

Habermas, Jürgen. 1989a. *The New Conservatism: Cultural Criticism and the Historians' Debate.* Ed. and trans. Shierry Weber Nicholsen. Cambridge: MIT Press.

Habermas, Jürgen. 1989b. *The Structural Transformation of the Public Sphere.* Cambridge, MA: Polity Press.

Habermas, Jürgen. 1992. "Citizenship and National Identity: Some Reflections on the Future of Europe." *Praxis International* 12 (1): 1–19.

Halbwachs, Maurice. 1992 [1952]. *On Collective Memory.* Trans. Lewis A. Coser. Chicago: University of Chicago Press.

Hall, Stuart, and Tony Jefferson. 1976. *Resistance through Rituals: Youth Subcultures in Post-War Britain.* London: Hutchinson.

Hall, Stuart. 1980. "Encoding/Decoding." In Stuart Hall et al., eds., *Culture, Media, Language.* London: Hutchinson.

Hansen, Miriam. 1991. *Babel and Babylon: Spectatorship in American Silent Film.* Cambridge: Harvard University Press.

Hansen, Miriam. 1993. "Early Cinema, Late Cinema: Permutations of the Public Sphere." *Screen* 34 (3): 179–210.

Havel, Vaclav. 1986. "The Power of the Powerless." In Jan Vladislav, ed., *Vaclav Havel, or Living in Truth.* London: Faber and Faber.

Hayden, Tom. 1967. "A Letter to the New (Young) Left." In M. Cohen and D. Hale, eds., *The New Student Left,* rev. ed. Boston: Beacon Press.

He Manzi. 1994. "'Guoxue' jie" (Interpreting "Chinese studies"). *Liaowang* 39:40–41.

He Manzi. 1995. "'Houguoxue' xutuo zheng" (The collapse of "post–Chinese studies"). *Suibi* (Essay) 5:59–63.

He Yi. 1995. "Quntixing jingshen taowang" (Collective spiritual escapism). *WYZM* 3:25–31.

Hebdige, Dick. 1988. *Hiding in the Light*. New York: Routledge.

Hermans, Theo, ed. 1985. *The Manipulation of Literature: Studies in Literary Translation*. London and Sydney: Croom Helm.

Hewson, Lance, and Jacky Martin. 1991. *Redefining Translation: The Variational Approach*. London: Routledge.

Hong Zicheng. 1995. "Wenxue 'zhuanxiang' he jingshen 'bengbai'" ("Changes" in literature and "collapse" of the spirit). *ZHDSB*, May 3.

Horkheimer, Max, and Theodor W. Adorno. 1972. *Dialectic of Enlightenment*. Trans. John Cumming. New York: Herder and Herder.

Howard, Dick. 1988. *The Politics of Critique*. Minneapolis: University of Minnesota Press.

Howe, Irving, 1963, "1984: History as Nightmare." In Irving Howe, ed., *Orwell's Nineteen Eighty-Four*. New York: Harcourt, Brace and World.

Hu Bin. 1993. "Yiren shengya, cuiren leixia: guan yingpian *Bawang bieji*" (The soul-stirring life of an artist: viewing *Farewell My Concubine*). *Shenzhen tequ bao* (News of the Shenzhen special zone) June 11.

Hu Shi. 1921. "Shiyanzhuyi" (Experimentalism). In *Hu Shi wencun* (Collected essays by Hu Shi), 2 vols. Shanghai: Yuandong tushuguan. First published in *Xin qingnian* (New youth), 6, no. 4 (1919): 385–401.

Hu Shi. 1989. *Hu Shi de riji* (Diary of Hu Shi), vol. 11 (December 22, 1933). Taibei: Yuanliu.

Hu Xiaoming. 1994. "Zhen jia guoxue de shijinshi" (The test of genuine and false Chinese scholarship). *Dongfang* 6:79–83.

Huang Baosheng. 1994. "Waiguo wenxue yanjiu fangfa tan" (Methodology of the studies of foreign literature). *WGWXPL* 3:123–26.

Huang Hao. 1995. "Wenxue piping zai danxin shenme?" (What is literary criticism worrying about?). *WYB*, August 27.

Huntington, Samuel. 1993. "The Clash of Civilizations." *Foreign Affairs* 72 (3): 21–49.

Jacoby, Russell. 1987. *The Last Intellectuals: American Culture in the Age of Academe*. New York: Basic Books.

Jameson, Fredric. 1986. "Third World Literature in an Age of Multinational Capitalism." *Social Text* 15:65–88.

Jameson, Fredric. 1991. *Postmodernist: Or, the Cultural Logic of Late Capitalism*. Durham, NC: Duke University Press.

Jameson, Fredric. 1994. *The Seeds of Time*. New York: Columbia University Press.

Ji Guangmao. 1995. "Nanyuan yu beizhe zhijian—cong liangpian wenzhang luekui baoshouzhuyi yu jijinzhuyi de xunxi" (Trying to go south by driving the chariot north: reading two articles on conservatism and radicalism). *WYZM* 4:12–20.

Ji Xianlin, et al. 1995. "'Wenhua zhiminzhuyi' xianxiang hai xu shenru toushi" (See through the phenomena of "cultural colonialism"). *Jingji ribao*, November 3.

Jiang Yin. 1991. "Xueshushi yanjiu yu xueshu guifanhua" (Research of scholarship history and academic normalization). *Xueren* 1:39–45.

Jin Chongzhi, Hu Shengwu, and Lin Huaguo. 1996. "Zhengque renshi zhongguo jindaishi shang de geming yu gailiang" (For a correct understanding of revolution and reform in modern Chinese history). *GMRB*, March 12.

Jin Dacheng. 1991. "Dui lishi de chongxin chanshi yu jijinzhuyi fan chuantong de xueshu shenhua" (Revaluating history and the academic myth of radical anti-traditionalism). *Xueren* 1:15–20.

Johnson, Chalmers. 1968. "China: The Cultural Revolution in Structural Perspective." *Asian Survey* (January): 1–15.

Johnson, Randall. 1989. "Tupy or Not Tupy: Cannibalism and Nationalism in Contemporary Brazilian Literature." In John King, ed., *Modern Latin American Fiction: A Survey*. London: Faber and Faber.

Kim, Samuel S. 1989. *The Third World in Chinese World Policy*. Princeton, NJ: Center of International Studies, Princeton University.

Kim, Samuel S. 1990. "Thinking Globally in Post-Mao China." *Journal of Peace Research* 27 (2): 191–209.

Kim, Samuel S. 1991. *China in and out of the Changing World Order*. Princeton, NJ: Center of International Studies, Princeton University.

Kim, Samuel S. 1992. "International Organizations in China's Foreign Policy." *Annals of the American Academy of Political and Social Science* 519:140–57.

Kinston-Mann, Esther. 1988. "'Perestroika' with a Human Face?" *Socialist Review* 18 (1): 7–15.

Kluge, Alexander. 1981–82. "On Film and the Public Sphere." *New German Critique* 24–25:206–20.

Kluge, Alexander. 1988. "On New German Cinema, Art, Enlightenment, and the Public Sphere: An Interview with Alexander Kluge." *October* 46:23–59.

Kohn, Hans. 1961. *The Idea of Nationalism: A Study in Its Origins and Background*. New York: Macmillan.

Kraus, Richard Curt. 1981. *Class Conflict in Chinese Socialism*. New York: Columbia University Press.

Kristof, Nicholas D. 1995. "The Rotting State." In Nicholas D. Kristof and Sheryl Wudunn, *China Wakes: The Struggle for the Soul of Rising Power*. New York: Vintage Books.

Kuhn, Thomas S. 1970. *The Structure of Scientific Revolutions*, 2d ed. Chicago: University of Chicago Press.

Kwong, Julia. 1988. "The 1986 Student Demonstrations in China: Democratic Movement?" *Asian Survey* 10:970–85.

Laclau, Ernesto, and Chantal Mouffe. 1985. *Hegemony and Socialist Strategy: Democratic Politics*. London: Verso.

Laclau, Ernesto. 1990. *New Reflections on the Revolution of Our Time.* London: Verso.

Larson, Magali Sarfatti. 1977. *The Rise of Professionalism.* Berkeley: University of California Press.

Lattas, Andrew. 1996. "Memory, Forgetting and the New Tribes Mission in West New Britain." *Oceania* 66 (4): 286–304.

Lefort, Claude. 1986. *Political Forms of Modern Society.* Cambridge, MA: Polity Press.

Lei Yi. 1995. "Beijing yu cuowei" (Background and dislocation). *Dushu* 4:16–20.

Lei Yi. 1997. "Shenme shi baoshou? Shui fandui minzhu?" (What is conservatism? who opposes democracy?) *ESYSJ* 39:121–25.

Li Bin. 1994. "Fanguan dianshi: yizhong pipan xuepai de guandian" (Reflection on film: a critical view). *Xuexi* (Study) 3:73–79.

Li Hang. 1987. "Huayu, quanli, zuozhe: Fuke houjiegouzhuyi lilun guankui" (Discourse, power, and writer: a glimpse at Foucault's post-structuralist theory). *WXPL* 4:138–44.

Li Jiefei, et al. 1995. "Jiushi niandai de wenxue jiazhi he celue" (Values and strategies of 1990s literature). *SHWX* 1:66–70.

Li Lianke. 1995. "Menwai tan 'guoxue' " (An amateur's notes on "Chinese scholarship"). *GMRD,* June 5.

Li Shenzhi. 1994. "Bian tongyi, he dongxi: zhongguo wenhua qianjing zhanwang" (Similarity/difference, East/West: outlook of Chinese culture). *Dongfang* 3:4–9.

Li Shenzhi. 1995. "Yazhou jiazhi yu quanqiu jiazhi" (Asian values and global values). *Dongfang* 4:4–9.

Li Zehou. 1986. *Zou wo ziji de lu* (Go my own way). Beijing: Sanlian shudian.

Li Zehou. 1994. "Li Zehou dawen" (Interview with Li Zehou). *Yuandao* (In search of the spirit of the Chinese culture) 1:1–3.

Li Zehou, and Liu Zaifu. 1995. *Gaobie geming* (Farewell to revolution). Hong Kong: Cosmos Books.

Li Zehou, and Wang Desheng. 1994. "Guanyu wenhua xianzhuang, daode chongjian de duihua" (Dialogue on the current cultural situation and moral reconstruction). *Dongfang* 5:69–73; 6:85–87.

Liu Dong. 1991. "Butong jiafa" (Against the discipline). *Xueren* 1:20–27.

Liu Dong. 1993. "Zhongguo nengfou zoutong 'dongya daolu'?" (Can China march on the "Asian road"?). *Dongfang* 1:7–16.

Liu Fangping. 1995. "Jingti 'zhimin wenhua' de chenzha fanqi" (Watch out for the coming back of "colonial culture"). *Jiefang ribao,* November 25.

Liu Jianjun. 1993. "Wenhua de zhengzhi kunjing" (The political dilemma of culture). *Dushu* 12:75–78.

Liu Junning. 1993. "Xinjiapo: rujiao ziyouzhuyi de tiaozhan" (Singapore: challenge of Confucian liberalism). *Dushu* 2:9–15.

Liu Kang, et al. 1996. *Zai yaomohua zhongguo de beihou* (Behind the scene of demonizing China). Beijing: Zhongguo shehui kexue chubanshe.

Liu Kang. 1996a. "Quanqiu geju xia de dangdai wenhua piping" (Contemporary cultural criticism of a globalist pattern). *WYLLYJ* 1:66–68.

Liu Kang. 1996b. "Quanqiuhua yu zhongguo xiandaihua de butong xuanze" (Globalization and alternative paths of Chinese modernization). *ESYSJ* 38:140–46.

Liu, Lydia. 1995. *Translingual Practice: Literature, National Culture, and Translated Modernity—China, 1900–1937.* Stanford, CA: Stanford University Press.

Lu Peng. 1993. "Zui shi wenren you ziyou" (The freest is the intellectual). *Dushu* 8:62–66.

Lu, Sheldon Hsiao-peng. 1997. "Global Postmodernization." *Boundary 2* 24 (3): 65–98.

Lu Xun. 1973. "Nalaizhuyi" (Grablism), *Lu Xun quanji* (The complete works of Lu Xun), 20 vols. Beijing: Renmin chubanshe.

Lull, James. 1991. *China Turned On: Television, Reform, and Resistance.* London: Routledge.

Lyotard, Jean-François. 1984. *The Postmodern Condition: A Report on Knowledge.* Trans. Geoff Bennington and Brian Massumi. Minneapolis: University of Minnesota Press.

Ma Chenghua. 1993. "Fangsong qineng you ziji" (Is relaxation self-chosen?). *Dushu* 12:132–34.

Ma Ning. 1987. "Notes on the New Filmmakers." In George Stephen Semsel, ed., *Chinese Film: The State of the Art in the People's Republic.* New York: Praeger.

Madsen, Richard. 1990. "The Public Sphere, Civil Society, and Moral Community: A Research Agenda for Contemporary China Studies." *Modern China* 19 (2): 183–93.

Manning, Stephen. 1994. "Social and Cultural Prerequisites of Democratization: Generalizing from China." In Edward Friedman, ed., *The Politics of Democratization: Generalizing East Asian Experiences.* Boulder, CO: Westview Press.

Marx, Karl. 1973. *Grundrisse: Foundation of the Critique of Political Economy* (rough draft). Trans. Martin Nicolaus. New York: Vintage Books.

Mattelart, Armand. 1992. *La Communication-monde: histoire des idées et des stratégies.* Paris: Edition la Découverte.

Matustik, Martin J. 1993. *Postnational Identity: Critical Theory and Existential Philosophy in Habermas, Kierkegaard, and Havel.* New York: Guilford Press.

Meisner, Maurice. 1977. *Mao's China: A History of the People's Republic.* New York: Free Press.

Meisner, Maurice. 1989. "The Deradicalization of Chinese Socialism." In Dirlik and Meisner 1989.

Meng Fanhua. 1994. "Wenhua bengkui shidai de taowang yu guiyi—jiushi niandai wenhua de xinbaoshouzhuyi jingshen" (Escape and support in an age of cultural collapse: neoconservative spirit of the 1990s culture). *ZGWHYJ* 4:52–54.

Meng Fanhua. 1995. "Xinlixiangzhuyi yu jingshen wutuobang" (New idealism and spiritual utopianism). *ZHDSB*, May 24.

Merleau-Ponty. 1968. *Résumés de cours*. Paris: Gallimard.

Meschonnic, Henri. 1973. *Pour la Poétique II*. Paris: Gallimard.

Migdal, Joel S. 1988. *Strong Societies and Weak States: State-Society Relations and State Capacities in the Third World*. Princeton, NJ: Princeton University Press.

Miyoshi, Masao. 1991. "A Borderless World? From Colonialism to Transnationalism and the Decline of the Nation-State." *Critical Inquiry* 19:726–51.

Morse, Richard M. 1979. "The Americanization of Languages in the New World." *Cultures* 3:25–37.

Mouffe, Chantal. 1988a. "Hegemony and New Political Subjects: Toward a New Concept of Democracy." In Cary Nelson and Lawrence Grossberg, eds., *Marxism and the Interpretation of Culture*. Urbana: University of Illinois Press.

Mouffe, Chantal. 1988b. "Radical Democracy: Modern or Postmodern?" In Andrew Ross, ed., *Universal Abandon?* Minneapolis: University of Minnesota Press.

Mouffe, Chantal. 1991. "Democratic Citizenship and the Political Community." In the Miami Theory Collective, ed., *Community at Loose Ends*, Minneapolis: University of Minnesota Press.

Murphy, Peter. 1990. "Socialism and Democracy." *Thesis Eleven* 26:54–77.

Nan Fan, et al. 1994. "Renwen huanjing yu zhishifenzi" (Environment of the humanities and the intellectual). *SHWX* 5:76–80.

Nan Fan. 1994. "Huayu quanli yu duihua" (Discursive supremacy and dialogue). *SHWX* 8:69–73.

Nandy, Ashis. 1983. *The Intimate Enemy, Loss and Recovery of Self under Colonialism*. New Delhi: Oxford University Press.

Nandy, Ashis. 1987. *Traditions, Tyranny and Utopias: Essays in the Politics of Awareness*. New Delhi: Oxford University Press.

Negt, Oskar, and Alexander Kluge. 1993. *Public Sphere and Experience: Toward an Analysis of the Bourgeois and Proletarian Public Sphere*. Minneapolis: University of Minnesota Press.

Nickel, James W. 1987. *Making Sense of Human Rights: Philosophical Reflections on the Universal Declaration of Human Rights*. Berkeley: University of California Press.

Nie Zhenbin. 1994. "Ya su zhi bian yu wenyijia de zeren" (The distinction between the elegant and the vulgar, and the responsibility of writers and artists). *WYYJ* 1:25–27.

Nora, Pierre. 1992. "General Introduction: Between Memory and History." In *Realms of Memory*, trans. Authur Goldhammer. New York: Columbia University Press.

Oakeshott, Michael. 1975. *On Human Conduct*. Oxford: Oxford University Press.

Ong Jieming, et al. 1996. *Yu zongshuji tanxin* (A heart-to-heart talk with the general secretary). Beijing: Zhongguo shehui kexue chubanshe.

Pan Shaomei. 1993. "Yizhong xinde piping qingxiang" (A new critical orientation). *Dushu* 9:18–21.

Pei, Minxin. 1994. *From Reform to Revolution: The Demise of Communism in China and the Soviet Union.* Cambridge: Harvard University Press.

Pickowicz, Paul G. 1990. "The Chinese Anarchist Critique of Marxism-Leninism." *Modern China* 16 (4): 450–67.

Pickowicz, Paul G. 1994. "Huang Jianxin and the Notion of Postsocialism." In Nick Brwone et al., eds., *New Chinese Cinemas: Forms, Identities, Politics.* New York: Cambridge University Press.

Poster, Mark. 1989. *Critical Theory and Poststructuralism: In Search of a Context.* Ithaca, NY: Cornell University Press.

Prybyla, Jan S. 1996. "China's Economic Reforms: A Synoptic View." *Journal of Northeast Asian Studies* 15 (1): 69–88.

Pye, Lucian W. 1971. "Identity and the Political Culture." In Leonard Binder et al., eds., *Crises and Sequences in Political Development.* Princeton, NJ: Princeton University Press.

Qi Shuyu. 1995. "Wufa huibi de chonggao" (Nobility that cannot be avoided). *WYZM* 3:12–17.

Qian Jun. 1993. "Saiyide tan wenhua" ([Edward] Said on culture). *Dushu* 9:10–17.

Qian Wenzhong. 1991. "Youyidai ren de xueshushi yanjiu" (A new generation of research of scholarship history). *Xueren* 1:10–15.

Qian Xun. 1986. "Weirao 'xiti zhongyong' de zhengming" (Controversy over "Western substance and Chinese application"). *Tuanjie bao*, December 6.

Qu Xuewei. 1994. "Zouchu bentuhua liangnan de kunjing" (Beyond the dilemma of indigenization). *Dongfang* 6:71–74.

Ricoeur, Paul. 1965. *History and Truth.* Trans. Charles A. Kelbley. Evanston, IL: Northwestern University Press.

Robins, Devin. 1991. "Tradition and Translation: National Culture in Its Global Context." In John Corner and Sylvia Harvey, eds., *Enterprise and Heritage: Crosscurrents of National Culture.* London: Routledge.

Rorty, Richard. 1991. *Essays on Heidegger and Others: Pilosophic Papers, Volume 2.* New York: Cambridge University Press.

Ruiz, Lester Edwin J. 1991. "After National Democracy: Radical Democratic Politics at the Edge of Modernity." *Alternatives* 16 (2): 161–200.

Rupnik, Jacques. 1989. *The Other Europe.* New York: Pantheon Books.

Said, Edward W. 1975. *Orientalism.* New York: Pantheon Books.

Said, Edward W. 1983. *The World, the Text, and the Critic.* Cambridge: Harvard University Press.

Said, Edward W. 1988. "Forward." In Ranajit Guha and Gayatri Chakravorty Spivak, eds., *Selected Subaltern Studies.* New York: Oxford University Press.

Said, Edward W. 1989. "Representing the Colonized: Anthropology's Interlocutor." *Critical Inquiry* 15:205–25.

Said, Edward W. 1993. *Culture and Imperialism.* New York: Alfred A. Knopf.

Sakamoto, Yoshikazu. 1991. "Introduction: The Global Context of Democratization." *Alternatives* 16 (2): 119–27.

Sapir, Edward. 1956. *Culture, Language and Personality.* Berkeley: University of California Press.

Sautman, Barry. 1992. "Sirens of the Strongman: Neo-Authoritarianism in Recent Chinese Political Theory." *China Quarterly* 129 (March): 72–100.

Schlesinger, Philip. 1987. "On National Identity: Some Conceptions and Misconceptions Criticized." *Social Science Information* 26 (2): 219–64.

Schreiter, Robert J. 1985. *Constructing Local Theologies*. Maryknoll, NY: Orbis Books.

Schwarcz, Vera. 1986. *The Chinese Enlightenment: Intellectuals and the Legacy of the May Fourth Movement of 1919*. Berkeley: University of California Press.

Sciolla, L., ed. 1983. *Identità: percorsi di analisi in sociologia*. Torino: Rosenberg and Sellier.

Scott, David. 1996. "The Aftermaths of Sovereignty: Postcolonial Criticism and the Claims of Political Modernity." *Social Text* 14 (3): 1–26.

Sennett, Richard. 1980. *Authority*. New York: Alfred A. Knopf.

Sha Jiansun. 1996. "Zenyang pingjia wusi shiqi de xinwenhua yundong" (How to evaluate the new culture movement during the May Fourth period). *WYLYP* 1:41–49.

Shao Jian. 1994. "Dongfang zhi wu" (The fallacy of the orient). *WYZM* 4:10–16.

Shao Jian. 1995. "Shijimo de wenhua pianhang" (The cultural deviation at the end of the century). *WYZM* 1:25–35.

Shao Yanjun. 1994. "Zhang Chengzhi tan wentan duoluo" (Zhang Chengzhi on the decadence of writers). *Zuopin yu zhengming* (Works and debates) 10:77–78.

Shi Zhong. 1993. "Weilai de chongtu" (Conflicts in the future). *ZLYGL* 1:46–50.

Shi Zhong. 1996. "Xifangren yan zhong de 'zhongguo minzuzhuyi'" ("Chinese nationalism" in the eyes of westerners). *ZLYGL* 1:20–26.

Shohat, Ella. 1992. "Notes on the 'Post-Colonial'." *Social Text* 31–32:99–113.

Smith, Paul. 1988. *Discerning the Subject*. Minneapolis: University of Minnesota Press.

Smith, Paul. 1991. "Laclau's and Mouffe's Secret Agent." In the Miami Theory Collective, ed., *Community at Loose Ends*. Minneapolis: University of Minnesota Press.

Song Qiang, et al. 1996. *Zhongguo keyi shuo bu* (China can say no). Beijing: Zhongguo gongshang lianhe chubanshe.

Song Zhongfu, Zhao Jihui, and Pei Dayang. 1991. *Ruxue zai xiandai zhongguo* (Confucian studies in modern China). Beijing: Zhongzhou guji chubanshe.

Spivak, Gayatri Chakravorty. 1990a. "Gayatri Spivak on the Politics of the Subaltern." Interview by Howard Winant. *Socialist Review* 23 (3): 81–98.

Spivak, Gayatri Chakravorty. 1987. *Other World: Essays in Cultural Politics*. New York: Methuen.

Spivak, Gayatri Chakravorty. 1990b. *The Post-Colonial Critic*. New York: Routledge.

Steiner, George. 1975. *After Babel: Aspects of Language and Translation*. London: Oxford University Press.

Stromberg, Roland N. 1975. *An Intellectual History of Modern Europe*, 4th ed. Englewood Cliffs, NJ: Prentice-Hall.

Su Wei. 1996a. "Heliu de jijie: dalu dangxia renwen fengshang yipie" (The season of coming together: a glimpse at humanities trends in contemporary China). *Kaifang zazhi* (Openness) 4:94–97.

Su Wei. 1996b. "Jinqi zhongguo dalu de 'Chen Yinke re' yu 'Gu Zhun re'" (Recent "fever of Chen Yinke" and "fever of Gu Zhun" in mainland China). *Shijie ribao: Shijie zhoukan* (World journal weekly), October 27 and November 3.

Su Wen, and Bian Wu. 1998. "Jianchi zhengyi bi 'gaobie geming' geng zhongyao" (Upholding justice is more important than bidding farewell to revolution). *ESYSJ* 47:160.

Sun Shengtao. 1993. "Minzu yuyan: disan shijie wenben de jiedu shiyi" (National allegory: interpreting the third-world text). *WGWXPL* 4:27–32.

Sun Yongmeng. 1994. "Ya yu su: zhongguo wenhua de kunjing he chulu" (The elegant and the vulgar: the plight and the future of Chinese culture). *Zhongguo wenhua bao* (Chinese culture bulletin), April 15; *XHWZ* 6:162–64.

Sun Zhanguo. 1994. "Lun shichang jingji dachao zhong de yansu wenyi" (Serious literature and art in the big wave of market economy). *RMRB*, February 24.

Tang Xiaobing. 1987. *Houxiandaizhuyi yu wenhua lilun* (Postmodernism and cultural theory). Taiyuan: Shanxi shifan daxue chubanshe (Press of Shanxi Teachers University).

Tang Xiaobing. 1993. "Orientalism and the Question of Universality: The Language of Contemporary Chinese Literary Theory." *Positions* 1 (2): 389–413.

Tang Yijie, and Min Huiquan. 1996. "Wenhua licheng de fansi yu zhanwang" (Looking back on the course of culture and into its future). *Xiandai chuanbo* (Modern communication), Humanities edition, 3:1–8.

Tang Yijie. 1994. "Lun wenhua zhuanxing shiqi de wenhua heli" (Cultural converging force in a period of remoulding of cultures). *Zhongguo wenhua* (Chinese culture) 10:220–31.

Tang Yijie. 1995. "'Wenhua re' yu 'guoxue re'" ("Culture fever" and "fever of new Chinese scholarship"). *ESYSJ* 31:32–35.

Tao Dongfeng. 1994. "Zhongxin yu bianyuan de weiyi: Zhongguo zhishi jingying neibu jiegou de bianqian" (Move from the center to the periphery: structural changes of Chinese intellectual elites). *Dongfang* 4:18–22.

Tao Dongfeng. 1996a. "Chaoyue lishizhuyi yu daodezhuyi de eryuan duili: lun duidai dazhong wenhua de disanzhong lichang" (Beyond the categorical dichotomy of historicism and moralism: a third position on the popular culture). *Shanghai wenhua* 3:20–28.

Tao Dongfeng. 1996b. "Jiushi niandai wenhua lunzheng de huigu yu fansi" (Reflection on the 1990s cultural controversies). *Xueshu yuekan* (Academic monthly) 4:34–39.

Tao Shuiping. 1994a. "'Shiyuzheng' yu 'huayuquan' de beilun" (The dilemma of "amnesia" and "discursive possession"). *WLB*, June 5.

Tao Shuiping. 1994b. "Tan houxiandai wenhua zai zhongguo xingqi de yuanyin" (Reasons of the rise of postmodern culture in China). *WYYJ* 6:33–36.

Taylor, Charles. 1985. *Philosophy and the Human Sciences*. Cambridge: Cambridge University Press.

Treadgold, Donald W., ed. 1967. *Soviet and Chinese Communism: Similarities and Differences*. Seattle: University of Washington Press.

Tsou, Tang. 1986. *The Cultural Revolution and Post-Mao Reform*. Chicago: University of Chicago Press.

Tsou, Tang. 1996. "Du *Gaobie geming*" (Reading *Farewell Revolution*). *Yuandao* 3:388–405.

Tu Weiming. 1986. "Ruxue disanqi fazhan de qianjing wenti" (Prospect of third-stage Confucian studies). *Mingbao yuekan* (January): 27–32; (February): 36–38; (March): 65–68.

Viereck, Peter. 1978. *Conservatism*. Westport, CT: Greenwood.

Wang Binbin. 1995. "Shidai neibu di diren" (The enemy within our time). *Beijing wanbao* (Beijing evening news), June 15.

Wang Desheng. 1994. "Minjian de xueshuguan—jiushi niandai dalu 'xuekan xianxiang'" (Non-official academic views—"phenomena of learned periodicals" in the 90s' mainland). *Dongfang* 5:56–58.

Wang Guangdong. 1994. "Xiaoshuo zhuanxingqi de meixue tezheng yu wenti" (Aesthetic qualities and problems in the transitional period of fiction writing). *DDZJPL* 3:40–45.

Wang Hui. 1994. "Wenhua pipan lilun yu dangdai zhongguo minzuzhuyi wenti" (Cultural criticism theory and contemporary Chinese nationalism). Interview with Zhang Tianwei. *ZLYGL* 4:17–20.

Wang Hui. 1997. "Dangdai zhongguo de sixiang zhuangkuang yu xiandaixing wenti" (Intellectual condition and modernity problem in contemporary China). *Tianya* 4:133–50.

Wang Jiaxin. 1995. "'Lixiangzhuyi' yu zhishifenzi xiezuo" ("Idealism" and the intellectuals' writing). *ZHDSB*, June 14.

Wang, Jing. 1996. *High Culture Fever: Politics, Aesthetics, and Ideology in Deng's China*. Berkeley: University of California Press.

Wang Jisi, ed. 1995. *Wenming yu guoji zhengzhi: Zhongguo xuezhe ping Hengtingdun de wenming chongtu lun* (Civilization and international politics: Chinese scholars on Huntington's theory of civilization clash). Shanghai: Shanghai renmin chubanshe.

Wang Lixiong. 1994. "Dui xinqi wuxiuzhi de milian" (Endless fascinations with the new). *Dongfang* 5:51–55.

Wang Meng, et al. 1995. "'Wenhua zhiminzhuyi' xianxiang buke dengxian shizhi" (Never neglect the phenomena of "cultural colonialism"). *Jingji ribao*, October 20.

Wang Meng. 1993. "Duobi chonggao" (Avoiding nobility). *Dushu* 1:10–17.

Wang Meng. 1994a. "Zongtan jingji dachao xia de wentan xianzhuang" (The current situation of literature under the influence of the economic boom). Interview with a reporter of *Wenxue bao* (Literary news). *WXB*, March 24.

Wang Meng. 1994b. "Renwen jingshen wenti ougan" (Random thoughts on the humanist spirit). *Dongfang* 5:46–50.

Wang Meng. 1995. "Xiangqi le Ridannuofu" (Thinking of Zhdanov). *Dushu* 4:21–27.

Wang Ning. 1987. "Houjiegouzhuyi yu fenjie piping" (Poststructuralism and deconstructive criticism). *WXPL* 6:143–50.

Wang Ning. 1992. "Jicheng yu duanlie: zouxiang houxinshiqi wenxue" (Heritage and discontinuity: toward the post–New Era literature). *WYZM* 6:11–12.

Wang Ning. 1993. "Houxiandaizhuyi: cong beimei zouxiang shijie" (Postmodernism: from North America to the world). *Huacheng* 1:194–206.

Wang Ning. 1994. "Houxinshiqi yu houxiandai" (Post–New Era and postmodernity). *WXZYT* 3:53–55.

Wang Ning. 1995. "'Houxinshiqi': yizhong lilun miaoshu" (Post–New Era: a theoretical description). *Huacheng* 3:201–8.

Wang Ning. 1997a. "Orientalism versus Occidentalism?" *New Literary History* 28 (1): 57–68.

Wang Ning. 1997b. "The Mapping of Chinese Postmodernity." *Boundary 2* 24 (3): 19–40.

Wang Shan. 1994. *Disanzhi yanjing kan zhongguo* (Looking at China through a third eye). Hong Kong: Mingbao chubanshe.

Wang Shenzhi. 1994. "Wenhua shichang lun" (On cultural market). *XHWZ* 8:162–65.

Wang Shouchang. 1991. "Xueshushi yanjiu chuyi" (A comment on research of scholarship history). *Xueren* 1:6–10.

Wang Shuo. 1989. "Yidian zhengjing meiyou" (An attitude). *Zhongguo zuojia* (Chinese writers), 6.

Wang Shuo. 1990. "Wanzhu" (The operators). *Wang Shuo xiequ xiaoshuo xuan* (Wang Shuo: selected comic fiction). Beijing: Zuojia chubanshe.

Wang Shuren. 1994. "Wenhua de weiji, ronghe yu chongjian" (Cultural crises, integration and reconstruction). *Yuandao* 1:95–114.

Wang Wei. 1992. "Haidegeer guanyu jishu de benzhi zhi si" (Heidegger on the essence of technology). *Xueren* 3:483–510.

Wang Xiaoming, ed. 1996. *Renwen jingshen xunsi lu* (Thoughts on the humanist spirit). Shanghai: Wenhui chubanshe.

Wang Xiaoming, et al. 1993. "Wenxue yu renwen jingshen de weiji" (Crises of literature and humanistic spirit). *SHWX* 6; *XHWZ* 11:119–23.

Wang Yi. 1991. "Liumang zhengzhi ji Zhang Tiesheng xianxiang" (Liumang politics and the Zhang Tiesheng phenomenon). *ESYSJ* 8:132–37.

Wang Yichuan, et al. 1994. "Bianyuan, zhongxin, dongfang, xifang" (Periphery, center, east, and west). *Dushu* 1:146–51.

Wang Yuanhua. 1993. "Introduction" to *Du Yaquan wenxuan* (Selected works of Du Yaquan). Shanghai: Huadong shifan daxue chubanshe.

Wang Yuanhua. 1995a. "Guanyu jinnian de fansi wenda" (Reflective dialogue about the year [1994]). Interview with Fu Jie. *WYLLYJ* 1:2–8.

Wang Yuanhua. 1995b. "Guanyu ren de suzhi deng wenti dawen" (Dialogue on issues of human quality). *Wenhui dushu zhoubao* (Wenhui reading weekly), July 1.

Wang Yuanhua. 1995c. "Jinnian de fansi" (Reflections of recent years). *Dongfang* 1:72–76.

Wang Yuechuan. 1992. *Houxiandaizhuyi wenhua yanjiu* (Postmodern cultural studies). Beijing: Beijing daxue chubanshe.

Wang Yuechuan. 1993a. "Houxiandai wenhua xianxiang yanjiu" (On postmodern cultural phenomena). *WYYJ* 2:139–49.

Wang Yuechuan. 1993b. "Houxiandai wenxue: jiazhi pingmian shang de yuyan youxi" (Postmodern literature: language games of values). *WXPL* 5:133–43.

Wang Yuechuan. 1994. "Zhishi puxi zhuanhuan zhong zhishifenzi de jiazhi xuanze" (Value choices of the intellectual in the transformation of knowledge genealogy). *Dongfang* 3:22–27.

Wang Yuechuan. 1995. "Zhongguo bainian xueshu sixiang shanbian de jiben wenti" (Basic issues in the transformation of this century's Chinese academic ideas). *Shehui kexue zhanxian* (Front of social sciences) 4:37–46.

Wang Yuechuan, and Shang Shui, eds. 1992. *Houxiandaizhuyi wenhua yu meixue* (Postmodernist culture and aesthetics). Beijing: Beijing daxue chubanshe.

Wasserstrom, Jeffrey N., and Elizabeth J. Perry, eds. 1992. *Popular Protest and Political Culture in Modern China: Learning from 1989*. Boulder, CO: Westview Press.

Weeks, Priscilla. 1990. "Post-Colonial Challenges to Grand Theory." *Human Organization* 3:236–44.

Welch, S. D. 1985. *Communities of Resistance and Solidarity*. Maryknoll, NY: Orbis Books.

Wen Liping. 1995. "Guanyu 'renwen jingshen' taolun zongshu" (A synthetic summary of the humanist spirit discussion). *WYLYP* 3:119–34; 4:123–38.

White, Stephen. 1986. "Economic Performance and Communist Legitimacy." *World Politics* 38 (3): 462–82.

Whiting, Allen S. 1995. "Chinese Nationalism and Foreign Policy after Deng." *China Quarterly* 142:295–316.

Williams, Raymond. 1961. *The Long Revolution*. New York: Columbia University Press.

Williams, Raymond. 1976. *Keywords: A Vocabulary of Culture and Society*. New York: Oxford University Press.

Williams, Raymond. 1977. *Marxism and Literature*. New York: Oxford University Press.

Williams, Raymond. 1989. *Resources of Hope*. London: Verso.

Womack, Brantly, ed. 1991. *Contemporary Chinese Politics in Historical Perspective*. Cambridge: Cambridge University Press.

Wong, Young-tsu. 1993. "The Fate of Liberalism in Revolutionary China: Chu Anping and His Circle, 1946–50." *Modern China* 19 (4): 457–90.

Wu Xiaoming, and Meng Yue. 1987. "Lishi, benwen, jieshi: Jiemuxun de wenyi lilun" (History, text, and interpretation: literary theory of Fredric Jameson). *WXPL* 1:157–64.

Wu Xuan, et al. 1994. "Women xuyao zenyang de renwen jingshen—renwen jingshen xunsilu zhisi" (What kind of humanist spirit do we need?—reflections on the humanist spirit, IV). *Dushu* 6:66–74.

Wu Xuan, et al. 1995. "Zhishifenzi de jiazhi dingwei" (Positioning the value of the intellectual). *WYZM* 5:19–28.

Wu Xuan. 1995. "Piping de zhengjie zai nali?" (Where lies the crux of criticism?). *ESYSJ* 29:125–29.

Wu Yuanmai. 1995. "Yetan waiguo wenxue yanjiu fangxiang yu fangfa" (A reconsideration of the orientation and methodology in studies of foreign literature). *WGWXPL* 4:125–29.

Xiao Gongqin. 1993. "Zouxiang chengshu—dui zhongguo dangdai zhengzhi gaige de fanxing yu zhanwang" (Toward maturity: reflection on and outlook of political reform in contemporary China). *Beijing qingnian bao*, May 13.

Xiao Gongqin. 1994. "Minzuzhuyi yu zhongguo zhuanxing shiqi de yishi xingtai" (Nationalism and ideology in China during the period of transformation). *ZLYGL* 4:21–25.

Xiao Gongqin. 1995. "Wuxu bianfa de zai fanxing: jianlun zaoqi zhengzhi jijinzhuyi de wenhua genyuan" (Reexamination of the reform movement of 1898: also on the cultural origin of the early political radicalism). *ZLYGL* 4:11–20.

Xiao Gongqin. 1996. "Zhongguo minzuzhuyi de lishi yu qianjing" (The history and prospect of nationalism in China). *ZLYGL* 2:58–62.

Xiao Gongqin. 1997. "Dangdai zhongguo xinbaoshouzhuyi de sixiang yuanyuan" (The ideological roots of neoconservatism in contemporary China). *ESYSJ* 40 (April): 126–35.

Xie Mian. 1995. "Lixiang de zhaohuan" (Call of the ideal). *ZHDSB*, May 3.

Xie Yong. 1993. "Bushi zebei wenren de shihou" (This is not the time to blame the intellectual). *Dushu* 12:130–32.

Xin Qi. 1996. "'Zhongguo quan': yige lilun yu xianshi de zouxing" (The "China circle": an undeveloped theory versus reality). *ZLYGL* 3:1–7.

Xing Bensi. 1996. "Jianchi makesizhuyi bu dongyao—huaqing makesizhuyi yu fan makesizhuyi" (Upholding Marxism unwaveringly—making a clear distinction between Marxism and anti-Marxism). *RMRB*, June 6.

Xu Ben. 1989. "Renwen kexue de pipan zhexue: Fuke he ta de huayu lilun" (Critical philosophy of the humanities: Foucault and his theory of discourse). In Gan Yang 1989.

Xu Ben. 1994. "Houxiandai, houzhimin pipan lilun he minzhu zhengzhi" (Postmodern, postcolonial critical theories, and democratic politics). *Qingxiang* (Tendency) 2–3:172–201.

Xu Ben. 1995. "'Disan shijie piping' zai dangjin zhongguo de chujing" (The predicament of "third-world criticism" in China today). *ESYSJ* 27:16–27.

Xu Ben. 1996a. "'Women' shi shui? Lun wenhua piping zhong de gongtongti shenfen rentong wenti" (Who are "we"? problem of identity in cultural criticism). *Dongfang* 2:69–73.

Xu Ben. 1996b. "Cong 'houxinshiqi' gainian tan wenxue taolun de lishi yishi" ("Post–New Era" and the historical consciousness of literary studies). *WXPL* 5:56–65.

Xu Ben. 1996c. "Wenhua taolun he gongmin yishi" (Cultural discussion and civil society). *Dushu* 7:3–11.

Xu Ben. 1996d. "Cong bentuzhuyi shenfen zhengzhi dao zhishi gongmin zhengzhi" (From nativist identity politics to intellectual civil politics). *Qingxiang* (Tendency) 7–8:247–71.

Xu Ben. 1996e. "Shenmo shi zhongguo de houxinshiqi" (What is the post–New Era of China?). *ESYSJ* 36:74–83.

Xu Ben. 1998. *Wenhua piping wang hechu qu? 1989 nian hou de zhongguo wenhua taolun* (Whither cultural criticism? Chinese cultural discussion after 1989). Hong Kong: Cosmos Books.

Xu Jialu. 1995. "Jingti yuwen shenghuo zhong de 'zhimin wenhua' qingxiang" (Watch out for the tendency of "colonial culture" in the daily life of Chinese language). *Zhongguo jiaoyu bao*, November 14.

Xu Jilin, et al. 1994. "Daode, xuetong yu zhengtong—renwen jingshen xunsilu zhisan" (Moral, scholastic, and political traditions—reflections on the humanist spirit, III). *Dushu* 5:46–55.

Xu Jilin. 1994. "Houzhimin wenhua piping mianmian guan" (Aspects of post-colonial cultural criticism). *Dongfang* 5.22–26.

Xu Jilin. 1995. "Bi piping geng zhongyao de shi lijie" (Understanding is more important than criticism). *ESYSJ* 29:130–36.

Xu Jilin. 1996. "Ji lingren xingfen you chongman yihan—jinqi wenhua piping huigu" (Excitement and regret: looking back on recent cultural criticism). *Dongfang* 2:40–43.

Xu Ming. 1991. "Yanjiu luoji, xueshu guifan, zhishi zengzhang" (Logic of research, academic norms, and knowledge building). *Xueren* 1:45–48.

Xu Ming. 1994. "Wenhua jijinzhuyi lishi weidu" (The historical dimension of cultural radicalism). *WXPL* 4:114–20.

Xu Youyu. 1995. "Guanyu houxiandai sichao de yizhong zhexue pinglun" (A philosophical reflection on the postmodern trend). *GMRB*, March 2.

Xu Youyu. 1997. "Baoshou yu cuowei" (Conservation and misplacement). *ESYSJ* 39:28–34.

Yang Chunshi. 1996. "Xinbaoshouzhuyi yu xinlixingzhuyi" (Neoconservatism and neorationalism). *Hainan shiyuan xuebao* (Journal of Hainan Teachers College) 2:8–11.

Yang Yuxi. 1993. "Bu ziyou chu you ziyou" (Finding freedom in an unfree place). *Dushu* 12:136–39.

Yao Wenfang. 1994. "Zhongguo de houxiandai yishu qingxiang jiqi yiyi" (Trends in postmodern art and its significance in China). *Wen shi zhe* (Literature, history, and philosophy) 1:3–8.

Yau, Esther C. M. 1993. "International Fantasy and the 'New Chinese Cinema.'" *Quarterly Review of Film and Video* 14 (3): 95–107.

Ye Wen. 1997. "Ying qubie zhengzhi de baoshouzhuyi he wenhua de baoshouzhuyi" (To differentiate between political and cultural conservatism). *ESYSJ* 40 (April): 136–37.

Yi Dan. 1994. "Chaoyue zhimin wenxue de wenhua kunjing" (Beyond the cultural dilemma of colonial literature). *WGWXPL* 2:111–16.

Yi Dan. 1996. "Chaoyue 'zhimin wenxue' wenhua kunjing de zai sikao" (Rethinking beyond the cultural dilemma of "colonialist literature"), *Zhongwai wenhua yu wenlun* (Chinese and foreign cultures and literary theory), vol. 1. Chengdu: Sichuan daxue chubanshe.

Yi Shuihan. 1988. "Wuchanjieji de liumang yishi weihai shehui" (The *Liumang* mentality of the proletariat threatens society). *Jingjixue zhoubao* (Economics weekly), November 27.

Yin Changlong. 1995. "'Guilai de' Zhang Wei" (Zhang Wei, the "returned"). *ZHDSB*, February 8.

You Xilin. 1994. "Shouhu lixiang yu xiaojie quanwei" (Defend the ideal and deconstruct the authority). *Dongfang* 2:39–40.

Yu Xinjiao. 1995. "Chonggao shi laodong suode" (Nobility is earned from work). *ZHDSB*, June 21.

Yu Yingshi. 1987. *Shi yu zhongguo wenhua* (Intellectuals and Chinese culture). Shanghai: Shanghai renmin chubanshe.

Yu Yingshi. 1993. "Zhongguo jinbainian jiazhiguan de bianqian" (Change of values in the past hundred years in China). *Mingbao yuekan* (Mirror monthly) 4:60–66.

Zang Li. 1995. "Lixiang de yuanwang" (Wish of the ideal). *ZHDSB*, May 24.

Zhang Chengzhi. 1993. "Yibi weiqi" (Using the pen as a banner). *Shiyue* (October) 3:52–53.

Zhang Chengzhi. 1994a. "Qingjie de jingsheng" (The clean spirit). *Shiyue* (October) 1:50–55.

Zhang Chengzhi. 1994b. *Huangmo yingxiong lu* (The hero's road in the desert). Beijing: Zhishi chubanshe.

Zhang Dainian. 1995. "Guoxue yu shidai" (Chinese scholarship and our times). *Zhongguo shehui kexueyuan yanjiushengyuan xuebao* (Journal of the Graduate School of the China Academy of Social Science) 5:1–3.

Zhang Dexiang. 1994. "'Houxiandai' lun: shijimo de lilun moshu yu wenhua yiyu" ("Postmodern" theory: fin-de-siècle theoretical magic shows and cultural ravings). *WLB*, June 5.

Zhang Enhe. 1995. "Ping jinnianlai 'guoxue re' zhong dui wusi xinwenhua yundong de piping" (Review of criticism of the May Fourth new cultural movement in recent "fever of Chinese studies"). *Lu Xun yanjiu yuekan* (Monthly of Lu Xun studies) 8:4–9.

Zhang Fa, Zhang Yiwu, and Wang Yichuan. 1994. "Cong 'xiandaixing' dao 'zhonghuaxing'" (From "modernity" to "Chineseness"). *WYZM* 2:10–20.

Zhang Fa. 1997. "Tantan houxiandai ji qi yu zhongguo wenhua de guanlian" (On postmodernism and its relevance in China). *WYYJ* 11:17–22.

Zhang Hong. 1994. "Waiguo wenxue yanjiu zenyang zouchu kunhuo?" (How shall foreign literature studies come out of its dilemma?). *WGWXPL* 4:122–29.

Zhang Hong. 1996. "Ping 'zhiminhua' de wenhua yujing" (On the cultural context of "colonization"). *Zhongwai wenhua yu wenlun* (Chinese and foreign cultures and literary theory), vol. 2. Chengdu: Sichuan daxue chubanshe.

Zhang Huimin. 1995. "Wenxue xuyao lixiang jingshen" (Literature needs ideal spirit). *ZHDSB*, May 3.

Zhang Jingyuan. 1990. "Bi yu ci: pingjie Aidehua Saiyide de *Dongfangzhuyi*" (Other and self: review of Edward Said's *Orientalism*). *WXPL* 1:129–34.

Zhang Kuan. 1993. "Oumeiren yan zhong de 'feiwo zulei' " (The "others" in the eyes of Europeans and Americans). *Dushu* 9:3–9.

Zhang Kuan. 1994. "Lijing pandao: yichang duoyuan wenhua de lunzheng" (Rebellion: controversy on multi-culturalism). *Dushu* 1:117–23.

Zhang Kuan. 1995a. "Saiyide de 'dongfangzhuyi' yu xifang de hanxue yanjiu" (Said's "Orientalism" and Western sinology). *Liaowang* 27:36–37.

Zhang Kuan. 1995b. "Jiaqiang women dui xifang zhuliu huayu de pipan" (Strengthen our criticism of Western mainstream discourses). *Zuojia bao* (Writers' news), June 24.

Zhang Kuan. 1996. "Guanyu houzhimin piping de zai sikao" (Re-thinking post-colonial criticism). *Yuandao* 3:406–24.

Zhang Longxi. 1994. "Guanyu jige shixin timu" (On some fashionable topics). *Dushu* 5:89–98.

Zhang Longxi. 1996. "Duoyuan shehui zhong de wenhua piping" (Cultural criticism in a pluralistic society). *ESYSJ* 33:18–25.

Zhang Qiqun. 1994. "Delida xueshuo sixiang shuping" (Introduction to Derrida's thoughts). *Xueren* 6:445–73.

Zhang Rulun, et al. 1994a. "Renwen jingshen: shifou keneng he ruhe keneng—renwen jingshen xunsilu zhiyi" (The humanist spirit: whether and how is it possible?—reflections on the humanist spirit, I). *Dushu* 3:3–13.

Zhang Rulun, et al. 1994b. "Wenhua shijie: jiegou haishi jiangou—renwen jingshen xunsilu zhiwu" (Cultural world: deconstruction or construction—reflections on the humanist spirit, V). *Dushu* 7:49–56.

Zhang Rulun. 1994. "Lun dazhong wenhua" (On mass culture). *Fudan daxue xuebao*, Social Science edition, 3:16–22.

Zhang Wei. 1994a. "Yu daxuesheng de malasong changtan" (A marathon talk with university students). *Xiaoshuojia* (Novelists) 3:86–99.

Zhang Wei. 1994b. "Wenxue shi shengming de huxi" (Literature is the breath of life). *Zuojia* (Writers) 4:25–33.

Zhang Wei. 1995. "Jujue kuanrong" (Refusing tolerance). *ZHDSB*, February 15.

Zhang Xudong. 1997. *Chinese Modernism in the Era of Reform: Cultural Fever, Avant-Garde Fiction and the New Chinese Cinema*. Durham, NC: Duke University Press.

Zhang Yiwu, and Meng Fanhua. 1993. "Chen Kaige / Zhang Yimou: Yingxiong he qiutu" (Chen Kaige / Zhang Yimou: heroes and prisoners). *WLB*, September 11.

Zhang Yiwu, et al. 1994. "Chonggu 'xiandaixing' " (Re-evaluating "modernity"). *Huanghe* (Yellow river) 4:195–207.

Zhang Yiwu, Wang Ning, and Liu Kang. 1994. "Houxinshiqi de wenxue piping: dangdai wenhua zhuanxing de yige fangmian" (Literary criticism of the

post–New Era: a paradigm shift in contemporary culture). *Zuojia* (Writers)
6:71–74.

Zhang Yiwu. 1992. "Houxinshiqi wenxue: xinde wenhua kongjian" (Literature
of the post–New Era: a new cultural space). *WYZM* 6:9–10.

Zhang Yiwu. 1993a. *Zai bianyuan zhuisuo: disanshijie wenhua yu dangdai
zhongguo wenxue* (Search at the periphery: third-world culture and contemporary Chinese literature). Changchun: Shidai chubanshe.

Zhang Yiwu. 1993b. "'Houxiandaixing' yu zhongguo dalu dangdai wenhua de
zhuanxing" ("Postmodernity" and contemporary cultural transition in
mainland China). *Zhongguo bijiao wenxue* (Chinese comparative literature)
2:10–24.

Zhang Yiwu. 1994a. "Fan yuyan/xin zhuangtai: houxinshiqi wenxue xin qushi"
(Anti-allegory / new condition: new trends of the post–New Era literature).
Tianjing shehui kexue 4:57–63.

Zhang Yiwu. 1994b. "Xinbaoshouzhuyi: jiazhi zhuanxing de biaozheng" (Neoconservatism: signs of value transformation). *ZGWHYJ* 4:55–56.

Zhang Yiwu. 1994c. "Chonggu 'xiandaixing' yu hanyu shumianyu lunzheng"
(Re-evaluating the argument of "modernity" and written Chinese). *WXPL*
4:109–13.

Zhang Yiwu. 1995a. "Chanshi zhongguo de jiaolu" (Anxiety of interpreting
China). *ESYSJ* 28:128–35.

Zhang Yiwu. 1995b. "Zhang Chengzhi shenhua: houxinshiqi de renjian xiju"
(The myth of Zhang Chengzhi: the human comedy in the post–New Era).
WXZYT 2:31–35.

Zhang Yiwu. 1995c. "Kongju yu taobi" (Fear and escape). *Zuojia bao*, May 27.

Zhang Yiwu. 1995d. "Xuanze de tiaozhan" (The challenge of choice). *Tianjin
shehui kexue* (Tianjin social sciences) 5:41–46.

Zhang Yiwu. 1996. "Zaishuo 'chanshi zhongguo de jiaolu'" (Revisiting "Anxiety
of interpreting China"). *ESYSJ* 35:121–26.

Zhang Yiwu. 1997. "Postmodernism and Chinese Novels of the Nineties."
Boundary 2 24 (3): 247–59.

Zhang Zhizhong. 1994. "Weiji, xuanze yu ziyou" (Crisis, transformation, and
liberty). *DDZJPL* 4:88–97.

Zhao Yanqiu. 1995. "Minzu wenhua yu waiguo wenxue yanjiu de kunjing" (The
dilemma of national culture and studies of foreign literature). *WGWXPL*
2:127–31.

Zhao Yao, and Wang Zhengping, eds. 1994. *Renquan wenti yanjiu* (Studies of
human rights). Beijing: Zhonggong zhongyang dangxiao chubanshe (Press
of the Academy of CCP Central Committee).

Zhao Yiheng (Zhao, Henry Y. H.) 1997. "Post-Isms and Chinese New Conservatism." *New Literary History* 28 (1): 31–44.

Zhao Yiheng. 1995. "'Houxue' yu zhongguo xinbaoshouzhuyi" ("Post-studies"
and China's neoconservatism). *ESYSJ* 27:4–15.

Zhao Yingyun. 1995. "Jingti 'zhiminzhuyi' de miaotou" (Watch out for signs of
"colonialism"). *RMRB*, September 22.

Zheng Min. 1993. "Shijimo de huigu: hanyu yuyan biange yu zhongguo xinshi chuangzuo" (A retrospective in the late 20th century: the transformation of Chinese language and the creation of Chinese new poetry). *WXPL* 3:5–20.

Zheng Min. 1995. "Hewei 'dalu xinbaoshouzhuyi?'" (What is the "neoconservatism of mainland China"?). *WYZM* 5:40–48.

Zheng Ning. 1994. "Shui shi zhishifenzi" (Who is the intellectual?). *Dongfang* 2:37–38.

Zhou Baozheng. 1985. "Xiaoshuo chuangzuo de xin qushi—minzu wenhua yishi de qianghua" (New currents in fiction writing: the strengthening of national consciousness). *WYB*, September 7.

Zhou Suyuan. 1995. "Guanyu 'guoxue' yanjiu he taolun zhong de jige wenti" (Problems of "Chinese studies"). *Jiangxi shehui kexue* (Jiangxi social sciences) 7:184–85.

Zhou Xian. 1995. "Dangqian wenhua quwei de shehuixue fenxi" (A sociological analysis of the current cultural interest). *WYLLYJ* 5:20–30.

Zhou Xiaoming, et al. 1996. "Xinbaoshouzhuyi yu xinpipanzhuyi" (Neoconservatism and new criticism). *Zhongshan* 6:191–200.

Zhou Xiaoming. 1996. "Yizhong zhide zhuyi de sixiang wenhua qingxiang: xinbaoshouzhuyi" (A noticeable intellectual and cultural trend: neoconservatism). *HZSFXB* 5:1–2.

Zhu Huaxin. 1994. "Jiushi niandai dushuren de sanzhong xuanze" (Three choices of the 1990s intellectuals). *XHWZ* 7:207.

Zhu Xueqin. 1993. "Lusuo, dageming qianxi de jingshen fenwei" (Rousseau, the spiritual aura before the [French] revolution). *Xueren* 4:357–90.

Zhuang Sihui. 1994. "Wenhua nengfou shichanghua?" (Can culture be marketed?). *XHWZ* 8:165–68.

Žižek, Slavoj. 1991. *For They Know Not What They Do: Enjoyment as a Political Factor*. London: Verso.

Subject Index

Antagonistic ideology. *See* Ideology
Anticolonial theory
    democracy and, 127–28
    manichean terms of, 124–25, 127
Antiradicalism
    antiliberalism versus, 167
    cultural traditionalism and, 172,
        175–78
    depoliticizing and, 175–76
    dread of democratic principle, 190
    as ideology integral to post-1989
        reality, 182
    as intellectual self-positioning in
        1990s, 167
    issues disguised by, 170
    logic of, 177–78
    new social evolutionism and,
        179–80
    realistic thinking and, 171–75
    in relation to Edmund Burke,
        168–69, 220–21n. 1
    as superior model of intellectual
        sensibility, 172
    usage of conservatism and, 182–83
    See also Conservatism; New cul-
        tural conservatism; Radicalism
Asian miracles, 13, 177, 219n. 2
Asian modernity, 3, 177
Authoritarianism, 11–12, 45, 54, 168
    apology of, 108
    Asian and Chinese values and,
        221nn. 2, 4
    centralized planed economy and,
        40, 45
    coercion of, 79

control of public sphere by, 138–39
cooption of post-ist theory by, 12,
    21, 123
critique of, 15–16, 176, 199–200
democracy versus, 1
economic marketization and, 168
government of, 2–3, 168
hypocrisy of, 31
modernity and, 100
nationalist excuse of, 21
party-state and, 54, 81, 103–4, 127
paternalism and, 30–31
post-Tiananmen responses to, 11–14
repression of, 215–16n. 21
socialism in China and, 10–11
status quo, 182
symbolic basis of, 30
Authority
    arbitrary, 31
    of humanist intellectuals, 37, 48
    political parental, 25, 30–31
    state-people fusion and, 30–31

Campaign against "spiritual pollu-
    tion," 28, 92
Censorship
    discussion of Cultural Revolution
        and, 214n. 14
    mass culture and state, 135–36
    post-ist theory and, 102
    posttotalitarian, 214nn. 14, 15
Chineseness
    cultural conservatism and, 114–15
    idealistic homogeneity of, 115–16
    limitations of, 116–18

251

Chineseness (*continued*)
 as model (paradigm) of knowledge,
  112
 as new subjectivity, 111–12
 as reaction to Western culture, 115
 re-centralizing effort of, 115–16
 as reverse of Orientalism, 118
 rime of Chinese culture and, 115–16
 social features of, 114–15
 xiaokang (comparatively well-off)
  and, 114
Citizenship, 80, 83–84
 as articulating principle, 83
 civil society and, 83, 84
 defined by essentialist nationalists,
  83
 defined by party-state, 83
 liberal, 83, 84
 public sphere and, 137
 radical democracy and, 83
 social resistance and, 84
 sociopolitical criticism and, 83
Civil society, 20, 84, 137
Class
 configuration in China, 47–48
 social stratification and, 47–49
 struggle as antagonistic ideology,
  103–4
Colonialism, 16, 17, 34, 107, 119, 123,
  124, 126, 127, 191, 192, 193, 215n.
  20
Communist Party, 9, 10, 14, 24, 25, 27
 as national representative, 218n. 4
 parental authority of, 25, 30–31
 party-state and, 30–31, 54
Confucianism, 12–13, 24, 30, 51, 60,
  66–67, 93, 116, 155, 171, 203n. 7
 New, 12–13, 115, 221n. 2
Conservatism, 13, 21, 58, 69, 102, 110,
  114–15, 117, 166–70, 182–91, 206n.
  4, 215–216n. 21
 contrast before and after 1989, 167
 as ideology integral to post-1989
  reality, 182–83
 intellectual activism versus, 184–91
 in 1990s, 171–84

 political utopianism and romanticism versus, 169, 170
 pseudo-binary of radicalism and,
  182–84
 rhetoric maneuver of, 167, 206n. 4
 rivalry-complicity relations to official ideology, 183–84
 sociopolitical problems disguised
  by, 182
 usage of, 182
 See also New cultural conservatism
Constitution, 8, 203n. 4
Cross-cultural theorizing
 antagonistic terms of, 129–31
 foreign reference of, 129
Cultural anxiety
 issues obscured by, 130
 nativist consciousness and, 129–31
 post-ist theory and, 129–31
 twofold concerns of, 129–31
Cultural comparison
 cognitive containment in, 148
 May Fourth Movement and, 147,
  219n. 11, 219–20n. 12
 in 1980s, 147
 in 1990s, 147
 relativism in, 148
 viewed by post-ist theory, 147,
  148
Cultural conservatism. *See* Conservatism; New cultural conservatism
Cultural criticism
 change after May Fourth Movement, 57
 character and contour of, 70
 compared with Western cultural
  studies, 2
 condition in 1990s, 3–4
 democratic postcolonial theory and,
  14–18, 123–28, 191–200
 enlightenment and, 179–80
 ethics of, 109
 forbidden zones of, 102
 inscribed in Chinese cultural discussion, 2

intellectual activism and, 184–90
politics and, 19–20
public sphere and, 138–39
rational discourse and, 75–76
regarding social change, 185
retreat from sociopolitical issues, 76
revitalization of, 18–20
silence on postsocialist and posttotalitarian condition, 10–11
theory of domination and violence
and, 123–28
See also Cultural discussion; Culture Fever
Cultural discussion
against autocratic rule, 49
categorized by post-ist theory,
114–15
Chinese versus Western, 2
cultural comparison and, 147
democracy and quandary of, 14–15
dichotomies in, 46–47
intellectual neutrality and, 82–83
issues eclipsed in, 4–5
May Fourth Movement and, 90, 91,
221n. 3
memory and, 166–67
national-cultural identity and, 107–8
new historical factors of, 3–4
new trends in 1990s, 2–3, 20–21, 35,
46–47
in 1980s, 1, 18, 23, 24, 53, 64
political apathy and withdrawal in,
1, 23, 35, 197
politics and, 19–20
postcolonial perspective of, 16–17
post-theories and, 18–20
post-Tiananmen condition and,
5–7
pro-democracy principle of, 14–16
quest for democracy and, 14–15
translation theory and, 161–62
utopian ideology and, 170
See also Cultural criticism; Culture
Fever
Cultural identity, 156. See also
National identity

Cultural nativism
cultural traditionalism versus,
117–18
New Chinese Studies and, 118
Cultural politics, 13, 19–20, 129. See
also Politics
Cultural Revolution, 1, 2, 8, 23, 28, 29,
30, 35, 45, 47, 89, 95, 176, 177–78,
209n. 21
censorship of discussion of, 214n. 14
Marxist-Leninist ideology and,
95–96
mass movement and, 95–96
Tiananmen incident and, 89, 95,
96
totalitarian modernity and, 95,
212–13n. 5
Cultural studies. See Cultural criticism; Cultural discussion
Cultural subjectivity
defined by post-ist theory, 111
as might-have-been-ideal, 111–12
Cultural traditionalism
cultural nativism versus, 117–18
Cultural violence. See Violence
Culture
anthropocentric, 94
boundaries of, 156, 158, 159
of critical discourse, 36–37
decline of homogeneity, 43
deterioration in China, 36
different types of, 139
elite and mass, 36
ethico-mythical nucleus of, 155
heterogeneity of, 42–43
humanist unitary, 40, 42–49
language and, 43
polysystem of, 152–54
semiotic study of, 155
Culture Fever, 1, 2, 6, 11, 150, 151,
163, 172, 174, 175, 176, 179, 213n.
7, 222n. 12

Democracy
as afterthought of national empow-
erment, 15

Democracy (*continued*)
  change in modern world and,
    123–24
  citizen participation and, 84
  dilemma in China, 15–16
  disillusion with, 3–4, 8, 170
  enlightenment and, 93
  as forbidden zone, 102
  globalization of, 123
  humanistic ideals of modernization
    and, 11
  intellectual activism and, 165, 170,
    184–91
  intellectual politics and, 10–11,
    18–20, 182, 184–200
  intellectuals and, 209n. 23
  lack in post-liberation countries,
    199–200
  as linkage of anticolonial and anti-
    totalitarian struggle, 123–24, 127,
    128
  market economy and, 46, 180
  May Fourth Movement and, 90, 176
  modernity as condition of, 91
  modernization in 1980s and, 23–24,
    92, 93, 94, 95, 166–67, 176
  national claim and, 68–69
  nationalism and, 14–15
  neo-authoritarian attitude toward,
    13, 93, 170
  as new principle of cultural criti-
    cism, 10–11
  nullified by antagonist ideology, 106
  oppositional cultural criticism and,
    75–76
  as politico-ethical goal of moder-
    nity, 94
  postcolonial criticism and, 14–18,
    19, 123–28, 191–200
  post-ist attitude toward, 12, 13, 101,
    102, 111, 113, 121, 123, 147, 172,
    178, 179
  postsocialism and, 26, 27–28
  in post-Tiananmen age, 7, 8, 10–11,
    55

  post-Tiananmen legitimacy crisis
    and, 24–30
  as principle of coordination for
    post-theories, 18–20
  public sphere and, 137
  as question of community and iden-
    tity, 84
  radical-conservative contrast and,
    182
  rational discourse and, 75, 79
  in realist thinking, 174, 175
  re-conception of in China, 15
  reinvigoration of, 21–22
  retreat from, 1, 2–3, 8, 23, 54, 55, 78,
    170
  separation from economic modern-
    ization, 11
  socialism and, 26, 28
  third world and, 16, 127–28
  translation and, 154, 161
  totalitarianism versus, 88
  Westernization and, 34, 107, 110,
    206n. 7
Democratic postcolonial criticism, 18,
    123–28, 191–200
  anticolonial theory versus, 124–25,
    127
  as a changing critical perspective, 16
  Chinese cultural criticism and,
    14–18
  emancipatory value of, 16
  as expression of subalterns, 124
  global democracy and, 127–28
  intellectual opposition and, 17
  theory of domination and liberation
    and, 123–28
  See also Democracy, postcolonial
    criticism and
Deng Xioaping's 1992 inspection tour,
    5, 28, 98
Depoliticization, 100
Discourse, unitary, 42–49
Disenchantment
  with democracy (*see* Democracy,
    retreat from)

of intellectuals (*see* Intellectuals,
    political apathy of)
with politics (*see* Politics, apathy
    toward)
Domination
    intranational and international, 16,
        126, 204n. 9
    theory of, 125–28

Eastern Europe, 3, 5, 104, 168,
    212n. 5
Elitism
    democracy and 75, 79
    intellectual, 52–54, 74–75, 78
    political, 78
    popularism versus, 79–80
    rational discourse and, 75, 76
    traditional, 94
Enlightenment, 1, 3, 4, 7, 14, 15, 67,
        74, 90, 93, 102, 114, 179–80,
        181–82, 188
    conservative presentation of, 173
    democratic values and, 170
    emancipation of the mind and, 91,
        92
    enforced, 188
    as first principle of modernization,
        91, 94
    forgetting of, 166–67
    Li Zehou on, 180–82
    liberating versus enslaving, 188
    myth of, 4, 12
    new, 114–15
    in 1980s, 74, 93, 114, 161, 173
    post-, 6, 102
    post-ist hostility to, 99, 101, 102,
        120, 121, 178, 179
    revolution versus, 179–82
    social change and, 91
Everyday Life, 54, 55, 77, 121, 183,
        191, 209n. 23, 211n. 9
    cultivation of, 74, 75
    democracy and, 75
    intellectual authority and, 77–78
    quality of, 74–75

Farewell My Concubine
    alternative narrative of history in,
        134
    audiences of, 139–41, 218–19n. 8,
        219n. 9
    challenge to official historiography,
        134
    Cultural Revolution and, 219n. 9
    cultural self-reflection and, 141–46
    deterioration of political order
        reflected in, 141–42
    horizon of experience and, 141
    nativist criticism of, 131–34
    picture of tyranny and violence in,
        145–46
    political barbarity in, 142
    theme of prostitution in, 141–46
Feudalism, 23, 24, 35–36, 93–94, 95, 96,
        212n. 3, 222n. 7
Film
    audience subjectivity and, 140,
        218n. 7
    audiences of, 140–41
    dual focus of, 139–40
    Fifth Generation, 132–33
    globalization and, 134
    government-sponsored projects of
        mass education and, 134
    history of, 133–34
    as horizon of experience, 140–41
    lack of indigenous purity, 133
    language of, 133
    mass culture and, 134, 136, 137
    national, 133
    nationalism in Chinese, 218n. 4
    national literature versus, 133
    propagandistic function of, 135
    as public sphere, 136–41
    pure entertaining, 135–36
    state censorship of, 135–36
Foreign literature studies. *See* Transla-
    tion
Forgetting
    recent history, 67, 166
    social, 166

Forgetting (*continued*)
    state, 166
    See also Memory
Four Cardinal Principles, 9
Four Modernizations, 88, 91–92
    lack of humanistic ethics, 93–94
    nondemocratic character of, 92, 95
    separation from democracy, 95
    separation from enlightenment, 94
    technical definition of, 92

Gang of Four, 28, 140, 163–64
Geopolitics, 13
Globalism, 13, 17, 89, 98, 99, 129–30,
    135, 145–46, 168, 171, 191, 192,
    193, 194, 199

He shang (River Elegy), 24, 93
Hierarchy
    of arts, 47
    of intellectual speech, 45
    of knowing, 78
    political, 47–48
    professional, 48–49
    social, 47
    of status, 23
History
    construction of meaning and, 5
    of film in China, 133–34
    forgetting recent, 67, 166
    intellectual, 65–66, 70
    Marxist theory of, 62
    memory versus, 164
    originary relation of, 120, 216–17n.
        26
    postcolonial view of, 191–92
    of postmodernism in China, 97–103
    of scholarly research, 63–70, 73
Houxue. See Post-ist theory
Humanist spirit, 1, 10, 12, 13, 36–56,
    206–7n. 8, 208n. 19
    acivic and antipolitical implication
        of, 52–53
    as antidote to moral erosion, 50–51
    ethical attitude of, 49–56

on mass culture, 40
    as personal virtue, 51–52
    private conscience and, 51–52, 53
    professionalism and, 20
    as redemptive moral force, 50–51
    relations to the public, 49, 54–55, 56
    retreat from socialist humanism, 52,
        53
    as safety valve, 55
    ultimate concern of, 49–56
Hybridity, of Chinese postmodernity,
    7

Ideology
    authoritarian rule and antagonistic,
        103–4
    antagonistic, 103–4
    class struggle and, 103–4
    cultural discussion and utopian, 170
    Cultural Revolution and Marxist-
        Leninist, 95–96
    death of, 220–21n. 1
    democracy nullified by antagonist,
        106
    modernity defined by official, 88,
        91–92
    nationalism and official, 34, 98,
        103–7
    post-ist theory and post-Tianan-
        men, 103–6
    post-1989 conservative, 182–84
    posttotalitarian, 108
    statism and party, 10, 203n. 6
    totalitarian, 95–97
Imperialism, 21, 34, 99, 105–6, 107,
    108, 126, 191, 199, 215n. 20
Intellectual activism, 1, 4, 21–22, 64,
    66, 86, 163, 166, 170, 184–91
    democratic principle of, 189, 190
    democratic values of, 187, 189
    enforced radicalism versus, 187–88,
        189, 190
    ethical principle of, 126
    historical context of, 187
    humanist impulse of, 187, 188

intellectual radicalism and, 189
pro-democracy cultural criticism
    and, 170
relations to May Fourth Movement,
    187
revolutionary radicalism and, 189
self-criticism of, 187
subject of criticism and, 187
transformation in 1990s, 3–5
Intellectual humanism. *See* Humanist
    spirit; Intellectuals
Intellectual politics. *See* Intellectual
    activism; Politics
Intellectuals, 1, 2, 3, 14, 15, 19, 36–37,
    39–42, 52, 53–54, 55, 56, 80–87
academic institutions and, 48–49
activism of, 90, 91, 184–89
authority of, 37, 48
common people and, 54–56,
    209–10n. 24
of Confucian tradition, 13
cultural criticism and, 1–2, 124–25,
    126–28
culture of critical discourse and,
    36–37
democratic politics and, 80–87
dilemma in relation to democracy,
    14–15
disillusion with democracy, 2–3
efficacy of activity, 87
engagement of, 57, 58
enlightenment and, 7
escapism of, 58
humanism of, 50–51, 97
humanist, 36–37, 39–41, 42–56
ideal of emancipation, 48–49
identity of, 80, 81, 86
lack of choice in self-positioning,
    36–37, 57–58, 183
liberalism and, 81, 211n. 12
marginalization of, 70, 81, 83–84
on market economy, 39–40, 46
memory of, 163–67
modernization and, 23, 88, 89,
    90–95, 97

moral concerns of, 36–37, 39–41,
    49–56
myth of neutrality of, 83
national sentiments of, 3–4, 106–8
neo-authoritarianism and, 167–70
new trends in 1990s, 2–3, 4, 10–14,
    35, 97–103, 108
organic, 12
political apathy of, 1, 35, 80, 81,
    83–84, 197
politics and, 19–20, 49, 81, 86
post-Tiananmen condition of, 4–5,
    6, 10–14, 53–54, 89
pro-democracy criticism and, 14–15
quandary of identity, 36–37, 57–58
realistic thinking of 1990s and,
    171–82
relations to party-state, 48–49
responsibility to the public, 49,
    54–55
self-interest of, 51, 64–66, 68, 70–73,
    127
separation of the private from the
    public by, 51–53
social stratification and, 48–49
telos of opposition, 124–25, 126–28
unitary culture and, 40–41, 42–45

Language
centripetal and the centrifugal, 43
cultural criticism and, viii
culture and, 43–44
diversity of, 43–45
of film, 133
human consciousness and, 154–55
intellectual, 45
interlanguage reposition, 45
mass culture, popular culture and,
    208n. 14
national identity and, 217–18n. 3
Party, 45
public life and, 154
translation and change in public,
    154, 155
of Wang Suo, 44

Leaping Forward, 26, 45
Legitimacy crisis, 24, 26–27, 35, 37
  defined by Habermas, 33
  erosion of moral vision and, 33–35,
    36
  post-socialist crisis and, 27
  state-nation rift and, 30–33
  state-people fusion and, 26–27, 31
Leninism
  party-state and, 11, 25–26
  political-economic tradeoff of, 26
  social contract of, 26
  social system of, 25–26
Liberalism, 1, 24, 26, 167, 221n. 3,
    222–23n. 10
  combined with cultural traditional-
    ism, 12–13
  cultural pluralism and, 92
  democracy and, 198, 222n. 10
  intellectual, 211n. 12
  intellectual activism and, 186–88,
    189
Literature
  hoodlum and serious, 37–42
  mission of, 38–39

Mao Zedong, de-idolization of, 30
Market economy, 5, 36, 39, 98, 114
  authoritarian order of, 168
  democratization and, 46, 180
  humanist intellectuals on, 39–40,
    46
  mass culture and, 33, 34
  new cultural conservatism and,
    220–21n. 1
Mass culture, 5, 36, 40, 82, 134, 136,
    137, 173
  ambivalence in relation to high cul-
    ture, 137, 138
  function of sociocultural criticism,
    140
  as horizon of experience, 140–41
  mass education and, 134
  mass media and, 136, 138
  new social relations and, 138

popular culture and, 208n. 14, 209n.
    22
  state censorship and, 135–36
May Fourth Movement
  Chinese studies after, 61, 66
  cross-cultural interaction of, 147,
    149, 150, 151, 152, 154
  cultural criticism and, 90, 91, 221n.
    3
  iconoclasm of, 51
  intellectual activism and, 187, 190
  intellectual escapism after, 57
  lumped with the Cultural Revolu-
    tion, 171, 172, 175, 176, 177
  post-ist attitude to, 98, 105, 113,
    115, 178, 179
Memory
  active versus passive, 163
  collective, 163–64
  history and, 164
  new cultural conservatism and,
    165–84
  of 1980s, 21–22, 166–67
  of the Cultural Revolution, 163–64
  of Tiananmen incident, 164
  theorizing and, 163
  three modes of, 165
  See also Forgetting
Micropolitics, 13
Modernity
  anti-authoritarian impulse of, 94
  Asian, 3, 203–4n. 7, 221–22n. 4
  belated in China, 88
  China-specific and responses, 11,
    12–14, 17, 173, 176–77, 221–22n. 4
  as condition of social progress, 93
  contradictory legacy of, 88, 89–97
  critique of, 95–97
  defined by official ideology, 88,
    91–92
  definition alternative to official
    usage, 92–93
  dominator-dominatee relationship
    of, 89
  effect in the West, 2

enlightenment and, 91, 93, 94
five periods in China, 112–13
guoxue's ambivalent relations to, 58–63
humanist ethics of, 94
limits under the Deng regime, 88, 89–95
metamorphosis of, 97–103
moral theory of, 93–94
myth of, 4
neo-authoritarian concept of, 93
New Confucianism and, 177, 203n. 7
New Era and, 113, 114, 120
as new theme of cultural traditionalism, 77–78, 221–22n. 4
parochial model of, 11
philosophical-literary approaches to, 93 94
political, 11
political reform and, 93–94
regarding national identity, 32–34
relations to Western incursion, 90
in relation to postmodernism, 6
social forms and practical orientations of, 91–93
socialist and revolutionary, 89–90
struggle on definitions of, 88, 89–97
totalitarian mode of, 95–97
tradition versus, 94, 199
translated, 220n. 13
as trope of change versus that of revolution, 90–91
as victimizing force against China, 113–14
Western and Chinese cultural studies and, 2
Western hegemony and, 172, 178–79
See also Four Modernizations; Modernization
Modernization
democratization and, 190
of the mind, 23, 175
new conservatism and, 168
revolution and, 181–82, 186, 189

social change and, 185, 190
socialism and, 196–97
in technical terms, 92
Western ideas and, 176, 183
See also Modernity

Nation. *See* National identity
National culturalism, 117–18
National identity, 25, 32, 34, 156
boundaries of, 32
collective moral vision of, 33–34
crisis of, 24–30, 34–35, 36
erosion of moral vision and, 33–35, 36
modern, 33
as modern collective identity, 32, 33
moral content of, 31–33
national language and, 216–17n. 3
nation-state rift and, 30–33
normative principles of, 33
philosophic terms of, 32–33
postsocialist, 35
primordial quantities of, 32, 34
reference group of, 32
responses to crisis of, 35–37
socialism and, 34
world culture and, 32
Nationalism
antagonistic ideology of, 98, 103–7
binary opposition of China versus the West, 98
Chineseness and, 112–18
different kinds of in China, 104, 214–15n. 17
elite and popular consensus on, 106
ideological orthodoxy and, 34, 98
patriotism and, 105, 215n. 19
post-Cold War complexion of, 106
post-ist theory and, 98, 112–18
rise of, 103–8
Tiananmen incident and, 104
undemocratic quality of, 106, 107
Neo-authoritarianism, 12–13, 93, 167–70. *See also* Authoritarianism

New Chinese Studies, 1, 10, 12, 13, 20,
    57–87, 118, 210n. 3
  challenge to, 58, 61–63, 73
  civic virtues and, 75, 79
  commercialism and, 62, 71, 211n. 6
  cultural discussion of 1980s and,
    64–65, 70, 71, 72
  cultural patriotism and, 58–59
  as disciplinary paradigm, 71, 72
  epistemological status of natural
    science in, 68
  history of scholarly research and,
    63–70, 73
  icons of, 67, 68
  intellectual elitism and, 74–75,
    78–79
  intellectual history and, 65–66, 70
  intellectual identity and, 61
  lack of indigenous purity, 61–62,
    210n. 5
  market economy and, 62
  Marxian definition of, 60
  Marxist historiography and, 62
  methodological issues of, 67, 68
  nationalism and, 69
  national spirit and, 60
  normative imperative of, 74
  official endorsement of, 58–59, 69
  political conservatism and, 68–69
  as post-*guoxue*, 58–63, 210n. 4
  professional definition of, 61
  professional identity entailed in,
    70–73
  professional standardization and,
    63, 71, 73
  publications of, 59
  as reaction to cultural iconoclasm,
    64, 65, 66
  reaction to intellectual activism, 66,
    70
  in relation to social morality, 74–80
  in relation to social reform, 66–67
  resistance to moral degeneration,
    74–80
  rise of, 58–60

  scholarly meaning versus social
    meaning in, 68–70
  sociology of scholarship and, 69–70,
    71, 72
  Western methodology and, 62–63,
    68
New Confucianism. *See* Confucianism, New
New cultural conservatism, 167, 171,
    175–84, 220–21n. 1
  ambivalent relations to modernity,
    62–63
  anti-enlightenment stance of, 179
  authoritarianism and, 168–69
  components of, 173
  concept of enlightened authority in,
    169
  concept of revolution in, 180–82
  Confucian values and, 177
  on the Cultural Revolution, 176
  cultural traditionalism and, 175–78,
    184, 221nn. 2, 4
  indigenous quality of, 60
  liberalism and, 167
  new pragmatism and new enlighten-
    ment versus, 114–15
  in 1980s and 1990s, 168
  normative and methodological
    issues in, 68
  post-Cold War age and, 168
  post-ist theory and, 178–79
  realistic thinking of, 172–75
  in relation to status quo, 183–84
  rivalry-complicity relationship to
    official ideology, 183–84
  self-description of, 171, 173
  social evolutionism and, 179–83
  view of 1980s intellectual activism,
    171, 172
  See also Conservatism; Radicalism
New Culture Movement, 2, 90, 113,
    150
New Epochalism, 119–23
  depoliticizing the post-Tiananmen
    era and, 120

new national consciousness and,
114
in post-ist theory, 119–23
postmodern politics and, 121, 122,
123
post-New Era and, 99, 113–14,
119–29
as smug rhetoric of historical
progress, 120
stylistic definition of, 120
as temporal framework of post-ist
theory, 119
Tiananmen incident and, 120
See also Post-New Era
New Era, 113, 114, 120

Opium War, 105, 113, 215n. 19
Oppositional criticism. *See* Intellectual
activism
Orientalism, 11, 22, 99, 108, 117, 118,
122–23, 130, 133, 204n. 9, 216n.
24, 217n. 1

Politics
active citizenship and, 83–84, 209n.
21
apathy toward, 1, 3, 23, 34–35, 77,
80, 81, 83–84, 100, 164, 197,
213–14n. 11
Chinese, 192
cultural, 13, 19–20, 129
cultural criticism and, 19–20
democracy and intellectual, 10–11,
18–20, 80–87, 182, 184–200
geopolitics, 13
of ideas, 19–20
micropolitics, 13
national identity crisis and withdrawal from, 35–36
of parental authority, 25, 30–31
personal conscience versus,
209n. 21
the political and, 19, 204n. 10
post-ist theory and, 109, 121–23
postmodern, 13, 14

professional, 13
of truth and values, 205n. 10
Popular culture, 3
humanist intellectuals and, 55, 56
mass culture and, 208n. 14, 209n. 22
public opinion and, 138
Post-Cold War, 106, 168
Postcolonialism, 17, 89, 119, 192
anticolonialism versus, 124–25, 127
applicability in China, 16–17, 119
as changing critical perspective, 125
as conjunction of world history,
191–92
as critique of totalitarianism and
party-state, 127
as ethics of opposition, 17
democracy and, 199–200
democratic, 14–18, 19, 123–28
multidimensional framework of,
17–18
postmodernism versus, 192–94
postsocialism and, 193–98
relations to Marxism, 119
theory of violence and domination
and, 127
See also Post-ist theory
Post-ist theory, 1, 7–8, 13, 16, 19,
20–21, 88–123, 129–36, 146–49,
178–79, 217n. 28, 217n. 1
academic politics of, 109, 121–23
anti-Western rhetoric of, 103–12,
216n. 24
attack on *luikmu*, 131 32
attention to mass culture, 98–99
attitude to May Fourth Movement,
98, 147, 148
bifurcations of, 102, 214n. 13
on Chineseness, 112–16
contrast-effect of, 100–103
criticism of, 108–10, 215–16n. 21,
217n. 27
cultural anxiety of, 129–30
as cultural nativism, 117–18
dualism of, 100
in foreign literary studies, 146–49

Post-ist theory (*continued*)
  formative moments of, 98–100
  lack of theory of domination, 127
  nativist formation of, 103–12
  negative attitude to democracy, 12,
    13, 101, 102, 111, 113, 121, 123,
    147, 172, 178, 179
  negative attitude to enlightenment,
    99, 101, 102, 120, 121, 178, 179
  as new cultural conservatism, 102,
    110, 114–15, 117, 215–16n. 21
  new epochalism and, 119–23
  new realism and, 99–100
  official nationalism and, 105–7,
    215n. 20
  party-state censorship and, 102
  political implication of, 109, 121–23
  post-New Era and (*see* Post-New
    Era)
  post-Tiananmen antagonistic ideol-
    ogy and, 103–6
  as post-Tiananmen phenomenon,
    97–112
  pro-mainstream nationalism and,
    98, 103–7
  related to postmodernism and post-
    colonialism, 1, 2, 6, 7, 8–9, 13, 14,
    17, 20–21, 88, 89, 90, 97–112,
    116–23, 129, 178
  rhetoric-as-politics of, 121
  rise of, 97–112
  self-contradiction of, 122
  silence on authoritarian modernity,
    100
  third-world concerns of, 21, 88, 101,
    102, 106, 108, 110, 114, 118, 121,
    123
  transformation of, 97–103
  use of globalism by, 89
  See also Postcolonialism; Postmod-
    ernism; Post-New Era
Postmodernism, 1, 2, 6, 13, 17, 88, 89,
  119, 178, 216n. 23
  as antitotalitarian strategy, 88
  capitalism and, 192–93

  celebratory and evasive rhetoric of,
    7
  contestation over, 88–89
  contradiction of, 88, 97
  debate in China, 88, 97–112, 116–23
  defined by Lyotard, 8–9
  different responses to, 18–19
  dubious definition of, 89–90
  history in China, 97–103
  integration with postcolonial the-
    ory, 101–2
  lack of fitness in China, 109
  as modernist discourse, 97
  politics of, 14
  in post-ist theory, 20–21, 88, 89, 90,
    97–112, 119
  postsocialism and, 196–97, 222n. 9
  in postsocialist and posttotalitarian
    condition, 7–14
  prehistory in China, 97, 103
  as "reaction to socialist and revolu-
    tionary modernity," 89–90
  in relation to China's modernity,
    97–98
  semantic complexities of, 8–9, 88–89
  sensibility of in China, 88–89
  theory of socialism and, 28
  transformation into nativist theory,
    97–103
  as Western discourse, 192–93
  See also Post-ist theory
Post-New Era, 99, 114, 119–23
  as age of national authenticity, 114
  defined by post-ist thinkers, 114,
    216n. 25
  smug rhetoric of historical progress,
    120
  supposed intersection with post-
    modern age, 99, 120, 121
  See also New epochalism
Postsocialism, 9, 10, 17, 25–30, 194–98
  as alternative to socialism, 195,
    205n. 2
  beyond parameters of Western
    democracy, 58

capitalism and, 198
decolonization and, 199–200
defined by Dirlik, 27, 28
defined by Pickowicz, 27
definition of, 27
democracy and, 197
disillusion of common people and,
  27
failure of socialism and, 27
legitimacy crisis in China and,
  26–27
political dimension of, 56
postcolonialism and, 194–98
post-liberation countries and,
  199–200
postmodernism and, 195–96, 222n. 9
as post-Tiananmen condition,
  27–28, 29
posttotalitarian control and, 10, 29
Post-Tiananmen dark period, 4, 5, 6,
  8, 99–100
Posttotalitarianism, 7, 9–10, 17, 21,
  29–30, 89, 206n. 4
control and domination of, 10
intellectual evasion of, 12–14
postsocialism and, 10, 29, 205–6n. 3
post-Tiananmen official ideology
  and, 108
See also Totalitarianism
Pro-democracy. See Democracy
Pro-enlightenment. See Enlightenment
Professionalism
alternative authority of, 77–78
club spirit of, 74–75, 76, 79
codification of knowledge by, 72
commercial interests and, 62, 71
commodity of knowledge and, 71
as critical discourse, 75–78
democratic potential of, 75–76
elitism and, 74–75, 78–79
intellectual enclosure and, 74–75,
  76, 79
moral benefits for society, 75–76, 77
new hierarchy involved in, 78
political apathy and, 77

as rational discourse, 75
self-discipline of, 74
as social space, 75–76
standardization of, 63, 71, 73
See also New Chinese Studies
Public sphere, 135, 137, 138, 139, 140
defined by Habermas, 136
defined by Oskar Negt and Alexander Kluge, 136
democracy and, 137
industrial-commercial, 138
normative function of, 136, 137, 139
of production, 138
weakness in China, 138
See also Civil society

Radicalism, 21, 166, 167, 184–91
absence of in 1990s, 184–85
ambivalence of, 190–91
democratic principle of, 189, 190–91
intellectual activism and, 184–91
intellectual versus enforced, 188,
  189, 190
liberalism and, 167
as modern phenomenon in China,
  185
pseudo-binary of conservatism versus, 182–85, 186–87
as reaction to foreign incursion,
  185, 186
See also Conservatism; New cultural conservatism
Realism, 90–100, 104
critical thinking versus, 173–75
routes of transformation, 173
thinking of, 173–75
variations of, 175–84
renwen jingshen taolun. See Humanist
  spirit
Revolution, 179–82, 187–89
democracy and, 188–91
enforced community and, 188
modernization versus, 90–91, 185,
  186
priorities and basic values of, 36

Revolution (*continued*)
  rationality of, 188
  as trope of change, 90–91
  of the 20th century, 180–81, 188

Socialism, 9, 10, 25–30
  appeal in China, 25
  capitalism and, 205–6n. 3
  with Chinese characteristics, 27,
    28
  crisis of, 25–28
  democracy and, 198, 199, 222–21n.
    10
  discrepancy with democracy,
    198–99
  egalitarianism and, 10, 194, 195,
    198–99, 222n. 8
  elements of Chinese, 10, 194
  failure of Maoist, 28
  humanist promise of, 28
  Leninist, 25–26
  party-state parental authority and,
    25, 30–31
  postsocialism and, 195, 205n. 2
  statism in Chinese, 10, 194, 195
  transformation into postsocialism,
    25–30
  See also Postsocialism
Soviet Union, 3, 5, 168
State. *See* Legitimacy crisis; Statism
Statism
  official ideology and, 10, 203n. 6
  parental authority and, 25
  socialism and, 10, 194, 195
Subject, 82–87
  as active agent, 84–85
  civil society and, 83–84
  identity and, 82
  multifarious positions of, 84, 85
  new social movements and new
    positions of, 85
  political nature of, 82
  political resistance and, 84, 85
  relations to China's sociopolitical
    order, 82, 84–85, 86

Taiwan, 4, 106, 116, 131, 177, 199,
    215n. 19
Technology
  as liberator of humanity, 93
  as means of authoritarian power, 92
Third world
  asymmetrical relations to first
    world, 129, 158–59
  China's status and, 15, 16, 32,
    33–34, 88, 191, 194, 196
  critics in, 131
  in cross-cultural interaction, 130,
    131, 146, 162, 217n. 2
  film and, 133
  lack of democracy in, 127–28
  modernization in, 186
  new dependency theory and, 158–59
  official attitude to China's status of,
    119
  postcolonial criticism and, 16, 192,
    193
  post-ist concerns for, 21, 88, 101,
    102, 106, 108, 110, 114, 118, 121,
    123
  postmodernism in, 7–8
  post-New Era and consciousness of,
    119
  as prototype of the colonized, 124
  specificities in, 125
Tiananmen incident, 5, 6, 8, 9, 10, 23,
    88
  post-1989 and, 5–7
  as reference of time passage, 7
Tibet, 4, 106
Totalitarianism, 8, 9, 10, 45, 89, 95–97,
    212n. 4, 212–13n. 5
  Cultural Revolution and Tiananmen
    incident and, 95–97
  dynamic core of, 9
  main features of, 9
  operative means of, 9
  rational, 96, 213n. 6
  silence on, 10–14
  two-level syndrome of, 9
  See also Posttotalitarianism

Translation, 148–62
  active periods of, 150–51
  baihua literature and, 151, 152,
    219–20n. 12
  change in politico-ethical values
    and, 155
  change in public-life language and,
    154, 155
  conceptual and nominal innovation
    and, 154
  as converting operator between cul-
    tures, 150
  cross-cultural interaction and,
    149–50, 156–62
  cultural comparison and, 150
  cultures involved in, 149
  donor-receiver relationship entailed
    in, 157, 220n. 14
  as intercultural and intracultural
    mediation, 152, 220n. 15
  in May Fourth Movement, 150
  naming of parties involved in,
    156–57, 158
  neologisms and, 155
  new dependency theory and, 158–59
  new theory of (Benjamin, Derrida),
    160, 161
  in 1980s, 150–51, 220n. 12
  old theory of, 160, 161–62
  personal purpose of, 150
  as process rather than terminal
    result, 156

  redefinition of, 149
  in relation to cultural polysystem,
    152–54
  as sociocultural event, 153
  sociocultural purpose of, 150
  sociocultural reconstruction and,
    155

Utopianism, 169, 170

Violence
  cultural, 16, 125
  direct, 125
  grand narratives of, 127
  imperialism and, 126
  intranational and international, 16,
    126
  as meeting place of colonialism and
    totalitarianism, 16, 126
  opposition to, 124–25, 127–28
  postcolonial criticism and, 124–25,
    127–28
  structural, 125, 126
  structures of, 125–26
  theory of, 125–28
  totalitarianism and, 126
  See also Domination

xiaokang (comparatively well-off),
  114
xin guoxue. *See* New Chinese
  Studies

Name Index

Adam, Ian, 124
Adamson, Walter, 165
Adorno, Theodor W., 188
Agresto, John, 57, 210n. 1
Ai Nong, 184
Althusser, Louis, 192
Amin, Samir, 197, 198
Anagnost, Ann, 29
Appadurai, Arjun, 218n. 6
Arac, Jonathan, 2, 203n. 2, 217n. 1
Arendt, Hannah, 53, 95, 209n. 21
Armes, Roy, 133

Bai Hua, 28, 92
Bakhtin, Mikhail, 43, 44
Balibar, Etienne, 192
Barber, Benjamin R., 212n. 4, 213n. 5
Barmé, Geremie, 42, 44, 207n. 10
Barthes, Roland, 97, 144
Bassnett, Susan, 157, 158, 159, 160, 162
Baudelaire, Charles, 142, 143, 160, 162
Benjamin, Walter, 160
Berlin, Isaiah, 112
Bernheimer, Charles, 142, 143
Berry, Chris, 29, 222n. 9
Beverley, John, 7
Bhabha, Homi, 204n. 8
Bian Wu, 222n. 6
Bonnin, Michel, 212n. 3
Booth, Wayne C., 21n. 10
Bourdieu, Pierre, 47
Brieder, Jerome B., 68
Brunner, José Joaquin, 13
Burke, Edmund, 168, 169, 221n. 1

Cai Zhongde, 221n. 3
Chang, Maria Hsia, 213n. 6
Chen Feng, 12, 182
Chen Jianhua, 222n. 5
Chen Kaige, 132, 211n. 7, 218n. 4
Chen Lai, 71, 80, 175, 176, 177, 210nn. 4, 5, 211n. 6, 221n. 3
Chen Pingyuan, 64, 71, 74
Chen Shaoming, 221n. 3
Chen Sihe, 50, 209n. 20
Chen Song, 219n. 11
Chen Xiaoming, 99, 102, 131, 132, 135, 183, 214n. 13, 216n. 25, 217n. 2
Chen Yaohong, 109
Chen Yinke, 64, 211n. 12
Chevrier, Yves, 212n. 3
Chow, Rey, 16, 17, 119
Collins, Jim, 42, 43, 44
Curtis, Michael, 212n. 4, 212–13n. 5

Dai Jinhua, 131, 132
Dallmayr, Fred R., 20
Deng Shaoji, 211n. 11
Deng Xiaoping, 5, 8, 28, 92, 98, 104, 114, 213n. 9, 214n. 16
Derrida, Jacques, 97, 160, 193
Ding Dong, 207n. 8
Dirlik, Arif, 17, 27, 28, 29, 30, 89, 90, 195, 196, 205nn. 1, 2, 205–6n. 3
Dittmer, Lowell, 31, 32
Dong Zhilin, 37
During, Simon, 119, 193
Du Yaquan, 177
Du Yeli, 107

Edel, Abraham, 75, 79
Evan-Zohar, Itamar, 151, 153

Fang Keli, 183
Fang Zizhou, 206n. 4, 216n. 24
Fanon, Frantz, 199, 200
Fan Qinlin, 81
Farquhar, Mary Ann, 29, 222n. 9
Featherstone, Mike, 218n. 6
Feng Youlan 177
Fiske, John, 80, 218n. 7
Flower, Elizabeth, 75, 79
Foucault, Michel, 97, 162
Frankel, Charles, 57, 210n. 1
Friedman, Edward, 203n. 6
Friedrich, Carl J., 212n. 4, 213n. 5
Fu Kuiyang, 207n. 12
Fu Sinian, 66

Galtung, Johan, 125, 126
Gambles, Ian, 6, 166
Gan Yang, 212n. 3, 213n. 7
Gao Ruiquan, 51, 209n. 19
Gao Yuanbao, 208n. 18
Gasster, Michael, 185, 189
Ge Hua, 97
Ge Zhaoguang, 211n. 12
Goldfarb, Jeffrey C., 96, 206n. 4
Goldman, Merle, 97, 102, 212nn. 1, 2,
  213–14n. 11, 220n. 12
Gong Shuduo, 184
Gouldner, Alvin W., 76, 77, 78
Grossberg, Lawrence, 2
Gu Jiegang, 61, 66, 67, 68
Guo Jian, 216n. 21, 217n. 27
Guo Sujian, 9
Gu Xin, 182

Habermas, Jürgen, 24, 137
Halbwachs, Maurice, 164
Hall, Stuart, 2, 218n. 7
Hansen, Miriam, 135, 136, 139, 218n.
  6
Havel, Vaclav, 29, 206n. 4
Hayden, Tom, 187

Hebdige, Dick, 18
He Manzi, 61, 62, 71, 210n. 5
Hermans, Theo, 153
Hewson, Lance, 149, 150, 160, 161,
  162, 220n. 15
He Yi, 57, 58, 69
Hong Zicheng, 38, 39, 207n. 11
Horkheimer, Max, 188
Hosking, Geoffrey, 203n. 6
Howard, Dick, 216n. 26
Howe, Irving, 96
Huang Baosheng, 219n. 10
Huang Jianxin, 222n. 9
Hu Bin, 217n. 9
Huntington, Samuel, 81, 107, 217n. 1
Hu Shengwu, 184
Hu Shi, 58, 60, 61, 62, 66, 67, 68, 219n.
  12
Hu Xiaoming, 81

Jacoby, Russell, 48
Jameson, Fredric, 2, 97, 193
Jiang Yin, 74
Jia Pingwa, 42
Ji Guangmao, 183
Jin Chongzhi, 184
Jin Dacheng, 64, 66, 67, 68, 72
Ji Xianlin, 107
Johnson, Randall, 157, 213n. 5

Kang Youwei, 66, 67, 177
Kim, Samuel S., 31, 32, 119
Kinston-Mann, Esther, 26
Kluge, Alexander, 136, 138
Kohn, Hans, 15
Konrak, György, 214n. 15
Kraus, Richard Curt, 47, 48, 194
Kristof, Nicholas D., 54
Kuhn, Thomas S., 72, 211n. 9
Kwong, Julia, 24

Lachner, Norbert, 13
Laclau, Ernesto, 204n. 10, 212n. 16
Larson, Magali Sarfatti, 71
Lee, Leo Oufan, 220n. 13

Lefort, Claude, 204n. 10
Lei Yi, 109, 178, 217n. 27
Liang Qichao, 67, 211n. 7
Liang Shumin, 177
Li Hang, 97
Li Jiefei, 207n. 12
Li Lianke, 81, 210n. 3
Lin Huaguo, 184
Link, Perry, 97
Lin Yusheng, 210n. 3
Li Shenzhi, 107, 222n. 4
Li Tiangang, 50
Liu, Lydia, 154, 219n. 12, 220nn. 13, 14
Liu Dong, 73, 107, 222n. 4
Liu Fangping, 107
Liu Junning, 81, 222n. 4
Liu Kang, 102, 107, 120, 216n. 23,
    217n. 28
Liu Shipei, 177
Liu Zaifu, 181, 212n. 3
Li Zehou, 180, 181, 182, 183, 184,
    212n. 3, 222n. 5
Lu Peng, 211n. 12
Lu Xun, 158
Lu Zhichao, 212n. 2
Lull, James, 206n. 7
Lyotard, Jean-François, 2, 8, 9, 193,
    196

Ma Chenghua, 211n. 12
Ma Ning, 218n. 5
Madsen, Richard, 137
Maistre, Joseph de, 168, 169
Manning, Stephen, 26
Mao Zedong, 206n. 5
Martin, Jacky, 149, 150, 160, 161, 162,
    220n. 15
Mattelart, Armand, 218n. 6
Mei Guangdi, 177
Meisner, Maurice, 204n. 10, 222n. 8
Meng Fanhua, 171, 207n. 11, 217n. 2
Meng Yue, 97
Merleau-Ponty, 5
Meschonnic, Henri, 149, 150, 161
Migdal, Joel S., 127

Min Huiquan, 222n. 7
Miyoshi, Masao, 192, 201
Morse, Richard M., 217n. 3
Mouffe, Chantal, 83, 84, 85, 212nn. 14,
    16
Mowitt, John, 85, 212n. 15
Murphy, Peter, 222n. 10
Mu Zongsan, 177

Nan Fan, 81, 217n. 27
Nandy, Ashis, 200
Negt, Oskar, 136, 138
Nelson, Cary, 2
Nie Zhenbin, 208n. 15
Nora, Pierre, 164

Oakeshott, Michael, 212n. 14
Ong Jieming, 13, 221n. 4
Oviedo, José, 7

Pan Shaomei, 99
Pei, Minxin, 203n. 5
Pei Dayang, 13
Pickowicz, Paul G., 10, 27, 28, 29, 195,
    196, 205n. 1, 222n. 9
Prybyla, Jan. S., 8
Pye, Lucian W., 35

Qian Jun, 99, 109
Qian Wenzhong, 63
Qi Shuyu, 207n. 9
Qu Xuewei, 107

Ricoeur, Paul, 155
Riesenberg, Peter, 57
Robins, Devin, 218n. 6
Rorty, Richard, 221n. 1
Ruiz, Lester Edwin J., 16, 127, 204n. 9
Rupnik, Jacques, 214n. 15

Said, Edward W., 2, 99, 108, 109, 124,
    131, 193, 199, 216n. 24, 217n. 1
Sakamoto, Yoshikazu, 128
Sapir, Edward, 160
Sautman, Barry, 12, 93

Schlesinger, Philip, 156
Schreiter, Robert J., 155
Sciolla, L., 156
Scott, David, 100, 101
Sennett, Richard, 30
Sha Jiansun, 184
Shang Shui, 213n. 8
Shao Jian, 117, 118
Shi Zhong, 107
Shohat, Ella,124
Simon, John, 218n. 8
Smith, Paul, 82, 84, 85, 212nn. 15, 16
Song Qiang, 107
Song Zhongfu, 13
Spivak, Gayatri Chakravorty, 131, 192
Steiner, George, 149, 150
Stromberg, Roland N., 65
Sun Min, 207n. 8
Sun Yat-sen, 180, 181
Sun Yongmeng, 208n. 15
Sun Zhanguo, 207n. 12
Su Wei, 97, 211n. 7, 216n. 24
Su Wen, 222n. 6

Tang, Xiaodu, 206n. 4
Tang Yijie, 222n. 7
Tao Dongfeng, 81, 183, 209n. 22
Tao Junyi, 177
Tao Shuiping, 109
Tao Xisheng, 177
Taylor, Charles, 32, 206n. 6
Tiffin, Helen, 124
Treichler, Paula, 2
Tsou, Tang, 102
Tu Weiming, 13, 210n. 3

Viereck, Peter, 168, 169

Wang Binbin, 208n. 18
Wang Desheng, 173, 181, 183
Wang Guangdong, 216n. 25
Wang Guowei, 211n. 7
Wang Hui, 107, 178, 179
Wang Jiaxin, 207n. 11
Wang Jisi, 107

Wang Meng, 37, 38, 40, 107, 207nn. 9, 12, 13
Wang Ning, 7, 97, 98, 120, 216n. 25, 217n. 1
Wang Ping, 42
Wang Ruoshui, 212n. 3
Wang Shan, 221n. 4
Wang Shenzhi, 207n. 12
Wang Shouchang, 63, 74
Wang Shuo, 37, 38, 41, 42, 44, 45, 207n. 10, 208n. 16
Wang Wei, 211n. 8
Wang Xiaoming, 39, 50, 51, 52, 207n. 8, 209n. 20
Wang Yi, 45
Wang Yichuan, 99, 109, 112, 113, 183
Wang Yuanhua, 180, 211n. 13
Wang Yuechuan, 81, 210n. 3, 213n. 8
Wang Zhengping, 215n. 20
Weeks, Priscilla, 159
Welch, Sharon D., 22
Wen Liping, 206n. 8
White, Stephen, 26
Whiting, Allen S., 104, 214n. 17
Whorf, Benjamin Lee, 160
Williams, Raymond, 2, 89, 139, 145, 146
Wittgenstein, Ludwig, 154
Wong Young-tsu, 211n. 12
Wu Mian, 177
Wu Xiaoming, 97
Wu Xuan, 81, 209n. 19
Wu Yuanmai, 219n. 10

Xiao Gongqin, 106, 167, 168, 169, 170, 221n. 4
Xie Mian, 38, 207n. 11
Xie Yong, 211n. 12
Xing Bensi, 184
Xiong Shili, 177
Xu Ben, 97, 209n. 23, 216nn. 21, 25
Xu Jialu, 107
Xu Jilin, 46, 51, 209n. 19, 217n. 27
Xu Ming, 64
Xu Youyu, 222n. 7

Yang Chunshi, 172
Yang Yuxi, 211n. 12
Yau, Esther C. M., 218n. 4
Ye Wen, 178, 206n. 4
Yi Dan, 146, 147, 148, 149, 150, 151,
152, 216n. 23, 219n. 10
Yin Changlong, 208n. 18
Yi Shuihan, 207n. 10
You Xilin, 81
Yuan Shikai, 180
Yu Xinjiao, 207n. 9
Yu Yingshi, 13, 210n. 3

Zang Li, 207n. 11
Zhang Chengzhi, 46, 208n. 18
Zhang Dainian, 60, 61, 66, 69, 211n.
11
Zhang Dexiang, 109, 110
Zhang Enhe, 221n. 3
Zhang Fa, 112, 113, 183, 203n. 3
Zhang Hong, 148, 149, 150, 219n. 10
Zhang Huimin, 207n. 11
Zhang Jingyuan, 99
Zhang Kuan, 99, 109, 110, 111, 179,
216n. 24
Zhang Longxi, 216nn. 21, 24, 217n. 27
Zhang Qiqun, 211n. 8
Zhang Rulun, 47, 50, 51, 52, 209nn.
19, 20

Zhang Shizhao, 177
Zhang Taiyan, 177
Zhang Wei, 208nn. 15, 18
Zhang Xudong, 89, 90
Zhang Yimou, 132, 218n. 4
Zhang Yiwu, 7, 102, 112, 113, 120,
131, 132, 133, 151, 152, 171, 179, 183,
208n. 18, 214nn. 12, 13, 216nn. 23,
25, 217n. 28, 217n. 2, 218n. 3, 222n.
5
Zhang Zhizhong, 81
Zhang Zongxian, 215n. 19
Zhao Jihui, 13
Zhao Yanqiu, 219n. 10
Zhao Yao, 215n. 20
Zhao Yiheng (Zhao, Henry Y. H.),
183, 203n. 1
Zhao Yingyun, 107
Zhao Yuanren, 211n. 7
Zheng Min, 151
Zheng Ning, 81
Zhong Chengxiang, 208n. 17
Zhou Suyuan, 210n. 3
Zhou Xian, 47, 208n. 15
Zhuang Sihui, 207n. 12
Zhu Xueqin, 211n. 8
Žižek, Slavoj, 19, 204–5n. 10